Customs Duties in the Qing Dynasty, ca. 1644–1911

Global Economic History Series

VOLUME 13

The Quantitative Economic History of China

VOLUME 2

The titles published in this series are listed at *brill.com/qehc*

Customs Duties in the Qing Dynasty, ca. 1644–1911

By

Ni Yuping

BRILL

LEIDEN | BOSTON

Cover illustration: Displayed is the left part of the eighteenth-century remake of the twelfth-century original painting *Along the River During the Qingming Festival* by Zhang Zeduan. The remake is created by five Qing dynasty court painters (Chen Mu, Sun Hu, Jin Kun, Dai Hong and Cheng Zhidao) and is currently in the National Palace Museum in Taipei. The painting captures the daily life of people and the landscape of the capital, Bianjing (today's Kaifeng) from the Northern Song period. LICENSED UNDER PUBLIC DOMAIN, VIA WIKIMEDIA COMMONS.

The Library of Congress Cataloging-in-Publication Data is available online at http://catalog.loc.gov
LC record available at http://lccn.loc.gov/2016042758

Typeface for the Latin, Greek, and Cyrillic scripts: "Brill". See and download: brill.com/brill-typeface.

ISSN 2405-870X
ISBN 978-90-04-32487-9 (hardback)
ISBN 978-90-04-32488-6 (e-book)

This book is printed on acid-free paper and produced in a sustainable manner.

Contents

Foreword

This book was written in the belief that one cannot make full sense of the commodity circulation taxes—i.e. customs duties—of the Qing Dynasty, or indeed of political economy of Qing China more generally, without understanding the history that produced it.

There is no need to justify the importance of finance in world history. Modern finance is the breeding ground of modern economic history and modern state formation.

This book describes and analyzes developments in Qing finance, focusing on commodity circulation taxes, one of major sources of modern public revenues. In traditional agrarian societies, land and head taxes made up the bulk of state revenues, while commodity circulation taxes provided only a small part of the revenues. In Western Europe of early modern times, commodity circulation taxes sprang up rapidly and finally replaced land and head taxes as the most important source of state revenue. A similar change took place in China in the mid-nineteenth century. That change is part of the story of China's economic transformation in the decades that followed.

In the Qing times, commodity circulation taxes were charged on all goods in domestic and foreign trade. These were collected separately by two institutions: *Changguanshui*, or ordinary custom ports that had the responsibility of taxing goods taking part in domestic trade; and *Yangguanshui*, or custom ports that focused on foreign trade. In this book, the taxes collected by both institutions were sometimes called by the Chinese name of *guanshui*.

Though there were clearly defined responsibilities for *Changguan* and *Yangguan*, in some cases these overlapped. In late-nineteenth-century China, moreover, domestic commodity circulation taxes were mainly composed of *lijin* (*Likin* taxes), which were in many cases collected by local authorities, while a modern custom service in charge of levying import and export duties was introduced and managed by modern West. To avoid any misunderstanding that may arise from the different meanings of these taxes in Qing China, it can be useful to use their original name – *guanshui*, not its English translation of "custom duties".

The issue of *guanshui* held a special position in the finances of the Qing state. Before the mid-nineteenth century, *guanshui* was already responsible for a considerable share of Qing financial revenues,[1] although land tax was the

1 According to Shen Xuefeng, *guanshui*'s share in Qing financial revenue was 11–12% in the second half of the eighteenth century and early nineteenth century. See Shen: *Qingdai cai-*

cornerstone of state finances, accounting for three-quarters of the total. In the second half of the nineteenth century, however, *guanshui* rose steeply to become the No. 1 financial source of revenue in the final decade of the Qing dynasty.[2] In this sense, we can say that without *guanshui*, the Qing state couldn't have run the country properly, or, for that matter, even survived. There can be little doubt, therefore, that the concept of *guanshui* is crucial to understanding the political economy of Qing China.

The Qing dynasty witnessed significant changes in *guanshui*. In the first two centuries of the Qing (1644–1850), the state followed the traditional basic principles of Chinese finance of "fitting one's spending to one's income", and there were little changes to speak of in this period. During the mid- and late Qing periods, however, the traditional financial system, as well as the country as a whole, faced great challenges. To cope with these challenges, great changes were initiated in the state's finances, among them was the rapid development of *guanshui*. As a result, this tax, together with land taxes and salt taxes, formed the financial pillars of the Qing state.[3]

This change took place in an era of great transformation in world history, recently referred to as the "Great Divergence". Angus Maddison has also argued that the mid-nineteenth century was the turning point of China's economy, from the previous centuries-long prosperity to the long-term decline that followed.[4] Coincidentally, it was in this very period that China's rocky road to

---

zheng shuru guimo yu jiegou bianhua shulun (On the changes of the sizes and structures of Qing finance), in *Beijing shehui kexue* (Beijing), no.1, 2002.

2 Shen Xuefeng suggested that in 1811 *guanshui* and *lijin* together accounted for 47% of Qing financial revenue. This share is much bigger than that of Land Tax (27%) and Salt Tax (26%), other major sources of Qing financial revenue (ibidem). R. Bin Wong argued that Qing financial revenue was 42.5 million taels of silver in 1849, 77% of which came from agriculture, with the rest coming from commerce. Financial revenue rose to 77 million taels in 1885, mainly due to a great increase in commercial taxes, which tripled during the period. In 1911, the last financial year of the Qing, revenue went up to 301 million taels, including agricultural taxes of 50 million taels (increasing from 30 million taels in 1885), miscellaneous taxes of 45 million taels, and commercial taxes of more than 207 million taels (R. Bin Wong: *China Transformed-Historical Change and the Limits of European Experience*, Ithaca: Cornel University Press, 1998. Chapter 3).

3 Among the others, the tax on opium accounted for 10% of total financial revenue. See Zhou Yumin: *19 shiji 60–90 niandai qingchao caizheng jiegou de bianhua* (Changes in the financial structure of the Qing in the 1860s through to the 1890s), in Shanghai shifan daxue xuebao (Shanghai), no. 4, 2000.

4 Angus Maddison: *Chinese Economic Performance in the Long Run* (Second edition). Paris: Development Centre of the Ogranisation for Economic Co-Operation and Development, 2007. Chapter 1.

modernization began, and the financial reforms already underway were able to play a key role in the transformation. Because of the special position of *guanshui* in Qing state finances, the changes it underwent serve as a showpiece of the Qing state's efforts to ensure the survival of the regime and modernize the country in this period.

The beginnings of modern scholarship focusing on Qing guanshui go back a century. In the century that has followed increasing efforts have been made to find new approaches for studying the phenomenon, particularly in the last decade, coinciding with rising interest in research on historical GDP. Significant achievements have been booked as a result, but it cannot be denied that major problems and flaws still exist, both in the availability of data and methods for processing them, and because some fields are still uncharted. For this reason, so far we still don't have really reliable and complete knowledge of *guanshui* and the roles it played in Qing political economy. In this book, Ni Yuping sets out to address and iron out some of these problems and flaws, in particular by setting up a reliable and usable database for the study of *guanshui* and by explaining the background to and importance of the data.

Professor Ni Yuping has spent years compiling and analyzing data on *guanshui* collected in the first half of the nineteenth century; his results were published in the form of book in 2010.[5] The book was a new attempt to study *guanshui* of the Qing based completely on first-hand inspection of archive materials and in doing so the author laid a solid foundation upon which to pursue further his research. After publication of the book, the author continued to compile new data and improve his research methods. His years of hard work have borne fruit, a fact to which this new book testifies.

This book presents several important findings in the field of *guanshui* that prove to be very helpful for our understanding of the Qing political economy. First, the book reveals trends for changes in *guanshui* during the Qing. In the early and mid-Qing, *Changguanshui* (*guanshui* collected by *Changguan*) remained stable, but dropped by half after the Taiping Rebellion. In contrast, *Yangguanshui* (*guanshui* collected by *Yangguan*) grew dramatically. When the two are added, we see that the total amount of *guanshui* collected increased from 5 million taels of silver per year in the early Qing to 35 million taels per year by the end of the Qing, i.e. a seven-fold increase. In that period, *Changguanshui* arising from trade along the Yangtzi River and Grand Canal still accounted for most of the revenues levied at *Changguan*, although *Yangguanshui* from *Yangguan* on the coast was growing much more rapidly. This

5 The book is titled *Qingchao jiadao guanshui yanjiu* (A study of guanshui of the Qing in the reigns of Jiaqing and Daoguang), Beijing: Beijing shiifan daxue chubanshe, 2010.

trend reflects the shift of the gravity of China's trade from inland to coastal regions.

Second, using population and price data, the author has made important corrections to—as well as supplementing—the published figures on Qing *guanshui*. The close relationship between political-institutional and financial developments defines the periodization of Qing financial history. In the book, two periods are distinguished: one from 1644 to 1850; and the other from 1850 to 1911. The author found out that per capita *guanshui* remained stable in the pre-1850 period, but rocketed by a factor of 7–8 times in the post-1850 period. Moreover, after correcting for inflation, the author found that real per capita *guanshui* decreased in the first half of the nineteenth century as compared to the second half of the eighteenth century, which confirms the occurrence of the "Daoguang Depression". After 1850, amounts of *guanshui* rose dramatically, although the real increase was 4–5 times, rather than the nominal growth of 7 times.

Third, starting with the tariffs used to levy *guanshui*, the author has estimated commercial output in the selected benchmark years of 1724, 1766, 1812, 1840, 1850, 1887, and 1910, both in terms of total and per capita outputs. He arrives at the conclusion that commercial output in both respects reached its peak in 1766, followed by a slow and smooth fall in the first half of the nineteenth century. Thereafter it rose dramatically to reached a new peak in 1887. Although it fell once more in 1910, it was still double what had been in the pre-1850 period. These findings offer new perspectives for the historical GDP study of China that is currently underway.

Fourth, Professor Ni argues that the evolution of *guanshui* changed the nature of Qing state finances, moving them on from their traditional, agricultural base to a new, commercial base, as well as setting off the evolution of its fiscal regime from a traditional to a modern one in the course of the seventeenth to the nineteenth centuries. In this sense, China was not as "exceptional" as people usually think. Indeed, the evolution of China's political economy has never been far from of the general path followed by the rest of the world.

Fifth, it is common knowledge that China had been "closed" to other parts of the world, in particular to the modern West, until the early 1840s, when Britain defeated China and forced it open up to the West. This centuries-old conventional wisdom has been challenged recently, and a new convention has been taking shape, which is expressed clearly by Jonathan Spence: "China's destiny as a nation has been entwined, at least since 1600 on, with others in the search for scarce resources, the exchange of goods, and the expansion of knowledge".[6] Inspired by global history, the author has placed special emphasis on changes

6 Jonathan D. Spence: *The Search for Modern China*. New York: Norton, 2012, preface.

in *Yangguan* and their influence on the political economy of the Qing. It is in fact an effort to put China in a global historical context.

To conclude, this book represents a new achievement in the field of China's financial history. What emerged in China during the Qing, in particular the late Qing, was a rich variety of institutions that were willing to experiment with sophisticated instruments such as foreign debt and modern custom duties, thus challenging the notion of a typical pre-modern stage of fiscal development. The book reveals patterns across a great temporal and spatial context that shed light on the basic factors driving the intensification, abatement, and innovation of the Chinese fiscal regime. In broad terms, this book aims to provide an understanding of the patterns and evolution of China's state finances as seen against the backdrop of long-term global economic and political developments, and I can say that it achieves this purpose admirably.

Bozhong Li
Professor of History, Tsinghua University, China

Foreword

This book demonstrates a couple of things. In the first place, it shows how important language still is in historical research. Large parts of China's fascinating history remain hidden from the outside world because there are not enough international researchers that are both masters of Chinese and English and have the opportunity to undertake wide-ranging archival research on this vast empire. This book is based on extensive work in different Chinese archives spanning a period of more than ten years. And that is the second thing this book demonstrates: the importance of doing historical research using primary sources, i.e. the value of accessing original records, found in collections and archives, brought together with care to combine quantitative data with qualitative information. The result of Ni Yuping's efforts is a overview of more than 250 years of China's domestic and international trade that is mirrored in its fiscal revenues. Starting at the beginning of Qing dynasty (and sometimes a bit earlier), Professor Ni follows the development of customs revenues to the end of this era. He shows how important customs duties were for the Qing state, how the fiscal regime was organized to achieve the highest revenue, how it was adapted to changing circumstances, and how Chinese tax officials reported on their work. This book gives an indication of China's trade flows during one of the most decisive periods in the country's history.

The data series of custom duties presented in this book were collected from a variety of archives; the duties were levied at the country land borders, at harbors along the Yangtze River and the Grand Canal, which connected southern and central China, and at maritime harbors on the country's eastern coast. Little of this material has been accessible for non-Chinese reading scholars.

The original source materials for those parts of the series that have been published in Chinese before have been checked first-hand by Professor Ni. The series have been constructed with great care and precision and put into context. The results are presented to the reader in the form of tables and graphs, followed by a discussion on what caused fluctuations in revenues and how contemporaries (such as the emperor and tax officials) reflected on these explanations in their letters and reports. An assessment of this material at the end of the book leads to a critical and cautious interpretation of the development of Chinese trade, as well as an evaluation of its relevance to overall economic performance.

Behind this study is the author's ambition to add to our understanding of one of the most pressing historical issues today: what explains the diverging economic developments that took place in Europe and China in the early modern and modern periods? What were the 'how's' and 'why's' of this 'Great Divergence'? Of course, there are a number of answers to be found in the literature, but the issue has different dimensions, and debate is ongoing about the relative significance of various aspects and the precise sequence and interrelatedness of events. Apart from that strand of literature that attributes the rise of Great Britain, and the consequent relative decline of China, to geography and other natural causes, most literature concentrates on changes in Europe and Great Britain to explain the Great Divergence. These publications point to the emergence of modern economic growth, the rise of capitalist institutions, the techniques of industrialization, the sustained European urban growth, the variety in state formation, the building of empires and colonial relations, plus the cultural exceptionalism of Europe. Often, and not just for sake of argument, Chinese society is presented as being almost inert, the Chinese agrarian economy as being captured in a kind of homeostasis, without any impulses to, or incentives for, change. And, in addition, Chinese authorities are portrayed as conservative, focused on keeping the status quo, avoiding any change in the traditional way of doing things, and obsessed by a preference for small and lean government, unwilling or not able to raise more taxes or to borrow money on capital markets. Admittedly, the book will not solve the entire debate on taxation and state formation, but it does offer a new and refreshing element to what we know about the topic, and in doing so, it changes the state of the art.

Economic and fiscal history are the fields to which Professor Ni's book makes a valuable contribution. While the institutional system of taxation is not the main focus of the book, his contextualizing approach ties in a lot of information on the practicalities and bureaucracy involved. In doing so, he provides us with an understanding of their broader societal effects, the relations between economic development, taxes and state formation. This was also a topic that Charles Tilly worked on. One of his famous quotes is: "Broadly speaking, internal struggles such as the checking of great regional lords and the imposition of taxation on peasant villages produced important organizational features of European states: the relative subordination of military power to civilian control, the extensive bureaucracy of fiscal surveillance…".[1] This observation was explicitly made on Europe, but it provides an interesting framework of understanding for the Chinese developments. In China, military considerations were extremely important. Especially in the reign of Youngzhen, the empire pushed westwards, and in the late Qing period the empire

1 C. Tilly, 'War Making and State Making as Organized Crime' in: Peter Evans, Dietrich Rueschemeyer, and Theda Skocpol (eds.) *Bringing the State Back in* (Cambridge: Cambridge University Press, 1985).

witnessed the Taiping Rebellion and several wars with Western powers, all of which drew heavily on the dynasty's existing resources. This created a need for new taxes, in addition to the wish to reorganize existing ones, such as land taxes, salt taxes and customs duties. As a paradox, one could point out the unfortunate results of the Opium wars, which forced the Chinese to redesign the commercial and fiscal organization of their sea ports on the east coast.

In this book Ni Yuping argues that during the Qing dynasty customs revenues reflected the general development of the Qing fiscal system. Tax revenues, such as custom duties on various forms of trade, may mirror Chinese economic development, but the reflection is complex, sometimes blurred and even cracked. It is a task for the careful historian to unravel the way this reflection came about—how the mirror has become distorted. In the book this is done through a detailed and critical examination of sources on the organization of the taxation system and ensuing correspondence on the revenue collected. This critical reading adds to the combination of sources of quantitative data in different collections. A clear picture arises of the numerous small adjustments made to taxation procedures and, from the middle of the 18th century onwards, the growing importance of taxes on trade. Not just as a result of a new tax administration: trade itself became more important. The exchange of commodities across the empire was stimulated as an addition to the agrarian base of society, as well as creating security for it. Probably, trade was not seen as an instrument for economic change, nor as a tool for obtaining a fortune – at least not beyond ambitions of the individual merchant. On the contrary, the official policy was to use trade as a balance for agrarian shortages that followed disasters in particular regions by directing surpluses from elsewhere. In late Qing, however, somewhere between 1840 and 1880, a new situation emerged. Trade became a real economic engine, leading to greater societal effects, one of which was the virtual tripling of state incomes derived from the custom duties. In these years China's domestic trade fluctuated greatly, due to wars and rebellions, but on average it showed a slow rise. A new sun was rising in the east, however. The higher tax revenues were derived from international trade in the Shanghai region, and this quickly became important for Chinese society as a whole. A general change in the tax regime followed, supporting one of the conclusions drawn in the book: that with foreign pressure and foreign aid the Qing state changed from 'a state with a tax system' to become 'a fiscal state'.

Maarten Duijvendak
Professor of Economic & Social History, Director of Studies MHIR,
University of Groningen, Netherlands

Emperors of the Qing Dynasty

Shunzhi	1644–1661
Kangxi	1662–1722
Yongzheng	1723–1735
Qianlong	1736–1795
Jiaqing	1796–1820
Daoguang	1820–1850
Xianfeng	1851–1861
Tongzhi	1862–1874
Guangxu	1875–1908
Xuantong	1909–1911

List of Maps, Figures and Tables

Maps

Figures

Tables

List of Abbreviations

FHAC	The First Historical Archives of China
ZPZZ	*Zhupi Zouzhe* (Palace Midrange Rescript Memorials)
TB	*Tiben* (Reports to the Emperor)
LFZP	*Lufu Zouzhe* (Extra Copies of Grand Council Memorials)
Chaodang	Copy of the Archives, which was stored in the library of the Institute of Economics, the Chinese Academy of Social Sciences.They include: Guanshui Baogao Biao: *Qingdai Guanshui Shouzhi Baogao Biao* (Revenue and Expenditure Reports of Customs in the Qing Dynasty); Tiben Guanshui: Customs Duties Reports to the Emperor
SYD	*Shangyu Dang* (Edict Records)
GXCZP	*Guangxu Chao Zhupi Zouzhe* (Palace Midrange Rescript Memorials of the Guangxu Reign)
GZDQLC	*Gongzhongdang Qianlong Chao Zouzhe* (Palace Midrange Rescript Memorials of the Qianlong Reign)
GZDGXC	*Gongzhongdang Guangxu Chao Zouzhe* (Palace Midrange Rescript Memorials of the Guangxu Reign)
SQYJ	*Shi Qu Yu Ji*, wroted by Wang Qingyun
YZCHW	*Yongzheng Chao Hanwen Zhupi Zouzhe Huibian* (Collection of the Palace Midrange Rescript Memorials in Han Language of the Yongzheng Reign)
LMGS	*The List of Money and Grains Sent to and from the Provinces in the Seventeenth Year of Jiaqing in the Qing Dynasty*

List of Chinese Terms

Baijiu (白酒), Chinese liquor, literally "white wine".
Buzhengshi (布政使), the nominal head of the civil service and the treasurer of the provincial exchequer.
Changshui (常税), also called changguan shui(常关税), referring to the collection of Chinese Regional Customs.
Dao (道), an official responsible for multiple prefectures.
Daqian (大钱), large coins/token metal coins issued during the late Qing period.
Diding (地丁), an agricultural land tax collected in silver.
Ewai Yingyu (额外盈余), additional Yingyu, add an Yingyu to ordinary Yingyu in some ports.
Ezheng Shu (额征数), the regular quota of a tax.
Gongbu (工部), the Ministry of Works.
Guan Shui (关税), customs duties.
Guangchu Si (广储司), the Storage Office, a section under the Department of Internal Affairs.
Hubu (户部), the Ministry of Revenue.
Jiandu (监督), the highest official in some customs ports.
Jiangni Zhizhao (江宁织造), the official responsible for weaving the emperor's clothes, located in Jiangni, today known as Nanjing.
Jingxiang (京饷), Provisions to the capital by provinces.
Li (厘), a unit of weight (also that of length and area). One li= 1/1000 of a tael.
Liangtou (樑头), a boat's skipper.
Likin (厘金), an ad valoren tax levied in the late Qing and early Republic of China.
Neiwu Fu (内务府), Department of Internal Affairs, an organization responsible for the affairs of the royal family.
Pingyu (平余), balancing surplus.
Qinglisi (清吏司), a division of the Ministry of Revenue.
Shilang (侍郎), an official title, assistant minister, for officials holding the rank of grade two within the traditional nine-grade civilian rank system. There were twelve assistant ministers in the Six Ministries of the central government (each ministry had two Zuo Shilang左侍郎, meaning Left Shilang, and two You Shilang右侍郎, meaning Right Shilang).
Tong Jin Shui Jiao (铜斤水脚), a copper transport fee, a fee to be paid by those who bought copper and sent it to Beijing.
Xian (县), county, the lowest provincial administrative district of ancient China.
Xunfu (巡抚), Viceroy, the highest official in a province. If there was a Zongdu (总督) (governor) appointed in a province, than the Zongdu outranked the Xunfu.

Yamen (衙门), government office.
Yangshui (洋税), also called Yangguan shui (洋关税), maritime customs duties.
Yanli (盐厘), salt Likin.
Yanglian Yin (养廉银), anti-corruption allowance.
Yingyu (盈余), surplus of Zheng'e.
Yinku (银库), the Silver Treasury.
Zheng'e (正额), the regular amount of government revenues and expenditures.
Zhou (州), prefecture, the provincial administrative district of the Qing China above Xian (县).
Zongdu (总督), Governor, the highest ranking official in one or several province(s).
Zongli Yamen (总理衙门), the Prime Minister of Foreign Affairs Yamen.
Zongren Fu (宗人府), Imperial Clan Court, an organization responsible for the affairs of the royal family.
Zouxiao (奏销), submitting financial reports to the throne for approval.

About the Guan (Customs Office)

In Chinese characters, the word "Guan" (关) has two different meanings. One means port, another means gate. Customs ports are customs offices where ships can enter. Customs gates are customs offices without a harbor being present.

In this book, I classify them as follows:

1. All the coastal customs will use the word "port": Tianjin Guan, Tianjin Haiguan, Jianghai Guan, Zhehai Guan, Minhai Guan, Yuehai Guan and Donghai Guan.
2. Land border customs are indicated with the word "gate" since they are located on dry land: Shanhai Guan, Zhangjiakou, Shahukou, Guihuacheng, Dajianlu, Chihli Pantaokou, Wuyuancheng, Gubeikou,Tungyongdao, Shengjing Mushui, Jilin Mushui and Yili Mushui. However, for Wu Chang, Xun Chang and Chen Guan I will use the word port since they are located near a river.
3. Most of the Grand Canal and Yangtze River customs will use the word "port" as the control the flow of river shipping: Zuoliangtin, Huai'an Guan, Hushu Guan, Yangzhou Guan, Wuhu Guan, Fengyang Guan, Longjiang Guan, Xixing Guan, Jiujiang Guan, Gan Guan, Beixin Guan, Nanxin Guan, Linqin Guan, Taiping Guan, Wuchang Guan, Jingzhou Guan, Hubei Xinguan, Kui Guan and Yu Guan. However, for Chongwenmen, Zuoyi and Youyi I will use the word "gate" since they are located on dry land.

Introduction

When doing research on China's political affairs one needs to take into account economic factors, just as one needs to consider political factors when doing research on China's economic affairs: these two threads in the social fabric of a country are closely intertwined.

Given the paucity of knowledge about economic activity in Qing China, especially before 1840, can we use the government's financial state as a gauge to evaluate the state of the economy? Even when one has taken into consideration all aspects of the special complexity of China's history, is it acceptable to estimate the country's economic development by studying its fiscal data? Maybe yes, maybe no. I intend to discuss the appropriateness of the various items of state finance for deriving information about the aggregate economy in Qing China.

China in its late imperial era (1644–1911) was still an agrarian society, albeit one in the process of great change. From a fiscal point of view, it was the period in which China moved from being "a state with a fiscal system to becoming a fiscal state". The fiscal system of the Qing dynasty (1644–1911) before 1850 comprised two basic elements: conventional financial revenue and expenditure; and temporary financial revenue and expenditure. Conventional financial revenue came from five main sources:

1. *Tian Fu* (Land Tax)
2. *Cao Liang* (Tribute Grain)
3. *Yan Shui* (Salt Tax)
4. *Guan Shui* (Customs duties)
5. *Za Fu* (Miscellaneous taxes, including a fish tax, a tea tax, mineral taxes, and so on)

Of these five sources, Land Tax was the most important and generated the largest portion of financial revenues. In the early Qing (before 1840), total annual revenue was about 45 million taels of silver, with land taxes accounting for about 25 million taels, about 50% of total annual revenues. The Land Tax was to a large extent determined by external factors such as weather, harvest and natural disasters, as well as arable area and the yields per hectare. However, the elasticity of Land Tax was very small, so revenue from land taxes did not change much over the business cycle. For this reason, it is very difficult to use Land Tax to estimate the actual economic situation and economic development in the country.

 | DOI 10.1163/9789004324886_002

Tribute Grain, the second item on the list of revenue sources, was collected from only eight provinces: Jiangsu, Zhejiang, An'hui, Jiangxi, Hubei, Hu'nan, Shangdong, and Hennan. All of these were located near waterways, in particular the Grand Canal and the Yangtze River. The annual quota of Tribute Grain to be collected was 3-4 million dans (a dry unit of measure for grain of approximately 50 kg) of rice. The transport of grain in traditional China was a relatively simple process as the only convenient way of transporting such large amounts of rice was on waterways.

Before 1850, collection of Tribute Grain was almost never reduced or waived. The Taiping Rebellion (1851–1864), the biggest rebellion in the Qing dynasty, brought a change in this policy, however. When the rebellion broke out, the eight provinces were devestated to varying extents. Activities to retrieve Tribute Grain after the Taiping Rebellion had been suppressed were carried out by Zeng Guofan (1811–1872), Li Hongzhang (1823–1901), and Zuo Zongtang (1812–1885), among the most powerful governors of the late Qing. Ultimately, by the final year of the Qing dynasty (1911), the annual contribution from Tribute Grain had fallen to as little as 1 million dans of rice. Clearly, it would be difficult to estimate economic activity in the Qing from the amounts of Tribute Grain collected.[1]

The third item on the list conventional sources of fiscal revenue is Salt Tax. Amounts raised from this tax were strongly influenced by two factors: population numbers; and per capita consumption of salt. Although population increased quickly during the Qing, per capita consumption of salt did not change very much. So, did revenues from the Salt Tax increase significantly in the early Qing? This seems not to have been the case. During the early Qing, the government divided the salt-producing areas into several geographical regions, each of which could only sell the salt it produced in its own territory. If they sold their salt in another region, this was considered to be "smuggling", which the government punished severely. Nevertheless, smuggling was wide spread and endemic, and this prevented substantial increases in revenue being made from the Salt Tax. In general, in the early Qing the Salt Tax consistently generated revenues of around 5 million taels of silver per year. Only in the late Qing, when *Likin* (taxing all commercial transactions by 1% of the goods value) was introduced, did tax revenues from salt—called *Yanli* ("salt Likin")—increase substantially. Of course, this also makes it very difficult to derive levels of economic activity from revenues arising from the Salt Tax in the early Qing.

Miscellaneous taxes, the fifth item on the list, could be quickly changed or adapted if the government wanted to do so. All sorts of fiscal revenue arose

1 More detail could be seen in the book of Ni Yuping (2005).

from Miscellaneous taxes, with several new kinds being created in the late Qing. In terms of total revenue, however, fiscal income arising from Miscellaneous taxes in the early Qing was very small. Indeed, it only yielded 1 million taels of silver a year, some 2% of total annual revenue. In their papers, many Chinese historians even ignore the influence of Miscellaneous taxes.

Unlike the taxes discussed so far, Customs duties, the fourth item on the list, were a very important and also flexible form of taxation. In general, the government would increase customs duties if it needed more money, this being the easiest and most effective way of expanding fiscal revenues. For example, a boat passing through a customs port could be taxed at a fixed ratio, which would range from about 2 to 5% of the value of the goods. If the economic situation was good, commercial activity would expand, and when the situation was poor, activity would decline. So, in theory, if one was looking for an indicator of fiscal income that could reflect the level of social and economic development in Qing China, Customs duties would have to be the first choice.

Following the Taiping Rebellion, the traditional financial system of the Qing dynasty faced challenges which were so great that the system could not be maintained without change. Increasing fiscal revenue as much as possible became the most important task of the government. In order to avoid financial collapse, the Qing government introduced many measures, the two most important of which were the system of *Likin* and a substantial increase in customs tarrifs, which together changed China's traditional fiscal structure tremendously. Land Tax was no longer as important a contributor to total fiscal revenues as before, while Customs duties, together with Likin and Salt Tax, grew to become almost three times as large as Land Tax. Further, Customs duties had been changed so much that it became one of the late Qing's most powerful fiscal instruments.

In traditional China, Customs duties, along with other flexible taxes, were the most powerful tool available for keeping governments alive. After the reforms introduced in the late Qing, one could say that China had changed from being an agricultural fiscal state to become a modern, commercial fiscal state. In particular, it had undergone a change in character, evolving from a stationary to an expansionary fiscal state, and from a conservative fiscal state to a progressive, adaptive one. In short, it changed "from a state with a fiscal system to becoming a fiscal state". In this sense, researching customs duties of the Qing dynasty is much more of an all-encompassing task than meets the eye.

Having said that, there have been many brilliant achievements reached over the past 100 years using modern academic methods to research Chinese economic history. In recent years, with interdisciplinary communication developing, more and more scholars with an economics background have begun researching economic history, and theory-based historical research has become more and more popular. Especially in the past 10 years, with the development of historical GDP research, the desire for access to sound historical data has become stronger and stronger. But obviously, many time series have their flaws and much work still needs to be done. Although some information is missing, of all the fiscal categories of the Qing dynasty the data on Customs duties is still the most complete time-series data available. By verifying archive materials at first hand and explaining their background and meaning, I have attempted in this book to set up a database of customs duties that answers previous short-comings in the data.

Considering that all former research on customs duties during the Qing dynasty mainly focused on the political structures in which these activities were embedded, I have decided to invest more effort in collection of the data. Although some customs duties were collected at customs gates situated at points along the dynasty's land borders, in the early Qing customs duties were mainly levied at outposts along domestic canals and rivers. In addition, some customs revenues on domestic goods were also raised at several coastal ports, including Tianjin Guan, Tianjin Haiguan, Donghai Guan, Jianghai Guan, Zhehai Guan, Minhai Guan and Yuehai Guan.

All ports serving waterborne trade were named *Haiguan* (maritime port) in the Qing dynasty. Of all of these, for most of the time customs duties on foreign goods were only imposed at Yuehai Guan. After the signing of the Sino-British Treaty (1842), however, one by one many ports serving foreign trade were opened. In previous research, scholars preferred to focus only on some of these; I consider them all. I call the customs ports for domestic trade *Changguan* (ordinary ports, taxing domestic goods) and those customs offices serving foreign trade *Yangguan* (ports for taxing foreign trade).

After 1861, when the Imperial Maritime Customs Service was established, Yuehai Guan was divided into two parts: one for levying duty on domestic goods; and one for levying customs duties on foreign goods. For the convenience of my research, I regard Yuhai Guan as *Yangguan* before 1861, and after 1861 I add its figures for domestic duties into *Changguan* and add its figures for foreign duties into *Yangguan*.

I believe that these time-series data of customs duties deliver a significant contribution in their own right, especially when one considers that all former books on fiscal revenues and expenditures of the Qing rely on data from reference years only. One final remark: the expression month in historical sources refers to lunar and not solar months.

CHAPTER 1

Research Approach

1.1 Previous Research

Although research into the role of the institution of customs and customs duties in the economic and political history of China has a long tradition, much of this has been done without employing modern techniques from disciplines such as economics and statistics. This situation has only changed in recent years.

The first book to be published on customs duties appeared in 1937: *Zhong Guo Guan Shui Shi* (History of Chinese Customs Duties), written by Wu Zhaoshen. Unfortunately, limitations of the period prevented him from using archival material of the Qing dynasty, and in addition his analysis was quite simplistic. Since then many other books have been published, but all remain relatively superficial in their analysis, as well as being inadequately short. For example, Peng Yuxin's book *Qing Dai Guan Shui Zhi Du* (The System of Customs Duties of the Qing Dynasty), published in 1956, counts only 44,000 words.

Since then a number of books have been published on the subject, albeit with their focus limited on specific periods and locations. In 2000, Huang Guoxin published *Ya Pian Zhan Zheng Qian De Dong Nan Si Hai Guan* (The Four Custom Ports in South-East China before the Opium War), which analyzes customs duties levied in Yuehai Guan, Jianghai Guan, Zhehai Guan and Minhai Guan during the early Qing dynasty. In 2004, Qi Meiqin published her book *Qing Dai Que Guan Zhi Du Yan Jiu* (The *Changguan* System of the Qing Dynasty), which describes the Qing's system of customs duties and the concept of central ports and local ports it used. Four years on, in 2008, Deng Yibin published her book *Qing Dai Qian Qi Guan Shui Zhi Du Yan Jiu* (The System of Customs Duties of the Early Qing Dynasty), which analyzes in great detail the system of customs duties in place during the period 1644–1840. Later, in 2010, *Qin Dai Chang Guan Yu Qu Yu Jing Ji Yan Jiu* (The *Changguan* and the Regional Economy of the Qing Dynasty) was published, in which the author, Liao Shengfen, expressed the belief that there is almost no relationship between customs duties and regional economic development in China. There are also a number of Japanese scholars, such as Kasaka Masaki, Kishimoto Mio and Takino Shojiro, who have written many articles, but no books, about various ports of the Qing.[1]

1 Kosaka Masanori (1991), Kishimoto Mio (1997), and Takino Shojiro (2001).

 | DOI 10.1163/9789004324886_003

Among the large number of journal articles that have also been written about this topic the most recent ones are: *Jin Nian Lai Ming Qing Shi Qi De Queguan Yanjiu* (Review of research in recent years on the *Changguan* of the Ming and Qing dynasties) by Liao Shengfen, in *ZhongguoShi Yanjiu Dongtai* (Trends of recent research on the history of China), Volume 11 (November 1997); *Qing Shi Qi De Que Guan Yan Jiu Zong Shu* (Review of research on the *Changguan* of the Qing dynasty) by Hei Guangju, in *Lishi Jiaoxue* (History of education, Volume 4 (April 2004); and *Jin Shi Nian Qing Dai Que Guan Yan Jiu Zong Shu* (Review of research in the last ten years on the *Changguan* of the Qing dynasty) by Yang Jianting, in *ZhongguoShi Yanjiu Dongtai* (Trends of recent research on Chinese history), Volume 4 (August 2009).

Generally, I have found that many researchers are mostly interested in describing the Qing's customs system, rather than providing and analyzing data on duties paid. There are, however, two series of customs data that have been highly valuable in preparing this book. The first was compiled by Tang Xianglong and published in his well-known book *Zhong Guo Jin Dai Hai Guan Shui Shou He Fen Pei Tong Ji: 1861–1910* (Statistics of Customs Revenue and their Distribution: 1861–1910). In particular, Tang's works provide the data for *Yangguan* between 1861–1910. His material stems from a large number of *Chaodang* (Copies of the Archives), which were compiled by him and other scholars in the 1930s; these are now stored in the library of the Institute of Economics, the Chinese Academy of Social Sciences.[2] *Chaodang* were copied from the First Historical Archives of China (Beijing, FHAC), which includes the Palace Midrange Rescript Memorials (*Zhupi ZouZhe*), and extra copies of grand council memorials (*Lufu Zouzhe*). As to be expected, Tang's data does contain some errors, something I will go into in Chapter 6. The other series was compiled by me and published in 2010 under the title *Qing Chao Jia Dao Guan Shui Yan Jiu* (Research on customs duties during the reigns of the Qing emperors Jiaqing and Daoguang); it includes data from 1795 to 1850. These two books are the most important sources for this monograph on customs duties from 1644 to 1911.

2 In the 1930s, thanks to the efforts of Tao Menghe (Head of the Peiping Institute of Social Survey, which merged with the Institute of Social Sciences of Academia Sinica in 1934), Tang Xianglong was able to send workers to many places where remaining Qing archives had been stored since 1911, including the Office of Documentation of the Palace Museum and the Institute of Arts at Peking University, in order to copy these Yellow Registers. The copies made at that time later became part of the Qing archive collection stored at the Institute of Economics, Chinese Academy of Social Sciences (CASS).

1.2 Data Sources

With the exception of Tang and myself, most researchers have drawn their data from two sources: *Shi Qu Yu Ji* (SQYJ) by Wang Qingyun; and *The List of Money and Grains Sent to and from the Provinces in the Seventeenth Year of Jiaqing in the Qing Dynasty* (LMGS). I have shown, however, that these sources are unreliable because customs data are missing for many historical periods and major ports of entry (on land borders or domestic waterways, and along the eastern coast). By inspecting archives from the First Historical Archives of China (FHAC), I found that data in SQYJ for Chongwenmen, Zuoyi, Youyi, Nanxin Guan and Zhehai Guan are inaccurate for the years 1841, 1842, 1845 and 1849, while the data in LMGS for Zhangjiakou, Shanhai Guan, Shahukou, Chongwenmen, Huai'an Guan, Hushu Guan, Yangzhou Guan, Xixing Guan, Jiujiang Guan, Longjiang Guan and Beixin Guan are inaccurate for the years 1811 and 1812. When customs data from the above mentioned less reliable data points are added, the data in LMGS is higher by more than 200,000 taels of silver per year and higher in SQYJ by more than 1,000,000 taels.[3]

From Table 1.1 one can see that the data in 1811 should be 4736461.453 taels of silver, not 459846.2 in LMGS; and the data in 1812 shoud be 4920342.212, not 4810340.5. These discrepancies demonstrate the importance of using materials gathered at first hand when analyzing customs revenues for the period 1644 to 1911.

In preparing this book I have drawn material from three main sources. One of these is the First Historical Archives of China (Beijing), which includes:

- *Zhupi Zouzhe* (Palace Midrange Rescript Memorials), for which the archive accession numbers always begin with the numeral 4, for example, 4-1-35-326-43. Archive accession numbers give complete information about the archived item. The example just given indicates that the item belongs to *Zhupi Zouzhe* and refers to a report submitted by Gao Chen, a Shanhai Guan district officer, on 22 December (Chinese lunar calendar) in the year 1750.
- *Tiben* (Reports to Emperors), whose archive accession numbers always begin with 2, for example 2-1-4-14795-17. Archive accession numbers give complete information about the archived item: the example refers to an item belonging to *Tiben* and identifies a report submitted by Jiangfu, a minister of the Ministry of Revenue, on the 10 May (Chinese lunar calendar) in the year 1754.

3 Ni Yuping,(2008 A & B).

TABLE 1.1 *Customs duties levied in 1811 and 1812 (in taels of silver)*

Ports of entry	Year	LMGS	Archive data	Ports of entry	Year	LMGS	Archive data
Chongwenmen	1811	290544.6	322655.34	Zhehai Guan	1811	79952.4	79943.155
	1812	253409.4	286126.5		1812	79960.5	79952.48
Zuoyi	1811	13676.9	20748	Minhai Guan	1811	208368.2	187060.997
	1812	14320.2	37060		1812	232440.6	189539
Youyi	1811	12571.9	23929.92	Taiping Guan	1811	134352.9	134352.9
	1812	12949.2	23951.02		1812	134383.5	134383.5
Huai'an Guan	1811	274531	221727.208	Yuehai Guan	1811	1165263.1	1165263.126
	1812	223848	272894.376		1812	1347936.8	1347936.891
Hushu Guan	1811	409445.2	373176.946	Zuoliangtin	1811	13367.5	13367.5
	1812	430231	392801.945		1812	12379.6	12379.6
Yangzhou Guan	1811	154270.7	153955	Shanhai Guan	1811	61810	114231.405
	1812	144568.5	144360	Zhangjiakou	1812	61867.1	111598.091
Wuhu Huguan	1811	230047.8	230047.88		1811	20004.3	60643.14
	1812	230049.5	230049.58		1812	20004.6	60644.04
Xixing Guan	1811	51969.9	52888.576	Shahukou	1811	16919.9	45677.408
	1812	53234.9	51969.912		1812	16919.9	45755.338
Fengyang Guan	1811	107227	107227.095	Guihuacheng	1811	26767.5	26767.5
	1812	95488.8	95488.826		1812	26666.1	26666.1
Jianghai Guan	1811	73612.7	73606.635	Longjiang Guan	1811	135371.9	134428.554
	1812	73606.6	73612.767		1812	133984.4	135371.996
Tianjin Guan	1811	83942	96291.833	Wuhu Gongguan	1811	117204.6	117204.66
	1812	82533.8	94884.583		1812	117201.8	117201.86
Linqin Huguan	1811	37539.5	32285.42	Linqin Gongguan	1811	4472.4	4375.3
	1812	36466.1	33151.01		1812	5418.9	5157.27
Jiujiang Guan	1811	492123.3	514948.258	Nanxing Guan	1811	25465	29444.939
	1812	584005.4	492123.389		1812	25465	29474.059
Ganguan	1811	122136.3	122136.3	Tianjin Haiguan	1811	–	46500
	1812	121610.8	121610.8		1812	–	50119
Beixing Guan	1811	196125.3	203362.284	Jingzhou Guan	1811	–	28214.174
	1812	190343.2	200125.391		1812	–	23952.888

Source: Ni Yuping (2008 B).

- *Lufu Zouzhe* (Extra Copies of Grand Council Memorials), whose archive accession numbers always begin with 3, for example 3-604-40. Archive accession numbers always give complete information about the archived item: the example refers to an item belonging to *Lufu Zouzhe* and identifies a report submitted by Chang Fu, a Shanhai Guan district officer, on 12 November (Chinese lunar calendar) in the year 1789.
- *Shangyu Dang* (Edict Records), the emperors' orders; when cited in this book these will be followed by the date of issuance as given in the archive.

To save space and facilitate ease of use, when I cite *Zhupi Zouzhe, Tiben* or *Lufu Zouzhe* I only give the archive accession numbers of items, and thus omit the reporter's name and the date on which the report was submitted.

A second major source is a selection made from a variety of published records which was edited by the First Historical Archives of China and the National Palace Museum in Taiwan, that includes:

- *Gong Zhong Dang Kang Xi Chao Zou Zhe* (Palace Midrange Rescript Memorials of the Kangxi reign);
- *Gong Zhong Dang Guang Xu Chao Zou Zhe* (Palace Midrange Rescript Memorials of the Guangxu reign);
- *Gong Zhong dang Qian Long Chao Zou Zhe* (Palace Midrange Rescript Memorials of the Qianlong reign);
- *Gong Zhong Dang Yong Zheng Chao Zou Zhe* (Palace Midrange Rescript Memorials of the Yongzheng reign);
- *Guang Xu Chao Zhu Pi Zou Zhe* (Palace Midrange Rescript Memorials of the Guangxu reign);
- *Guang Xu Xuan Tong Liang Chao Shang Yu Dang* (Edict Records of Guangxu and Xuantong reigns);
- *Jian Qing Dao Guang Liang Chao Shang Yu Dang* (Edict Records of Jiaqing and Daoguang reigns);
- *Jian Qing Dao Guang Liang Chao Shang Yu Dang* (Edict Records of Jiaqing and Daoguang reigns);
- *Kang Xi Chao Man Wen Zhu Pi Zou Zhe Quan Yi* (Translation of the Palace Midrange Rescript Memorials recorded in Manchu language of the Kangxi reign);
- *Kang Xi Chao Han Wen Zhu Pi Zou Zhe Hui Bian* (Collection of the Palace Midrange Rescript Memorials recorded in the Han language of the Kangxi reign);
- *Qian Long Chao Shang Yu Dang* (Edict Records of the Qianlong reign);

- *Xian Feng Tong Zhi Liang Chao Shang Yu Dang* (Edict Records of the Xianfeng and Tongzhi reigns);
- *Yong Zheng Chao Man Wen Zhu Pi Zou Zhe Quan Yi* (Translation of the Palace Midrange Rescript Memorials recorded in the Manchu language of the Yongzheng reign).

As before, to save space and promote ease of use, I only state page numbers if I actually cite material on those particular pages.

The third, and last, source is *Chaodang* (Copies of the Archives), which is stored in the library of the Institute of Economics, the Chinese Academy of Social Sciences. As some archives have been lost throughout the centuries, sometimes I have had to rely solely on *Chaodang* as a data source. Of course, as a rule I normally give priority to inspecting archives first hand, rather than copies, and I only cite *Chaodang* instead if I cannot find the original archive or data is missing in that archive.

Chaodang includes several important sources:

- The most important source is *Qingdai Guanshui Shouzhi Baogao Biao* (Revenue and Expenditure Reports of Customs in the Qing dynasty).
- The second-most important is *Tiben·Guanshui* (Customs Duties Reports to Emperors).
- I have also used a copy of the book of *Geguan Changshui Shizheng Duanzheng Yinliang Shumu* (The amount of silver raised by taxation and taxation shortfalls for each *Changguan*), which is stored in the library of the Institute of Economics, the Chinese Academy of Social Sciences.

Needless to say, in addition to archives, there are many kinds of official books, gazetteers and other historical records (such as published collections written by individual officials) that also have had high value in my research. I will provide the details of these when I cite them.

CHAPTER 2

The System of Customs Duties under the Qing Dynasty

2.1 The System of Customs Duties in Traditional China

China's system of customs duties has a long history. Indeed, *Liji* (礼记, Book of Rites) reported that before the Zhou dynasty (BC 1029–BC 256) "There was no tax on the market",[1] although we have no more detail than just that. Of the Zhou dynasty, *Zhouli* (周礼, Rites of the Zhou dynasty) noted that "The system of customs duties determines taxes on goods, and the officials are responsible for the people and collecting the tax. If goods do not pass through the customs port, and duty is not paid, the officials can punish any offending merchants and confiscate their goods."[2]

During the Spring and Autumn periods (BC 770–BC 476,), Kongzi (Confucius), the founder of Confucianism, suggested that the emperor should not tax goods at all, in order to create more benefits for the people.[3] This shows that a system was already in existence at that time. During the Qin (BC 221–BC 207) and Han (BC 202–220) dynasties the system of the customs duties developed rapidly, at which time customs ports such as Tongguan, Hanguguan and Yumen Guan became quite famous. During the Sui (581 AD–618 AD) and Tang (618 AD–907 AD) dynasties, as a result of economic development, customs revenues also increased and Xuanzhong (712 AD–756 AD), the seventh emperor of the Tang dynasty, set up Guangzhou Shiboshi (the predecessor of Yuehai Guan of the Qing dynasty) to levy duty on foreign goods.

In 960, the Song dynasty (960–1279) published *Shangshui Zheli* (Customs Duty Regulations), which stipulated that customs duties were to be levied at 2% rate of the value of the goods. These were the first customs rules in China and included the names of all goods that would attract duty; these items were listed publically on notice boards.[4] The Song dynasty also kept in place the Shiboshi system, which gave officials powers to examine goods, buy goods needed by the government, and sell special goods to the people. During the Song dynasty, customs duties became one of the government's most important

1 Wang Pingzhen (1983), p. 3.
2 Li Xueqing (1999), p. 383.
3 Yang Chaomin (2009), p. 66.
4 Sun Xuewen (2003), p. 45.

 | DOI 10.1163/9789004324886_004

sources of fiscal revenue, as the records show: "The benefits of Shiboshi are very large. And if it is managed well, we can easily raise one million coins of tax annually."[5] The Song government also set up special customs gates called *Quechang* in the northern part of China to regulate trade with northeastern and northwestern minorities, mostly taxing trade in tea and horses. Following the Song, the Yuan dynasty (1206–1368), the largest and most powerful empire of China, levied duty on goods at a rate of 1/30, as well as maintaining the Shiboshi system. It provided more explanations of its customs rules than the Song dynasty did.[6]

At the beginning of the Ming dynasty (1368–1644) the system of customs duties was simple: duty was levied at a rate of 1/30. Later, in 1375, the Ming government began to publish the money called Daming Notes, a kind of paper currency. To force people to use this paper money, the government stipulated that it should be used to pay customs duties. However, with the passing of time Daming Notes were used less and less. So in 1439, the government stated: "Since merchants are unwilling to pay tax and always act to avoid the law, we shall use former methods and tax them five-fold in the following 33 prefectures and counties: Shuntian, Yintian, Shuozhou and Songjiang, Zhengjiang, Huai'an, Changzhou, Yangzhou, Yizheng, Hangzhou, Jiaxin, Huzhou, Fouzhou, Jiannin, Wuchang, Jingzhou, Nanchang, Ji'an, Ninjiang, Qinjiang, Guangzhou, Kaifeng, Ji'nan, Ji'ning, Dezhou, Ninqing, Guilin, Taiyuan, Pingyang, Puzhou, Chengdu, Chongqing and Luzhou. At the same time, we will also create seven new ports for levying customs along the Grand Canal, i.e. at Huoxian, Ji'ning, Ninqing, Xuzhou, Huai'an, Yangzhou and Nanjing."[7] Soon, the Ministry of Revenue (*Hubu*) closed the customs offices of Ji'ning and Xuzhou because they were too close to other ports and in 1446 the Ministry of Revenue transferred the customs port at Huoxian to Hexiwu. During the reign of Jintai (1450–1457), the government set up another four offices: Hushu, Beixin, Jiujing and Jinshazhou. In 1493, the customs gate at Chongwenmen was established, followed two years later by the port of Fengyang. Much later, in 1629, the port of Wuhu was established. Finally, some ports were also established by local governments, such as that of Gan Guan in Jiangxi province.

In 1562, the Ming government ordered that customs duties should be levied at a fixed rate, and that if customs revenues surpassed the offices's quota, the excess should be handed over to the central treasury.[8] In 1572, the government

5 Xu Song (1957), Volume 44.

6 Sun Xuewen (2003), p. 77.

7 Yang Shiqi (1438), Volume 50.

8 Li Dongyang (1529), Volume 35.

ordered that all taxes must be paid in silver. Following the reign of the emperor Wanli (1572–1620), the quota for each port was made payable in silver: "There were customs quotas of 325,000 taels of silver, to which in 1597 another 80,000 taels of silver were added. However (due to war and natural disasters), customs revenues decreased after 1599. In 1601, these revenues were 266,000 taels."[9] In the late Ming, tax revenues increased again.

TABLE 2.1 *Customs duties of the Ming dynasty (in taels of silver)*

Ports / Year	1580	1599	1621	1625
Linqin Guan	44,700	83,800	63,800	63,800
Hexiwu	14,600	46,000	32,000	32,000
Hushu Guan	17,400	45,000	67,500	87,500
Jiujiang Guan	10,900	25,000	37,500	57,500
Beixin Guan	36,800	40,000	60,000	80,000
Huai'an Guan	11,400	22,000	29,600	45,600
Yangzhou Guan	9,600	13,000	15,600	25,600
Total	145,400	274,800	306,000	392,000

Source: Zhang Tingyu (1936), Volume 26.

Table 2.1 shows that customs duties increased greatly during the late Ming, although the proportional contribution to fiscal revenue was not as great as during the Song dynasty.

In addition to the Ministry of Revenue, the Ministry of Works (*Gongbu*) also set up some ports for customs purposes, but only to levy duty on bamboo and wood. The first three of these were located at Wuhu, Jingzhou and Hangzhou; all revenues collected were to be used by the Ministry of Works. Following these three, another 12 ports were established.[10] The rate of taxation also changed over time: during the Hongwu era (1368–1398) customs duty was levied at a ratio of 1/30, but during the reign of Yongle (1402–1424) it was raised to 2/30. In 1435–1449 it was raised again, this time to 4/30, and in 1457–1464 once more to 6/30. Then, in 1464–1487, the trend was reversed and it was cut to 1/30. Even so, this tax burden was still very light: in 1471, only several thousands of taels of silver were collected by the Ministry of Works, and by the last year of

9 Zhang Tingyu (1974), Volume 81.
10 Li Dongyang (1529), Volume 204.

the Ming dynasty this had only increased to several tens of thousands of taels.[11] Indeed, when compared with ports set up by the Ministry of Revenue, the duties raised by the Ministry of Works were small, and this was also the case during the Qing.

2.2 The *Changguan* System of the Qing

The Qing government (1644–1911) believed that customs duties should be levied at all ports, and when it inherited the customs system of the Ming dynasty it even introduced a number of innovations to improve the system.[12] Like the Ming, the Qing government had two types of customs offices: those belonging to the Ministry of Revenue (*Hubu*), called *Huguan*; and those belonging to the Ministry of Works (*Gongbu*), called *Gongguan*. Generally, each custom port or gate managed several gates at the same time. Such as Zuoyi was responsible for An'ding, Dongzhi, Chaoyang, Dongbian, Guangqu, and Zuo'an gates, and Youyi was responsible for Desheng, Xizhi, Fucheng, Xibian, Guang'an, You'an, and Yongding gates.

Wang Qingyun, a very famous official and scholar during the reign of Daoguang (1821–1850), is recorded to have said that "Our government levied customs duties according to the system of the former dynasty, starting in the year 1645."[13] The Qing government set up another 19 *Huguan* very soon after 1644, the year that it entered Beijing and established its empire. These extra gates of entry were located at Chongwenmen, Zuoyi, Youyi, Tianjin Guan, Zhangjiakou, Longqun, Fengtian, Shahukou, Linqing Guan, Huai'an Guan, Fengyang Guan, Wuhu Guan, Yangzhou Guan, Xixing Guan, Hushu Guan, Beixin Guan, Jiujang Guan, Gan Gan and Min'an Guan. During the reign of Kanxi (1661–1722), the government added a further 11 Huguan, located at Zuoliangtin, Shanhai Guan, Wuchang Guan, Dajianlu, Kui Guan, Taiping Guan, Yuehai Guan, Jianghai Guan, Zhehai Guan, Minhai Guan and Fenghuangcheng Zhongjiang. During the reign of Yongzheng (1723–1735), Wu Chang and Xun Chang, another two new Huguan, both located in Guangxi province, were set up. During the reign of Qianlong (1736–1795), the government also established two new Huguan: one at Guihuacheng and and one at Dolon Nuur. In total, in the early Qing there were 34 Huguan. Of these, most had been inherited from the Ming: only several customs offices—including Zuoyi, Youyi, Wuchang

11 Zhang Tingyu (1974), Volume 81.

12 Fu Heng (1764), Volume 16.

13 Wang Qingyun (1985), Volume 6.

Guan, Dajianlu and Guihuacheng—were new. Of course, the Qing government made adjustments to a number of Ming policies. During the Kangxi, for example, several small ports were transeferred under the management of Yangzhou Guan and Huai'an Guan.

During Jiaqing's reign (1796–1820), the Huguan were mainly managed by *Guizhou Qinglisi* (a division of the Ministry Revenue with the title of Guizhou province), and included 24 ports of entry: Chongwenmen, Zuoyi, Youyi, Zuoliangtin, Tianjin Guan, Zhangjiakou, Shanhai Guan, Shahukou, Guihuachen, Linqing Guan, Jianghai Guan, Hushu Guan, Huai'an Guan (including Miaowan Guan), Yangzhou Guan, Xixing Guan, Fengyang Guan, Wuhu Guan, Jiujiang Guan, Gan Guan, Minhai Guan, Zhehai Guan, Beixin Guan, Yuehai Guan and Taiping Guan. At the same time, *Shandong Qinglisi* (another division of the Ministry Revenue with the title of Shandong province) managed Fenghuangcheng Zhongjiang and Fengtian Niumashui; *Fujian Qinglisi* (another division of the Ministry Revenue with the title of Fujian provnice) managed Tianjin Haishui; *Hubei Qinglisi* (yet another division of the Ministry Revenue with the title of Hubei province) managed Wuchang Guan; *Sichuan Qinglisi* (still another division of the Ministry Revenue with the title of Sichuan province) managed Kui Guan and Dajianlu; and *Guangdong Qinglisi* (one more division of the Ministry Revenue with the title of Guangdong province) managed Wu Chang and Xun Chang. Altogether, there were 32 Huguan during the Jiaqing period.

Besides Huguan, there were also *Gongguan* (Ministry of Works) ports. According to Li (1908), there were Linqing Gongguan in Sandong province, Longjiang Gongguan in Jiangsu province, Wuhu Gongguan in Anhui province, Nanxin Gongguan in Zhejiang province, Jinzhou Gongguan in Hubei province, Chen Guan Gongguan in Hu'nan province, and Yu Guan Gongguan in Sichuan province.

Gongguan were established at Suqian Gongguan (under the jusrisdiction of Huai'an Guan), Youzha Gongguan (belonging to Yangzhou Guan), Tongyongdao Gongguan, Pantaokou Gongguan, Guobeikou Gongguan in Zhili province, Shahukou Mushui in Shanxi province, Shengjin Mushui in Liaoning province, Jilin Mushui in Jilin province and Yili Mushui in Xingjiang province. However, since Youzha Gongguan fell under the jurisdiction to Yangzhou Guan, Suqian Guan Gongguan to Huai'an Guan, and Shahukou Mushui to Shahukou Huguan, one may conclude that by 1840 there were in total 46 Huguan and Gongguan offices.[14]

14 Li Hongzhang (1908), Volume 942.

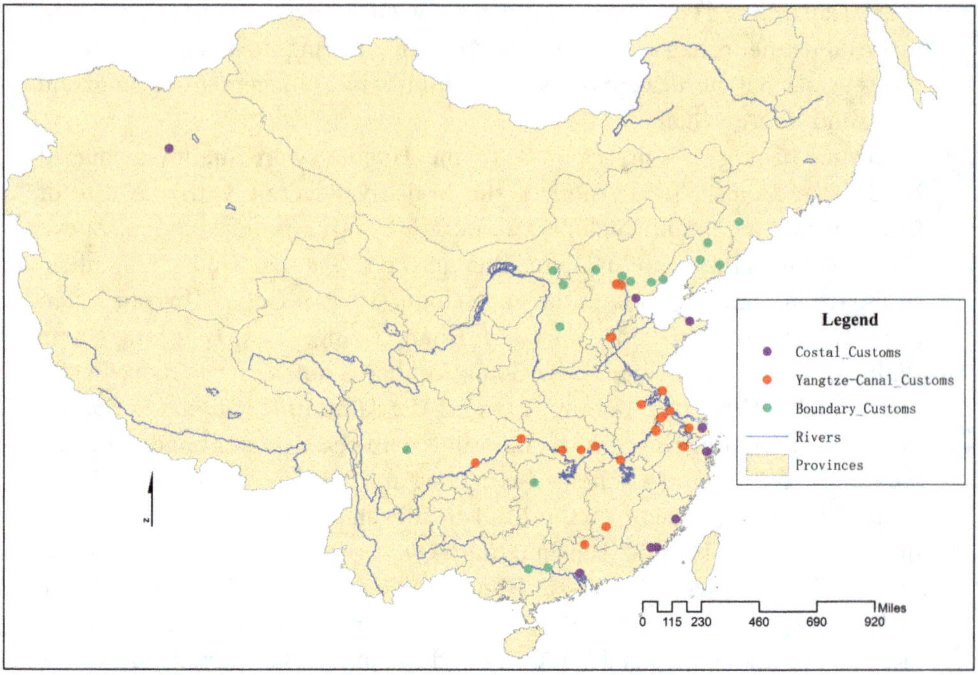

MAP 2.1 *Customs offce at which customs duty was collected before 1840*

Huguan and Gongguan are referred to collectively as *Changguan*, i.e. ordinary customs ports (as compared with *Yangguan*, or foreign trade offices). I have divided *Changguan* into three kinds, according to their geographic positions: gates of entry on land borders; ports on or near the Grand Canal and Yangtze River; and coastal ports. If gates were located along land borders, or if duties were mainly levied on trade with ethnic minorities, they fell under the jurisdiction of Land Border customs. Offices located close to or on the Grand Canal or Yangtze River fell under the jurisdiction of Canal and Yangtze River customs, and, finally, coastal offices fell under the jurisdiction of Coastal customs. Of course, this is only a very rough classification, but by regrouping the data according to this classification does not affect our results in any significant way.

Land Border customs raised duty at 17 gates and points of entry: Shanhai Guan, Zhangjiakou, Shahukou, Guihuacheng, Wuyuancheng, Gubeikou, Tungyongdao, Chihli Pantaokou, Shengjing Mushui, Jilin Mushui, Yili Mushui, Dajianlu, Fengtian Niuma Shui, and Fenghuangcheng Zhongjiang being customs gates; only Wu Chang, Xun Chang and Chen Guan being ports in the nautical sense of the word.

Customs duty was levied by Canal and Yangtzi River customs at 23 entry points: Zuoliangtin, Huai'an Guan, Hushu Guan, Yangzhou Guan, Wuhu Huguan, Wuhu Gongguan, Longjiang Guan, Xixing Guan, Fengyang Guan, Linqin Huguan, Linqin Gongguan, Jiujiang Guan, Gan Guan, Beixin Guan, Nanxin Guan, Yu Guan, Kui Guan, Taiping Guan, Wuchang Guan and Jingzhou Guan being offices in the true sense of the word; and Chongwenmen, Zuoyi and Youyi being customs gates.

Finally, Coastal customs collected duty at seven ports: Tianjin Guan, Tianjin Haiguan, Jianghai Guan, Zhehai Guan, Minhai Guan, Yuehai Guan (after 1861) and Donghai Guan.

2.3 Policy Adjustments

In June 1644, Manchurian soldiers entered Beijing to end the turmoil of rebellion and war and unite the country under the Qing emperor Shunzhi. The new government proclaimed that "No duties will be levied this year but, as stipulated in the late Ming, all ports should be taxed *Zheng'e* (according to a predetermined quota) as from the 1 January of 1646."[15] Since a quota of about 360,000 taels of silver was set in the late Ming, I estimate that the quota during the reign of Shunzhi was also at about that level. It was, however, very difficult to collect this quota due ongoing warfare.

From archives we know that in the year 1680, during the Kangxi, the government said that "Since our county needs money so badly, it is only logical that we increase the quota." Thus, the quota of Wuhu Huguan was increased from 45,300 to 50,300 taels, Beixin Guan from 2,400 to 3,400 taels, and Longjiang Guan from 39,300 to 43,800 taels.[16]

There were some subsequent adjustments made to *Zheng'e*, but the percentage change was not too large and *Zheng'e* grew in total to about 2 million taels of silver.[17] In addition to *Zheng'e*, some ports also charged *Tong Jin Shui Jiao* (a copper transport fee), a fee to be paid by those who bought copper and sent it to Beijing. Shipping copper through ports stopped in 1707, yet the fee continued to be collected. According to the records, the annual transport fee was 7,692 taels of silver for Chongwenmen (8,536 taels per year if an additional lunar month was included); in Tianjin Guan, Linqin Huguan and Xixing Guan the fee was 7,692 taels; in Jianghia Guan it was 2,500 taels; in Hushu Guan it was 22,442 taels; in Huai'an Guan it was 15,384 taels; in Fengyang Guan it was

15 Liu Jingzhao (2000), Volume 26.

16 TB of FHAC: 2-1-4-13560-19.

17 Kun Gang (1990), Volume 23.

10,320 taels; in Wuhu Huguan it was 18,423 taels; in Jiujiang Guan it was 18,392 taels; in Gan Guan it was 5,346 taels; in Minhai Guan it was 7,000 taels; in Zhehai Guan it was 3,750 taels; in Beixin Guan it was 15,384 taels; in Taiping Guan it was 5,846 taels; and in Yuehai Guan it was 3,564 taels of silver. In total, *Tong Jin Shui Jiao* collected annually amounted to 166,811 taels of silver. Since it was regarded as part of the quota, I consider it to be a part of *Zheng'e* and do not mention it as a separate item.[18]

Yingyu (surplus) was created when the duties collected surpassed *Zheng'e*; *Yingyu* also contributed to government income. Speaking of *Yingyu,* Qianlong emperor said: "Each customs port has its quota and all the money it collects has to be sent to the government. We created *Yingyu* because we were afraid that some officials would embezzle any excess *Zheng'e* that had not been collected directly from merchants and the people. However, the harvest of each province may vary, and the quality of goods traded may also vary. How could we fix *Yingyu* for each port in advance? The Ministry of Revenue (*Hubu*) would be happy to find that *Yingyu* was greater than that of the previous year; yet if there was a loss, it would criticize the officials responsible. Thus, the officials need to increase *Yingyu* year by year to avoid criticism, which in turn disadvantages merchants and the people. We need to reconsider the balance between the people and taxation."[19]

In 1744, Yan Shisheng, the Hubei viceroy, reported the *Yingyu* collected from Jingzhou Guan. It made Qianlong emperor very angry. In his report, Yan said that *Yingyu* collected between 1741 and 1744 was 13,049.9, 14,755, 27,571.5 and 24,247.2 taels, consecutively. Qianlong's response to Yan Shisheng was direct: "This report is only about money and ways to make even more. What do you really want? Don't forget that you are the father of your province. Even a loss would be acceptable—provided you taxed properly. You should feel ashamed for that."[20] This archival record gives us an insight into the emperor's attitude towards customs duties.

As the economy grew, with it grew*Yingyu*. In order to control this source of revenue, the government made several adjustments. In 1749, at the beginning of Qianlong's reign, the government stipulated that *Yingyu* be levied at a rate no less than that of 1736, the last year of Yongzheng's reign and the first year of Qianlong's. Referring to the 1736 measure, Qianlong explained that "*Hubu* wants to compare the tax with that of the year before, and if there is a shortfall the officials responsible should be punished. Comparison with the previous

18 Kun Gang (1990), Volume 23.

19 SYD of FHAC: 3 December, 6th year of Qianlong.

20 ZPZZ of FHAC: 4-1-35-316-22.

year is good but the result will be terrible. If an office raised 10,000 taels in revenue this year, it has to raise 15,000 taels the following year, and 20,000 the year after that. Where will this end? All money would be transferred from the people, increasing their tax burden, which is not a good measure. I think we should compare taxes collected with those of 1736, which is an adequate benchmark as it is not too big and not too small."[21]

However, as time passed, almost all *Yingyu* coming from the ports either surpassed or fell short of *Yingyu* collected in 1736. In 1777, when Yangzhou Guan and Fengyang Guan once more experienced a gap as compared to the 1736 benchmark, the emperor had to admit that comparison with *Yingyu* collected in 1736 had not been a good idea. He instead created a triennial system of comparison: "Customs revenues are linked to harvests and cannot be changed spontaneously. If revenues in a year are lower than those of the previous year, they should then be compared with another two former years. If it is not smaller than in any of these three previous years, it will be acceptable. I had good intentions when ordering a comparison with *Yingyu* collected in 1736, but now I know it may not fit every port. So a triennial comparison will replace comparison with *Yingyu* in 1736 ."[22] Nevertheless, in practice *Hubu* always compared the *Yingyu* collected with the highest amount amassed in the three years previous. If the *Yingyu* was less, the responsible officials would have to make up the shortfall from their private means.

Obviously, the system of triennial comparison was not a good policy because it did not take any account of the reason for increases or decreases in *Yingyu*. In practice, it drove officials to increase taxes by any means possible. Furthermore, trade patterns during the late Qianlong changed significantly and with them the customs duties collected. There were some obviously expected revenue increases from customs offices near the rivers and the coast. However, some other ports close to the Grand Canal experienced decreases in customs revenues, and nobody wanted to be an official at these ports since they had to pay any short falls out of their own pockets. So, in 1799, during the reign of Jianqing, the government was forced to adjust its policy and cancel the system of triennial comparisons: instead the new *Yingyu* was set at a fixed amount (*Zheng'e* was not changed). This was a very important event in the history of customs duties in the Qing.

On 18 March 1799, emperor Jiaqing declared:

21 ZPZZ of FHAC: 4-1-35-325-39.

22 SYD of FHAC: 3 August, 42nd year of Qianlong.

> The amount of customs duties collected has been judged according to a system of triennial comparison. If the revenues collected were considered to be insufficient, the responsible officials would be punished and they would have to make up the shortfall out of their own pockets. Obviously, this has already resulted in officials taxing the people heavier than their rulers have asked of them, to avoid shortfalls occurring. But most of the time, the shortfall would not be made up so easily (since the volume of economic transactions fluctuated over time), and this system was based on guesses rather than estimates. I have examined the list of customs offices under the jurisdiction of the Ministry of Revenue and found that different offices face different sets of circumstances. I will introduce a new policy in which *Yingyu* for each port will be fixed and the system of triennial comparison will stop permanently. If tax revenues are too low, the responsible officials should then pay the shortfall. And this system is not only applicable for Huguan, but also for Gongguan.[23]

According to this new policy, a fixed amount of *Yingyu* was stipulated: Zuoliangtin was 6,000 taels of silver; Tianjin Guan was 20,000; Linqing Huguan was 11,000; Jianghai Guan was 42,000; Hushu Guan was 235,000; Huai'an Guan was 111,000; Miaowan Guan was 2, 200(under the jusridiction of Huai'an Guan); Yangzhou Guan was 68,000; Xixing Guan was 29,000; Fengyang Guan was 15,000; Wuhu Huguan was 73,000; Jiujiang Guan was 347,800; Gan Guan was 38,000; Minhai Guan was 113,000; Zhehai Guan was 39,000; Beixin Guan was 650,00; Wuchang Guan was 12,000; Kui Guan was 110,000; Yuehai Guan was 855,500; Taiping Guan was 75,500; Wu Chang was 7,500; Xun Chang was 5,200; Guihuacheng was 1,600; Shanhai Guan was 49,487; Shahukou was 15,414; and Zhangjiakou was 40,561. In total these ports collected 2,387,762 taels of silver as *Yingyu*.

Five years later, the government once more changed the *Yingyu* of some ports. The Ministry of Revenue reported at the time: "After our examination, we find that since 1799 most customs ports have raised more taels of silver than their tax quota stipulates. At ports such as Yuehai Guan, Tianjin Guan, Beixin Guan, and Gan Guan custom duties collected have even doubled, thus meeting the 1799 quota with ease, so we need not worry about these ports anymore. Also, customs collected at some places, such as Jianghai Guan, Taiping Guan, Wuchang Guan, and Guihuacheng have surpluses of 1,000 to 10,000 taels of silver each year, and that is alright too. However, there are still some offices, like Zhehai Guan, Yangzhou Guan, Fengyang Guan, Jiujiang Guan, Hushu Guan, Huai'an Guan, Kui Guan and Linqing Guan, whose customs revenue is always

23 SYD of FHAC: 18 March, 4th year of Jiaqing.

short of the quota."[24] In keeping with this report, Jiaqing adjusted the *Yingyu* of some ports: Xixing Guan's *Yingyu* was increased from 29,000 to 33,000 taels of silver, Jiujiang Guan from 347,800 to 367,000 taels, Zhehai Guan from 39,000 to 44,000 taels, Yangzhou Guan from 68,000 to 71,000 taels, Fengyang Guan from 15,000 to 17,000 taels, Hushu Guan from 235,000 to 250,000 taels, and Huai'an Guan from 111,000 to 131,000 taels of silver. *Yingyu* of the other offices was not changed. After this change, the total amount of *Yingyu* collected increased from 2,387,762 to 2,455,962 taels of silver.[25]

Up until 1831, quotas set for *Yingyu* remained very stable. In 1831, however, because duties collected at the ports of Huai'an Guan and Hushu Guan always fell short of their fixed quotas, the government reduced the *Yingyu* at these two ports from 131,000 to 110,000 taels, and from 250,000 to 230,000 taels of silver, respectively.[26] From then on, up until the end of the Qing, there were no major changes in *Yingyu* quotas.

TABLE 2.2 *Customs duty quotas in the late Qing (in taels of silver)*

Port of entry	*Zheng'e*	*Yingyu*	Total
Chongwenmen*	102,175	212,789	314,964
Zuoyi	10,008	18,000	28,008
Youyi	10,005.12	7,321.4	17,326.52
Zuoliangtin	6,339.26	6,000	12,339.26
Huai'an Guan	254,363.602	110,000	364,363.602
Hushu Guan	191,151.388	230,000	421,151.388
Yangzhou Guan	92,791.3	71,000	163,791.3
Wuhu Huguan	156,919.08	73,000	229,919.08
Xixing Guan	41,376.325	33,000	74,376.325
Fengyang Guan	90,159.6	17,000	107,159.6
Jianghai Guan	23,980.33	42,000	65,980.33
Tianjin Guan	48,156.313	20,000	68,156.313
Linqing Huguan	37,376.313	11,000	48,376.313
Jiujiang Guan	172,281.306	367,000	539,281.306
Gan Guan	46,470	38,000	84,470
Beixin Guan	123,053.65	65,000	188,053.65
Zhehai Guan	35,908.23	44,000	79,908.23
Minghai Guan	73,549.547	113,000	186,549.547

24 LFZZ of FHAC: 3-1767-64.

25 Li Hongzhang (1908), Volume 238.

26 SYD of FHAC: 13 August , 11th year of Daoguang.

TABLE 2.2 *Customs duty quotas in the late Qing (in taels of silver)* (cont.)

Port of entry	*Zheng'e*	*Yingyu*	Total
Taiping Guan	52,675	75,500	128,175
Yuehai Guan	43,564	855,500	899,064
Shanhai Guan	61,642.379	49,487	111,129.379
Zhangjiakou	20,000	40,561	60,561
Shahukou	16,919.95	15,414	32,333.95
Guihuacheng**	15,000	1,600	16,600
Tianjin Haiguan	26,000	14,000	40,000
Fengtian	3,307	Not fixed	3,307
Fenghuangcheng Zhongjiang	4,000	1,000	5,000
Wuchang Guan	33,000	12,000	45,000
Kui Guan	73,740.491	110,000	183,740.491
Dajianlu	20,000	Not fixed	20,000
Wuchang	60,913	7,821	68,734
Xunchang	43,741	5,565	49,306
Chen Guan	12,500	3,800	16,300
Wuyuancheng	1,231	2	1,233
Linqing Gongguan	4,572.74	3,800	8,372.74
Wuhu Gongguan	70,146.16	47,000	117,146.16
Longjiang Guan	57,607.225	55,000	112,607.225
Jinzhou Guan	17,687.156	13,000	30,687.156
Tongyongdao	7,115	3,900	11,015
Yu Guan	5,000	No fixed	5,000
Nanxin Guan***	30,247.5	-77.981	30,169.519
Gubeikou	1,212.51	Not fixed	1,212.51
Shengjing Mushui	2,000	Not fixed	2,000
Jilin Mushui	656	Not fixed	656
Pantaokou	6,445	Not fixed	6,445
Yilin Mushiu	Not fixed	Not fixed	Not fixed
Total	2,206,991.475	2,792,982.419	4,999,973.894

* Chongwenmen's *Zheng'e* was 8536 tales higher in lunar month and became 110,710 taels of silver.
** Guihuacheng also had to tax coins, collecting some 9,000, 000 coins of *Zheng'e* and 137,610 coins of Yingyu. These amounts were not included in the total quota.
*** Nanxin Guan's *Yingyu* was fixed at 3,922.019 taels of silver but each year it received an additional 4,000 taels from Beixing Guan.
Sources: materials come from various sources including *Shilu*, *Huidian*, *Hubu Zheli* and archives.

In addition to ordinary *Zheng'e* and *Yingyu*, some offices also had to supply *Ewai Yingyu* (additional Yingyu), such as Tianjin Guan, which was required to send 12,000 taels of silver to the imperial palace each year.

In 1853, when the Taiping Rebellion broke out, almost all customs ports near to Jiangsu, Zhejiang, and the Yangtze River asked the central government to waive the quota they were normally required to meet. Even though these offices faced dangerous situations, still the Ministry of Revenue (*Hubu*) answered: "We think that different ports have to deal with different situations. Longjiang Guan, Yangzhou Guan, Wuhu Guan and Jiujiang Guan were occupied by the rebels and could not be taxed, and we have had to agree that they collect duties without having to meet a specific quota. Although rebels are active close to Hushui Guan, Huai'an Guan and Fengyang, these ports have still been able to trade. If we agree to lift their quota, there would be no difference between them and the occupied ports. So Hushui Guan, Huai'an Guan and Fengyang Guan must be taxed just as before."[27] In other words, the customs officials in these ports had to solve the difficulties by themselves—at least this was what the central government hoped.

2.4 Rate of Taxation and Surtaxes

In 1644, the year that the Qing entered Beijing, and also the first year of the emperor Shunzhi, no taxes were levied. But one year later, Shunzhi's government, in addition to starting to levy taxes, also made changes to the rules in force under the Ming dynasty. There were two major changes: duty was to be paid in units of taels instead of coins; and some items were deleted from, and others added to, the list of goods to be taxed. According to research done by Xu Tan and Jing Junjian,[28] during the reign of Yongzheng the duty to be charged on 30 kinds of goods was changed for the port of Chongwenmen, i.e. 2.6% of a total of 1173 goods. During the Qianlong, the duty on 36 kinds of goods was changed, i.e. 3% of a total 1,192 goods.

At the port of Linqin Guan, duty was kept for ony 180 of the 1,900 dutiable items under the Ming dynasty. Some kinds of goods that were very popular in the Ming were no longer traded in the Qing, such as, for example, golden silk

27 LFZZ of FHAC: 3-4376-49.

28 Xu Tan and Jing Junjian, Qing Dai Qian Qi, Shang Shui Wen Ti Xing Tan (New Research about the Customs Duties in the Early Qing) in Researches In Chinese Economic History, vol. 2 (May 1990), p. 93.

from Nanjing and Hangzhou and golden silk yarn from Suzhou.[29] In the reign of Daoguang, some new goods were added to the list of dutiable items at Yuehai Guan, such as wheelbarrow—attracting a duty of 2 taels—and canary cages covered with glass—attracting a duty of 3 taels.[30]

The Qing government abandoned the policy of fixing the price of goods in advance, as was done by the Ming, and instead taxed goods by the piece or by volume. Such units included the *dan* (one dan of rice equals approximately 50 kg), the *che* (one cart full of goods), the *jin* (0.5 kg), the *pi* (a horse, donkey or mule), the *jian* (one piece of something), the *fu* (a pair of items), the *xiang* (one box of things), and the *bao* (one bag of something).

In general, there were four kinds of customs duty on goods: clothing duty, duty on food, duty per article, and duty on groceries. However, the actual goods subject to duty varied from office to office. In Beixin Guan, 2,100 different varieties of dutiable goods were divided into 50 categories that included silk, cotton, cloth, copper, china, hats, iron, lacquerware, medicinal materials, groceries, and foreign goods.[31] There were 217 kinds of medicinal materials and 50 kinds of cloth, many items of which have no real equivalent in English. It has been said that "The system of customs duties of the Qing was very complicated. Many items were referred to as *Changguan*, but they had different names for the purposes of customs duty. Especially the rates of taxation and the kinds of tax were so dazzling that it was hard for us to understand."[32]

In addition, the *Liangtou* (referring to a boat's skipper) was also taxed at the same time as were the goods being transported. In effect, a tax was levied on the boat itself. To do this, officials checked the length and width of the boat and compared these with a variety of scales. As it was paid in silver, this tax was known as *Liangtou* silver. In Jiujiang Guan, middle-sized and larger boats would be taxed according to a quota of 17.5 taels of silver, which along with other surtaxes could reach 47-48 taels and 37-42 taels in total per boat. Boats for transporting salt would be taxed 146 taels each.[33] In Hushu Guan, *Liangtou* silver could be levied depending on the goods carried: *Ping Liao* (ordinary goods), *Jia Ping* (ordinary goods plus *liangtou*), *Bu Liao* (*liangtou* still to be added), and *Jia Bu* (special *liangtou* still to be added). Table 2.3 shows the relationship between *Liangtou* silver and boat lengths for Hushu Guan.

29 Tiben Guanshui of Chaodang, 2 September, 11th year of Qianlong.

30 Wo Ren (1865), Volume 68.

31 Jiang Zhaochen (2002), p. 409.

32 Li Jingming (1936), pp. 358–359.

33 FHAC (1991), Volume 14, pp. 111–112.

TABLE 2.3 Liangtou *silver related to boat length, as applied at Hushu Guan in 1686 (in taels of silver)*

Boat length (Chinese feet)	Pingliao	*Jiaping*	*Buliao*	*Jiabu*
7	1.7	8.1	9.1	11.1
8	3.1	11.2	12.2	16.2
9	4.2	14.3	15.3	24.3
10	5.3	16.4	17.4	29.4
11	7.4	20.5	21.5	34.5
12	8.5	24.6	25.6	39.6
13	9.6	28.7	29.7	44.7
14	10.7	33.3	33.8	49.8
15	11.8	37.9	38.9	53.9
16	12.9	42.1	43.1	59.1
17	14.1	46.2	47.2	63.2
18	15.2	51.3	52.3	67.3

Note: 3 Chinese feet = 1 meter.
Source: Ling Shouqi (1992), Volume 5.

In Yuehai Guan, there were three types of *Liangtou* silver: one for Chinese boats (four grades, taxed per Chinese foot), one for Japanese boats (four grades) and one for Western boats (three grades), as shown in Tables 2.4a and 2.4b.

TABLE 2.4a Liangtou *silver applicable to Chinese boats at Yuehai Guan*

Grade	Length (Chinese feet)	Width (Chinese feet)	Tax per 10 (Chinese feet)
1	74	22	15
2	70	20	13
3	60	18	11
4	50	16	9

Source: Liang Tingzhan (1935), Volume 9.

TABLE 2.4b Liangtou *silver applicable to Japanese and Western boats at Yuehai Guan (Chinese feet/tael)*

Grade	Japanese boats		Western boats		Tax per boat (taels)
	Length (Chinese feet)	Width (Chinese feet)	Length (Chinese feet)	Width (Chinese feet)	
1	74	23	74	23	1,400
2	70	21	72	22	1,100
3	60	20	65	20	600
4	50	15	–	–	400

Source: Liang Tingzhan (1935), Volume 9.

Xu Tan and Jing Junjian wrote that "The customs rules and quotas of the Qing were very stable as a whole, although the rate of taxation of the Qing had a declining trend".[34] However, it is difficult to tell the exact rate of duty at each port in the Qing dynasty since rates were connected to customs rules, and each port had its own set of rules to be applied. Yangzhou Guan, for instance, levied in 1756 a duty of 0.02 taels for each *dan* of beans, rice, wheat and sesame passing through it. At that time the price of ordinary rice varied between 2.4-2.5 taels and 3.1-3.2 taels per *dan*, so the rate of taxation (duty) ranged between 0.63% and 0.83% of the value.[35] Although this was a special case, it does demonstrate the wide variation in rates.

During the reign of Yongzheng, customs duty at Kui Guan was fixed such that "All goods with the price of 1 tael should be taxed 3 Fen (0.03 taels)".[36] In other words, the taxation rate was 3% of the value. This rate was maintained during the Qianlong, Daoguang and Tongzhi.

In 1728, Shandong province reported that "All grains should be taxed 0.011 taels per *dan*, but taxes on rice and wheat are more expensive. Rice and wheat should be taxed 0.022 tael per *dan*."[37] Considering the price of rice varied from

34 Xu Tan and Jing Junjian (1990), p. 95.

35 GZDQLC, Volume 13, p. 710.

36 Wo Ren (1865), Volume 70.

37 National Palace Museum in Taiwan (1978), Volume 11, pp. 649–650.

0.5 to 07. taels per *dan*, Deng Yibin estimated the taxation rate of rice at Linqin Guan to have been about 2.2% to 5.5% of its value.[38]

Kishimoto Mio found that during the reign of Yongzheng, the rate of taxation for rice at Hushu Guan varied from about 3.7% to 6.7% of its value.[39] According to Deng Yibin's research, the rate of taxation for rice at Hushu Guan was about 2.2% to 4% of its value during the Qianlong and 2.5% during the Daoguan.[40] Takino Shojiro used the price of beans (1.2 taels per *dan*) to estimate that the rate of taxation (0.05 taels) of Huai'an Guan was 4.2% in 1778; in the beginning of the 19th century the rate of taxation was even lower.[41]

He Befang estimated that goods passing through the offices of Zuoyi, Youyi, Fengtian Niuma Shui, and Fenghuangcheng Zhongjiang were taxed at a rate of about 3% of their value, while the rate of taxation at Yuehai Guan was kept at about 5.76% for imported goods and 3.74% for exported goods.[42] Peng Zeyi calculated that the rate of taxation maintained at Jianghai Guan, Zhehai Guan, Minhai Guan, and Yuehai Guan would have been about 2% of value.[43] Deng Yibin also estimated the taxation rate for white wax at Kui Guan to have been 3.75% of its value. For cotton at Hushu Guan, he estimated the rate to be 2.7% of its value, and at Shanhai Guan the rate for green tea to be 1.8%-2.4%.[44] Kosaka Masanori estimated the taxation rate for ordinary silk in the port of Beixin Guan to have been about 1.3%.[45]

Since this material is very scattered and recorded in unsystematic manner, most scholars prefer to do case studies. Their research indicates that taxation rates during the Qing dynasty were somewhere between about 2% and 5%.

Some goods were duty-free. In 1737, Shahukou began to lift duty on brooms, bamboo baskets, vegetables, food, rice, shoes, and socks if they were carried by hand.[46] In 1739, officials at the ports of Longjiang Guan and Xixin Guan wrote that "All kinds of baskets and brooms that were used in farmers' houses; chicken, ducks, pigs, dogs and other livestock that facilitated the accumulation of manure; all kinds of sandals, belts, arrowheads, water chestnuts, cherries,

38 Deng Yibin (2003), pp. 217–218.
39 Kishimoto Mio (1997), pp. 118–119.
40 Deng Yibin (2003), p. 217.
41 Takino Shojiro (2001), pp. 116–156.
42 He Befang (1984), p. 75.
43 Peng Zeyi (1984), pp. 136–141.
44 Deng Yibin (2003), pp. 219–220.
45 Kosaka Masanori (1991), pp. 34–57.
46 Wo Ren (1865), Volume 55.

grapes, sugarcane, white gourds, pears, eggs and other things that constituted the only source of income for the poor. So these things should be tax-free."[47]

When major natural disasters occurred, rice would be declared duty-free. There are a large number of references to duty-free rice boats in the records of the Qing dynasty. More about that later. In addition, with the pressure of population expansion being felt, the government also agreed as from 1743 to discount customs duty to be paid on rice boats from Thailand by 20%-50%.[48]

The third kind of duty-free commerce under the Qing was the trade of tribute. In 1663 the government ordered that "All goods on tribute boats should be tax-free, stipulating that the tribute only needed to be recorded."[49] The Qing government, in addition, permitted 126 dans of tax-free goods to be loaded onto grain boats carrying tribute, such as rice, to Beijing. When the boats returned from Beijing they were permitted to have 86 dans of tax-free goods on board. I have estimated that each year more than 900,000 dans of tax-free goods were transported on tribute boats.[50]

A surtax was generally collected in each port, albeit in a variety of ways and at various rates: These revenues were mainly used to meet the ordinary administrative expenses of each port, since the Qing government did not provide officials with the funds needed to employ subordinates and manual laborers. Although surtaxes were permitted by the central government, the amounts collected would not be included in the formal tax report; I have included these surtaxes in Appendix A (Customs revenues collected at *Changguan,* 1723–1910) of this book. Different ports used different names for this surtax, such as *Fan Shi* (food allowance) silver in Xixing Guan and Huai'an Guan, *Kan Cang Gui Fei* (warehouse safeguarding fee) in Yangzhou Guan, *Fa Liao* (penalty for tax evasion) in Minhai Guan, and *Gui Li* (rulers' gifts) in Yuehai Guan.

Hushu Guan, for example, had a surtax called *Ping Yu* (balancing surplus) silver. The silver exchange system of the Qing dynasty was very complicated and *Pingyu* was a part of it. By law, all silver sent to the central government was weighed with a treasury-standard scale *Kuping* (treasury balance). However, for some time the central government continued to use the market-standard scale *Shiping* (market balance) to weigh any silver being payed out. Since the weight of *Shiping* silver was lower than that of *Kuping* silver, the central government would benefit from the difference in weight between the two scales, while the local governments or tax authorities would suffer the loss. To

47 He Changling (1992), Volume 51.

48 Liu Jingzhao (2000), Volume 27.

49 Li Hongzhang (1908), Volume 239.

50 Ni Yuping (2005), p. 228.

compensate for such losses the port of Hushu Guan introduced a surtax it called *Pingyu* silver: the surtax was levied at a rate of 5.8% for each tael of regular taxes collected. With the passing of time, *Pingyu* silver became an important source of income of Hushu Guan. Later, it even became a minor income source of the Imperial Household (*Neiwu Fu*).

There were three types of *Pingyu*: one of a fixed rate, which would be collected in ports; one that was used to pay *Jiangni Zhizhao* (the official responsible for weaving the emperor's clothes, located in Jiangni, today known as Nanjing), which amounted to no more than 3,000 taels each year; and one that was any *Pingyu* remaining, which would be sent to the Imperial Household.

TABLE 2.5 Pingyu *silver per type for Hushu Guan during the reigns of Jiaqing and Daoguan (in taels of silver)*

Year	Port	*Zhizhao*	*Neiwu Fu*	Total *Pingyu*
1796	8156.36	2834.483	16381.797	27372.64
1797	8190.59	2207.012	16951.138	27347.74
1798	7409.09	2991.487	12975.703	23376.28
1799	7734.11	1672.76	15458.41	24865.28
1800	7619.28	2162.786	15412.364	25194.43
1801	7482.67	2993.41	13310.81	23786.89
1802	6946.48	2913.494	11338.026	21198
1803	7349.34	2299.707	13453.933	23102.98
1804	7528.89	2922.904	13588.516	24040.31
1805	6828.21	1348.479	12666.611	20843.3
1808	6481.06	2955.156	10644.384	20080.6
1809	7148.93	2994.912	12684.228	23008.07
1810(1)	7031.27	2920.058	12220.412	22171.74
1810(2)	5582.51	1067.925	9069.925	15720.36
1811	6665.77	2986.898	10761.402	20414.07
1812	6896.113	2978.209	11670.908	21545.23
1814	5747.7	2959.468	7530.152	16237.32
1816	7125.17	2986.688	12882.462	22994.32
1817	7310.15	3000	13189.64	23499.79
1818	7328.92	3000	13152.88	23481.8
1819	7287.97	3000	13171.87	23459.84
1820	6822.57	3000	11290.84	21113.41

TABLE 2.5 *Pingyu silver per type for Hushu Guan* (cont.)

Year	Port	*Zhizhao*	*Neiwu Fu*	Total *Pingyu*
1821	7005.76	3000	11973.82	21979.58
1822	6533.26	3000	1018.65	19719.77
1823	6124.9	1667.925	10070.975	17863.8
1824	6313.58	2480.15	10000.71	18794.44
1825	6534.5	1906.179	11321.641	19761.87
1826	6643.24	2000.364	11697.226	20340.83
1827	6299.71	1998.721	10314.399	18612.83
1828	6671.24	2315.845	11470.305	20457.39
1829	6701.43	2831.203	10991.137	20524.27
1830	6755.42	2524.878	11512.082	20792.38
1832	5357.14	2669.737	6252.013	14278.89
1833	5237.94	1839.304	6984.266	14061.51
1834	5956.96	1718.315	9894.395	17569.67
1835	5148.32	1250.869	7300.91	13700.09
1837	5785.55	2897.319	7690.311	16373.18
1838	5643.84	1368.799	8702.531	15715.17
1839	5484.55	1427.684	8123.706	15035.94
1840	5158.78	2223.275	6114.805	13496.86
1841	4933.85	1899.685	5679.655	12513.19
1843	5469.04	1134.015	8535.175	15136.23
1845	5648.82	1216.963	8802.407	15668.19
1846	5679.3	1225.075	8911.785	15816.16
1847	5184.32	1359.757	9900.743	16444.82
1848	5902.9	3000	11006.15	16909.05
1850	4434.45	301.131	5526.79	10264.29

Sources: ZPZZ, LFZZ and Chaodang. There are two data entries for duties in 1810, due to the Chinese Lunar year.

Table 2.5 shows that the port of Hushu Guan would send large amounts of *Pingyu* silver to the Imperial Household each year, making this a very important income source for the Imperial Household. As I have indicated, surtaxes were used to meet the costs of administering each port, and according to Deng

Yibin's research this surtax delivered about 11%-24% of the total income of each port.[51]

2.5 *Yangguan*

For *Yangguan*, i.e. customs offices for foreign trade, the year 1861 is a significant milestone. Indeed, when researching the customs systems in place for *Yangguan*, one distinguishes between two significantly different periods in their existence: the period before 1861, and the period after 1861, for it was in that year that the Chinese Maritime Customs Service was founded.

Before 1842 Yuehai Guan was the only customs port to hold the privilege of trading with foreigners. In 1843, following the First Opium War (1840–1842), though, four new ports were opened to foreigners: Jianghai Yangguan, Zhehai Yangguan, Fouzhou Yangguan, and Xiamen Yangguan. Later, during and after the Taiping Rebellion, the infrastructure relating to ports and harbors changed again, and more *Yangguan* were set up. Also, gradually *Yangguan* came to be placed under the control of Western administrators. In 1861, the Chinese Maritime Customs Service was set up under the auspices of *Zong Li Ge Guo Shi Wu Ya Men* (The Prime Minister Foreign Affairs Yamen). From that moment, by law *Yangguan* were to be managed by Western administrators, the most notable of these being the Englishman R. Hart. *Yangguan* ports maintained their own system of customs and became a special source of fiscal revenue of the Qing, because they were managed separately by Western administrators who had been appointed to the service. Table 2.3 presents an overview of the establishment of *Yangguan* ports.

TABLE 2.6 *The establishment of* Yangguan *customs ports by year and treaty*

Port	Opening	Treaty
Yuehai Guan	1685	–
Jianghai Yangguan	1843	Sino-British Treaty (1842)
Zhehai Yangguan	1843	Sino-British Treaty (1842)
Fuzhou Yangguan	1843	Sino-British Treaty (1842)
Xiameng Yangguan	1843	Sino-British Treaty (1842)
Suzhou Guan	1/10/1896	Sino-Japanese Treaty of Shimonoseki (1895)

51 Deng Yibin (2008), p. 173.

TABLE 2.6 *The establishment of Yangguan customs ports by year and treaty* (cont.)

Port	Opening	Treaty
Zhenjiang Guan	1/5/1861	Treaty of Tientsin (1858)
Jinling Guan	1/5/1899	Treaty of Tientsin (1858)
Wuhu Yangguan	1/4/1877	Sino-British Yantai Treaty (1876)
Jiujiang Yangguan	1/1/1863	Treaty of Tientsin (1858)
Jianghan Guan	1/1/1863	Treaty of Tientsin (1858)
Yuezhou Guan	13/12/1899	initiative of the Qing government
Changsha Guan	1/7/1904	Sino-British Another Ship Treaty (1902)
Shashi Guan	1/10/1896	Sino-Japanese Treaty of Shimonoseki (1895)
Yichang Guan	1/4/1877	Sino-British Yantai Treaty (1876)
Chongqing Guan	2/3/1891	Yantai Treaty (1890)
Hangzhou Guan	1/10/1896	Sino-Japanese Treaty of Shimonoseki (1895)
Ouhai Guan	4/1877	Sino-British Yantai Treaty (1876)
Taiwan	18/7/1862	Treaty of Tientsin (1858)
Wuzhou Yangguan	4/6/1897	Sino-British Treaty of Burma (1897)
Nanning Guan	1/1/1907	initiative of the Qing government
Zhennan Guan	1/6/1889	Sino-French commercial treaty (1887)
Mengzi Guan	13/8/1889	Sino-French commercial treaty (1887)
Simao Guan	1/1/1897	Sino-French special commercial treaty (1896)
Tengyue Guan	8/5/1902	Sino-British Treaty of Burma (1897)
Donghai Yangguan	20/8/1861	Treaty of Tientsin (1858)
Jinhai Guan	23/3/1861	Treaty of Beijing (1860)
Qinhuangdao Guan	1/1/1902	initiative of the Qing government

Port	Opening	Treaty
Niuzhuang Guan	1/1/1863	Treaty of Tientsin (1858)
Andong Guan	14/3/1907	Sino-Japanese Ship Treaty (1903)
Ha'erbin Guan	5/2/1908	Sino-Japanese Agreement following the Treaty of Portsmouth (1905)

Source: Tang (2005), pp. 54-60.

As Table 2.3 shows, *Yangguan* ports were opened gradually and that just before the end of the Qing dynasty there were more than 30 *Yangguan* ports in existence. In 1902, during the negotiation of the Boxer Protocol, *Changguan* ports became a very important collateral to secure the Chinese payments: "All *Changguan* income collected near *Yangguan* trading ports should be managed by *Yangguan* administrators."[52] After 1902 *Changguan* ports were divided into two kinds: ports within 25 km of a trading port would be managed by the Inspector-General of the Chinese Maritime Customs Service; ports more than 25 km from a trading port or mainland port would continue to be managed by their current administration. Nevertheless, customs revenues were still being reported to the Imperial Court, so for our accounting records this makes no relevant difference.

In addition to these changes, in 1906 the government ordered that the collection period for *Changguan* be changed from 12 Chinese lunar months to "one Chinese lunar year", regardless of whether it comprised 12 or 13 months. With the accumulation of leap-months, some lunar years would have 13 months and, therefore, two sets of tax revenues. If the first tax year ended in January and the current year was a leap year, then the second tax year would end the following December. Such cases would occur every 32-33 years. This meant, for instance, that in 1938 there would have been income from an additional new year. However, the Qing dynasty did not last that long.

52 Wang Yanwei (1987), Volume 156.

CHAPTER 3

Land Border Customs

As already described in Chapter 2, there were three types of *Changguan* customs ports in the Qing: Land Border customs, Canal and Yangtze River customs, and Coastal customs. Gates and ports that were located on land borders, and those whose customs revenues came mainly from trade with ethnic minorities, fell under Land Border customs.

3.1 Shanhai Guan

Shanhai Guan was located in the northeastern part of Zhili province (now Hebei province), with the Bohai Sea situated to the west. It had a very important geographical position in Qing China since it connected the three northeastern provinces of China, and being near to Korea it guarded the approaches of Beijing. "The significance of Shanhai Guan for Beijing is just like that of the throat to the body or the key to a door. Each year, countless merchants and boats cross Shanhai Guan, so it is very important to tax goods very carefully, not only to collect duties, but also to make people obey the law," wrote a gazetteer.[1]

The customs office of Shanhai Guan was set up during the reign of Jiajin (1521–1567) in the Ming dynasty. In the beginning it collected 900 taels of silver, which led to the disappearance of merchants from the port because nobody wanted to pay customs duty. So in 1529, the gate was closed down by the Ming government.[2] After that this cycle repeated itself from time to time: in 1680 (the early Qing) the emperor Kanxi set the customs gate up once more, only to close it again two years later, just as the Ming had done. Nevertheless, some taxation data are available for Shanhai Guan. In 1695, it levied duty amounting to about 25,000 taels of silver.[3] By 1715 this had increased to 28,000 and by 1720 it had risen to 29,000.[4]

It was not until 1794 that officials were appointed here for the first time, a symbol of the formal establishment of Shanhai Guan in the Qing dynasty. In the following year the government set Shanhai Guan's taxation quota at 25,000

1 Shi Xiaofeng (1999), p. 608.
2 Zhan Rong (1534), Volume 2.
3 Zhang Tingyu (1936), Volume 26.
4 Zhang Tingyu (1732), Volume 52.

 | DOI 10.1163/9789004324886_005

taels of silver, rising by 1765 (reign of Qianlong) to 100,000 taels of silver (including *Zheng'e* and *Yingyu*). Of this income, 22,600 taels were allotted to pay the soldiers stationed in Shanhai Guan, and a further 10,800 was ear-marked as salary for local officials. Any revenue remaining would be sent to the Beijing.

There were more than 30 locations in the area that fell under the jurisdiction of Shanhai Guan customs, most important among them being Jingzhou and Niuzhuang.[5] In the early Qing, the customs revenues from Shanhai Guan increased, as did economic development in general. In 1797, De Xin, the Administrator of Shanhai Guan, reported to the Imperial Court that Shanhai Guan's *Yingyu* had been growing quickly in previous years. He said that he would be able to increase *Yingyu* to 20,000 taels of silver. However, the emperor Jiaqing responded saying that "[…] It was totally unacceptable to increase *Yingyu*. Customs duty collected in Shanhai Guan is affected by how many boats went through its multiple gates. In recent years, tax revenues from Shanhai Guan have increased greatly, but only because harvests were—fortunately—good. How could it be possible to increase *Yingyu* continuously by a fixed annual amount?"[6] From this quote we are able to gain a deeper understanding about how the emperor saw customs duties and how he thought about financial matters.

After the Taiping Rebellion, customs duties levied in Shanhai Guan increased steeply once again, since many merchants' activities had to be moved to the north in order to avoid the rebellion. Thus, its fate differed from that of most other customs ports in the late Qing. Since there was more and more *Yingyu*, in 1860 the Ministry of Revenue was able to add another 80,000 taels of silver as *additional Yingyu*.[7]

TABLE 3.1 *Quotas of customs duties for Shanhai Guan during the Qing dynasty (in taels of silver)*

Year	1695	1715	1720	1732	1770	1780	1799
Zheng'e	25,000	28,000	29,000	32,000	33,309	61,642	61,642
Yingyu	–	–	–	–	–	–	49,487
Total	25,000	28,000	29,000	32,000	33,309	61,642	111,129

Sources: materials from *Shilu, Huidian, Hubu Zheli* and archives (see text for archival references).

5 National Palace Museum in Taiwan (1978), Volume 20, p. 365.
6 Liu Jingzhao (2000), Volume 29.
7 LFZZ of FHAC: 3-4872-14.

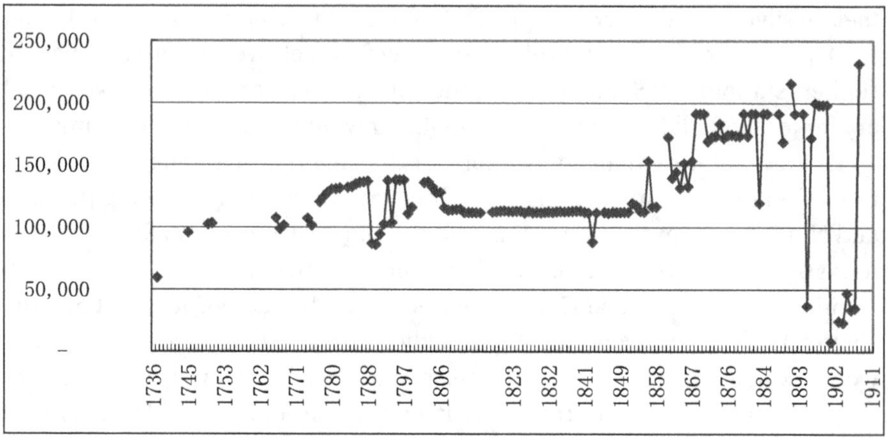

FIGURE 3.1 *Tax revenue trends of Shanhai Guan, 1736–1911*

As I have already said previously, in Shanhai Guan each tax year consisted of 12 months, but with the accumulation of leap months some years would have 13 months and, thus, two sets of tax figures; this would occur every 32-33 years. In Figure 3.1 I show the individual figures, but in the Appendix table A these figures together to show the total fiscal revenue. The archives show that in 1781, 1814, 1846 and 1879 there are two tax data entries for Shanhai Guan.[8]

Figure 3.1 indicates that tax revenues of Shanhai Guan experienced striking changes. Before 1788 there was a clear increase that paralleled population and economic development—although, since the officials seldom explained why changes occur, we can only guess at the reasons for this. During the period 1788–1809 annual tax revenues varied greatly, ranging from 80,000 to 130,000 taels of silver, due to climatic fluctuations; this can be concluded from archival evidence.[9]

After the three-years-comparison measure was stopped, the tax revenues of Shanhai Guan remained stable for more than 50 years. It is quite easy to make sense of this stability: simply, the quota system worked extremely well. The tax revenues of Shanhai Guan thus reflected the stability of political power rather than economic development. Only during the First Opium War did tax revenues drop, because the merchants dared not to travel by sea in times of war.[10]

8 ZPZZ of FHAC: 4-1-35-319-21, 4-1-35-326-43, 4-1-14-35-43, 4-1-35-348-19, 4-1-35-349-51; SYD of FHAC: November 17th, 54th year of Qianlong. And so on.

9 LFZZ of FHAC: 3-604-40, 3-605-37; ZPZZ of FHAC: 4-1-35-359-18, 4-1-35-364-31.

10 ZPZZ of FHAC: 4-1-35-379-56.

When the Taiping Rebellion broke out in 1850 the tax revenues of Shanhai Guan were greatly affected. The largest change occurred during the late Qing. As I have already indicated, this was because in 1860 the Ministry of Revenue asked the Imperial Court to add 80,000 taels of silver of additional *Yingyu* to the quota, there was a steep rise in taxes. Nevertheless, there were some fluctuations during the period 1862–1866. One cause of these was the creation in 1861 of the position of Inspector-General of Chinese Maritime Customs Service. From that time on, *Yangguan* were controlled by Western administrators, and the foreign customs office of Niuzhuang Yangguan levied duty on many goods that had previously fallen under Shanhai Guan. A further cause of fluctuation was the prevalence of horse bandits roaming Fengtian province during this period. Because they no longer felt safe, merchants avoided travelling as much as possible.[11]

There were two more instances of falling revenues, one being the Sino-Japanese War in 1894–1895, and the other being the Boxer Rebellion in 1899–1900. In 1894–1895, Shanhai Guan was occupied by Japanese armies, bringing the levying of customs duties to a halt.[12] In relation to the Boxer Rebellion, a 1901 report states: "As a result of the Boxer Rebellion, taxes collected in Shanhai Guan have fallen steeply. On 10 July, Russian soldiers occupied Yinkou, the most important port of Shanhai Guan, which was then closed. After negotiations, the port was reopened and levying of customs duty resumed. Nevertheless, because of the presence of foreign soldiers and prevalence of bandits, merchants dared not to travel there. So tax revenues are very low."[13]

3.2 Zhangjiakou

Zhangjiakou, the site of another customs gate, was located during the Qing in the northern part of Zhili province. Situated to its east was Chengde City, to its southeast was the capital Beijing, to the west was Shanxi province, and to its north lay Inner Mongolia. Zhangjiakou was, as a result, one of the most important customs offices of the Great Wall for many years. Han people (especially those from Shanxi province) always traded cloth and tea for cows and horses with other ethnic groups (especially Mongolians). It also was the best place for trips to Kyakhta, which held a concession for pursuing the Sino-Russian trade.

11 LFZZ of FHAC: 3-4871-33, 3-4873-49, 3-4875-54, 3-4875-85.

12 ZPZZ of FHAC: 4-1-35-1038-2.

13 GXCZP, Volume 74, p. 382.

In short, during the early Qing, Zhangjiakou held a strategic position on Sino-Russian and Han-Mongolian trade routes, making it a very prosperous commercial city in the north of China.

Zhangjiakou had already been a point of entry for goods during the Ming dynasty. In 1644, the Qing government appointed Manchu officials to collect duty there, and to begin with set a *Zheng'e* quota of 10,000 taels of silver.[14] In 1663 the *Zheng'e* quota was reduced to 6,000 taels,[15] only to be raised in 1677 to 12,000 taels, to which a further 763 taels of silver were added in the following year. In 1685, yet another 2,236 taels were added, bringing *Zheng'e* to a total of 15,000 taels.[16]

In 1799, following on from the series of adjustments just described, *Zheng'e* was increased to 20,000 taels, and *Yingyu* to 40,561 taels. Finally, I want to point out that Zhangjiakou only taxed Chinese merchants, not Russian ones.

TABLE 3.2 *Quota of Zhangjiakou in the Qing dynasty* (*in taels of silver*)

Year	1661	1663	1677	1678	1685	1702	1723	1799
Zheng'e	10,000	6,000	12,000	12,763	15,000	16,000	20,000	20,000
Yingyu	–	–	–	–	–	–	–	40,561
Total	10,000	6,000	12,000	12,763	15,000	16,000	20,000	60,561

Sources: materials from *Shilu*, *Huidian*, *Hubu Zheli* and archives (see text for archival references).

Note that in the archival material there two data entries for taxes in the years 1822 and 1887.

Because bilateral trade developed so quickly, customs revenues collected at Zhangjiakou always remained stable in the early Qing. There were some falls after 1840, however, although when compared to the usual revenue of 60,500 taels, a fall of 500 taels is nothing that needs to be especially explained.[17] The biggest change occurred during the Taiping Rebellion, when the revenue fluctuated strongly, almost falling to half the level collected before the rebellion. In 1853, officials reported to the Imperial Court that the reduction was because "The Taiping bandits were still occupying the Yangtze Delta. No tea from the

14 *Qing Shilu* Kangxi Chao, Volume 3.

15 Yi Sang'e (1690), Volume 34.

16 Zhang Tingyu (1936), Volume 26.

17 LFZZ of FHAC: 3-3168-67; ZPZZ of FHAC: 4-1-12-467-134, 4-1-35-559-1, 4-1-12-478-84.

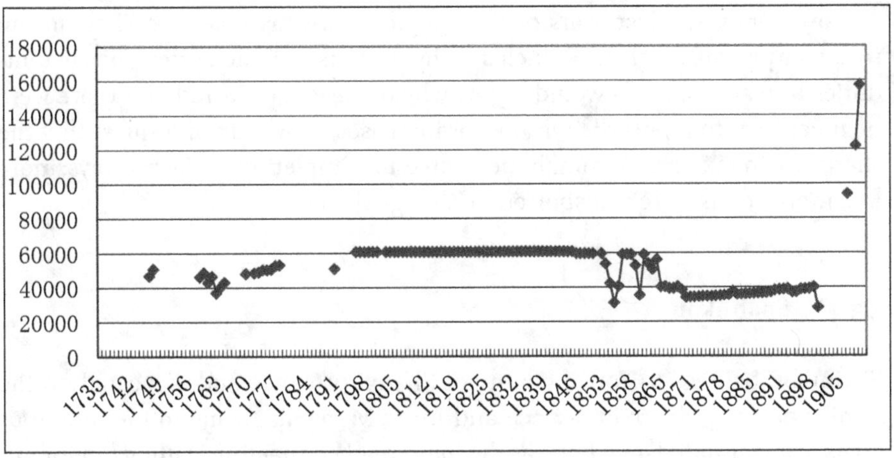

FIGURE 3.2 *Tax revenue trends of Zhangjiakou, 1735–1911*

southern part of China can reach the north, nor are goods from the northern part of China able to reach the south. As a result, tax revenues are falling rapidly without there being anything we can do about it."[18] This situation continued for a long time and even became worse when several *Yangguan* ports were established nearby, so that Zhangjiakou lost its power to tax foreign goods as it had done before.[19]

In 1900, Zhangjiakou's tax income was strongly affected by the Boxer Rebellion. It was reported that "The tax revenues of Zhangjiakou mainly depend on tea from southern China. However, after our government signed a trade contract with Russia all tea was transported by the Russians and Zhangjiakou no longer had power to tax it. Little by little Chinese businessmen are having to close their shops since they can no longer earn any money. [...] After the Boxer Rebellion broke out, foreign countries fought us, and Tianjin and Beijing were also involved in the war. Large numbers of troops were sent to Zhangjiakou to protect Beijing and the road could no longer be used. As a result, no merchants dared to travel to the city. This was especially the case in September 1900, when German and British soldiers advanced on Zhangjiakou: all shops were closed and the people fled. Then, after the foreign armies had returned to Beijing, bandits appeared, robbing people in the area. Merchants had no choice but to reduce their activities, so tax revenues fell very quickly."[20]

18 ZPZZ of FHAC: 4-1-35-382-14.

19 ZPZZ of FHAC: 4-1-35-382-59; LFZZ of FHAC: 3-4871-23, 3-4874-8, 3-4880-74.

20 GXCZP, Volume 73, pp. 200–201.

However, in the last years of the Qing dynasty, tax revenues Zhangjiakou rose sharply, although it is unclear why. Because of the system of customs duties in place, officials would report why decreases occurred, but there were no incentives to report the reasons for increases, so we can only guess that the sharp rise in tax revenues might be related to completion of the railways: more and more goods were transported to Zhangjiakou by rail.

3.3 Shahukou

Shahukou belongs to Youyu county of Shanxi province and is located on the border between Shanxi province and Inner Mongolia. Lying in mountainous terrain, it is situated on what was the main road connecting Datong (an important gate in the Great Wall) with Hohhot (Guihua city), a garrison town established to prevent Mongol tribes from attacking south into mainland China.

During the Ming dynasty, invasion by the Mongols was the most dangerous threat faced by the Imperial Court, and Shahukou was right on the frontier with Mongolia. When peace was established in the region, the Ming court built *Mashi* (horses markets) at Shahukou and began to collect taxes there. In 1651, during the Qing dynasty, the government began appointing officials who were to be held responsible for collecting taxes there.[21]

In general, customs duty collected at Shahukou came mainly from animals and fur being transported from the north, and from tobacco, tea and clothing from the south. Officials posted at Shahukou had only one-year terms and were, thus, changed frequently. Sometimes officials would leave—being replaced or even dying in their position—before completing their term, so taxation figures for any one year could cover the terms of several officials. Especially when compared with other gates, this was a very rare phenomenon in Qing China.

From Table 3.3 one can see that the *Zheng'e* in Shahukou had changed a lot between 1661–1696, ranging from 6,000 and 13,000 taels. During the Qianlong *Zheng'e* was fixed at the 16,919 taels, while *Yingyu* in 1799 was fixed at 15,414 taels. In addition, 3,358 taels of silver had to be collected to cover the office's own expenses, 7,200 taels were to be collected for *Gongbu* (Ministry of Works), and 446 taels was required as revenue for Guihua city. So, in total 43,338 taels of silver was required, most of which was sent to the Neiwu Fu (Imperial Household).

21 YZCHW, Volume 11, pp. 455–457.

TABLE 3.3 *Quota of Shahukou in the Qing dynasty (in taels of silver)*

Year	1661	1663	1667	1674	1677	1696	Qianlong (1735-95)	1799
Zheng'e	13,000	10,000	8,000	6,000	9,000	10,920	16,919	16,920
Yingyu	–	–	–	–	–	–	–	15,414
Total	13,000	10,000	8,000	6,000	9,000	10,920	16,919	32,334

Sources: materials from *Shilu, Huidian, Hubu Zheli* and archives (see text for archival references).

Note that there were two entries for tax data in 1835 and 1868.

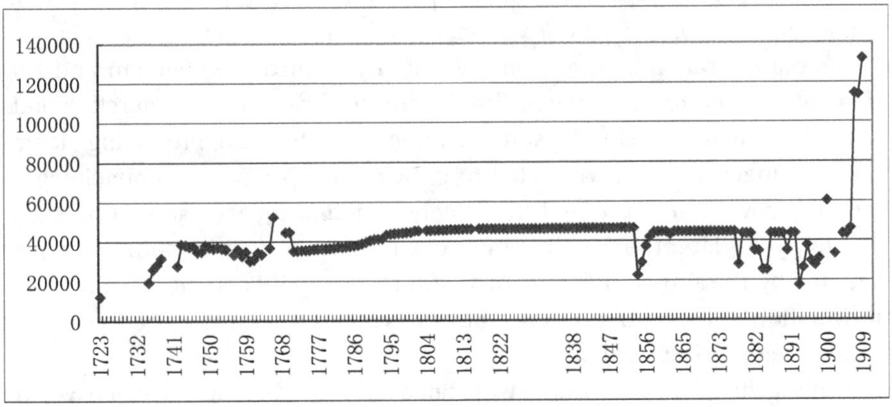

FIGURE 3.3 *Tax revenue trends of Shahukou, 1723–1911*

Clearly, tax revenues increased from 1723 to 1850. Of course, we can explain this with the increase of the population and economic development. The highest level reached was 52,236.525 taels of silver, in 1766. This was a special case because that tax year comprised one year and 25 days, almost 13 months.[22]

Between 1854 and 1856, tax collected at Shahukou declined quickly. The following explanation is given in the records: "Due to the Taiping Rebellion, no goods could come from the south, and no consumers could be found for the goods transported from the north to the south. All the rich merchants were worried by this situation and withdrew their money. Small businesses and

22 ZPZZ of FHAC: 4-1-35-337-4.

shops closed one by one."[23] Fortunately, soon after 1856 Shahukou's tax revenues recovered their normal levels, the result of Sino-Russian trade. Indeed, Shahukou even became quite prosperous as this trade flourished.[24] There was only one obvious drop, that during 1893–1898, due to the Sino-Japanese War.[25] A new taxation policy, among other things, led to a steep increase of tax revenues between 1907 and 1909.[26]

3.4 Guihuacheng

Guihuacheng (Guihua city), also named Hohhot, is the capital of the province of Inner Mongolia in China today. Building of Guihuacheng began under the Ming dynasty in 1572 and was finished in 1575. Its name was given by the Ming court, and means that it "likes to be a part of China". Although Guihuacheng was located in Mongolia, it was very close to the North China Plain, so it quickly became a densely inhabited commercial city of mixed Mongolian and Han population. Before the Kangxi, there were no duties on commercial goods. Later, Mongolia proved to be suitable for growing tobacco, producing alcohol and manufacturing oil, which led to growing prosperity in Guihuacheng. In 1761, the government ordered that alcohol, oil and tobacco should be taxed, and five years later the Administrator of Guihuacheng was appointed to oversee this by the Imperial Court. At first, in 1769, Guihuacheng fell under the jurisdiction of the Shanxi viceroy, but five years later it was placed under the local prefecture of Guisuidao.

Guihuacheng's *Zheng'e* quota was 15,000 taels of silver and 9,000,000 wens of coin. In 1799, *Yingyu* was set at 1,600 taels of silver and 137,610 wen of coin.[27]

There were two entries for tax data in the years of 1788, 1811 and 1842. The data for Guihuacheng after 1862 are missing.

From Figure 3.4 we can clearly see that there were some "gaps" in the years' bottom. It connects with two tax data in one year. For example, in 1778, there were two tax data, one from 13th January of 1777 to 12th January of 1778; another was from 13th January of 1778 to 12th December of 1778.[28] In this tax trend map

23 LFZZ of FHAC: 3-4378-28, 3-4379-30.

24 LFZZ of FHAC: 3-4380-17, 3-4382-16, 3-4383-8, and so on.

25 LFZZ of FHAC: 3-6506-21, 3-6573-8, 3-6405-26; TB of FHAC: 2-1-4-22558-28, 2-1-4-22625-4, 2-1-4-22650-19.

26 LFZZ of FHAC: 3-7508-45.

27 ZPZZ of FHAC: 4-1-35-373-12.

28 *GZDQLC*, vol. 42, p. 191; vol. 46, p. 753.

TABLE 3.4 *Quota of Guihuacheng in the Qing dynasty (taels / 1000 wen)*

Year	1761	1770	1799
Zheng'e taels	15,000	15,000	15,000
Zheng'e coins	9,000	9,000	9,000
Yingyu taels	–	1,548	1,600
Yingyu coins	–	137	–
Total taels	15,000	16,548	16,600
Total coins	9,000	9,137	9,000

Note: Materials from *Shilu, Huidian, Hubu Zheli* and archives (see text for archival references).

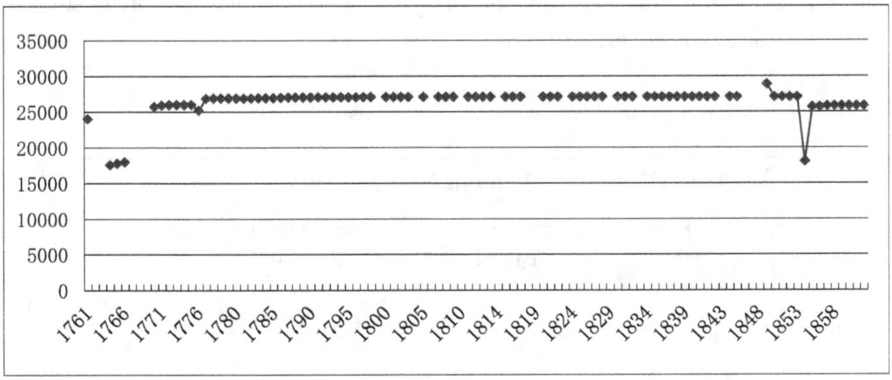

FIGURE 3.4 *Tax revenue trends of Guihuacheng, 1761–1862*

of Guihuacheng, if I added these two data together in 1778, the point of this year will look very high and very strange. So I show these two data separately. Of course, in the appedi table I add these two data in one year. I will deal with such thing in the whole book.

Figure 3.4 shows that the revenue trend in Guihuacheng was very stable for almost a century. Only during the period 1854–1856 did tax revenues fall very sharply. I could not find any explanation for this in the records and can only guess that the Taiping Rebellion had a negative influence on tax collection even in provinces far from the strife.[29]

29 The material for 1854 came from TB of FHAC: 2-1-4-21618-28. The material for 1855-1856 came from *Geguan Changshui Shizheng Duanzheng Yinliang Shumu* (The taxed silver

3.5 Dajianlu

Dajianlu was located in Sichuan province and has now the name Kangding. In the year 1701 (reign of Kangxi) the government appointed the Administrator of Dajianlu from the Ministry of Revenue to collect tax there. In 1777, the management of the customs was moved to the Zongren Fu (Imperial Clan Court).[30] In 1780, the customs gate was transferred again to the Sichuan Governor who appointed an official. After 1882, it belonged to the local prefecture and became permanently established.

Dajianlu mainly collected taxes for tea, generally at the rate of 0.18 tael of silver per 50 kg tea. During the reign of Jiaqing it collected about 18,958.32 taels of silver in customs duties on tea each year. In 1819, the government reduced the gate's quota by 1621.62 taels: it still had to collect 17,336.7 taels. There were no requirements set for the level of *Yingyu*. The request was simply to send all surplus money to the government.

TABLE 3.5 *Taxation quota of Dajianlu in the Qing dynasty (in taels of silver)*

Year	Kangxi*	Qianlong*	1801
Zheng'e	5,317	19,368	20,000
Yingyu	–	–	–
Total	5,317	19,368	20,000

*Exact year unknown.
Sources: materials from *Shilu, Huidian, Hubu Zheli* and archives (see text for archival references).

In the beginning, Dajianlu was being taxed per lunar year, so that the situation of one year with two data entries would not occur. In 1802, however, the government ordered that Dajianlu should be taxed per 12 months as were the other ports,[31] which led in 1808 and 1841 to two data entries. But in 1857 the government changed this practice again, and once more it only taxed per lunar year, regardless of whether it consisted of 12 or 13 months.

figures and insufficient silver figures in each Changguan), stored in the library of the Institute of Economics, the Chinese Academy of Social Sciences.

30 Zhang Tingyu (1936), Volume 27.

31 TB of FHAC: 2-1-4-20377-20.

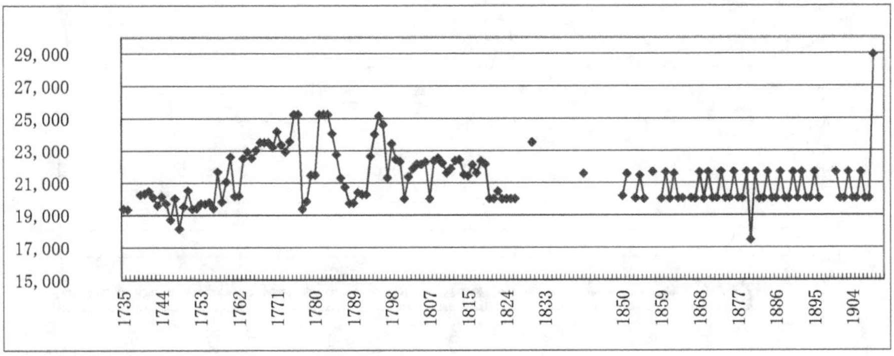

FIGURE 3.5 *Tax revenue trends of Dajianlu, 1735–1911*

From Figure 3.5 one can see that the tax revenues of Dajianlu ranged from almost 20,000 to 25,000 taels, and that this level was stable for most of the time. As I have already mentioned, after 1857 the government taxed once per lunar year, no matter whether it comprised 12 or 13 months. For this reason, the fluctuations after 1857 are reasonable, since they represent different periods of taxation.

3.6 Fenghuangcheng Zhongjiang

Fenghuangcheng (city of Phoenix) Zhongjiang was located in Shengjing, the second capital of the Qing dynasty. The city, which had been founded in 1481 by the Ming government, gradually became a prefecture during the Qing and it belongs to Fengcheng city of Liaoning province today. Fenghuangcheng was taxed twice a year, once in February and once in August, when there were horse markets. Most of the customs duties it collected were the result of the Sino-Korea trade.[32] In 1702 (reign of Kangxi) it had already collected 4,000 taels of silver.[33] In 1747, Zhongjiang's *Zheng'e* was fixed at 3,307 taels of silver. If more tax was raised, it would have to be sent to the government. No requirements were set for *Yingyu* because all tax revenue would be used to pay the city's soldiers.[34]

Owing to the Chinese lunar year, there are two data entries in the records for the years 1764, 1832, 1835, and 1843.

32 Min Nin (1831), Volume 39.

33 LFZZ of FHAC: 3-585-28.

34 Jin Fufu (2003), vol 146.

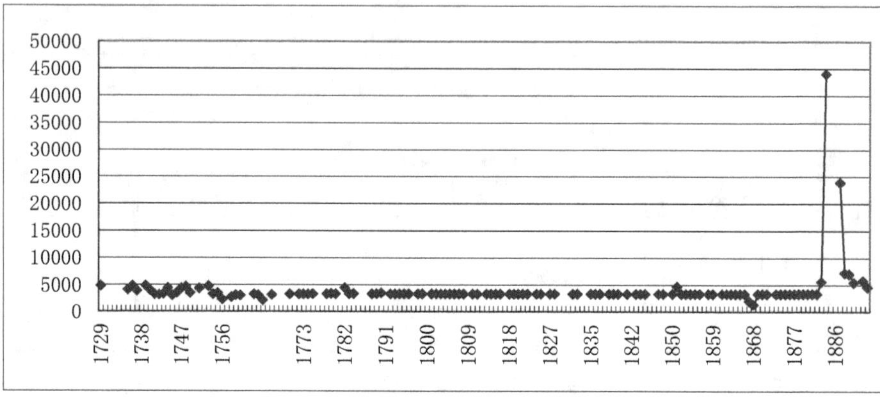

FIGURE 3.6 *Tax revenue trends of Zhongjiang, 1729–1892*

Figure 3.6 demonstrates that the tax figures remained very stable for more than a century. There was, however, a large increase in tax revenues in the years 1884 and 1887, the result of a change in the taxation rate. The rate for ordinary goods was about 5% of their value, but for red ginseng the rate was, following government orders, set at 10% of its value.[35] This subsequently led to a decline in the amounts of ginseng passing through this port, which in turn quickly led to the taxtion rate being reduced to its previous level.

3.7 Fengtian Niuma Shui

Fengtian Niuma Shui (Shengyan city today), the capital of Fengtian province, collected taxes mainly from the trade in horses and cows. The town was set up at the beginning of the Qing dynasty and in 1727 the Imperial Court ordered that an official be selected from the Shengjing Jiangjun Yamen (Mukden General Yamen) and appointed Administrator of Fengtian Niuma Shui. Later the responsibility of collecting taxes was transferred to Beijing. After 1768, the gate was managed by the Vice-Director of the Ministry of Revenue in Mukden. In 1780, the government fixed *Zheng'e* at the level of 4,000 taels of silver, and *Yingyu* at 1,000 taels of silver.[36]

There are, unfortunately, only a few data points for the period before the reign of Daoguang, and there are no data at all after 1847. Nevertheless, the graph shows that the trend was quite stable, suggesting that tax revenues were not influenced by either economic development or the political situation.

35 LFZZ of FHAC: 3-6352-21.

36 Li Hongzhang (1908), Volume 236.

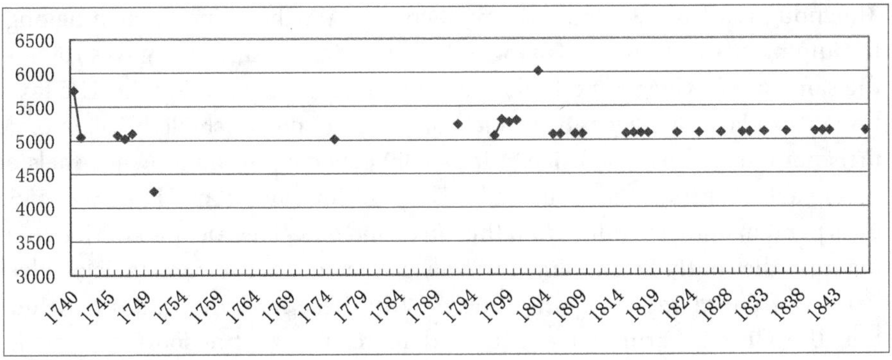

FIGURE 3.7 *Tax revenue trends of Fengtian Niuma Shui, 1740–1846*

3.8 Wu Chang and Xun Chang

The following two customs officies are treated in the same section, since they were treated as one financial unit by the Chinese Bureaucracy, and accordingly revenues were also reported together for the two locations. Wuzhou prefecture was located at the crossing of three rivers, Rong jiang, Xun jiang and Miao jiang, where the port was established by the Ming government in 1521. At the beginning of the Qing dynasty the tax quota to be collected was fixed by the government at 10,976 taels of silver. Thereafter the quota changed frequently, reaching by the reign of Jiaqing 68,734 taels (*Zheng'e* was 60,913 taels, and *Yingyu* was 7,821 taels of silver).[37]

TABLE 3.6 *Tax quota of Wu Chang in the Qing dynasty (in taels of silver)*

Year	Kangxi*	1730	1750	1774	1776	1799	1804
Zheng'e	10,977	46,828	46,828	63,008	54,621	54,621	60,913
Yingyu	–	–	17,335	–	7,500	7,500	7,821
Total	10,977	46,828	64,163	63,008	62,121	62,121	68,734

*Exact year unknown.
Sources: materials from Shilu, Huidian, Hubu Zheli and archives (see text for archival references).

37 LFZZ of FHAC: 3-1767-77.

Xunzhou prefecture was near the prefecture of Wuzhou, and today it belongs to Guiping city in Province Guangxi. The situation in Xun Chang was roughly the same as Wu Chang and both collected taxes mainly from grain. The taxation rate of Wu Chang was 0.078 taels of silver per dan of shelled rice, or 0.156 taels per dan of unshelled rice.[38] It usually collected 10,300 to 12,000 taels of silver each year from the grain trade. The taxation rate of Xu Chang was 0.162 taels per dan of rice coming from the north and 0.144 taels per dan of rice coming from the south. Xun Chang normally collected 6,000 to 7,100 taels of silver per year from taxing the grain trade.[39] With these rates in mind, I conclude that the Qing government encouraged merchants to transport rice to the northern part of China, where most of the population lived, and where more food was needed. During the Jiaqing, Xun Chang had a quota of 43,741 taels *Zheng'e* and 5,565 taels *Yingyu*.[40]

TABLE 3.7 *Quota of Xun Chang in the Qing dynasty (in taels of silver)*

Year	Kangxi*	1730	1750	1774	1776	1799	1804
Zheng'e	4,347	34,131	34,131	45,820	38,606	38,606	43,741
Yingyu	–	–	17,335	–	5,200	5,200	5,565
Total	4,347	34,131	51,466	45,820	43,806	43,806	49,306

* Exact year unknown.
Sources: materials from *Shilu, Huidian, Hubu Zheli* and archives (see text for archival references).

Because Wu Chang and Xun Chang always reported their tax revenues together, we have to add the data up. Also, there were two data entries in the years 1767 and 1832.

Figure 3.8 clearly shows that tax revenues were increasing during the reigns of Yongzheng and Qianlong. During the reigns of Jiaqing and Daoguang, tax revenues for these two cities stayed at almost the same level, the only exception being the several years in the beginning when the method of three-year comparisons was applied.[41] Wu Chang and Xun Chang were also affected by the Taiping Rebellion: tax revenues declined to some extent as early outbreaks

38 One dan of rice = approximately 50 kg.

39 LFZZ of FHAC: 3-1767-77.

40 LFZZ of FHAC: 3-1767-77.

41 LFZZ of FHAC: 3-1767-77; TB of FHAC: 2-1-4-18111-2.

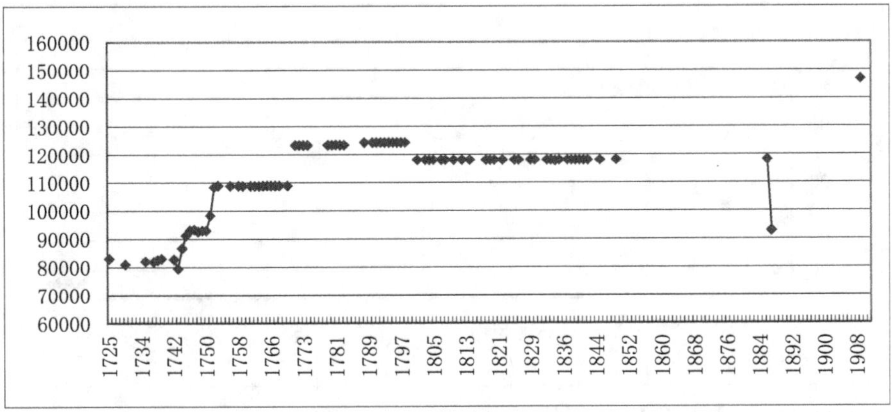

FIGURE 3.8 *Trends in tax revenue of Wu Chang and Xun Chang, 1725–1911*

of the rebellion took place in these cities .[42] However, there are a lot of missing data points between 1850 and 1911, which reduces the accuracy of our knowledge. As was so often the case, taxes did not change very strongly in this period.

3.9 Chihli Pantaokou

Chihli Pantaokou was located in Yongping prefecture and today belongs to Lulong county, in Hebei province. Chihli Pantaokou began collecting taxes in 1735: it only taxed wood, applying a tax rate of 10 of the goods' value.

The data of Chihli Pantaokou are quite incomplete. Neverthelss, from Figure 3-9 one can infer that during Qianlong the trend for tax revenues was basically flat. The lowest amount of revenues during Qianlong occurred in 1751, because taxes were not collected for a full year then.[43] Similarly, the greatest amount was collected in 1761, when the tax period consisted of 1 year and 68 days.[44] Tax revenues fell rapidly in the late Qing, when a shortage of wood led to a decline in the wood trade.[45]

42 TB of FHAC: 2-1-4-21474-16, 2-1-4-22429-19, 2-1-4-22653-15; ZPZZ of FHAC: 4-1-35-589-6; LFZZ of FHAC: 3-7513-37.

43 Tiben Guanshui of Chaodang, March 23th, 17th year of Qianlong.

44 ZPZZ of FHAC: 4-1-35-333-45.

45 LFZZ of FHAC: 3-4891-53.

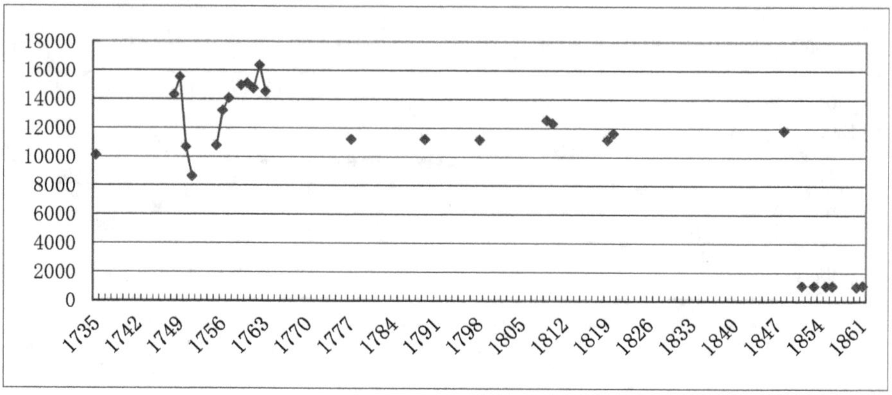

FIGURE 3.9 *Tax revenue trends of Chihli Pantaokou, 1735–1861*

3.10 Other Ports

Below I discus those customs ports, for which the archival material was too scarce to allow for a more detailed analysis.

Chen Guan

Chen Guan was located in Hu'nan province and belonged to *Gongbu* (Ministry of Works). It mainly collected taxes from the trade in wood and during the Kangxi reign it normally collected about 2,400 taels of silver.[46] Thereafter, tax revenues increased gradually to finally reach 12,500 taels of silver as *Zheng'e*. In 1799 Chen Guan's *Yingyu* was fixed at 3,800 taels of silver.[47]

During the Taiping Rebellion, in order to avoid influence of hostilities, administration of Chen Guan was transferred from Chenzhou prefecture to Changde prefecture. Despite this measure, taxes still dropped sharply. Because data from many years are missing, I have been unable to graph a trend for tax revenues for this port.[48]

Wuyuancheng

Wuyuancheng was located in Shanxi province, where it levied customs duty on wood: 1,231 taels of silver (*Zheng'e*) were collected every year; its *Yingyu* was 2 taels of silver. In 1799, Wuyuancheng's *Zheng'e* was raised to 1,269 taels; *Yingyu*

46 YZCHW, vol 7, p. 514.

47 TB of FHAC: 2-1-4-18726-18.

48 LFZZ of FHAC: 3-4400-8, 3-4880-174.

continued to be 2 taels of silver. As for Chen Guan, many data points are missing for Wuyuancheng.

Gubeikou

Gubeikou was located in Zhili province. Like Wuyuancheng, most of the duty it collected came from the wood trade. In 1729, the government set Wuyuancheng's quota 40,341.5 taels of silver, which was an exorbitant sum. As a result of declining availability of wood resources, the quota was lowered the following year to 1,021.51 taels of silver. In 1734, however, only 402.074 taels of silver were collected, once again due to shortages of wood supplies.[49]

Ports for which data is extremely sparse

There are several gates for which larger numbers of data points are missing. These have not been included in the Appendix Table A. The gates are Tungyongdao, Shengjing Mushui, Jilin Mushui, and Yili Mushui. Fortunately, their *Zheng'e* and *Yingyu* were very small, so the affect of missing data on the dataset is negligible, and for this reason I have left them out in Appendix A.

Tungyong Dao

Tungyong Dao was located in Zhili province. It had a *Zheng'e* quota of 7,115 taels and a *Yingyu* quota of 3,900 taels of silver. When tax was recorded per lunar month, *Yingyu* would increase by 592.98 taels. In 1799, records show that the quota was fixed at 11,015.76 taels of silver, but otherwise available archival material is sparse. The reports in the records tell us that from 1808 to 1841 the amounts of taxes collected were always less than the quota, but the exact amounts themselves are unknown.[50] Tax revenue figures for 1870 and 1903 are available, but neither of them was more than 2,800 taels.[51]

Shengjing Mushui

Shengjing Mushui was located at Shengjing area and had a *Zheng'e* quota of 2,000 taels of silver. This was mainly collected from customs duty on wood, levied at a rate of 1/15 of the wood's value.[52]

---

49 TB of FHAC: 2-1-4-12847-14.

50 LFZZ of FHAC: 3-3165-85.

51 TB of FHAC: 2-1-4-21917-31; GZDGXC: Volume 20, p. 518.

52 Li Hongzhang (1908), Volume 941.

Jilin Mushui

Jinlin Mushui was located in Jilin province and had a *Zheng'e* quota of 656 taels of silver, mainly collected from customs duty on wood, which was taxed at the ratio 1/10 of the wood's value.[53]

Yili Mushui

Yili Mushui was located in Xinjiang province. Tax revenue came mainly from customs duty on wood. Unlike many other customs offices, no quota was stipulated. The taxation rate was about 7% of the wood's value.[54]

3.11 Summary

It is time to draw together the data and present an overview of Land Border customs in the Qing. Many data points are missing from the customs gates and ports under Land Border customs, so I have constructed two separate trend lines. The first shows the data just as I compiled them from the archives, while the second line includes missing data points that have been extrapolated from data entries available for surrounding years. I have chosen to not split the extrapolated data into *Zheng'e* and *Yingyu* since these items were never actually collected as such; they were just amounts of the whole that were assigned to these categories. Moreover, there were always problems in actually collecting enough tax revenues to be able to meet stipulated quotas.

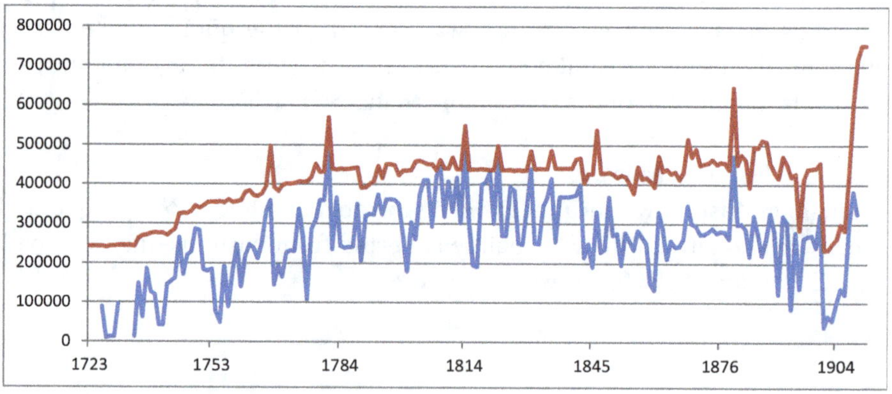

Note: The blue line represents data points reported in the archives; the red line represents data points from the archives to which have been added data for years that are missing.

FIGURE 3.10 *Tax revenue trends of Land Border customs, 1723–1911*

53 Li Hongzhang (1908), Volume 941.

54 Li Hongzhang (1908), Volume 941.

Figure 3.10 clearly shows that tax revenues rose steeply during the period 1723–1795 (the reigns of Yongzheng and Qianlong). Of course, this was influenced by population expansion, as well as economic development. Under the reigns of Jiaqing and Daoguang (1796–1850) there were almost no changes in revenues. In following years there was a small decline, especially during the period 1891–1902. This drop is most probably due to the ascendence of *Yangguan,* since they captured a large part of customs revenues that had previously been collected by *Changguan*, and to some extent due to the impact of the Sino-Japanese War. But generally speaking, one can say that Land Border customs were least affected by unfolding events in the late Qing (especially during the Taiping Rebellion). I think the geographical location of its customs ports, on the edges of the empire, was maybe the most important reason for this.

CHAPTER 4

Grand Canal and Yangtze River Customs

Up until the early twentieth century, when modern technologies were introduced, transportation on water was the cheapest way to carry goods. The Grand Canal and Yangtze River were the most important waterways of traditional China, so it is not surprising that Canal and Yangtze River customs was the major source of tax revenues in the early Qing. With the economic development of the coastal areas, however, Coastal customs gradually surpassed Grand Canal and Yangtze River customs, reflecting also the transformation of China's economy during the Qing.

4.1 Chongwenmen

Chongwenmen was the most important place of entry—in fact a customs gate in the city wall—of Beijing. "Beijing is the capital of the county. All over the country people would like to travel to here and all of the country's goods are sent here. As a result, the government has decided to set up a gate to collect taxes on the goods."[1] There is disagreement in the literature about when Chongwenmen was actually established. Some believe that it was inherited from the Ming dynasty, while others believe it was built at the beginning of the Qing. We do know from records that in 1666 the administration of Chongwenmen was placed under Shuntian prefecture. In 1668, however, administrative responsibility was returned to *Hubu* (Ministry of Revenue). In 1724, it was again placed under the administration of the Shuntian prefecture, only to be returned once more to the Ministry of Revenue in 1762. Finally, in 1822, the Imperial Court considered Chongwenmen to be so important that it decided to appoint a high-ranking official to manage the gate directly.

The customs duties levied in Chongwenmen were collected mainly from commercial activites, especially the trade in tea, alcoholic beverages, tobacco and clothing. At some time during the reign of Shunzhi the tax quota (*Zheng'e*) was set at 85,099 taels of silver. Later, in 1686, the quota for *Zheng'e* was increased to 102,175 taels, but *Yingyu* was not fixed.[2]

1 Mou Quansun (1886), Volume 11.

2 Mou Quansun (1886), Volume 11.

 | DOI 10.1163/9789004324886_006

TABLE 4.1 *Quota of Chongwenmen in the Qing dynasty (in taels of silver)*

Year	Shunzhi	1686	1723	1800	1804	1806	1822
Zheng'e	85,099	94,483	102,175	102,175	102,175	102,175	102,175
Yingyu	–	–	–	183,269	212,376	212,473	197,825
Total	85,099	94,483	102,175	285,444	314,551	314,648	300,000

Sources: materials from *Shilu, Huidian, Hubu Zheli* and archives (see text for archival references).

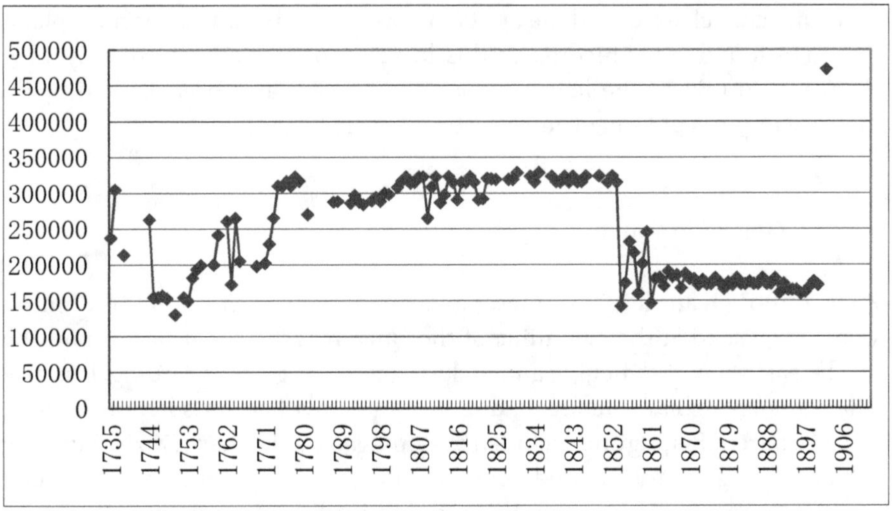

FIGURE 4.1 *Tax revenue trends of Chongwenmen, 1735–1911*

Chongwenmen's taxation year was not like that of most other gates, which was a 12-month year. Rather, its taxation year was strictly fixed from 3 August in a year to 2 August of the following year according to the traditional Chinese lunar calendar. Some years, therefore, comprised 13 lunar months.

As Figure 4.1 shows, tax revenues under the reigns of Yongzheng and Qianlong increased rapidly, almost doubling in 60 years. Of course, this was connected to population expansion and increasing economic development. During the Jiaqing and Daoguang, taxes were quite stable, also in part due to new tax policy. There were only three serious shortfalls during that time. Archival material reports a shortfall in 1813, due to the late arrival of the Tribute Grain boats.[3] The shortfall in 1821 was due to silk shortages in the south, such

3 LFZZ of FHAC: 3-1770-50.

that almost nothing was being transported to Beijing.[4] Finally, the shortfall in the tax year of 1822 was the result of a huge flood (that actually occurred in 1823).[5]

During the Taiping Rebellion, Chongwenmen was heavily affected. In 1853, Chongwenmen's official administrator reported to the emperor: "Tax revenues collected at Chongwenmen are falling quickly day after day, and this is totally due to the rebel army, which occupies the southern part of China to the extent that the roads cannot be used by merchants. Goods cannot be transported as usual, and tax revenues are declining accordingly."[6] The situation reoccurred repeatedly in following years.[7] In the late Qing, one year stood out: 1902. The tax revenue collected in the first nine months was already 472,497.62 taels of silver and as such exceeded the quota that had been fixed. There is no explanation to be found in the records for this, but the gate's administrator only asked the Court to reward the lower officials. I assume that it was affected by the increase imports of foreign goods trade after the Boxer Rebellion.[8]

4.2 Zuoyi and Youyi

Zuoyi ("zuo" means left in Chinese) and Youyi ("you" means right in Chinese) were established at the beginning of the Qing dynasty. Zuoyi was responsible for the eastern part of Beijing and included customs gates at An'ding, Dongzhi, Chaoyang, Dongbian, Guangqu, and Zuo'an. Youyi had jurisdiction over the western part of Beijing and included customs gates at Desheng, Xizhi, Fucheng, Xibian, Guang'an, You'an, and Yongding. In 1797, the government combined Zuoyi and Youyi to form one office, only to split them up again two years later.[9]

Zuoyi's quota was 6,000 taels of silver in the period 1644–1662, but in 1663 this was raised to 10,000 taels of silver. After that the quota changed several times: by 1799 its *Zheng'e* was fixed at 10,008 taels of silver and *Yingyu* at 18,000 taels. Apart from taxes on commercial goods, Zuoyi also taxed real estate (trade in housing) in the eastern part of Beijing, raising several hundreds to one thousand taels of silver each year.[10]

4 LFZZ of FHAC: 3-3155-32.
5 LFZZ of FHAC: 3-3156-28.
6 LFZZ of FHAC: 3-4376-23.
7 LFZZ of FHAC: 3-4376-23, 3-4378-33, 3-4379-48, 3-4381-22.
8 LFZZ of FHAC: 3-6513-95.
9 Li Hongzhang (1908), Volume 236.
10 Mou Quansun (1886), Volume 11.

TABLE 4.2 *Quota of Zuoyi in the Qing dynasty (in taels of silver)*

Year	1661	1663	1799
Zheng'e	6,000	10,000	10,000
Yingyu	–	–	18,000
Total	6,000	10,000	28,000

Sources: materials from *Shilu, Huidian, Hubu Zheli* and archives (see text for archival references).

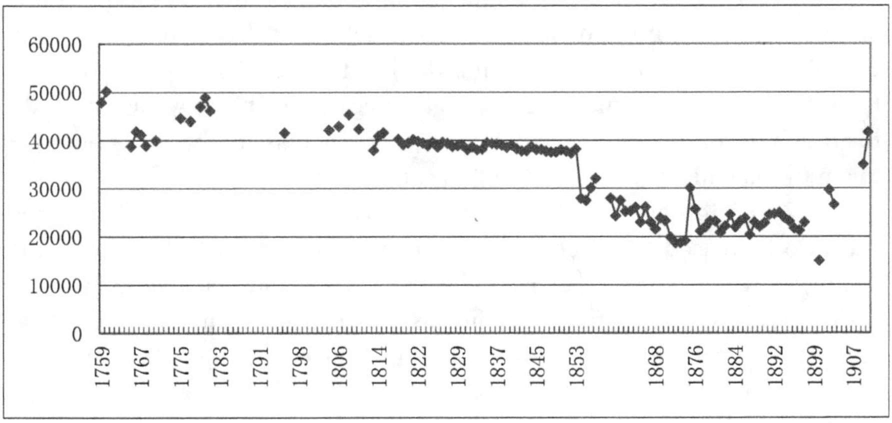

FIGURE 4.2 *Tax revenue trends of Zuoyi, 1759–1911*

There are two entries of tax data for the years 1792, 1827, 1860, and 1892, due to the use of the Chinese lunar year.

There are many data points missing in the first 50 years shown on Figure 4.2, even though I made allowances for the lack of data by only starting to plot data from 1759 onwards, rather than 1725 or 1735 as in many other figures. Nevertheless, from the scanty data available it appears that tax revenues in that period were fairly stable. Thereafter, from 1796 to 1850, however, the trend was declining. In fact, closer examination of the data shows that the drop was relatively small (amounting to only several thousand taels) when compared against the quota of 45,000 taels of silver.

The Taiping Rebellion brought significant decreases in Zuoyi's tax revenues. In 1855 the Administrator of Zouyi reported to the Imperial Court that "In recent years, the Taiping army has not been exterminated, and the roads are closed and goods do not reach the capital as easily as before".[11] From 1853 onwards, the government was forced to adopted inflationary measures to get through the fiscal crisis arising from the rebellion. It produced a large amount of copper coins and ordered everyone to use these, which quickly led to a depreciation of the coins. Although people had to use these coins in their daily lives, taxes had to be paid in silver, which had an enormous effect on people's personal wealth. This was probably the reason for the decline in tax revenues in Zuoyi. In 1856 the Adminsitrator of Zouyi reported that "It is mainly because the price of silver in the capital is very high when it is exchanged for coins. As a result, many merchants have lost large sums of money and many shops have had to close."[12] This observation was made repeatedly in reports.[13]

In 1900, during the Boxer Rebellion, Beijing was occupied by foreign armies and tax revenue from Zuoyi fell to an historic low, i.e. from an annual 50,000 taels of silver to 20,000 taels. During the last few years of the Qing dynasty, however, tax revenues increased strongly once more. This may have been due to growth in commercial activity following the increase of foreign goods arriving in China when the Boxer Rebellion came to an end.[14]

Like Zuoyi, initially Youyi had a quota of 6,000 taels of silver, which in 1663 was also increased to 10,000 taels. Thereafter the quota changed frequently, until 1799, when *Zheng'e* was fixed at 10,005.12 taels and *Yingyu* at 7,321.4 taels of silver. At the same time, Youyi, just as Zuoyi, also began taxing real estate (trade in housing) in the western part of Beijing, collecting each year several hundreds to one thousand taels of silver.[15]

TABLE 4.3 *Quota of Yuoyi in the Qing dynasty* (*in taels of silver*)

Year	1661	1663	1799
Zheng'e	6,000	10,000	10,005.12
Yingyu	–	–	7,321.4
Total	6,000	10,000	17,326.52

Sources: materials from *Shilu*, *Huidian*, *Hubu Zheli* and archives (see text for archival references).

11 LFZZ of FHAC: 3-4395-57.

12 LFZZ of FHAC: 3-4379-4.

13 LFZZ of FHAC: 3-4383-2, 3-4384-48, 3-4871-29, 3-4874-19, 3-4876-8.

14 Guanshui Baogao Biao of Chaodang, 5 April, First year of Xuantong. LFZZ of FHAC: 3-7507-4.

15 Mou Quansun (1886), Volume 11.

There are two entries of tax data in the years 1797, 1827, 1860, and 1892 in the material, once again due to the use of the Chinese lunar year.

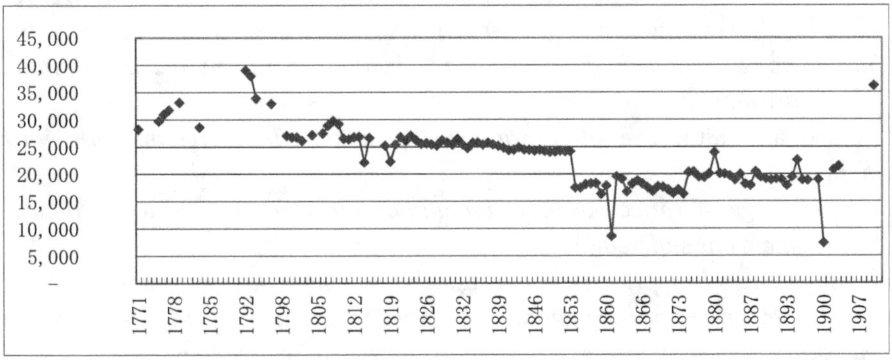

FIGURE 4.3 *Tax revenue trends of Youyi, 1771–1911*

Similarly for Zuoyi, in Figure 4.3 there are many data points missing for Youyi from 1735 to 1770, so I analyze the tax revenue trend only from 1771 onwards. Unlike the trend in Zuoyi, Youyi experienced a small increase in tax revenues from 1771 to 1795. During the period 1796 to 1850 there was a slight decline. In comparison with previous periods, Youyi experienced a serious decline from 1850 onwards—just as in Zuoyi, the impact of the Taiping Rebellion was great. In 1855, the Adminsitrator of Youyi reported to the Imperial Court that the cause of falling revenues was the Taiping Rebellion: "It was very dangerous in Zhili province and merchants dare not to come because of the war."[16] In following years, the decline was most often linked to the price of silver. This happened mostly because the central government, in order to make up for the loss of revenues as a result of the Taiping Rebellion, issued a large quantitiy of new coins of large denominations with reduced silver content. As people distrusted the new coins, they used them to pay their taxes.

1856: *taxes collected in Youyi were mainly in copper coin, not silver, as before. However, recently silver has become very expensive and as we have to change the newest coins of large denominations into silver, we have lost a lot of money.*[17]

1857: *The large-denomination coins are inconvenient for day to day transactions, which has led a steep rise in silver and food prices. Many merchants have had to close down their shops.*[18]

16 LFZZ of FHAC: 3-4395-62.

17 LFZZ of FHAC: 3-4379-14.

18 LFZZ of FHAC: 3-4396-21.

1858: *Silver price is so high that everything has become very expensive. Merchants don't dare come to trade.*[19]

1859: *Last year, British and French warships arrived at Tianjian (and the Second Opium War broke out) and merchants had become a rare occurrence. Also, the silver price was much higher in Beijing than in other provinces. Merchants have to pay a great deal of money to have their goods transported to the capital, so they are unwilling to trade in Beijing.*[20]

1860 and 1861: *The silver price was high and the merchants lost much money.*[21]

1862: *The silver price was very high and ordinary people have a very difficult life. Business has suffered.*[22]

1865: *The silver price is much higher in Beijing than in other provinces. Merchants have to pay a great deal of money to have their goods transported to the capital and so they dare not to come to trade in Beijing. In recent years, both soldiers and civilians have become very poor and business has been very bad.*[23]

1866: *The silver price is high and merchants have lost much money.*[24]

1867 and 1869: *The silver price is high and merchants have lost much money. At the same time, Inner Mongolia's grasslands have suffered from a severe drought, so horses and sheep could not be herded to Beijing as usual.*[25]

1872: *Major flooding occurred in Zhili and the Yongding River flooded, making roads impassible. At the same time, the price of silver was much higher in Beijing than in the provinces.*[26]

Obviously, the price of silver had become the most important factor behind the decline of tax revenues during that period. Revenues reached their lowest level in 1900, owing to the Boxer Rebellion: "Since the forces of the foreign alliance are in conflict with our army, all roads have been closed and cannot be used for trade. Merchants are worried about the situation and almost half the shops have closed, which has led to a decline in taxes collected. Later, troops of the Eight-Nation Alliance occupied and looted Beijing, so all tax records from Youyi disappeared, as did the tax money that had been collected."[27]

---

19 LFZZ of FHAC: 3-4397-10.

20 LFZZ of FHAC: 3-4382-2.

21 LFZZ of FHAC: 3-4383-3, 3-4888-71.

22 LFZZ of FHAC: 3-4888-70.

23 LFZZ of FHAC: 3-4872-82.

24 LFZZ of FHAC: 3-4874-18.

25 LFZZ of FHAC: 3-4876-7, 3-4879-15.

26 LFZZ of FHAC: 3-4880-193.

27 GXCZP, Volume 74, p. 282.

4.3 Zuoliangtin

Zuoliangtin, inherited from the Ming dynasty, was located in Tongzhou district of Beijing. In 1700, the government appointed one Han and one Manchu official to administer the port. Much later, in 1768, it was managed by the Vice-Minister of Revenue.[28] At the beginning of the Kangxi the quota for Zuoliangtin was set at 6,339.26 taels of silver.

Duties levied at Zuoliangtin were mainly based on the value of the goods. If the goods were to be sold in Tongzhou district, the taxation rate was 8% of their value. And if the goods were to be sent into Beijing, the taxation rate was 3%. In 1776, the Imperial Court changed the basis of its customs tarrifs for Zuoliangtin: rice was to be taxed according to its weight, and animals were to be taxed according to their number.[29]

TABLE 4.4 *Quota of Zuoliangtin in the Qing dynasty (in taels of silver)*

Year	1669	1699	Qianlong*	1799
Zheng'e	6,000	6,339	6,339	6,339
Yingyu	–	–	7,871	6,000
Total	6,000	6,339	14,210	12,339

* Exact year unknown.
Sources: materials from *Shilu, Huidian, Hubu Zheli* and archives (see text for archival references).

The tax year in Zuoliangtin comprised 12 months. There are two entries for tax data in the years 1751, 1784, 1816, 1849, and 1881, due to the use of the Chinese lunar year.

As Figure 4.4 shows, in general, customs revenue increased little from 1732 to 1795. In 1740, however, there was clearly a drop. According to the official records from 1739, the Qing government forbad the trading of rice, which was the main raw material for the production of Chinese liquor (baijiu, literally "white wine"). The government thought liquor production would use up too much rice, ultimately resulting in wide-spread hunger among the population. For Zuoliangtin, this ban meant a reduction in annual tax revenues of several thousand taels of silver.[30]

28 Wu Chunli (2002), Volume 3.
29 Li Hongzhang (1908), Volume 234.
30 TB of FHAC: 2-1-4-13254-10.

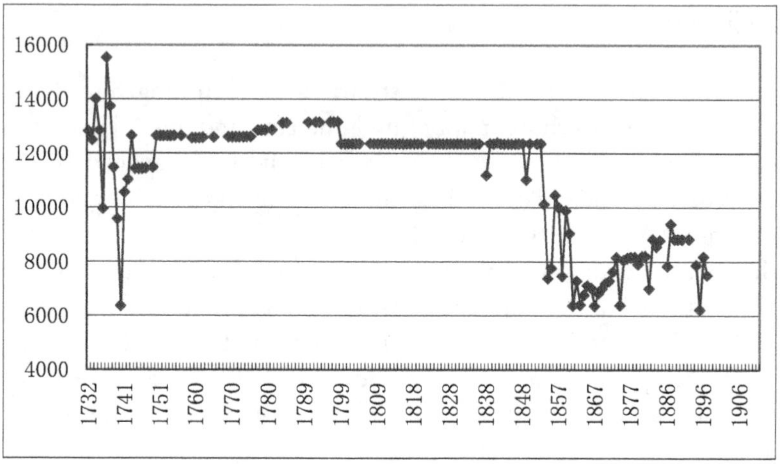

FIGURE 4.4 *Tax revenue trends of Zuoliangtin, 1732–1911*

There were also some steep falls during the period 1796–1850. The first decline occurred in 1799, the fourth year of the reign of Jiaqing, who stopped using the triennial comparison measure and set a new amount of *Yingyu* (*Zheng'e* was not changed). In 1838, tax revenues fell sharply, but I cannot find an explanation for this in the records.[31] This reoccurred in 1849, again without an explanation being recorded.

The outbreak of the Taiping Rebellion ushered in a permanent fall in tax revenues. The reason for this was that "Because of the war, tea shipments from the south declined year after year."[32]

4.4 Huai'an Guan

Huai'an Guan was located on the Grand Canal, in Huai'an prefecture, Jiangsu province. Huai'an Guan was originally established in 1429 (Ming dynasty), and in 1645 its office was re-established by the Qing government. The quota of Huai'an Guan in the Ming was 77,875 taels of silver. In 1646, under the Qing dynasty, its quota was set at 50,047 taels of silver, which was increased in 1690 to 119,523 taels. In 1706, the warehouses of Huai'an and Qingjiang Chang were combined with those of Huai'an Guan. This led to several further changes in its quota, which was finally fixed at a *Zheng'e* of 201,639.602 taels of silver. In addition to the warehouses just mentioned, Huai'an Guan also administered

31 TB of FHAC: 2-1-4-21049-25.

32 LFZZ of FHAC: 3-4875-30.

customs duties collected at two other ports, i.e. Suqian Guan and Miaowan Kou. Each of these three offices had different administrative systems for collecting customs duties, even though they were managed by the same Administrator. Huai'an and Miaowan Kou fell under *Hubu*, while Suqian Guan fell under *Gongbu*. In 1741, Suqian Guan's quota was 48,884 taels of silver; that of Miaowan Kou was 3,840 taels of silver.

In 1799, the *Yingyu* of Huai'an Guan was fixed at 101,000 taels of silver, Miaowan Kou at 2,200 taels, and Suqian Guan at 7,800 taels, in total 111,000 taels of silver. In 1804, Huai'an Guan's *Yingyu* was increased to 121,000 taels, but this was later, in 1831, reduced to 100,000 taels. Together with Miaowan Kou and Suqian Guan, this brought the entire quota (*Zheng'e* plus *Yingyu*) to 364,363 taels of silver. Even though they belonged individually to different branches of the Imperial Court, all three ports reported at the same time. *Hubu* administered the main part of this.

TABLE 4.5 *Quota of Huai'an Guan in the Qing dynasty (in taels of silver)*

Year	1645	1652	1669	1670	1686	1723	1799	1804	1831
Zheng'e	22780	58300	50000	80891	150728	135223	254363	254363	254363
Yingyu	–	–	–	–	–	–	111000	121000	110000
Total	22780	58300	50000	80891	150728	135223	365363	375363	364363

Sources: materials from Shilu, Huidian, Hubu Zheli and archives (see text for archival references).

There are two entries of tax data in each of the years 1740, 1767, 1800, 1832, 1865, and 1898, due to the use of the Chinese lunar year.

From Figure 4.5 one can see that customs duties collected at Huai'an Guan changed continuously. A contemporary observer during the late Qing explained why:

Huai'an Guan was located at the crossroads of southern and northern China; many boats and merchants have passed through this place. Formerly, there was no coastal sea transport, and all water transport was focused on the Grand Canal, so customs revenues were, of course, very high. After the Taiping Rebellion, though, the tax revenue declined quickly, and not only because of the hostilities. For example, when in the late Qing the Yellow River changed its course to the north, goods could be transported over land. Second, with more and more steamboats being used, more and more goods were transported through sea ports. Third, the transport of Tribute Grain was switched from the Grand Canal to sea transport, so less and less goods passed through Huai'an. Finally, the fourth, and

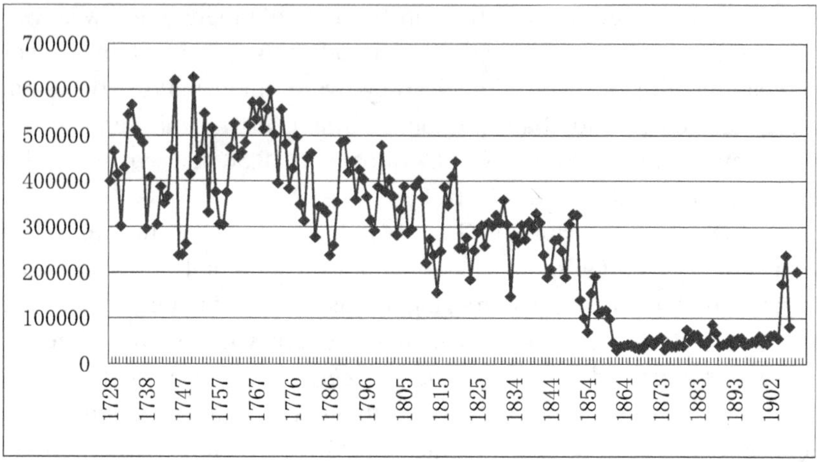

FIGURE 4.5 *Tax revenue trends of Huai'an Guan, 1728–1911*

most important, reason was that Yangshui (foreign tax) could be levied anywhere, while Changshui (domestic tax) could not.[33]

I can confirm that these reasons were generally the case. From my research on the period 1796–1850, there are two explanations for the fall experienced by Huai'an Guan. The first is that when the Yellow River flooded, the Grand Canal could not be used for short periods. This occurred for a total of 20 years: 1797, 1798, 1803, 1804, 1806–1807, 1811–1815, 1820–1821, 1825–1826, 1832, 1836, 1843–1844, and 1846. The second was because of the negative effect of natural disasters on the transport of grain and, thus, tax revenues. Natural disasters affected in this manner a total of 16 years: 1796, 1822–1824, 1827–1831, 1833–1835, and 1847–1850.[34]

During the Taiping Rebellion the situation changed drastically. Since Huai'an Guan was occupied by the Taiping army and serious battles were a daily occurrence, it was very dangerous for merchants and others to pass through the ports, so there was a rapid fall in customs revenues in that period. In 1853, reports to be found in the records state that "The Taiping troops have invaded Jiangsu province and the region along the Yangtze River is subject to martial law. Goods couldn't pass through, so we could hardly collect any taxes."[35] Again and again in the records, the same reasons were given for shortfalls in revenues collected. This was especially the case when the Yellow River changed

33 GXCZP, vol 74, p. 755.

34 Ni Yuping (2010), p. 47.

35 LFZZ of FHAC: 3-4376-8.

its course in 1855, affecting the Grand Canal accordingly.[36] Archived records of Huai'an Guan for the period 1856 to 1859 put it in the following way: "In recent years, commercial activities stopped due to the rebellion. At the same time, the Yellow River changed its course and this prevented the boats from passing through the port."[37]

After 1860, the Taiping army again occupied parts of Jiangsu province, in particular Suzhou city (the largest and most prosperous city in northern Jiangsu), making it once more impossible for merchants to pass through Huai'an Guan. During this period, the Qing government banned the grain trade to prevent food being suppied to Taiping troops; this made collecting taxes even more difficult.[38] When Suzhou prefecture was reconquered in 1863, the Nian rebellion (another large rebellion) followed. As a result of all these years of war, merchants and the people had become poorer and poorer, so commerce was adversely affected and tax revenues declined.[39] The situation was summarized as follows: "Huai'an Guan could still provide tax revenues of more than 10 thousand taels of silver even though the Yellow River changed its course. In the period after 1860, the rebellion expanded rapidly into this area. This, in addition to the parallel development of sea transport, caused tax collections to fall by 20-30 thousand taels each year. At the same time, the Likin bureaucracy was established in China. More and more goods were transported, therefore, via sea routes."[40] This trend continued into the last years of the Qing dynasty.

4.5 Hushu Guan

Hushu Guan was located in Suzhou prefecture of Jiangsu province and was close to Yanzhou Guan, Zhehai Guan and Beixing Guan. It was established in 1429, under the Ming dynasty. In 1645, the second year of the Qing, Hushu Guan was re-established. Management of the office was transferred from the central government to the viceroy of Jiangsu and later to the Suzhou Zhizhao (the official responsible for weaving in the prefecture).[41]

36 ZPZZ of FHAC: 4-1-35-382-15, 4-1-35-382-16; LFZZ of FHAC: 3-4378-19.

37 LFZZ of FHAC: 3-4379-27, 3-4392-26; ZPZZ of FHAC: 4-1-35-383-15, 4-1-35-383-50.

38 LFZZ of FHAC: 3-4383-7; ZPZZ of FHAC: 4-1-35-383-72, 4-1-35-384-24.

39 LFZZ of FHAC: 3-4871-54, 3-4873-36, 3-4875-21; ZPZZ of FHAC: 4-1-35-385-23, 4-1-35-385-77.

40 ZPZZ of FHAC: 4-1-1-899-27.

41 Ling Shouqi (1992), Volume 6.

TABLE 4.6 *Quota of Hushu Guan in the Qing dynasty (in taels of silver)*

Year	1645	1656	1669	1686	1694	1699	1723	1799	1804	1831
Zheng'e	113,947	149,000	140,000	159,709	179,709	159,709	191,151	191,151	191,151	191,151
Yingyu	–	–	–	–	–	–	–	235,000	250,000	230,000
Total	113,947	149,000	140,000	159,709	179,709	159,709	191,151	426,151	441,151	421,151

Sources: materials from *Shilu*, *Huidian*, *Hubu Zheli* and archives (see text for archival references).

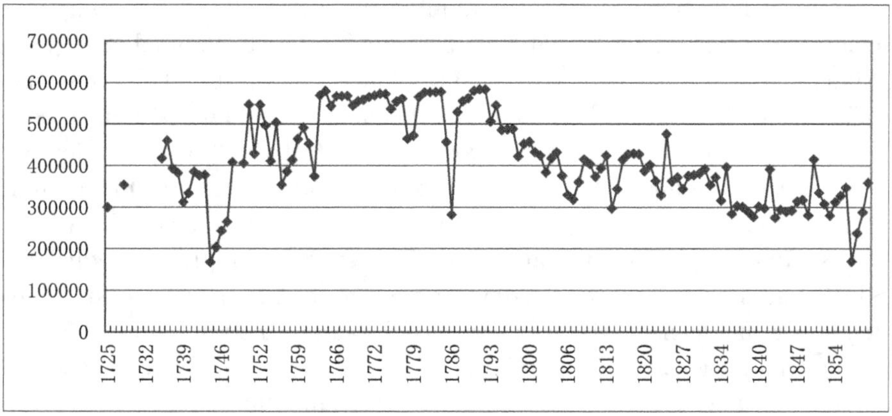

FIGURE 4.6 *Tax revenue trends of Hushu Guan, 1725–1860*

There are two entries of tax data for 1748, 1770, 1803, and 1835 because of the use of the Chinese lunar year.

For the reigns of Yongzheng and Qianlong, customs duties collected at Hushu Guan clearly show an increase trend, with a doubling of revenues between 1725 and 1760. The lowest point in that period was in 1744, because in that year Hushu Guan collected customs revenues only from 12 November 1743 to 9 March 1744, a little less than half a year.[42] The following taxation period changed accordingly. A second low point was in 1786, the result of a serious interruption in water transport.[43]

During the reigns of Jiaqing and Daoguang, tax revenues in Hushu Guan gradually declined. My research indicates that the reasons for the decline between 1796 and 1850 were the blocking of the Grand Canal and natural disasters such as flooding and drought, all of which were harmful for trade.[44]

42 ZPZZ of FHAC: 4-1-35-318-6, 4-1-35-318-7.

43 LFZZ of FHAC: 3-601-24.

44 Ni Yuping (2010), p. 62.

Of course, tax collection was affected by the First Opium War. In 1842, when British forces entered the Yangtzi River region, "Zhengjiang was occupied and the Grand Canal couldn't be used. We can only collect taxes of one to two hundred taels every day, so tax revenue has dropped sharply."[45] When, however, I take the social general background into consideration, I conclude that this drop was because of the economic shift from local inland micro-economies to coastal micro-economies, or, in other words, a shift in focus from the Grand Canal to the sea, which led to economic decline in the Hushu Guan area.

After 1850, tax revenues continued to drop, the Taiping Rebellion being the direct cause.[46] In 1860, Suzhou prefecture was occupied by the Taiping Army and the building of the customs office was destroyed. In such a situation, collection of taxes was absolutely out of the question, so this activity was terminated in that year.[47] Later the Qing government tried to re-establish taxation in an effort to collect more money. This plan was, however, repeatedly rejected by the local governor,[48] so there were no data records for Hushu Guan after 1860.

4.6 Yangzhou Guan

Yangzhou Guan was located in Yangzhou prefecture, Jiangsu province. It was originally established under the Ming dynasty in 1429. For a very long time Yangzhou Guan was managed by the central government. In 1723 the court decided to transfer its administration to the viceroy of Jiangsu province. Several changes followed, such as that in 1739, when its management was passed on to the Lianghuai Salt Syndicate. But not too long after that, it once again fell under the jurisdiction of Jiangsu's viceroy and remained so.

TABLE 4.7 *Quota of Yangzhou Guan in the Qing dynasty (in taels of silver)*

Year	1656	1669	1686	1723	1799
Zheng'e	36,500	30,000	44,884	52,576	92,791
Yingyu	–	–	–	–	71,000
Total	36,500	30,000	44,884	52,576	163,791

Sources: materials from *Shilu*, *Huidian*, *Hubu Zheli* and archives (see text for archival references).

45 LFZZ of FHAC: 3-9489-60.

46 LFZZ of FHAC: 3-4375-29, 3-4382-26, ZPZZ of FHAC: 4-1-35-382-42, 4-1-35-383-14, 4-1-35-383-51.

47 LFZZ of FHAC: 3-4872-31.

48 LFZZ of FHAC: 3-4889-89.

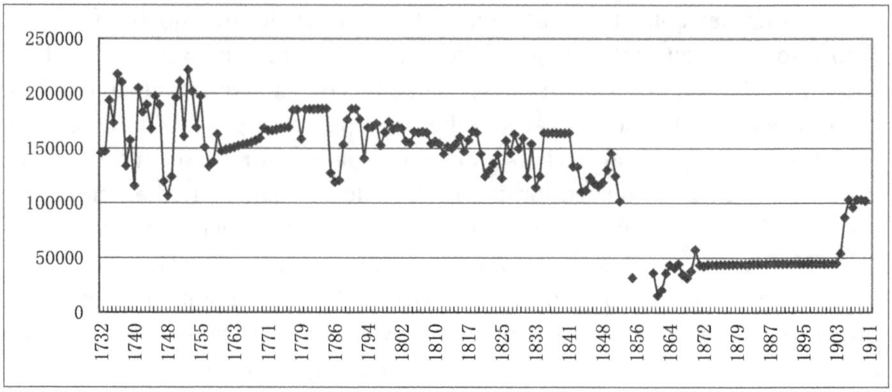

FIGURE 4.7 *Tax revenue trends of Yangzhou Guan, 1732–1911*

My research shows two entries of tax data in the years 1748, 1781, 1814, 1846 and 1876, due to the use of the Chinese lunar year.

As Figure 4.7 indicates, during the Qianlong tax levels were very stable. From the reign of Jiaqing onwards, however, tax revenue began to slowly decrease. The records from that period, i.e. 1796–1850, indicate that this decrease was caused by a blockage of the Grand Canal and poor harvests in Yangzhou prefecture and in neighboring provinces, all leading to less goods being transported. The same situation arose during the Daoguang's reign. Simlilarly, during the First Opium War tax revenues of Yangzhou Guan were adversely affected. The records in the archives state: "When the British army began hostilities, Qing soldiers had to travel to Jiangsu and Zhejiang provinces to defend the country, which makes it almost impossible for the merchants to pass. On 8 June of this year (using the Chinese lunar calendar), British warships sailed up the Yangtze River and occupied Zhenjiang city (Jiangsu province) for 84 days. In order to address this situation, the Qing government closed all rivers and no merchant dared to trade in that area. The customs shortfall was 30,000 to 50,000 taels in these years.[49]

There was an even more obvious decrease during the reigns of Xianfeng and Tongzhi, which was, of course, also caused by the Taiping Rebellion. Tax revenues could not be collected for four years (1856–1859) due to hostilities: gaps in the data are not due to missing records but rather due to this port being occupied by rebel forces.[50] After the Taiping Rebellion was put down, tax levels stabilized and remain that way for a long time, albeit at a level of around half of the quota decreed. The records always state that this decline could be explained by the ascendancy of *Yangguan*, which was very clear in the late

49 LFZZ of FHAC: 3-9489-41.

50 LFZZ of FHAC: 3-4376-1, 3-4876-11; ZPZZ of FHAC: 4-1-1-888-17.

Qing.[51] In addition to this, during the last seven years of the Qing dynasty tax revenues of Yangzhou Guan doubled compared to previous years, a result flowing on from the introduction of a new system of taxation.[52]

4.7 Wuhu Guan

Wuhu Guan consisted of *Huguan* and *Gongguan* offices, all of which were located in Wuhu prefecture of Anhui province. Wuhu Huguan and Wuhu Gongguan were established in the late Ming; up to 1471, Wuhu Gongguan levied customs duties on wood and bamboo. Initially, it was expected to collect taxes amounting to about 1,000 taels of silver, but this quota increased year by year. In 1502, for example, customs revenues amounting to about 37,000 taels were collected. In 1630, *Huguan* office was also set up at Wuhu. These *Huguan* and *Gongguan* initially belonged to *Hubu* and *Gongbu* respectively, and were, therefore, administered by different officials. In 1670, however, the management of both was assigned to the viceroy of Anhui province, even though their taxes still needed to be sent separately to *Hubu* and *Gongbu*. In 1733, during the reign of Yongzheng, the management of Wuhu Guan was passed on to Wuhu prefecture, where it remained permanently.

TABLE 4.8 *Quota of Wuhu Huguan in the Qing dynasty (in taels of silver)*

Year	Shunzhi*	1656	1669	1686	1691	1694
Zheng'e	87,338	123,100	120,000	135,396	138,496	158,496
Yingyu	–	–	–		–	–
–						
Total	87,338	123,100	120,000	135,396	138,496	158,496
Year	1699	1723	1735	1756	1799	–
Zheng'e	138,496	156,920	156,920	156,919	156,919	–
Yingyu	–	–	57,870	42,867	73,000	–
Total	138,496	156,920	214,790	199,786	229,919	–

* Exact year unknown.
Sources: materials from *Shilu*, *Huidian*, *Hubu Zheli* and archives (see text for archival references).

51 ZPZZ of FHAC: 4-1-35-391-17, 4-1-1-925-33.

52 GZDGXC: Volume 23, pp. 407–408; LFZZ of FHAC: 3-6439-11, 3-6445-60; ZPZZ of FHAC: 4-1-35-434-77, 4-1-35-437-7.

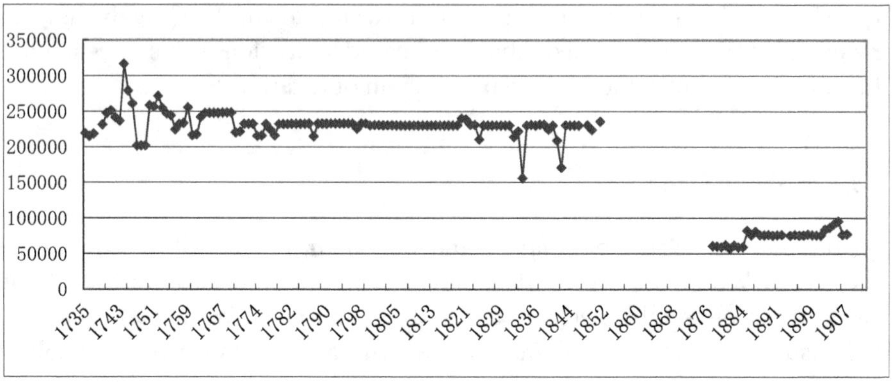

FIGURE 4.8 *Tax revenue trends of Wuhu Huguan, 1735–1911*

TABLE 4.9 *Quota of Wuhu Gonguan in the Qing dynasty (in taels of silver)*

Year	1658	1681	1686	1706	Qianlong*	1799
Zheng'e	45,300	50,300	55,530	70,145	70,146	70,146
Yingyu	–	–	–	–	57,453	47,000
Total	45,300	50,300	55,530	70,145	127,599	117,146

* Exact year unknown.
Sources: materials from *Shilu*, *Huidian*, *Hubu Zheli* and archives (see text for archival references).

Goods passing through Wuhu Guan were quite varied and included food, bamboo, salt and tea, which mainly came from Sichuan, Hubei, Jiangxi, Zhejiang, and Jiangsu provinces. Already during the reign of Kangxi, Wuhu Guan had become one of the most important ports along the Grand Canal.

There are two entries of tax data in the years 1767, 1800, 1832, and 1890, since they taxed for 12 months in one year, but the Chinese lunar year sometimes had 13 months.

Figures 4.8 and 4.9 illustrate that there was a slight decline in tax revenues during the Qianlong, with the transfer of economic activity from local areas in the interior to the coastal seaboard. There was also some decline during the Jiaqing and Daoguang, but stability was the most outstanding characteristic of the period. Explanations for this decrease can be found in the archives, for example the big flood in China of 1823: "Flooding is so extensive that all neighbouring areas have been covered by water, and there are few boats using the ports. After the autumn of 1823, the harvest from all areas was very poor and it

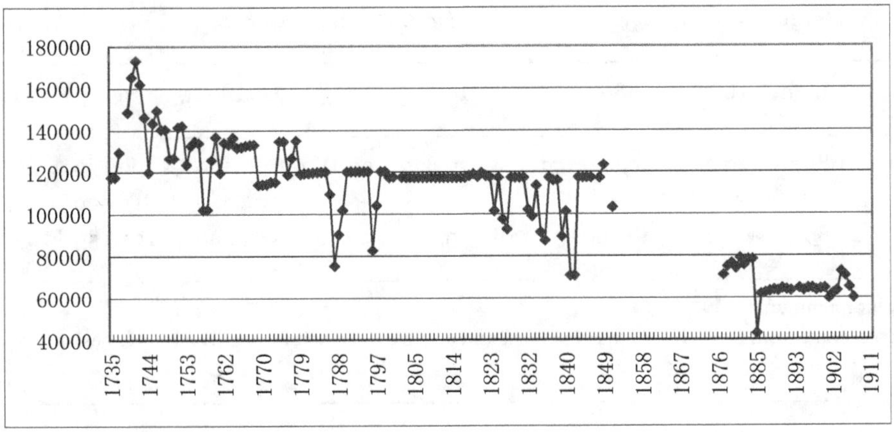

FIGURE 4.9 *Tax revenue trends of Wuhu Gongguan, 1735–1911*

is difficult to trade those goods that are available."[53] The tax revenues of the following year show the same results. Also, in 1841, during the First Opium War there was a shortfall of 67,573 taels of silver, to be followed the next year by a shortfall of 106,221 of taels of silver. Reports state that "There was a rumor that British warships have been in the Yangtze River and the local population has rushed to Hubei and Jiangxi provinces to escape. Commercial boats dare not to come to trade. This situation is a totally different reason from the shortfalls of other years, which were attributable to natural disasters."[54]

Of course, Wuhu Guan was strongly affected by the Taiping Rebellion. In 1851, records state: "Merchants dare not to come to trade since the Taiping Rebellion has broken out."[55] Also due to the rebellion, there were no tax revenues at all during the period 1853–1876. Even later, when economic activity recovered (after the rebellion had been put down), tax revenues remained low at around roughly half the level of the quota.

4.8 Fengyang Guan

Fengyang Guan was located in Fengyang prefecture of Anhui province and was the only port in the Huai River area. It was established by the Ming dynasty in 1465. Since Fengyang is the birthplace of Zhu Yuanzhang, the first Ming emperor, it is not surprising that its prosperity grew during the Ming Dynasty.

53 ZPZZ of FHAC: 4-1-35-373-23.

54 LFZZ of FHAC: 3-9489-56.

55 LFZZ of FHAC: 3-4375-30.

TABLE 4.10 *Quota of Fengyang Guan in the Qing dynasty (in taels of silver)*

Year	Shunzhi*	1669	1680	1681	1686	1723	Qianlong	1799	1804
Zheng'e	21,807	20,000	30,000	71,116	79,839	90,160	90,160	90,159	90,159
Yingyu	–	–	–	–	–	–	74,280	15,000	17,000
Total	21,807	20,000	30,000	71,116	79,839	90,160	164,440	105,159	107,159

* Exact year unknown.
Sources: materials from *Shilu*, *Huidian*, *Hubu Zheli* and archives (see text for archival references).

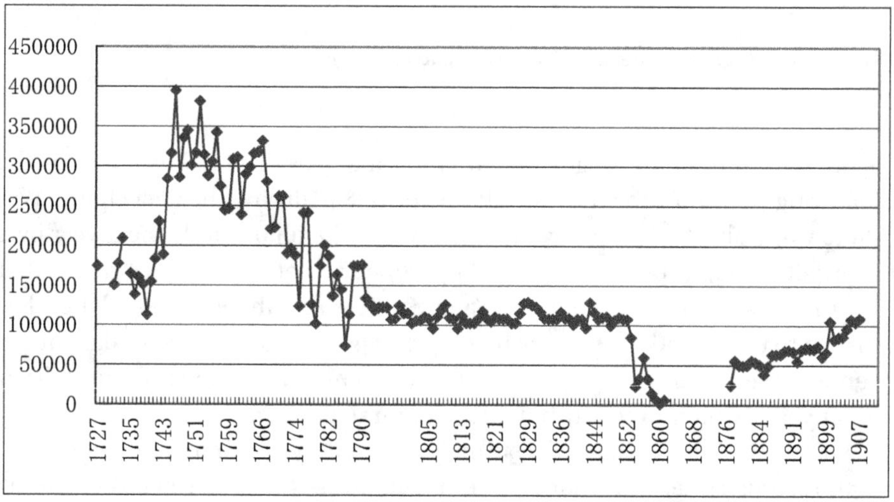

FIGURE 4.10 *Tax revenue trends of Fengyang Guan, 1727–1911*

In the Qing, it was first managed by the central government, but its administration was transferred to the provincial viceroy of Anhui in 1716. In 1749, however, the management of Fengyang Guan was permantly assigned to Lufeng prefecture.

There are two entries of tax data in 1765, 1797, 1830, and 1890, once more due to the use of the Chinese lunar year.

Figure 4.10 presents an interesting picture. In the early Qianlong, tax revenues increased very quickly. But after 1760 they began to gradually decline, reaching their lowest point in 1786 as a result of a natural disaster.[56] From my research, I conclude that the overall decline was due to the ongoing transfer of

56 GZDQLC, Volume 60, pp. 707–708.

economic activity to coastal areas, which meant that there was less traffic on the Grand Canal than before.

When the Qing government stopped using the system of triennial comparison, Fengyang Guan's quota was fixed at one-third of the highest point experienced during the reign of Qianlong, and as a result tax revenues stablized. Of course, some fluctuations occurred during the reigns of Jiaqing and Daoguang, due to natural disasters.[57] Fengyang Guan was also affected by the First Opium War: "The British warships entered the Yangtze River and since nobody dares to use the port, tax revenues fell short by 10,000 taels of silver".[58]

Even after the Taiping Rebellion had been put down, tax revenues continued to fall quickly. Contemporarly reports describe the decline:

1853: *There is much military activity. We have already recaptured Fengyang prefecture but the people have fled. At the same time, bandits are appearing everywhere to rob merchants. Tax revenues have declined very quickly.*[59]

1854: *We have only collected 23,026 tales of taxes; the shortfall is 84,133 taels of silver. Nobody dares to trade since the rebellion has completely devastated the area.*[60]

1855: *During the Taiping Rebellion, Anhui has been the most seriously affected province and it has also suffered the longest. All the ports of Fengyang Guan have been destroyed as a result of the rebellion and nobody dares to trade.*[61]

1856: *The shortfall has been caused by the rebellion; the people suffer as a result of the fighting and merchants are losing money.*[62]

1857: *The shortfall is even larger than last year, once again due to the rebellion.*[63]

1858: *The shortfall is even larger than last year because the main ports of Fengyang Guan are occupied by the rebels. All the roads are blocked as a result of the fighting and nobody dares to trade.*[64]

1859–1860: *The shortfall is even larger than last year. Rebels and bandits are everywhere and we will not be able to levy taxes properly for a long time.*[65]

1861: *The rebels occupy Fengyang, among other places. The use of rivers is severely hampered and merchants have scarcely been seen for several months.*

---

57 Ni (2010), pp. 77–79.

58 LFZZ of FHAC: 3-3166-44.

59 LFZZ of FHAC: 3-4376-31.

60 ZPZZ of FHAC: 4-1-35-382-40.

61 LFZZ of FHAC: 3-4378-15.

62 LFZZ of FHAC: 3-4379-22.

63 LFZZ of FHAC: 3-4380-18.

64 LFZZ of FHAC: 3-4381-15.

65 LFZZ of FHAC: 3-4382-22.

More than half of the customs officials of Fengyang Guan have run away and all its documents have been lost.[66]

Because the degree of fighting was very serious, there are no tax records at all for the period 1862–1876.[67] Fengyang Guan recovered in the period following the rebellion, such that tax revenues almost reached levels achieved in the Jiaqing and Daoguang.

4.9 Longjiang Guan and Xixing Guan

Longjiang Guan belonged to *Gongbu* and Xixing Guan belonged to *Hubu.* Both were located in Jianning prefecture (Nanjing today) of Jiangsu province; they were 10 km apart. They were established by the Ming dynasty before its conquest by the Qing. Before 1685 (Qing dynasty), each was administered by different officials, who were assigned separately to these ports by the central government. In 1689 the ports were combined under one administrator, although they still had separate tax quotas. In 1728, they fell under the jurisdiction of Jianning Zhizhao (the official responsible for weaving).

TABLE 4.11 *Quota of Longjiang Guan in the Qing dynasty (in taels of silver)*

Year	1658	1681	1686	1713	1735	1763	1764	1799
Zheng'e	39,300	43,800	46,838	57,607	57,607	57,607	57,607	57,607
Yingyu	–	–	–	–	102,399	93,299	87,340	55,000
Total	39,300	43,800	46,838	57,607	160,006	150,906	144,947	112,607

Sources: materials from *Shilu, Huidian, Hubu Zheli* and archives (see text for archival references).

For both Longjiang Guan and Xixing Guan, there are two entries of tax data for the years 1759, 1792, and 1824, because of the use of the Chinese lunar year.

Due to the Taiping Rebellion, there are no tax figures for Longjiang Guan and Xixing Guan after 1853, so it makes no sense to attempt to indicate a trend for the period 1851–1911.[68] Accounts of the tax revenues of Longjiang Guan and Xixing Guan were generally given by Jianning Zhizhao in a single report.

66 ZPZZ of FHAC: 4-1-12-492-11.

67 LFZZ of FHAC: 3-6334-18.

68 LFZZ of FHAC: 3-6347-55.

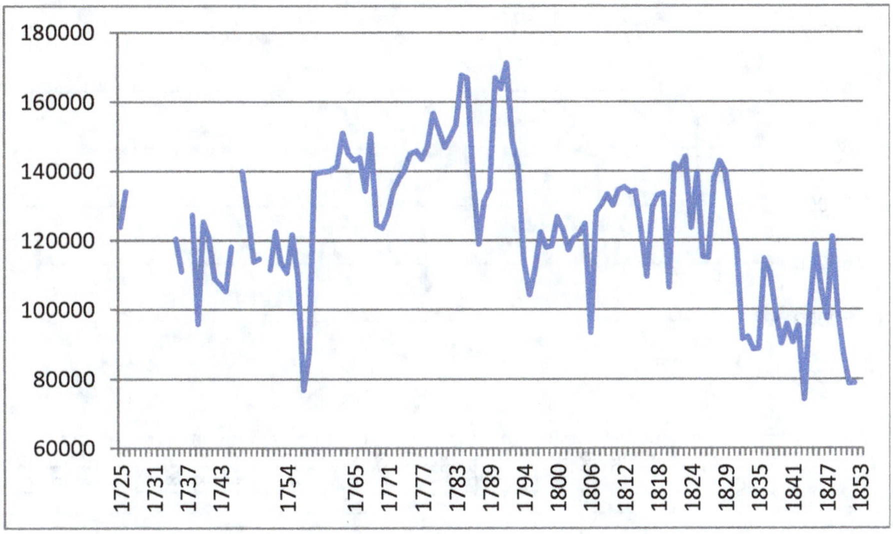

FIGURE 4.11 *Tax revenue trends of Longjiang Guan, 1725–1852*

TABLE 4.12 *Quota of Xixing Guan in the Qing dynasty (in taels of silver)*

Year	Shunzhi*	1656	1669	1681	1682	1686	1723	1799	1804
Zheng'e	18,269	28,300	20,000	30,800	28,300	33,684	41,376	41,376	41,376
Yingyu	–	–	–	–	–	–	–	29,000	33,000
Total	18,269	28,300	20,000	30,800	28,300	33,684	41,376	70,376	74,376

* Exact year unknown.
Sources: materials from *Shilu*, *Huidian*, *Hubu Zheli* and archives (see text for archival references).

As Figure 4.13 shows, during the reigns of Yongzheng and Qianlong tax revenues increased slightly, which of course was in keeping with economic development and population expansion of those times. The lowest point in the Qianlong, in 1757, was due to the occurrence of a natural disaster.[69]

After 1800, tax revenues began to fall gradually. From my research I conclude that, besides the occurrence of natural disasters, markets may have become depressed, causing more and more businesses to closed.[70] This point is important enough to warrant explanation.

69 ZPZZ of FHAC: 4-1-35-329-11.

70 Ni Yuping (2010), pp. 86–87.

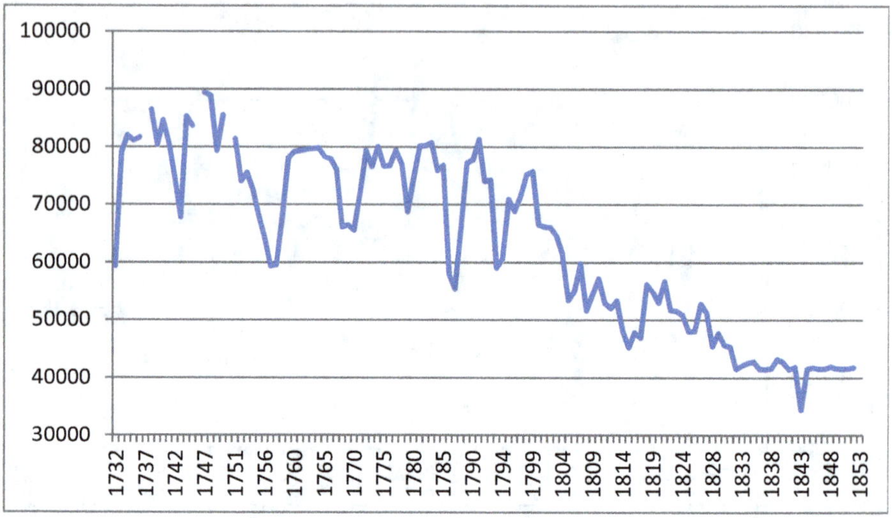

FIGURE 4.12 *Tax revenue trends of Xixing Guan, 1732–1852*

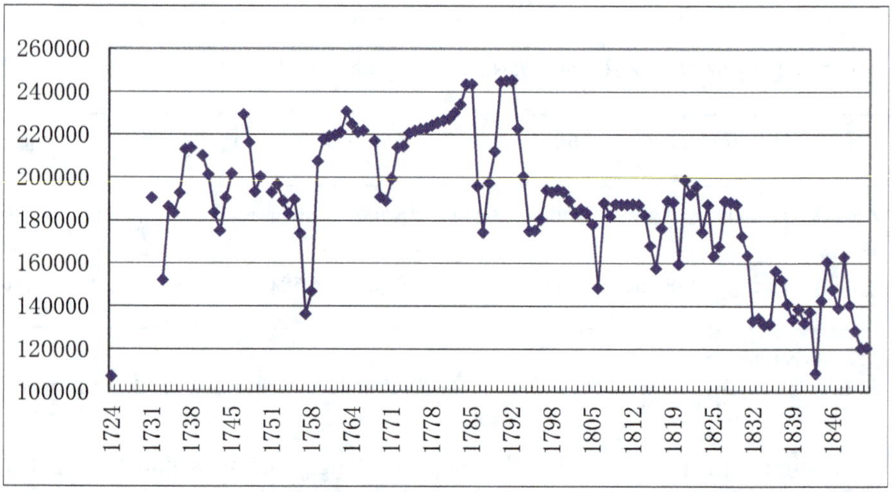

FIGURE 4.13 *Tax revenue trends of Longjiang Guan and Xixing Guan, 1724–1852*

In 1806, shortfalls in tax revenues of Longjiang Guan and Xixing Guan were explained as follows: "Tax revenues arise from the trading of silk, since Nanjing is the most important area of the silk sector. However, the silk harvest was poor and many silk industries had to close last year. Nobody wants to come here to trade."[71] The very same explanation appeared again in the records of 1808.[72]

71 ZPZZ of FHAC: 4-1-35-363-51.

72 LFZZ of FHAC: 3-1768-81.

In 1814, it was reported that "Customs revenues are mainly derived from the transport of silk from other areas, and from silk clothing being sent to other places. Silk is expensive and trading has been poor in recent years. Many silk-based industries have suffered big losses and factories have been forced to close; silk merchants are even becoming rare."[73] This reason was given again in 1817 and once more in 1820.[74]

In 1823, in the Daoguang reign, the most extensive flooding of the entire Qing period occurred. Records from 1824 explain the resulting shortfall in tax revenues: "The strong flooding ruined the harvest, and grain became very expensive."[75]

In 1832, a report explained that "Another large flood occurred in Hunan, Hubei, Jiangxi, Anhui, Jiangsu, and Zhejing provinces last year. The people have suffered great losses, from which it cannot be expected that they will recovered soon. Commercial trading has become intermittent."[76] This same reason was given again in 1834, 1835, and 1836.[77]

During the First Opium War, Nanjing was greatly affected by the hostilities and this had a negative influence on tax revenues collected in Longjiang Guan and Xixing Guan. In June 1842 it was noted that "British vessels entered the Yangtze River and martial law was declared along the river. No merchant dares to come. [...] On 28 June, British warships occupied the river of Nanjing and the levying of taxes had to stop for 67 days."[78]

In 1849 there was a shortfall in tax revenues because "There was strong flooding last year and Nanjing was under water. Goods for trading have become rare, and, in particular, half the silk industries have closed."[79]

During the Taiping Rebellion, tax revenues declined very quickly. In 1851 the records explain that "The market is subject to martial law and all commercial activities are forbidden."[80] In 1853, Nanjing became the capital of the Taiping army and it was impossible for the Qing government to collect taxes there. After the rebellion had been put down by the government, the customs revenues were still unable to recover because *Yangguan* was established nearby, and the local government was strongly against the central government's attempts to re-establish the old office.[81]

---

73 ZPZZ of FHAC: 4-1-35-368-13.

74 ZPZZ of FHAC: 4-1-35-368-54, 4-1-35-370-37.

75 ZPZZ of FHAC: 4-1-35-373-8.

76 LFZZ of FHAC: 3-3163-38.

77 ZPZZ of FHAC: 4-1-35-377-68, 4-1-35-378-33, 4-1-35-379-12.

78 LFZZ of FHAC: 3-3166-39.

79 ZPZZ of FHAC: 4-1-35-381-26.

80 LFZZ of FHAC: 3-4375-12.

81 LFZZ of FHAC: 3-4878-9, 3-6347-55.

4.10 Jiujiang Guan

Jiujiang Guan, located in Jiangxi province, on the Yangtze River, was situated where Jiangxi, Anhui and Hubei provinces meet. It was also situated at the confluence of the Poyang Lake, Ganjiang and Yangtze Rivers. In short, as a result of its very special geography it was a unique location for collecting customs duties.

Jiujiang Guan was established by the Ming dynasty in 1450. In 1645, the second year of Shunzhi, Jiujiang Guan was rebuilt. In 1665, Jiujiang Guan was managed by the Jiujiang prefecture, but later this changed and up until 1778 it was managed by the Jiujiang Bingbeidao (another official of Jiujiang prefecture). From the beginning under the Ming dynasty, tax revenues collected at Jiujiang Guan increased year by year. Up until 1840 it was the biggest domestic port of the Qing dynasty.

TABLE 4.13 *Quota of Jiujiang Guan in the Qing dynasty (in taels of silver)*

Year	Shunzhi*	1656	1669	1682	1685	1686	1723	Qianlong*	1799	1804
Zheng'e	79,784	99,799	90,000	120,907	141,015	153,890	172,281	172,281	172,281	172,281
Yingyu	–	–	–	–	–	–	–	148,598	347,800	367,000
Total	79,784	99,799	90,000	120,907	141,015	153,890	172,281	320,879	520,081	539,281

* Exact year unknown.
Sources: materials from *Shilu, Huidian, Hubu Zheli* and archives (see text for archival references).

There are two entries of tax data in years 1727, 1748, 1756, 1789, 1822, and 1890 to be found in the archival material, as in other cases, owing to the use of the Chinese lunar year.

Figure 4.14 clearly shows that during the reigns of Yongzheng and Qianlong, tax revenues quickly increased, reaching a peak in the late Qinglong as a result of population increase and economic development. During the reigns of Jiaqing and Daoguan, revenues were stable, however; declines were due to natural disasters or bumper harvests (the latter leading to low price, such that no boat was willing to berth at the port). Some archive material also points to depressed markets, because natural disasters led to reduced trading of rice and wood.[82] Jiujiang Guan was also strongly affected by the First Opium War

82 ZPZZ of FHAC: 4-1-35-363-48, 4-1-35-369-19, 4-1-35-379-50, 4-1-35-376-63.

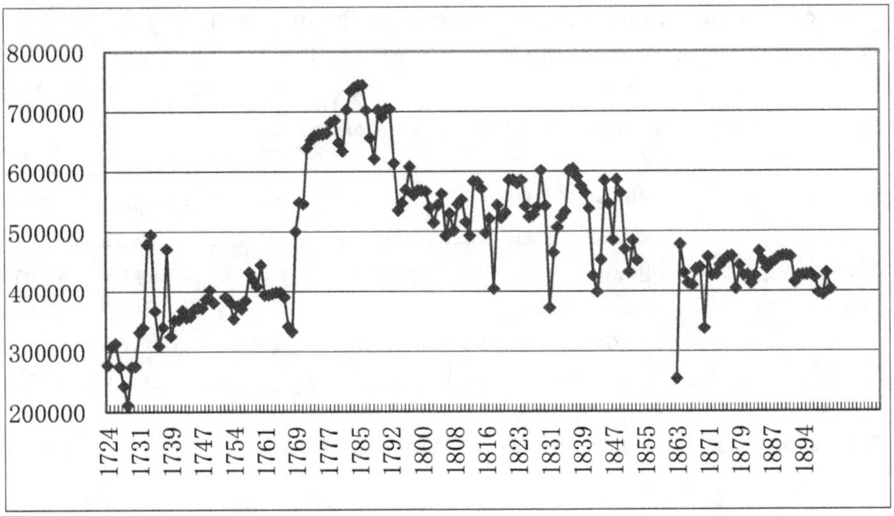

FIGURE 4.14 *Tax revenue trends of Jiujiang Guan, 1723–1901*

because military action took place on and along the Yangtze River, so no boats dared to come to trade.[83]

During the Taiping Rebellion, Jiujiang Guan again suffered since it was located at the middle point of the Yangtze River's course. It was even occupied by the rebels, and between 1854 and 1862 it remained closed.[84] At the cessation of hostilities it recovered only to some extent: tax revenues declined very quickly, dropping to between 200,000 and 300,000 taels of silver for many years. The influence of *Yangguan* also had a detrimental effect on Jiujiang Guan's ability to collect tax revenues.[85]

4.11 Gan Guan

Gan Guan was located in Ganzhou prefecture, which was the political, economic and cultural center of the southern part of Jiangxi province. Gan Guan was established in 1511 by the Ming dynasty and it management was permanently assigned to Ganzhou prefecture. Significantly, Gan Guan was on the main road along which goods were transported from inland China to Yuehai Guan, the only port for foreign trade before 1840. Gan Guan's geographical

83 ZPZZ of FHAC: 4-1-35-379-50.

84 ZPZZ of FHAC: 4-1-35-391-38.

85 ZPZZ of FHAC: 4-1-35-391-38, 4-1-35-392-44; LFZZ of FHAC: 3-4873-26, 3-4875-7, 3-4876-43, 3-4877-144, 3-4879-29.

position, therefore, had a large influence on its local economy. In the early Qing, the Gan Guan's tax quota increased gradually.

TABLE 4.14 *Quota of Gan Guan in the Qing dynasty (in taels of silver)*

Year	1656	1669	1680	1681	1723	Qianlong*	1799
Zheng'e	30,800	30,000	34,383	37,383	46,471	46,471	46,471
Yingyu	–	–	–	–	–	43,610	38,000
Total	30,800	30,000	34,383	37,383	46,471	90,081	84,471

* Exact year unknown.
Sources: materials from *Shilu, Huidian, Hubu Zheli* and archives (see text for archival references).

There are two entries of tax data in years 1754, 1786, 1819, 1851, and 1884, because of the use of the Chinese lunar year.

Figure 4.15 demonstrates that in the long run there was a declining trend for the tax revenues collected in Gan Guan, falling from 120,000 to 40,000 taels of silver annually. This was undoubtedly connected with the economic transformation of regions during the Qing dynasty. Reports from the late Qing state that "Gan Guan is situated in the interior. When Yuehai Guan was the only port to trade with foreigners, all goods had to pass through Gan Guan, on their journey further into the interior or to Western countries. After the First Opium War, five other ports were opened for foreign trade, allowing goods to flow freely to Jiujiang Yangguan or Shanghai Yangguan. With this development Gan Guan lost its advantageous position and tax revenues declined accordingly."[86]

During the reign of Qianlong, tax revenues of Gan Guan were stable, showing only a slight increase. During the reigns of Jiaqing and Daoguang, however, a declining trend set in. When the First Opium War broke out, Yuehai Guan was strongly affected. Since it was on the main route from the interior to Yuehai Guan, it is by no means strange that in 1841 Gan Guan suffered a shortfall of 9,728 taels of silver.[87]

Figure 4.15 also shows a major change occurred after 1850. Jiangxi province was one of the most important areas those were fought over by the Qing government and the Taiping army. Gan Guan was seriously affected by this. In

86 ZPZZ of FHAC: 4-1-35-390-45.

87 LFZZ of FHAC: 3-3165-90.

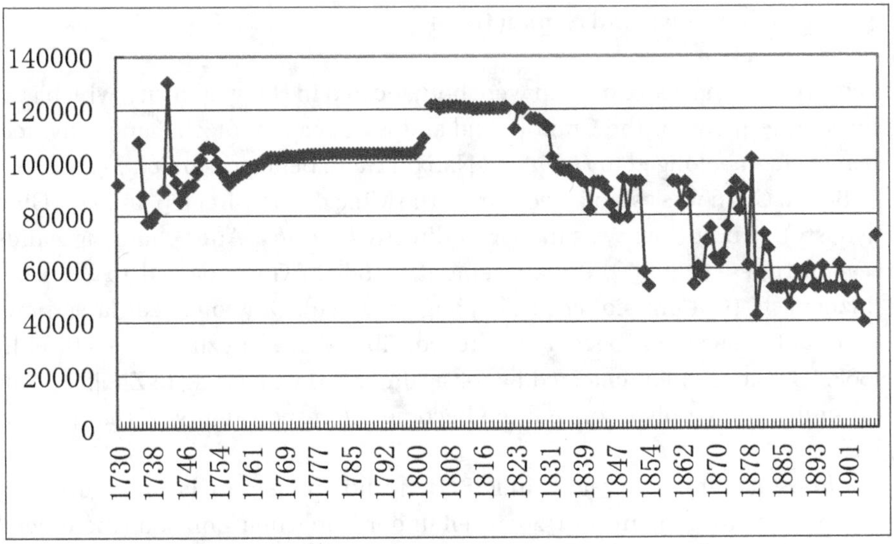

FIGURE 4.15 *Tax revenue trends of Gan Guan, 1730–1911*

1853, the official records state that "From April till now, the rebels wanted to take the capital of Jiangxi province (Nanchang) and innumerable battles took place in this area. Everywhere, all sorts of bandits appeared. Nobody dares to trade in Gan Guan anymore."[88]

Traditionally, Jianghai Yangguan was responsible for levying duties on silk, and it tranferred this revenue to Gan Guan after the First Opium War. In the years following 1842 the revnues from silk taxes contributed more than 10,000 taels to Gan Guan's annual quota. However, in August 1853 the Shanghai Xiaodao Hui (Small Sword Society) Uprising broke out and Jianghai Yangguan was occupied, preventing it from collecting taxes. Gan Guan immediately lost these revenues.

From 1855 to 1859, tax revenues could not be collected because of the Taiping Rebellion.[89] Even after the rebellion was put down, revenues continued to show some decline, which the records put down to the effect of *Yangguan*.[90]

88 ZPZZ of FHAC: 4-1-35-382-16.

89 LFZZ of FHAC: 3-4382-31.

90 LFZZ of FHAC: 3-4889-101, 3-4940-65, 3-4874-47, 3-4876-5, 3-4891-26; ZPZZ of FHAC: 4-1-35-391-30, 4-1-35-392-24.

4.12 Beixin Guan and Nanxin Guan

Beixin Guan and Nanxin Guan were both located in Hangzhou city, which is at the southern end of the Grand Canal and is the capital of Zhejiang province. Beixin Guan belonged to *Hubu* and Nanxin Guan belonged to *Gongbu*.

Beixin Guan was established during the Ming dynasty in 1429. In 1647 (Qing dynasty), Beixin Guan was managed directly by *Hubu*. After changing hands several times, in 1665 the management of Beixin Guan passed to Zhejiang Buzhengshi (Commissioner of Zhejiang province). Only one year later, however, its management became the responsibility of Hangzhou prefecture. In 1668, its management changed hands again, this time passing to Zhejiang Salt Administration, only to once more become the responsibility of *Hubu* a year later.

Almost a half century later, in 1718, Hangzhou prefecture became responsible for its management. In 1729, it fell under Hangzhou Zhizhao (the official responsible for weaving). It became the responsibility of the viceroy of Zhejiang in 1793 since it reported that Hangzhou Zhizhao was also made responsible for the administration of Zhejiang Salt and was unable to manage so many things at once. However, following the reign of Daoguang, the responsibility for Beixin Guan was transferred permanently back to Hangzhou Zhizhao again.

TABLE 4.15 *Quota of Beixin Guan in the Qing dynasty (in taels of silver)*

Year	Shunzhi*	1656	1669	1686	1721	1723	Qianlong	1799
Zheng'e	89,376	94,400	90,000	123,054	163,054	123,054	123,054	123,053
Yingyu	–	–	–	–	–	–	43,610	65,000
Total	89,376	94,400	90,000	123,054	163,054	123,054	166,664	188,053

* Exact year unknown.
Sources: materials from *Shilu, Huidian, Hubu Zheli* and archives (see text for archival references).

Because of the lunar calendar, there are double entries of tax data in the archival material for Beixin Guan in the years 1740, 1773, 1805, and 1838.

Tax revenues for Beixin Guan during the Qianlong hinge around the year 1764. In Figure 4.16, the period before 1764 shows an increase; the period after 1764 shows a stable trend. During the reigns of Jiaqing and Daoguang, there was some decline, apparently the result of natural disasters.[91] In 1842, Beixin

91 LFZZ of FHAC: 3-3159-32, 3-9487-20, 3-9487-43; Guanshui Baogao Biao of Chaodang, 30March, 14th year of Daoguang.

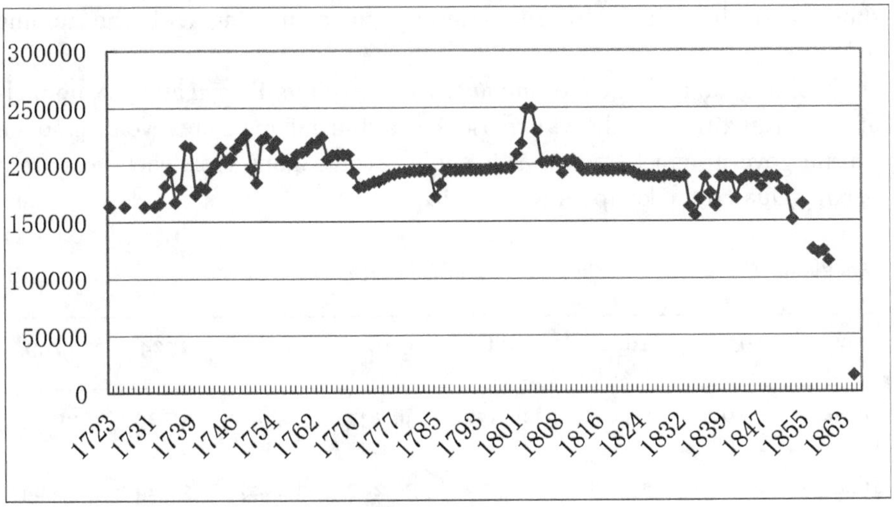

FIGURE 4.16 *Tax revenue trends of Beixin Guan, 1723–1865*

Guan recorded a big loss: "British warships have blocked the Yangtze River and military operations are in full swing. No merchant dares come here to trade."[92]

Zhejiang was one of the richest cities of Qing China, and it was also the most important source of fiscal revenue at that time. When the Taiping Rebllion started, the rebels invaded Zhejiang province and fought numerous fierce battles there against the Qing government. Taxes collected in Beixin Guan quickly fell. In 1853, it was reported in the records that "Rebellion has come to Jiangsu and its neighboring areas are being harassed. All roads connecting with Jiangsu and Zhejiang provinces have been cut. Merchants cannot trade their goods and tax revenues have dropped rapidly."[93] In April 1856 Ningbo was occupied by the Taiping army and the Qing government declared martial law: "All roads to Beixin Guan are closed."[94] The situation did not change in the years that followed.[95] Indeed, between 1861 and 1864 there were no tax revenues collected in Beixin Guan at all.[96] Between 11 July 1864 and 11 January 1865, a period of a little less than six months, there was some recovery in revenues. After that, however, Beixin Guan was closed down, never to be reopened.[97] Figure 4.16 clearly

92 ZPZZ of FHAC: 4-1-35-379-51.

93 LFZZ of FHAC: 3-4376-53.

94 ZPZZ of FHAC: 4-1-35-382-64.

95 ZPZZ of FHAC: 4-1-35-383-17, 4-1-35-383-53.

96 Unkonwn, Ge Guan Chang Shui Shi Zhen Duan Zhen Yin Liang Shu Mu (The Number of Taels of Real Tax and Tax Shortfalls in Different Changguan), Beixin Guan.

97 LFZZ of FHAC: 3-7120-111.

shows a decline in tax revenues after 1850, coinciding with the Taiping Rebellion.

Nanxin Guan belonged to *Gongbu*, which fixed its *Yingyu* at 3,922.019 taels of silver. Nanxin Guan always experienced a shortfall in its tax revenues, so the central government agreed that it could receive 4,000 taels each year from Beixing Guan to make up for the deficit.

TABLE 4.16 *Quota of Nanxin Guan in the Qing dynasty (in taels of silver)*

Year	1658	1681	1686	1707	1721	1724	1799
Zheng'e	24,000	25,000	26,572	30,247	36,247	30,247	30,247
Yingyu	–	–	–	–	–	–	–
Total	24,000	25,000	26,572	30,247	36,247	30,247	30,247

Sources: materials from *Shilu, Huidian, Hubu Zheli* and archives (see text for archival references).

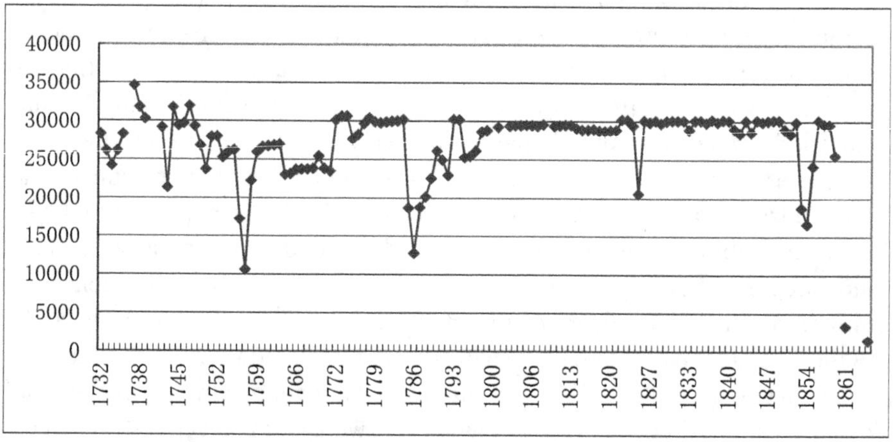

FIGURE 4.17 *Tax revenue trends of Nanxin Guan, 1732–1865*

There are two entries of tax data in 1767, 1800, and 1832 in the records, due to the use of the Chinese lunar year.

Considering the data for Nanxin Guan for the period 1732 to 1865 as a whole, one could say that the overall trend was stable. Of course, there were some dips in revenue before the Taiping Rebellion: 1757, 1786, and 1825.

The reason for the decline in 1757 was that: "The main income of Nanxin Guan was from bamboo and wood cutting in nearby areas. However, in recent years it was very difficult to find bamboo and wood that were big enough and useful enough to cut. Merchants have to travel deep into the forest, so there has been little trade."[98] More or less the same reason was given to explain the decline in 1786.[99] In the case of 1825, no explanation was even given.[100] I suspect it had something to do with the flooding of Hongze Lake in that year, which led to the closure of the Grand Canal and the first case of transporting Tribute Grain by sea during the Qing dynasty.[101]

After the Taiping Rebellion was put down, Nanxin Guan met the same fate as Beixin Guan: on 12 February 1865 Nanxin Guan closed, never again to be reopened.[102]

4.13 Linqin Guan

Linqin Guan was located in Shandong province, on the Grand Canal at the confluence of the Huitong, Wei, and Wen Rivers. It was located inbetween Huai'an Guan in the South and Tianjin Guan in the North. Linqin Guan was established by the Ming dynasty in 1429. In later years, it was closed and reopened, again and again. Linqin Guan actually consisted of two ports: Linqin Huguan and Linqin Gongguan, which belonged to *Hubu* and *Gongbu*, respectively.

In the Shunzhi time, Linqin Huguan and Linqin Gongguan were managed directly by the central government. In 1665, their management was transferred to the local Dongchang prefecture, only to be passed back to the central government four years later. In 1714, however, these ports were assigned to the viceroy of Shandong, but in 1756 they were made the responsibility of Linqin prefecture. Changes continued to be made until in 1803, when Dongchang prefecture was given permanent responsibility for their management.

Records for Linqin Huguan had two entries of tax data in the years 1748, 1781, 1814, 1846, and 1879, due to use of the Chinese lunar year. However, Linqin Gongguan generally collected taxes from January to December each year: usually ice in the canal would begin to melt in January, making it possible to transport goods by boat; in December the canal would freeze over, preventing transport by boat. So its period of taxation is one Chinese lunar year.

98 ZPZZ of FHAC: 4-1-35-19-919.
99 LFZZ of FHAC: 3-602-21.
100 LFZZ of FHAC: 3-3159-16.
101 More information could be seen in Ni Yuping (2005).
102 LFZZ of FHAC: 3-7120-111.

TABLE 4.17 *Quota of Linqin Huguan in the Qing dynasty (in taels of silver)*

Year	Shunzhi*	1656	1669	1686	1723	1799
Zheng'e	76,271	24,300	20,000	25,384	37,376	37,376
Yingyu	–	–	–	–	–	11,000
Total	76,271	24,300	20,000	25,384	37,376	48,376

* Exact year unknown.
Sources: materials from *Shilu*, *Huidian*, *Hubu Zheli* and archives (see text for archival references).

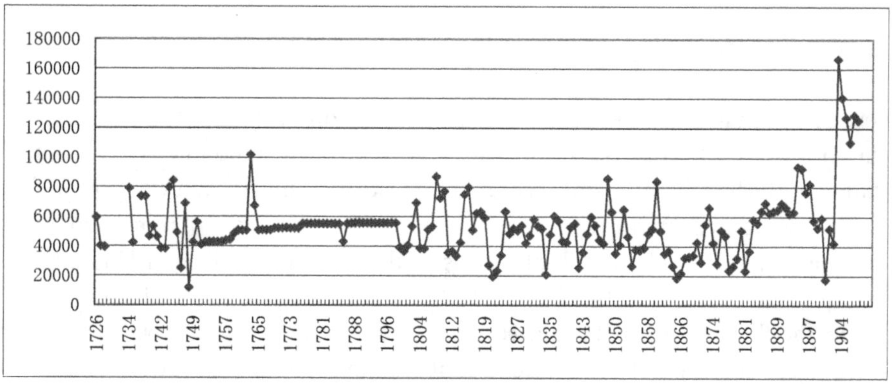

FIGURE 4.18 *Tax revenue trends of Linqin Huguan, 1726–1911*

As can be seen in Figure 4.18, the highest amount of tax revenue collected before 1850 occurred in the year 1763, and the reason given in the records was that "A large natural disaster has happened in Zhili province, but Henan and Jiangsu provinces have good harvests. Many merchants transport rice to Zhili to trade and therefore pass through Linqin Huguan. We have more chances to collect taxes than before. It is not a common phenomenon and we cannot hope to collect this amount again."[103] The lowest amount collected occurred in 1747, because that taxation year only ran from 2 April 1746 to the 3 February 1747, just a bit more than 10 months[104] For the period 1796–1850, my research indicates that the reasons for the decline are natural disasters and silting of the Grand Canal.[105]

103 LFZZ of FHAC: 3-591-105.

104 ZPZZ of FHAC: 4-1-35-381-11.

105 Ni Yuping (2010), pp. 106–114.

During the Taiping Rebellion, tax revenues changed significantly. Since these revenues were always reported together with other *Gongguan* (ports of the Ministry of Works) in the late Qing. Tax quotas and trends of revenue collected for Linqin Gongguan are given in Table 4.18 and Figure 4.19.

TABLE 4.18 *Quota of Linqin Gongguan in the Qing dynasty (in taels of silver)*

Year	1736	1799
Zheng'e	4,572	4,572
Yingyu	–	3,800
Total	4,572	8,372

Sources: materials from *Shilu*, *Huidian*, *Hubu Zheli* and archives (see text for archival references).

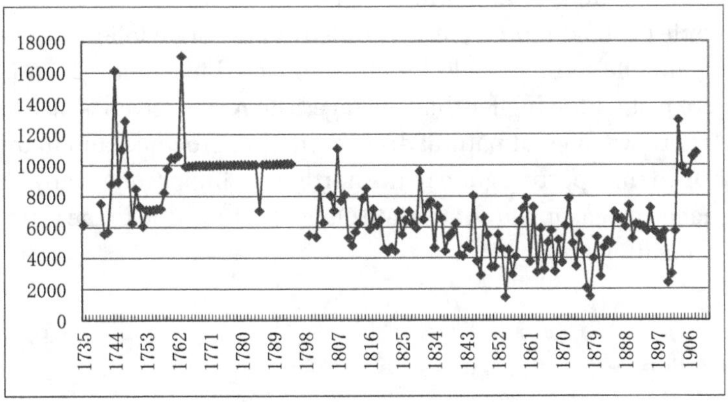

FIGURE 4.19 *Tax revenue trends of Linqin Gongguan, 1735–1911*

Figure 4.19 shows that there was some increase in tax revenues during the reign of Qianlong, especially in the early years. There are two peak years in the figure: 1744 and 1763. Reports state that in 1744 "The grain price in Zhili is so high that many merchants from Hennan rush to Zhili province to sell grain. Since this involves a large number of boats, customs duties collected are accordingly very high."[106] A similar reason was reported in 1763: "A big natural

106 ZPZZ of FHAC: 4-1-35-318-31.

disaster has occurred in Zhili province. Merchants from Henan and other provinces have heard the news and are sending a lot of rice to Zhili province. All goods pass through Linqin Huguan and customs revenues are, therefore, very high. It is not a common phenomenon and we cannot hope to collect this amount in the future."[107]

There was a strong decline in revenues during the reigns of Jiaqing and Daoguang, again due to the Grand Canal silting up and, linked to that, a reduction in the number of ships capable of transporting the Tribute Grain.[108]

During the Taiping Rebellion, tax income was also affected by the hostilities, both for *Huguan* and *Gongguan*. Records state that in 1853 the roads were closed.[109] One year later, Linqing city was occupied by the rebels and the prefecture's magistrate and his family members were even killed.[110] After Linqin city was recaptured, the following report was made: "Rebels still exist in the southern areas of Linqin's prefecture, and merchants dare not to come to trade."[111] After the rebels had been suppressed, the explanation given in the records changed: "The grain harvest of Henan province is very poor. No merchant is willing to send grain to Zhili province and boats rarely pass through the port. The people (in Linqin prefecture) are all in a poor state following the rebellion and are unable to buy goods."[112] Taxes collected in Linqin Guan in 1872 and 1873 were just a little higher than average. The reason given is also as we can image: "There was a great natural disaster in Zhili province, and many merchants have been transporting grain to the north (via Linqin Gongguan)."[113] Tax revenues reached a peak in 1903 of the late Qing, this time due to the introduction of a new taxation system.[114]

4.14 Taiping Guan

Taiping Guan was located on the Beijiang River of Shaozhou prefecture, in the northern part of Guangdong province. Taiping Guan was the second biggest port of Guangdong province, the biggest being Yuehai Guan. In the beginning,

107 LFZZ of FHAC: 3-592-3.

108 Ni Yuping (2010), p. 114.

109 LFZZ of FHAC: 3-4378-1.

110 LFZZ of FHAC: 3-4380-4.

111 LFZZ of FHAC: 3-4379-19, 3-4381-12, 3-4392-20, 3-4382-42, 3-4384-51, 3-4872-6, 3-4383-11, 3-4889-77; ZPZZ of FHAC: 4-1-35-383-9, 4-1-35-384-71, 4-1-35-383-72, 4-1-35-384-27.

112 LFZZ of FHAC: 3-4872-72, 3-4874-3, 3-4877-147, 3-4879-39, 3-4880-136, 3-4875-53, 3-4877-52, 3-4879-5.

113 LFZZ of FHAC: 3-4880-227, 3-4880-95.

114 GXCZP, Volume 74, pp. 532–533.

Taiping Guan was administered by Nanxiong prefecture, but it was transferred later, in 1669 of the Kangxi, to Shaozhou prefecture. The central government sent officials here for a term of one year to supervise the collection of taxes. In 1722, this measure was dropped and managerial responsibility was transferred to the viceroy of Gongdong province. In 1770 this responsibility was permanently assigned to Nanshao Dao (an official adminstrating Nanxiong and Shaozhou prefectures).

Unlike Yuehai Guan, at which foreign boats docked, Taiping Guan only collected customs duty on goods from the mainland. As the Qing government decreed that all goods for foreign trade must pass through Yuehai Guan, and as the Beijiang River was the main waterway for Guangdong province, this meant that prior to 1840 Taiping Guan prospered greatly. It became one of the most important staging ports for the transport of silk, tea and other goods on their way to Yuehai Guan.

TABLE 4.19 *Quota of Taiping Guan in the Qing dynasty* (*in taels of silver*)

Year	Shunzhi*	1669	1670	1681	1683	1686	1723	Qianlong*	1799
Zheng'e	26,626	40,000	37,524	38,987	41,987	46,829	52,675	52,675	52,675
Yingyu	–	–	–	–	–	–	–	72,045	75,500
Total	26,626	40,000	37,524	38,987	41,987	46,829	52,675	124,720	128,175

* Exact year unknown.
Sources: materials from *Shilu*, *Huidian*, *Hubu Zheli* and archives (see text for archival references).

There are two entries of tax data in the years 1743, 1775, 1808, 1841, and 1892, due to the use of the Chinese lunar year.

Figure 4.20 demonstrates that the tax revenues for Taiping Guan remained stable throughout the entire Qing dynasty, in particular for the reigns of Yongzheng through to Daoguang. Tax revenues severely declined during the last years of the Daoguang and the first years of the Xianfeng. These were impacted by the rise in importance of Shanghai Yangguan, and many goods would go straight to Shanghai instead of passing through Yuehai Guan as they had before. Since Taiping Guan's trade was closely linked with that of Yuehai Guan, its tax revenues declined accordingly. Taiping Guan was also strongly affected by the the Taiping Rebellion. Reports I found in archives continually repeated themselves: "Rebellion is continuing and roads are closed."[115] Because

115 LFZZ of FHAC: 3-4378-5, 3-4378-49, 3-4871-43.

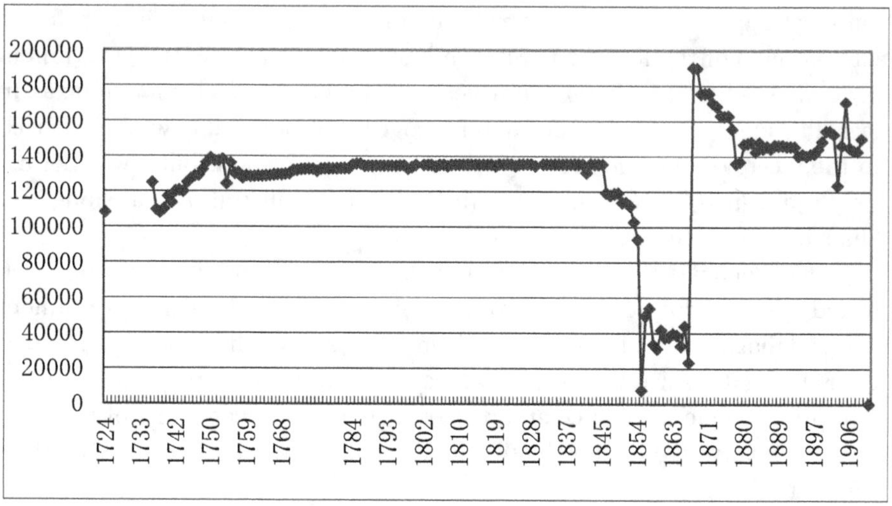

FIGURE 4.20 *Tax revenue trends of Taiping Guan, 1724–1911*

of the rebellion, tax revenues collected in Taiping Guan in 1855 declined to 7,467 taels of silver, i.e. about 5% of its quota.[116]

However, with the restoration of commerce after the rebellion had been quashed, and the introduction of a new taxation system, tax revenues in the late Qing increased significantly. There was a sharp increase in 1867, which was attributed to an adjustment of policies by the viceroy of Gongdong, who reduced the number of officials in Taiping Guan and put a stop to illegal activities, with the result that revenues rose.[117]

4.15 Wuchang Guan

Wuchang Guan was set up by the Qing dynasty in 1665. It was located on the Yangtze River and was the economic and political center of Hubei province. Initially, it was under the control of the viceroy of Hubei, but after several reorganizations, Wuchang Guan was transferred to the jurisdiction of Wuchang prefecture permanently.

116 TB of FHAC: 2-1-4-21590-9, 2-1-4-21609-1.

117 LFZZ of FHAC: 3-4877-6.

TABLE 4.20 *Quota of Wuchang Guan in the Qing dynasty (in taels of silver)*

Year	Kangxi*	Yongzheng*	1723	Qianlong*	1799
Zheng'e	10,000	13,000	13,000	33,000	33,000
Yingyu	–	20,000	6,419	–	12,000
Total	10,000	33,000	19,419	33,000	45,000

* Exact year unknown.
Sources: materials from *Shilu, Huidian, Hubu Zheli* and archives (see text for archival references).

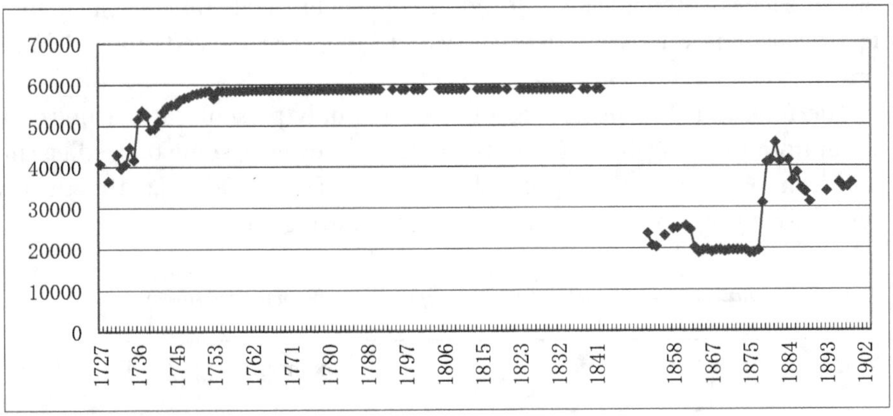

FIGURE 4.21 *Tax revenue trends of Wuchang Guan, 1727–1911*

There are two entries of tax data in the years 1751, 1784, 1816, 1849, and 1868, due to the use of the Chinese lunar year.

Interestingly, each of the data points plotted in Figure 4.21 (from the periods 1727–1795, 1796–1850, and 1850–1911) show an increase, but taken overall there is a decrease. One can definitely see that there was an increase in the early Qianlong and revenues remain stable afterwards.

Although Wuhan was the capital of Hubei province, it was occupied by the Taiping army for three times during the Taiping Rebellion, which explains the lack of tax records from 1851 to 1859.[118] After the rebellion was put down, tax revenues were collected but these declined to the half level reached before the rebellion. The explanation always given in the records was as follows: "Since it has been affected by the rebellion, and because the Yangtze River can hardly be

118 TB of FHAC: 2-1-4-21712-41.

safely used for trade, we have had to collect taxes without considering a quota."[119] The greatest amount collected in the late Qing was reached in 1889, the archives commenting that "In recent years, tax revenues of Wuchang Guan have always been severely affected by *Yangguan*. However, there was an increase this year because the port official has drastically cut expenditures and added the savings to tax revenues."[120]

4.16 Jingzhou Guan and Hubei Xinguan

Jingzhou prefecture, in Hubei province, was a very important region of the upper reaches of Yangtze River. Jingzhou Guan belonged to *Gongbu* and mainly levied customs duties on rice and wood being transported from Sichuan province.

The tables in the appendices to this book only present data of Jingzhou Guan from the Yongzheng onwards. There are, however, some data still available from before the reign of Yongzheng. One can see in Table 4.21 that the tax revenues of Jingzhou Guan fluctuated greatly during the early Qing.

TABLE 4.21 *Tax revenue of Jingzhou Guan during the Shunzhi (in taels of silver)*

Year	Period of taxation	Tax months	Tax revenue
1647	7/10/1646-25/4/1647	6	503.875
1648	26/4/1647-30/4/1648 (lunar month)	13	12,452.083
1649	1/5/1648-29/6/1649	13	12,382.6074
1650	1/7/1649-17/6/1650	12	8450.87
1651	18/6/1650-26/7/1651	14 (plus 10 days)	10,056.324

Sources: materials come from *Shunzhi Nianjian Sheguan Queshui Dang'an Xuan* (Archive collections of customs duties in the Shunzhi), in *Historical Archives, Volume 4, 1982, pp. 28–29.*

There are two entries of tax data in 1767 and 1800, due to the use of the Chinese lunar year.

As Figure 4.22 shows, there was a sharp increase in tax revenues during the early Qianlong, peaking in 1748. The records state that in 1748 "There was heavy

119 LFZZ of FHAC: 3-4376-51; ZPZZ of FHAC: 4-1-35-383-58.

120 TB of FHAC: 2-1-4-22445-9.

TABLE 4.22 *Quota of Jingzhou Guan in the Qing dynasty (in taels of silver)*

Year	1658	1686	1712	Yongzheng*	1735	Qianlong*	1768	1799	1860
Zheng'e	7,489	9,642	16,439	17,019	16,439	17,019	17,686	17,686	17,686
Yingyu	–	–	–	–	6,299	–	–	13,000	7,800
Total	7,489	9,642	16,439	17,019	22,738	17,019	17,686	30,686	25,486

* Exact year unknown.
Sources: materials from *Shilu, Huidian, Hubu Zheli* and archives (see text for archival references).

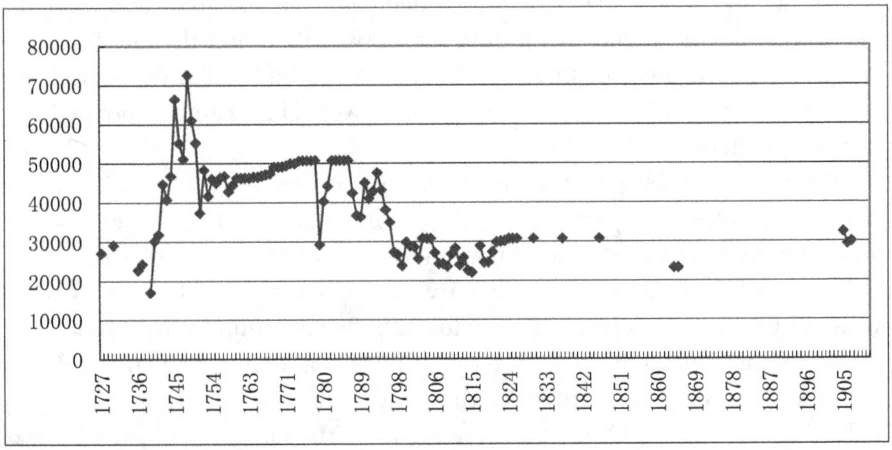

FIGURE 4.22 *Tax revenue trends of Jingzhou Guan, 1727–1911*

flooding along the Yangtze River and it was easy to ship large amounts of wood from Sichuan province. Customs revenues increased greatly."[121] There were some declines in revenues in the late Qianlong, however. Bi Yuan, the governor of Hubei and Hunan provinces, explained to the emperor the shortfall of tax revenues in 1792 in the following manner: "All the provinces neighboring on Sichuan province have had abundant harvests and the price of rice in these areas is similar to that in Sichuan province. As a result, no merchant is interested in transporting rice from Sichuan to the other provinces". The emperor Qianlong was dissatisfied with Bi's report, as his response demonstrates: "If each province has a good harvest, the price of rice will be low and this will stimulate merchants to trade. Hubei province has had good harvests in recent

121 ZPZZ of FHAC: 4-1-35-323-3.

years. How is it possible to collect less and less taxes? Several years before, Hai'an Guan and Yangzhou Guan reported that the reason for their lower tax revenues was poor harvests in Henan and Shandong provinces, and that merchants were unwilling to go to Jiangsu province. How are we supposed to imagine that both good harvests and poor harvests both lead to insufficient tax revenues? "[122]

Clearly, Figure 4.22 shows that tax revenues declined from the Jiaqing onwards. The decline could be firstly explained by the White Lotus Rebellion (1796–1804), which mainly broke out in Hubei, Sichuan and Shaanxi provinces. The records report that "During the rebellion, all the boats were used by the army and commercial boats became very rare. Customs revenues declined accordingly."[123] A second reason for the decrease was that less wood was coming from Sichuan province. The third reason was that after the late Daoguan, two of the main ports of Jingzhou Guan were so badly silted that no boats could pass through.[124] In 1841, these two ports were closed and harbor facilities were set up in other places.[125]

Of course, since Jingzhou Guan was located on the Yangtze River, it was also significantly affected by the Taiping Rebellion. Shortfalls in tax revenues were all too common at that time.[126] Taxation data for some years is also missing. In 1860, since Hubei Xinguan had been very successful in collecting its taxes, while Jingzhou Guan always had a shortfall, the government was prepared to decrease Jingzhou Guan's Yingyu by 5,200 taels to a total of 7,800 taels.[127]

Hubei Xinguan was created by the Qing government during the Taiping Rebellion. In 1856 the Qing government closed Yueguan, one of the offices of Jingzhou Guan. At the same time, they established Xinguan Guan at Mianyang and named it Hubei Xingguan.[128] Most of the tax collected at Hubei Xinguan came from customs duties levied on wood and bamboo. Since it had a better geographic position, Hubei Xinguan's tax revenues very quickly surpassed those of Jingzhou Guan.

Figure 4.23 clearly shows that during the latter years of the late Qing, tax revenues skyrocketed: they climbed to almost fives times those of previous periods. As the levels of tax collected at Hubei Xinguan were so high, the Qing

---

122 SYD of FHAC: September 13th, 57th year of Qianlong.

123 ZPZZ of FHAC: 4-1-35-359-6.

124 TB of FHAC: 2-1-4-20929-34.

125 TB of FHAC: 2-1-4-21374-13.

126 ZPZZ of FHAC: 4-1-35-383-48, 4-1-35-384-19.

127 ZPZZ of FHAC: 4-1-35-384-48.

128 TB of FHAC: 2-1-4-21804-50.

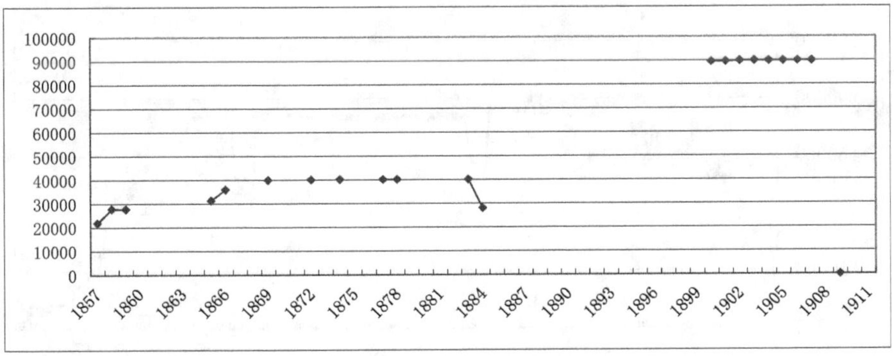

FIGURE 4.23 *Tax revenue trends of Hubei Xingguan, 1857–1911*

government agreed to decrease the *Yingyu* of Jingzhou Guan from 13,000 to 7,800 taels of silver.[129]

4.17 Kui Guan and Yu Guan

Kui Guan was established by the Ming dynasty in the prefecture of Kuizhou, Sichuan province. After the periods of warfare that raged during the late Ming and early Qing, Kui Guan was rebuilt during the reign of Kangxi. At first Kui Guan was managed by Kuizhou prefecture, but in 1728 this responsibility was transferred to the central government. In 1734, its management was returned to Kuizhou prefecture, only to be passed on in 1750 to Chuandong Dao (an official responsible for multiple prefectures). Three years later, however, Kuizhou prefecture was again made responsible for the management of Kui Guan, this time permanently.

TABLE 4.23 *Quota of Kui Guan in the Qing dynasty (in taels of silver)*

Year	Kangxi*	1723	Qianlong	1799
Zheng'e	1,542	73,740	73,740	73,740
Yingyu		23,445	17,063	110,000
Total	1,542	97,185	90,803	183,740

* Exact year unknown.
Sources: materials from *Shilu, Huidian, Hubu Zheli* and archives (see text for archival references).

129 TB of FHAC: 2-1-4-21804-50.

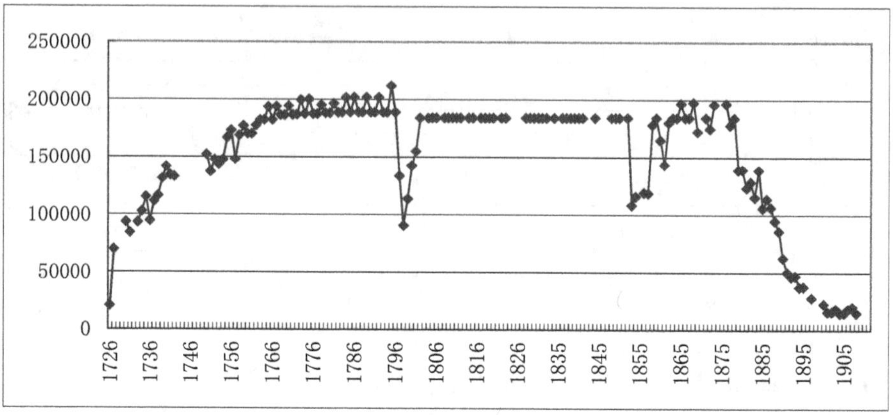

FIGURE 4.24 *Tax revenue trends of Kui Guan, 1726–1911*

Kui Guan changed its periods of taxation several times. At first, Kui Guan collected taxes over the period of one lunar year, no matter whether it consisted of 12 or 13 months. In 1799, the central government fixed Kui Guan's tax revenue quota, and four years later *Hubu* (Ministry of Finance) fixed the period of taxation at 12 months.[130] Ultimately, the taxation period was fixed at one Chinese lunar year. I did not, however, find any traces in the records of two periods of taxation in a single year.

Population and economic growth in Sichuan province during the reigns of Yongzheng and Qianlong produced the impressive increasing trend to be seen in Figure 4.24. This was followed from 1796 to 1802 by a dramatic decline, an influence of the White Lotus Rebellion.[131] The governor of Sichuan described in 1802 the situation during this period, noting that "There have been many shortages in Kui Guan in recent years. Before the White Lotus Rebellion began, goods were in ample supply and many merchants passed through Kiuzhou prefecture. At that time, tax revenues were sufficient. Now, during the rebellion, however, all roads have been closed and nobody dares to come. I was worried that illegal activities in the port might have led to the decline. However, after careful investigation I can say with confidence that the shortages of goods are totally due to the rebellion."[132]

Since it was located in the upper reaches of the Yangtze River, Kui Guan was also affected by the Taiping Rebellion. The official records state that "The rebels

130 TB of FHAC: 2-1-4-18641-5.

131 ZPZZ of FHAC: 4-1-35-359-37.

132 TB of FHAC: 2-1-4-18563-6.

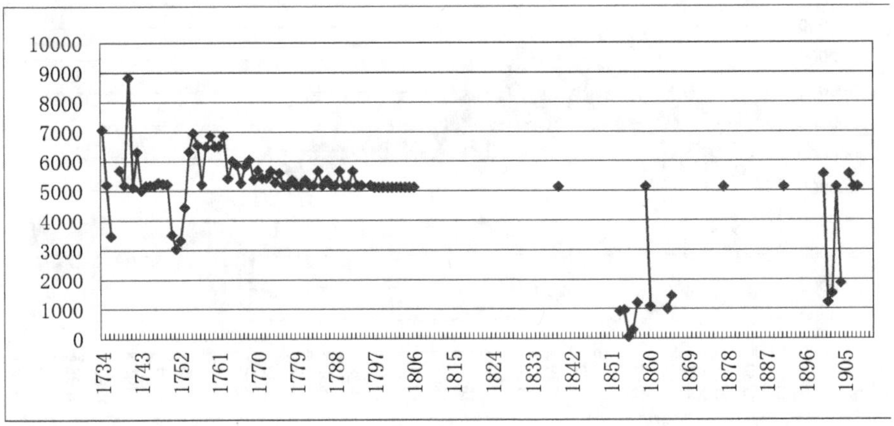

FIGURE 4.25 *Tax revenue trends of Yu Guan, 1734–1911*

have invaded Hubei and Hunan provinces, occupying several cities. The enitre region is under martial law and goods from Hubei province cannot reach Kui Guan. Likewise, goods cannot leave Sichuan province."[133] After the Taiping Rebellion was finally put down, Kui Guan's tax revenues still showed a negative trend, due to the increasing influence of *Yangguan*.

Yu Guan, located in Chongqing prefecture, Sichuan province, was established during the Ming dynasty and was already very famous at that time. Under the Qing dynasty, in 1707 the governor of Sichuan province rebuilt Yu Guan. Most customs revenue was collected from duties on wood. Total tax revenues collected amounted to about 4,705.9 taels of silver annually.[134] Yu Guan always reported its tax revenues to the Imperial Court together with those of Kui Guan.

As can be seen in Figure 4.25, tax revenue data are missing for many years, especially those in the late Qing. In the early years of Qianlong's reign, tax revenues were extremely volatile, which was related to shipping conditions and the success of the timber harvest. The lowest amount collected was in 1751,[135] and the highest in 1740.[136] Later in the reign of Qianlong, annual tax revenues stablized.

As for other ports, the Taiping Rebellion influenced tax revenues collected at Yu Guan, leading to a sharp decline in the late Qing. In some years, tax

133 ZPZZ of FHAC: 4-1-35-382-15, 4-1-35-382-67; LFZZ of FHAC: 3-4377-38.

134 ZPZZ of FHAC: 4-1-30-4-23.

135 TB of FHAC: 2-1-4-14520-15.

136 Tiben Guanshui of Chaodang, July 17th, 6th year of Qianlong.

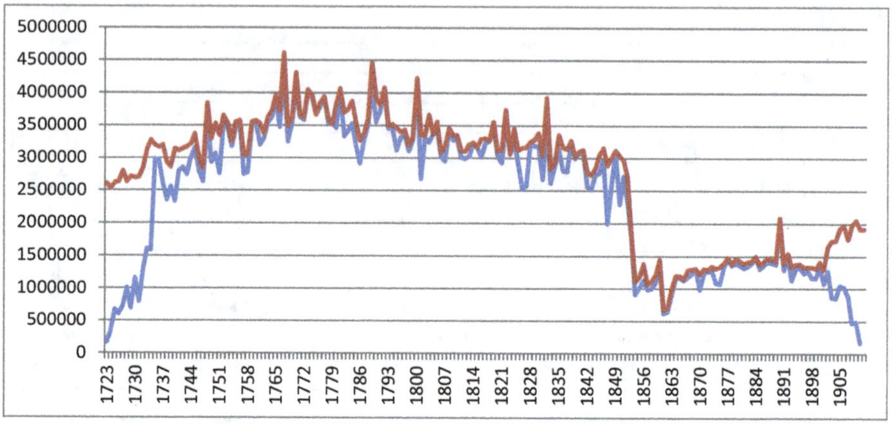

Note: The blue line represents data points reported in the archives; the red line represents data points from the archives to which have been added data for years that are missing.

FIGURE 4.26 *Tax revenue trends of the Grand Canal and Yangtze River customs, 1723–1911*

revenues almost reached the required quota, but this was only because officials made up the deficit with money paid from their own pockets.[137] This was a common occurrence in the Qing dynasty. From my observations, the relation between tax revenues and actual economic performance becomes extremely difficult to analyze when officals make up for deficits from their own funds.

4.18 Summary

There were also several data points missing among the Canal and Yangtze River Customs data. Similarly to Chapter 3 (Land Border customs), I show two trend lines in Figure 4.26. The lower line shows the data just as I compiled them from the archives; while the top line includes missing data points, which have been extrapolated from data entries available for surrounding years.

During the period 1723–1795 of the reigns of Yongzheng and Qianlong, customs duties clearly increased in total. Of course, customs revenues of ports along the Grand Canal and Yangtze River had benefited from population growth and economic expansion during that time. Under the emperors Jiaqing and Daoguang, a slight decline set in, the result of natural disasters, poor har-

137 TB of FHAC: 2-1-4-21677-38, 2-1-4-22101-6, 2-1-4-22532-9; LFZZ of FHAC: 3-6445-57; ZPZZ of FHAC: 4-1-35-579-74, 4-1-35-435-39; GXCZP, Volume 75, p. 171.

vests, and river blockages, as well as a shift of economic activity from inland regions to the coast.

As a direct result of the Taiping Rebellion, there was a sharp decline in tax revenues collected, falling from almost 3 million to 1 million taels of silver. These revenues remained low for several decades, negatively affected by *Yangguan* and the Sino-Japanese War. When I extrapolate all the data missing, I estimate that tax revenues continued to remain at this low level of 1 million taels throughout the rest of the Qing. This was actually a great achievement, especially when competition from *Yangguan* in the late Qing is taken into account.

CHAPTER 5

Coastal Customs

Even though the Grand Canal and the Yangtze River played a very important role in the collection of customs duties in the early Qing, the increasing importance of the Coastal customs was inevitable. With the economic development of coastal areas during the Qing, duties collected by Coastal customs eventually surpassed revenues levied in ports along the Grand Canal and Yangtze River.

5.1 Tianjin Guan

During the Ming dynasty, Hexiwu served as the sole customs port of Tianjin Tianjin city. In 1662, the Qing government established Tianjin Guan that was reposnible for multiple customs gates, among others Hexiwu. During the reign of Daoguang (1820–1850), Tianjin Guan had 13 customs ports under its jurisdiction.

Initially, Tianjin Guan was governed by the Ministry of Revenue (*Hubu*). The official appointed in 1716 to administer Tianjian Guan was He Se. Unfortunately, he fell ill that same year and the central government had to order the governor of Zhili province, Zhao Hongyan, to manage Tianjian Guan. However, as the governor of Zhili had too many other responsibilities, the government was later forced to transfer Tianjian Guan's management to Tianjin prefecture. In 1734 it was transferred permanently to the Changlu Salt Admininstration.

In addition to raising *Zheng'e* and *Yingyu*, Tianjin Guan was also required to collect taxes of about 12,000 taels as an additional surplus (*erwai yingyu*) for the Imperial Household.[1]

There are double entries of tax data in 1762, 1795, 1827, 1860, and 1892, due to the Chinese lunar year.

Tax revenues doubled during the Qianlong. However, the data points (see Table 5.1) from 1735 to 1752 are inadequate because exempted duty for the Tribute Grain boats is missing, which was generally about 10,000 taels of silver per year. If these annual amounts were to be added to the data, tax revenues of the Qianlong would show more stability—with an increasing trend. The peak during the reign of Qianlong occurred in 1764, and even though no explanation

1 ZPZZ of FHAC: 4-1-35-379-20/21.

 | DOI 10.1163/9789004324886_007

TABLE 5.1 *Quota of Tianjin Guan in the Qing dynasty (in taels of silver)*

Year	1656	1662	1669	1686	1717	Qianlong*	1799
Zheng'e	30,900	35,080	30,000	40,464	48,156	48,156	48,156
Yingyu						26,053	20,000
Total	30,900	35,080	30,000	40,464	48,156	68,156	

* Exact year unknown.
Sources: materials from *Shilu, Huidian, Hubu Zheli* and archives (see text for archival references).

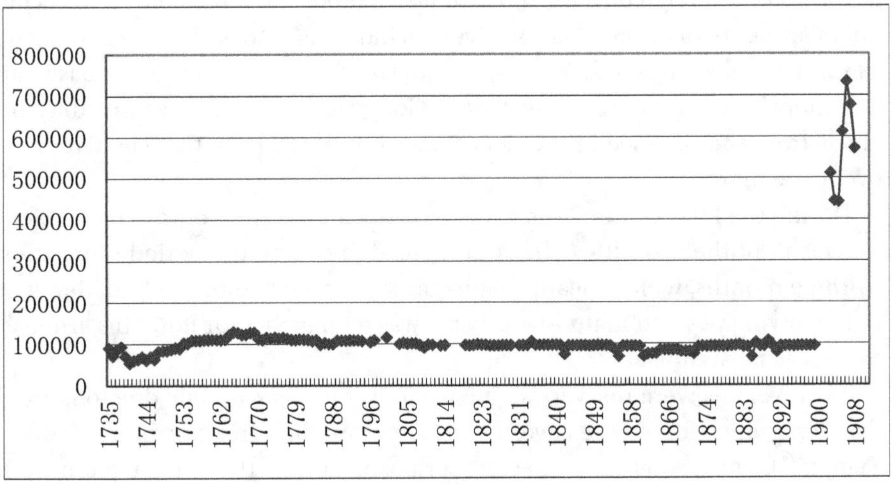

FIGURE 5.1 *Tax revenue trends of Tianjin Guan, 1735–1911*

could be found in the archives, it might well be the result of an increase in coastal trading.[2]

During the Jiaqing and Daoguang, tax figures were generally stable. There was a clear decline in 1842 due to the influence of the First Opium War. The records state that "From last year right up until now, travel on the sea lanes has been affected by British warships. Chinese trading boats dare not to come to Tianjin from Shanghai, or from other places."[3]

Tianjin was partly affected by the Taiping Rebellion. However, since it was far from the areas of conflict, the decline in tax revenues was not so serious.

2 LFZZ of FHAC: 3-592-40.

3 LFZZ of FHAC: 3-9489-50.

Records from that period consistently state that "The roads are blocked by the rebels, and no merchants dare to come".[4] After 1861, the reports would attribute shortfalls in tax revenues to the rise of *Yangguan*.[5] During the final years of the late Qing, tax revenues increased sharply in response to the introduction of a new system of taxation.[6]

5.2 Tianjin Haiguan

Tianjin Haiguan was established very late in the Qing dynasty and was managed by the governor of Zhili province. It was mentioned for the first time as late as 1807, the reign of Jiaqing, when it was reported to the court that its tax quota amounts to 40,000 taels of silver, including 26,000 as *Zheng'e* and 14,000 as *Yingyu*. Unlike most other ports, Tianjin Haiguan's tax year was not based on a 12-month period. Similarly to Linqin Gongguan, it levied customs duty on goods from the time ice in the river thawed until the time that the river iced over once more.

During the First Opium War, because tax revenues were always insufficient as a result of the hostilities, the court agreed to extend the period of taxation by three months, which meant that its tax year stretched through to March of the following year, no matter whether it was a lunar year or not. This arrangement was most unusual.[7]

Tax revenues were not very stable from 1807 to 1850, mainly due to natural disasters, which forced the government to permit duty-free transport of food.[8] Tianjin Haiguan was also affected seriously during the First Opium War. Records state that "Taxes raised in Tianjin Haiguan come mainly from the transport of tea and ordinary goods from Shanghai (the Northern China). However, in 1840 British warships closed the sea lanes for trading and no boats dared to come."[9] This situation continued into the next year because merchants were afraid of the British warships.[10] As I noted above, the government agreed to expand the period of taxation accordingly.[11]

---

4 ZPZZ of FHAC: 4-1-35-382; LFZZ of FHAC: 3-4378-8.

5 LFZZ of FHAC: 3-4845-31, 3-4872-86, 3-4874-20, 3-4869-74; ZPZZ of FHAC: 4-1-35-391-32.

6 LFZZ of FHAC: 3-6434-31, 3-6445-34, 3-6435-17,3-6440-64. GXCZP, Volume 74, p. 867; GXCZP, Volume 75, pp. 30–31, 210.

7 LFZZ of FHAC: 3-3166-8.

8 Ni Yuping (2010), pp. 122–123.

9 LFZZ of FHAC: 3-3166-8.

10 LFZZ of FHAC: 3-3166-8, 3-3166-30.

11 LFZZ of FHAC: 3-3166-8.

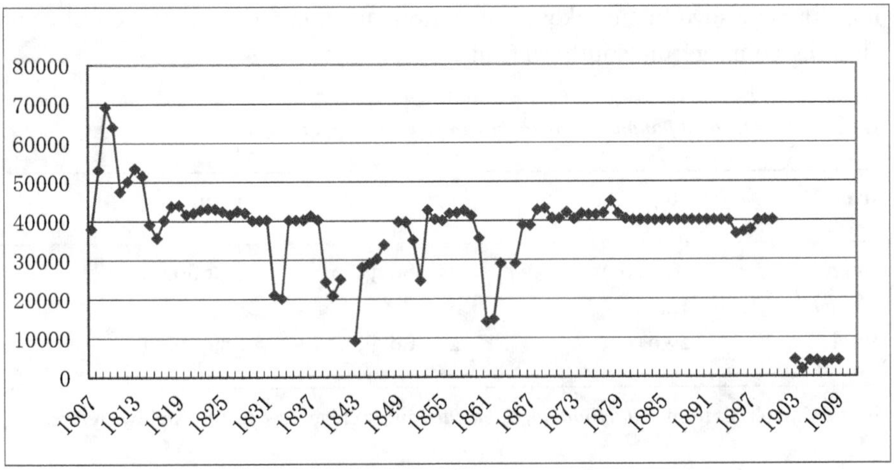

FIGURE 5.2 *Tax revenue trends of Tianjin Haiguan, 1807–1911*

After the Taiping Rebellion broke out in southern China, boats from Shanghai found it very difficult to travel to the north, and the tax revenues declined quickly.[12] And after 1861, reports would say that shortfalls in revenues were a consequence of the increasing activity of *Yangguan*.[13] In the last years of the Qing dynasty, tax revenues declined, this time because of the Boxer Rebellion, and following that the introduction of a new taxation system. Records from 1907 indicate that "As a result of the Sino-Japanese War and the Boxer Rebellion, almost half the sea-worthy boats have been destroyed. At the same time, railways can transport everything to anywhere. All merchants prefer to send their goods by train, and so the tax revenues of Tianjin Haiguan have declined accordingly."[14]

5.3 Jianghai Guan

Jianghai Guan was established in 1685, during the Qing dynasty. Initaially, it was located at Huating county but moved to Shanghai later. Intially, *Hubu* was directly responsible for its management. Later, in 1722, this was transferred to the viceroy of Jiangsu province. Jianghai Guan collected taxes mainly by levy-

12 LFZZ of FHAC: 3-4376-21, 3-4383-18, 3-4384-53.

13 LFZZ of FHAC: 3-4871-53, 3-4872-34, 3-4873-45, 3-4875-48.

14 GXCZP, Volume 75, p. 25.

ing duty on soya-bean cake coming from northern China and cotton and clothing coming from southern China.

TABLE 5.2 *Quota of Jianghai Guan in the Qing dynasty (in taels of silver)*

Year	1690	1729	1799
Zheng'e	23,016.33	23,980.33	23,980.33
Yingyu	42,000		
Total	23,016.33	23,980.33	65,980.33

Sources: materials from *Shilu, Huidian, Hubu Zheli* and archives (see text for archival references).

There are two entries of tax data in the years 1770, 1803, 1835, 1868, and 1900, due to the use of the Chinese lunar year.

Figure 5.3 displays a very interesting drop between 1746 and 1749. This was not because of a decline in tax revenues, but rather because an exemption of grain duty meant that this source of revenue was not included in the results as before.[15] If this factor is taken into account, there is no decrease in taxes collected. There were also declines in 1756 and 1757, due to the big flood in Jiangsu province that led to a poor harvest and which weakened people's ability to buy goods.[16]

Before 1840, during the reigns of Jiaqing and Daoguang, tax revenues remained stable. The first change occurred during the First Opium War (1840–1842): in June of 1840, the viceroy of Jiangsu reported to the Emperor that "In order to fight the British, we have closed Shanghai harbor and forbidden any boats to pass through."[17] This prohibition lasted for three months, coincidentally at the busiest time of the trading year. Two years later, British warships returned to Jiangsu province and Jianghai Guan was closed once again. Many commercial boats were stopped by British warships and were unable to trade.[18]

During the Taiping Rebellion tax revenues declined once again, since Jiangsu province was the scene of some serious battles. Concurrently, in 1854 Shanghai was occupied for two months during a rebellion by members of the

15 ZPZZ of FHAC: 4-1-35-322-17, 4-1-35-323-28, 4-1-35-325-2.

16 ZPZZ of FHAC: 4-1-35-329-15.

17 ZPZZ of FHAC: 4-1-35-379-42.

18 LFZZ of FHAC: 3-9489-69.

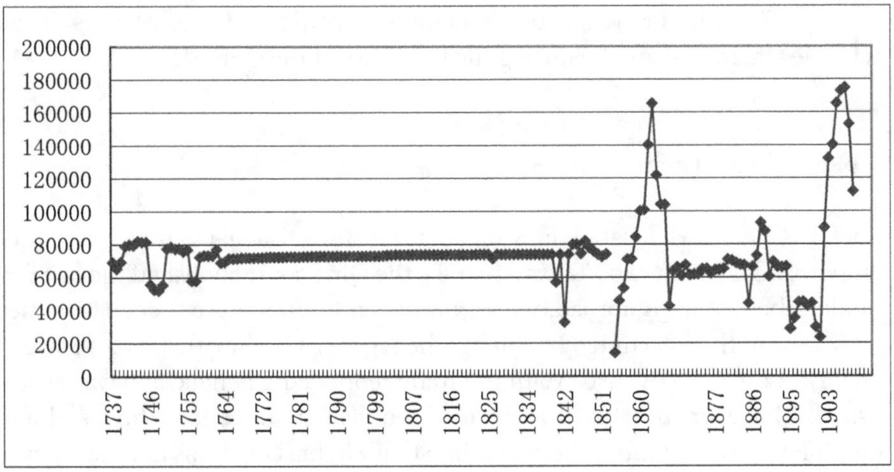

FIGURE 5.3 *Tax revenue trends of Jianghai Guan, 1735–1911*

Small Knife Society, and Jianhai Guan was unable to collect taxes at that time.[19] After that, Jianghai Guan was still threatened by the Taiping Rebellion. The records refer to this situation repeatedly.[20]

Tax revenues collected at Jianghai Guan from 1859 to 1865 exceeded its quota, with revenues peaking in 1863. This is a little strange if one considers the ongoing Taiping Rebellion at that time. After checking the relevant documents, I found that the increase in revenues was due to a new tax called "the newly added foreign tax". It meant that Jianghai Guan received 20,000 taels from Jianghai Yangguan during that time to compensate for revenue lost as a result of Jianghai Yangguan acquiring the right to tax foreign goods.[21] However, later these 20,000 taels were no longer included in the customs revenue figures reported for Jianghai Guan.

After 1865, Jianghai Guan's tax revenues returned to normal levels, although reports found in the archives say that it was affected by the ascendency of *Yangguan*: "Since our government has opened many ports, all types of traditional boats have been declining in numbers. People more and more often choose foreign ships for water transport."[22] The lowest amount of revenues collected was in 1901, because of the Boxer Rebllion (or Yihetuan Movement).[23]

19 TB of FHAC: 2-1-4-21639-34.

20 LFZZ of FHAC: 3-4379-15, 3-4845-22; ZPZZ of FHAC: 4-1-35-383-11,4-1-35-383-56.

21 LFZZ of FHAC: 3-4876-51.

22 LFZZ of FHAC: 3-4877-39, 3-4880-65; ZPZZ of FHAC: 4-1-35-391-79.

23 LFZZ of FHAC: 3-6380-26.

Shortly after this, a new taxation system was introduced, and as a result tax revenues increased greatly during the last years of the Qing.[24]

5.4 Zhehai Guan

Zhehai Guan was located in Ningbo prefecture, Zhejiang province. After emperor Kangxi annexed Taiwan in 1683, the Qing court abolished the law forbidding boats to sail abroad, which had been in effect to cut economic ties with Taiwan then occupied by Zheng Chenggong, a military leader and sworn enemy of the Qing dynasty. With the trade reopened, Zhehai Guan was established. However, because the records published in various books differ, opinions also differ about the exact time that Zhehai Guan was founded. Some believed that it was set up in 1684, while others believed it was founded in 1686.[25] After it was established, officials were sent to Zhehai Guan by the central government. In 1720, management of the port was passed on to the viceroy of Zhejiang. After changing hands again several times, Ningbo prefecture was finally assigned the responsibility of managing it permanently.

TABLE 5.3 *Quota of Zhehai Guan in the Qing dynasty (in taels of silver)*

Year	Kangxi*	1721	1724	1799	1804
Zheng'e	31,952	32,952	31,952	35,908	35,908
Yingyu				39,000	44,000
Total	31,952	32,952	31,952	74,908	79,908

* Exact year unknown.
Sources: materials from *Shilu*, *Huidian*, *Hubu Zheli* and archives (see text for archival references).

There are two entries of tax data in 1748, 1781, 1814, 1868, and 1900, due to use of the Chinese lunar year.

In general, tax revenues were stable in the Qianlong, with only one single decline, which occurred in 1736. Strangely, I can find no reason for this decline

24 LFZZ of FHAC: 3-6430-33, 3-6426-5, 3-6515-126, 3-6450-31; ZPZZ of FHAC: 4-1-35-434-54, 4-1-35-436-25; GXCZP, Volume 74, p. 764; GZDGXC: Volume 24, p. 312.

25 Li Hongzhang (1908, Volume 235) recorded it was in 1864, while Ji Zengyun (1736, Volume 86) said it was in 1866.

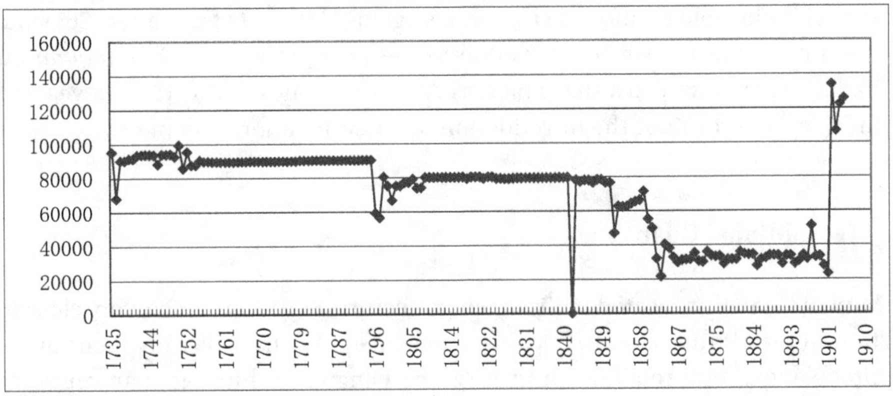

FIGURE 5.4 *Tax revenue trends of Zhehai Guan, 1735–1911*

in the archived documents.[26] Zhehai Guan was able to generally maintain that stability during the reigns of Jiaqing and Daoguang, with some interruptions in the early Jiaqing caused the pirate Cai Qian (active from 1794 to 1809 in Fujian and Zhejiang provinces). Archived reports state: "Pirates have been raiding the waters around Zhejiang. Seldom do boats from Fujian province risk the voyage to Zhejiang province".[27] Another major interruption occurred in 1842: due to the First Opium War, no customs duties were collected because the port was closed when it came under threat from British warships.[28] This is easy to understand because Zhejiang province was in the main theater of war at that time. Indeed, the British army occupied Dinghai county (a county close to Zhehai Guan) twice. Local officials were afraid that the Han people would cooperate with the British, and so it was decide to close the port completely.[29] The war also affected Zhehai Guan's period of taxation, just as it did that of Tianjin Haiguan. In 1841, Zhehai Guan's period of taxation was to begin on 9 March 1840 and end on 8 March 1841. However, owing to the declaration of martial law, the taxation year continued until 19 June 1841. So the next year's period of taxation began on 20 June 1841 and ended on 7 October 1842.

Due to the Taiping Rebellion, Zhehai Guan's tax revenues declined again, and even failed to reach half the level of its quota since Zhejiang province was also an important battlefield. Contemporary reports repeatedly mention that "There seems to be no end to hostilities, and the poor cannot recover fast

26 TB of FHAC: 2-1-4-12847-9.

27 LFZZ of FHAC: 3-1766-60; ZPZZ of FHAC: 4-1-35-360-8.

28 LFZZ of FHAC: 3-3166-63.

29 ZPZZ of FHAC: 4-1-35-379-27.

enough to be able to afford to buy goods again."[30] Reports from after 1861 state repeatedly that the decline was due to the rising influence of *Yangguan* on trade.[31] There was also a sharp increase in tax revenues during the last years of the Qing as a result of the introduction of a new taxation system.[32]

5.5 Minhai Guan

Minhai Guan was located in Xianmen prefecture, Fujian province, very close to Taiwan prefecture (later to become a province). As I have already mentioned, after Kangxi annexed Taiwan in 1683, the Qing court lifted its ban on boats landing there. The government immediately set up Minhai Guan in 1684 and it became the first coastal customs facility in the Qing dynasty.

Initially, the central government sent two officials—one a Han and the other a Manchu—to manage the port, each for a term of two years. Later, after 1690, only one official—who had to be a Manchu—was appointed, and then only for a term of one year.

In 1724, administration of Minhai Guan became the responsibility of the governor of Fujian. In the Qianlong, its management was passed on to the Minzhe Governor, but in 1738 it was permanently transfered to the Fuzhou General (commander of the military stationed in Fuijan province). Minhai Guan's *Zheng'e* amounted to 73,549.547 taels of silver. In 1799, the Imperial Court fixed its *Yingyu* at 113,000 taels, i.e. its quota totalled 186,549.547 taels.

There are two entries of tax data in the years 1748, 1781, 1814, 1846, and 1879, due to the use of the Chinese lunar year.

As Figure Figure 5.5 shows, tax revenues reached their peak in the late Qianlong, with a clearly increasing trend as from the reign of Yongzheng. From then on, a long decline sets in. I have analyzed the explanations for this during the reigns of Jiaqing and Daoguang (1796–1850). The first decline was due to large-scale marauding after 1805 by the pirate Cai Qian; he was finally defeated in 1809. The second decline occurred during the First Opium War.[33] Xiamen was attacked twice by the British army at that time. In 1840, the British tried to occupy Xianmen but were unsuccessful. Nevertheless, merchants still avoided the region and boats seldom came.[34] In 1842, Xianmen was finally occupied by

---

30 LFZZ of FHAC: 3-4379-15, 3-4845-22; ZPZZ of FHAC: 4-1-35-383-11, 4-1-35-383-56.

31 LFZZ of FHAC: 3-4877-39, 3-4880-65; ZPZZ of FHAC: 4-1-35-391-79.

32 GXCZP, Volume 74, pp. 501, 850; LFZZ of FHAC: 3-6431-50.

33 Ni Yuping (2010), pp. 134–135.

34 ZPZZ of FHAC: 4-1-35-379-44.

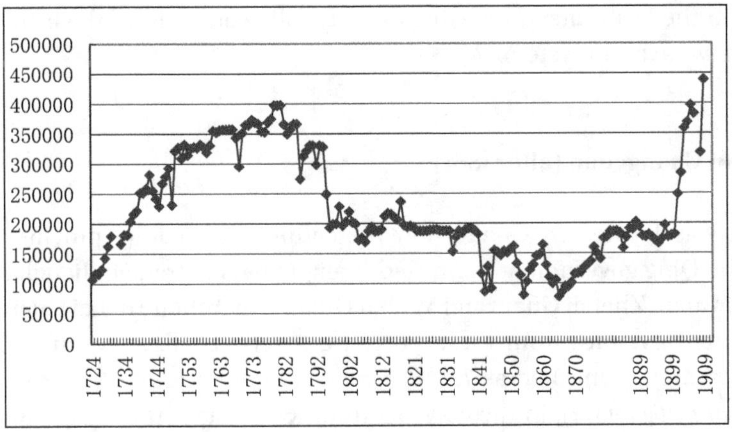

FIGURE 5.5 *Tax revenue trends of Minhai Guan, 1724–1911*

the British army and Minhai Guan was closed for 20 days (from 10 July to the end of July) in 1843. Archived records report that "Xianmen is the most flourishing place in Fujian province. However, the British army have occupied and looted it several times, such that the people fled for their lives. When the city was recaptured, those that had fled had no money to enable them to return back home. All shops were closed and all the boats were destroyed during the fighting. A shortfall in tax revenues for Minhai Guan was inevitable."[35]

Minhai Guan was also greatly affected by the Taiping Rebellion and by *Yangshui*. Records from that period report that "The rebellion has made people scared. Many of them have lost their jobs and merchants have lost their money".[36] At the same time, banditry sprang up everywhere: "They [bandits] occupy Xianmen and other areas, and all the merchants have had to move to other places. We cannot collect taxes to the extent that we did before."[37] After 1861, reports explain shortfalls by referring to the increasing influence of *Yangguan*.[38] Of course, the Likin bureaucracy, which was established everywhere in the late Qing, also had an effect: this increased the burden on merchants and they were became unwilling to trade.[39] The sharp increase in

35 LFZZ of FHAC: 3-3166-6.

36 ZPZZ of FHAC: 4-1-35-382-39; LFZZ of FHAC: 3-4378-56.

37 LFZZ of FHAC: 3-4376-60; ZPZZ of FHAC: 4-1-35-382-54.

38 ZPZZ of FHAC: 4-1-35-384-2, 4-1-35-384-44, 4-1-35-385-1, 4-1-35-385-29, 4-1-35-386-7, 4-1-35-386-63, 4-1-35-387-33, 4-1-35-388-3, 4-1-35-388-58.

39 ZPZZ of FHAC: 4-1-35-389-70, 4-1-35-390-40.

tax revenues in the last years of the Qing dynasty followed on from the introduction of a new taxation system.[40]

5.6 Yuehai Changguan (after 1861)

Yuehai Guan was located in Guangzhou prefecture, Guangdong province. Before 1757, the Qing government permitted foreign boats to trade in Jianghai Guan, Minhai Guan, Zhehai Guan, and Yuehai Guan. Other than Yuehai Guan, however, the tax revenues from these ports were very small. According to H.B.Morse's research, published as *The Chronicles of the East India Company Trading to China (1635–1834)*, in the 90 years from 1664 to 1753 there were 199 boats from the East India Company active in China, and of them 153 traded at Yuehai Guan (i.e. 77% of all the Company's boats). Minhai Guan only received 26 of these boats, Zhehai Guan only 17 boats, and Jianghai Guan only one boat.[41] After 1757, the emperor Qianlong ordered that all foreign boats must trade only in Yuhai Guan. This situation continued until 1842, when the Sino-British "*Nanjing Treaty*" arranged for five ports to be opened for foreign trade (including Yuehai Guan). Seen from a long-term perspective, Yuhai Guan was the only port that levied taxes on foreign trade; I will analyze this later.

To simplify the discussion, in this book I treat Yuehai Guan as the only port that was open for foreign trade before 1842. After 1861, Yuehai Guan was split into Yuehai Changguan and Yuehai Yangguan. In this section I only show customs revenues collected at Yuehai Changguan after 1861.

In the period 1861 to 1911, the only year that records for Yuehai Guan show two entries of tax data was 1879. As for other ports, this was due to the use of the Chinese lunar year.

As Figure 5.6 shows, on the whole, tax revenues collected at Yuehai Changguan increased gradually, but the climb became especially steep after 1902, when a new taxation system was adopted. Revenues peaked in 1905 because the collection period spanned 13 months and 27 days, considerably longer than other periods of taxation.[42]

40 LFZZ of FHAC: 3-6443-2, 3-6446-23, 3-6432-58, 3-6443-19, 3-7506-55; GZDGXC: Volume 24, pp. 578–579; GXCZP, Volume 75, p. 193.

41 Hosea Ballou Morse (1926), pp. 309–321.

42 LFZZ of FHAC: 3-6490-45.

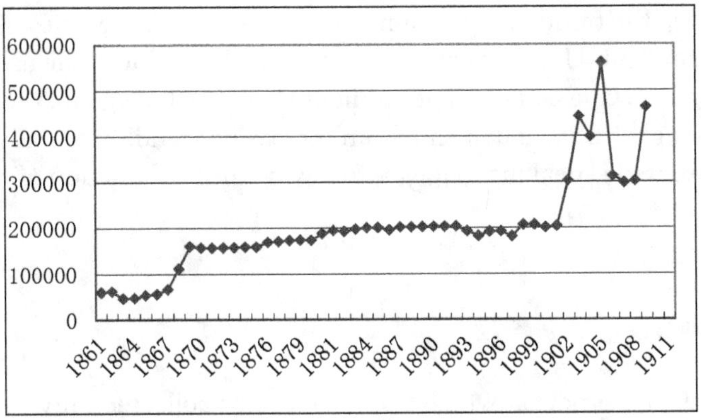

FIGURE 5.6 *Tax revenue trends of Yuehai Changguan, 1861–1911*

5.7 Donghai Guan

Donghai Guan was established on 18 June 1862, with the consideration that following the expansion of foreign trade Yantai needed its own tax office and the closest tax office in Tianjin was too far (about 600 km). Like Yuehai Guan, Donghai Guan was also split into two types of ports: *Changguan* (to collect taxes from domestic goods) and *Yangguan* (to collect taxes from foreign goods). At first no quota was set. It was only in 1875 that the government fixed Donghai Guan's quota: 70,000 taels of silver.[43]

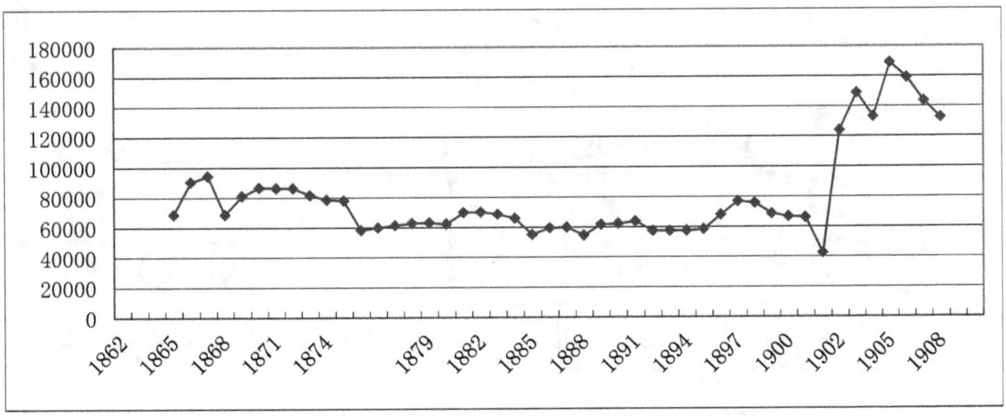

FIGURE 5.7 *Tax revenue trends of Donghai Changguan, 1861–1911*

43 GXCZP, Volume 72, p. 210.

Figure 5.7 shows the the trend only for Donghai Changguan. Two entries of tax data have only been found for the year 1876, as in other cases, due to the use of the Chinese lunar year. One can see that, similar to Yuehai Changguan, revenue collected at Donghai Changguan shows an increasing trend. Especially after 1902, revenues soared—peaking in 1905—following the introduction of a new taxation system.[44]

5.8 Brief Summary

Yuehai Guan was the largest port at which Coastal customs collected duty. To facilitate comparisons between *Changguan* and *Yangguan*, I have initially concentrated on revenues collected in years after 1861.

The first four peaks can generally be explained by the affects of Chinese lunar years, resulting in two entries of tax data in some years. For example, in 1781 there were two tax figures for Zhehai Guan and Minhai Guan, so these revenues were higher than usual. The trend displayed in Figure 5.8 is generally increasing, exceptions only occurring during periods when uncommon events

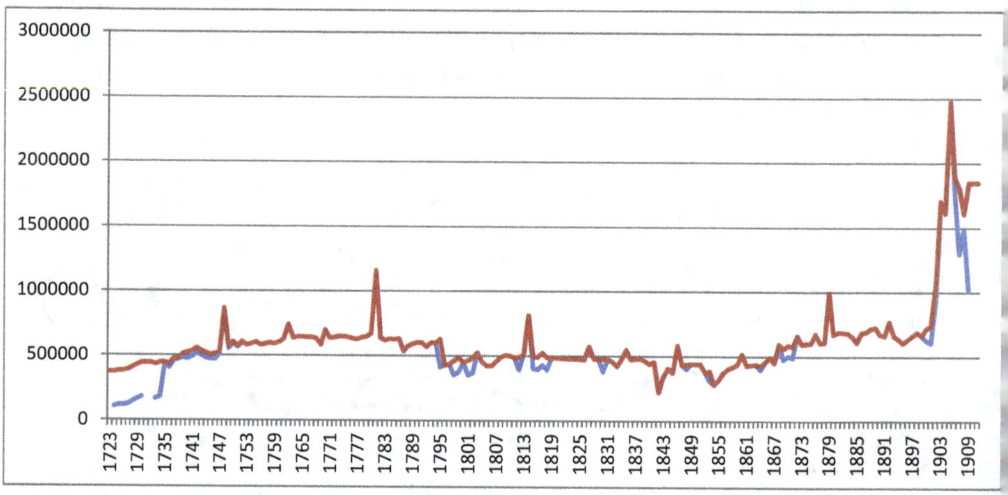

Note: Blue lines represent data points reported in the archives; the red line represents data points from the archives to which have been added data for years that are missing.

FIGURE 5.8 *Tax revenue trends of Coastal customs from customs duties levied on domestic goods, 1723–1911*

44 GXCZP, Volume 74, p. 715.

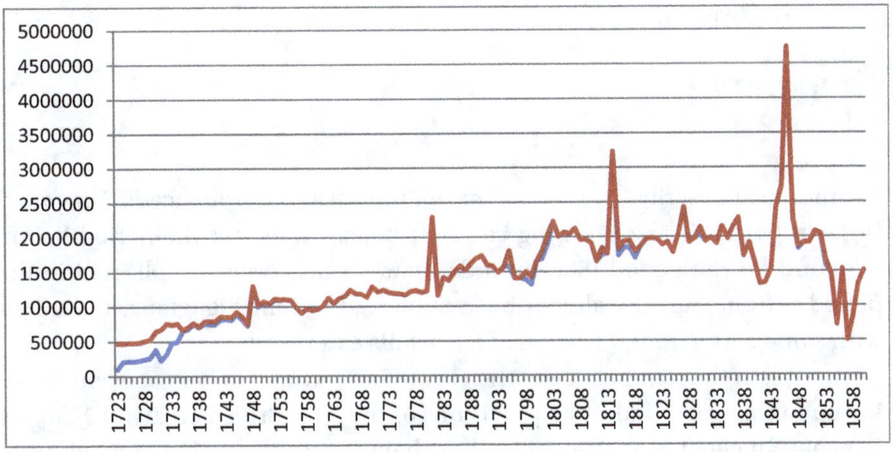

Note: Blue lines represent data points reported in the archives; the red line represents data points from the archives to which have been added data for years that are missing.

FIGURE 5.9 *Tax revenue trends of Coastal customs (including Yuehai Guan), 1723–1911*

took place, such as the First Opium War. The highest peak during the entire Qing occurred in 1905, following the introduction of a new system of taxation. Figure 5.8 also indicates that economic development in coastal areas was more successful and faster than that of inland economic regions.

Figure 5.9 shows the trend of tax revenues collected at Yuehai Guan when data from before 1861 are also added.

The difference between Figure 5.8 and Figure 5.9 is indicative of the impact of international trade passing through Yuehai Guan before 1861. In Figure 5.9 one can see that the coastal ports experienced even greater increases in customs revenue before 1796 (especially when compared against revenues collected at ports on the Grand Canal and Yangtze River). It also confirms the transformation of economic activity from inland regions to coastal areas duing the reign of Qianlong.

In the reigns of Jiaqing and Daoguang, tax revenues remained stable. After 1850, i.e. during the Taiping Rebellion, tax revenues collected from the coastal area declined quickly as Jianghai Guan and Zhehai Guan, in particular, were close to battlefields. Other coastal ports were affected to varying extents by the war.

CHAPTER 6

Yangguan

For reasons I describe a little further on, the fiscal performance of *Yangguan* (foreign ports) during the Qing can best be examined for the period before 1861, and for the period 1861 onwards. Data on tax revenues collected in the period as from 1861 have already been published by Tang Xianglong, and, albeit with some corrections, I have used his results extensively.

To explain the significance of the year 1861 it is useful to look at events leading up to that year. Under the provisions of the Sino-British Treaty of Nanjing, Jianghai Yangguan was opened at Shanghai towards the end of 1843. Just one month later, Zhehai Yangguan was opened. Then, Xiamen and Fuzhou were opened in 1844. Up until 1853 the Qing court still controlled these *Yangguan*.

However, in 1853 the Xiaodao Hui Uprising (an uprising of the Small Sword Society) broke out in Shanghai and it became more difficult to collect customs duty at Jianghai Yangguan. In response to the chaotic situation that developed, Britain, U.S.A and France decided to take over Jianghai Yangguan. The Qing government had no choice but to accept this fact and Jianghai Yangguan became, thus, the first foreign port in China to be controlled by the West.

After the Second Opium War (1856–1860), the Qing government signed the Treaty of Tianjin (1858) with Britain, U.S.A, France and Russia. Two years later, the Treaty of Beijing was signed with Britain, France and Russia. The Qing government had to open more ports to the West. Taking into consideration its conflicts with the Taiping rebels and the West, as well as the West's successful administration of Jianghai Yangguan, the Qing government decided to allow the West to help them levy customs duty in *Yangguan*. In 1855, the Qing government established the Chinese Maritime Customs Service and the Englishman H.N. Lay became its first Commissioner in 1858. In 1861, the post of Inspector-General of the Chinese Maritime Customs Service was established; its encumbant reported to Zongli Yamen (the Prime Minister of Foreign Affairs Yamen). From that time on—1861—*Yanggguan* were controlled by the West. In the years that Robert Hart—the service's most well-known inspector-general—was in charge, *Yangguan* evolved into an organization that governed a wide variety of services related to China's waterways and maritime transport, and it became one of the most important sources of fiscal revenue for the Qing government, albeit with the disadvantage it was separately managed by the West.

 | DOI 10.1163/9789004324886_008

In 1900, the Boxer Rebellion broke out. Hostilities came to an end after an alliance of eight western nations captured Beijing and thus lifted the siege of the foreign legations there. One of the conditions of the Boxer Protocol, signed in the following year, was that China had to pay war reparations to the Western allies that had lifted the siege. As a consequence, the Qing government had to allow *Changguan* close (within 25 km) to *Yangguan* to also be managed by the West. This was not only aimed at collecting more taxes, but was also meant to be a guarantee that China would meet the indemnity payments to the Western powers arranged under the Boxer Protocol. As we have seen in sections 3.11, 4.18 and 5.8, this new system did increase the tax revenues.

6.1 Yuehai Guan (before 1861)

Yuehai Guan was established in 1685 in Guanzhou city, Gongdong province, two years after emperor Kangxi annexed Taiwan. Yuehai Guan had its own official Yuehaiguan Jiandu (manager of Yuehai Guan), who held a rank as high as governor. Since it had monopolized foreign trade for such a long time, it is logical that before 1850 Yuehai Guan was the largest port in Qing China.

TABLE 6.1 *Tax quota of Yuehai Guan in the Qing dynasty (in taels of silver)*

Year	Kangxi*	1688	1699	1799
Zheng'e	91,740.5	82,362	39,030	43,564
Yingyu	855,500			
Total	91,740.5	82,362	39,030	899,064

* Exact year unknown.
Sources: materials from *Shilu, Huidian, Hubu Zheli* and archives (see text for archival references).

Under the Sino-British Treaty of Nanjing, the ports of Jianghai Yangguan, Zhehai Yangguan, Xiamen and Fuzhou were opened to foreign trade and were given the same rights as Yuehai Guan to tax foreign goods. Intially the Qing government was worried that these new ports would weaken and damage the position of Yuehai Guan. It ordered that "If Yuehai Guan cannot collect enough taxes to meet its quota, the other four ports must transfer some of their tax

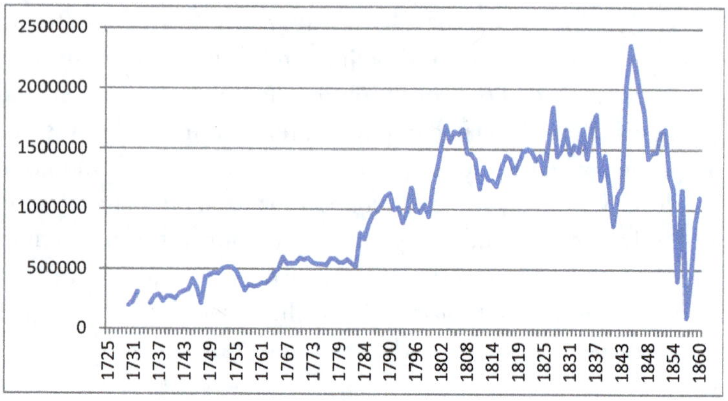

FIGURE 6.1 *Tax revenue trends of Yuehai Guan, 1725–1860*

revenues to recompense Yuehai Guan."[1] In short, the Qing government was worried that Yuehai Guan would be unable to raise as much tax revenue as it had before. However, after several years' practice, they found that tax revenues collected at Yuehia Guan had even increased and the old quota was kept.[2]

There are two entries of tax data in 1781, 1814, and 1846, due to the use of the Chinese lunar year.

During the reigns of Yongzheng and Qianlong tax revenues increased six-fold, from 200,000 to 1,200,000 taels of silver annually; see Figure 6.1. This great increase was the result of growth in Sino-foreign trade. During the reigns of Jiaqing and Daoguang, however, a number of incidents interrupted this rising trend. For example, as a result of wide-spread marauding by the pirate Cai Qian, in 1811 the viceroy of Guangdong decided to close all ports and forbade boats to leave.[3] Of course, tax revenues declined as trading came to a halt.

The First Opium War had a disasterous impact on Yuehai Guan's tax revenues, as can be clearly seen in Figure 6–1. In 1839, emperor Daoguang bestowed upon Lin Zhexu (1785–1850), an imperial commission, to abolish the opium trade, which he promptly set about doing. After he forbade the importation of opium the number of foreign vessels visiting Yuehai Guan declined from 138 to 93 (i.e. 33 fewer vessels), which led to a fall in tax revenues from 1,440,000 to 1,180,000 taels of silver (i.e. 19 less).[4] Soon afterwards the First Opium War broke out, and the number of foreign vessels calling at Yuehai Guan declined

1 Wen Qing (2007), Volume 67.

2 Wen Qing (2007), Volume 67.

3 ZPZZ of FHAC: 4-1-35-366-7.

4 ZPZZ of FHAC: 4-1-35-379-28.

even further to 13, since British warships blockaded the port.[5] Taxes collected in 1841 dropped to half of what they had been before the hostilities, reaching their lowest point during the reigns of Jiaqing and Daoguang.[6]

Under the conditions of the Sino-British Treaty of Nanjing, the Qing government was forced to adopt a more open policy towards foreign trade and as result tax revenues of Yuehai Guan increased in the years that followed. In 1846, due to the use of the Chinese lunar year, there were two periods of taxation—revenues were 2,186,530 and 1,972,089 taels of silver—so it is not surprising to find such high results for this year as a whole.[7] Nonetheless, other ports in Shanghai, Ningbo, Xiamen and Fuzhou had the same right to tax foreign merchants and soon after 1840 they began to challenge Yuehai Guan's position as the entrepôt port.

Following the outbreak of the Taiping Rebellion, tax revenues of Yuehai Guan decreased very quickly as most of its goods came from Jiangsu and Zhejiang provinces, where much of the hostilities were taking place; roads were closed and businesses were all but ruined.[8] Once the rebellion was put down, revenues recovered very rapidly, however.

6.2 Jianghai Yangguan (1844–1861)

Under the Treaty of Nanjing, Shanghai had to be opened up to trade with the West. Jianghai Yangguan was the first port to be opened under this treaty and it began to collect taxes on foreign goods towards the end of 1843.

In 1855, during the uprising of the Small Sword Society, rebels took control of Shanghai and all taxation activities came to a halt. Britain, U.S.A and France decided to take over Jianghai Yangguan, and they levied customs duties there on their own authority. The Qing government had no choice but to agree to the takeover, although the Western authorities did pass on the revenues they collected to the government after the rebellion had been quashed. In this way, Jianghai Yangguan became the first port to be controlled by the Western powers.[9] The same period of taxation was adopted as that of Yuehai Guan before 1861, and there were two entries of tax data in 1846 due the use of the Chinese lunar year.

5 ZPZZ of FHAC: 4-1-35-379-49.

6 ZPZZ of FHAC: 4-1-35-379-49.

7 ZPZZ of FHAC: 4-1-35-380-43.

8 ZPZZ of FHAC: 4-1-35-382-56; LFZZ of FHAC: 3-9491-31.

9 TB of FHAC: 2-1-4-21618-3.

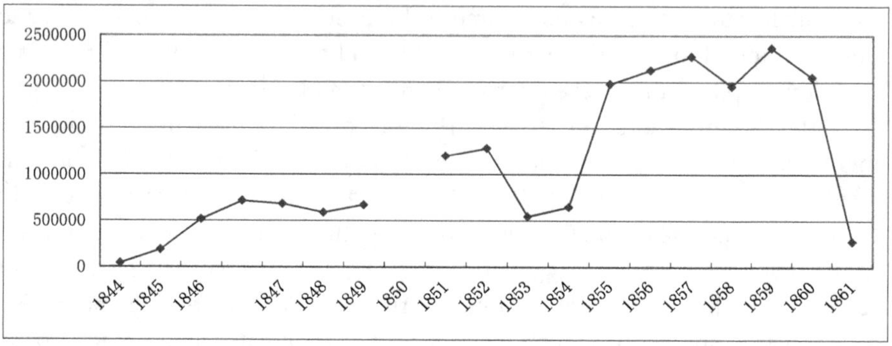

FIGURE 6.2 *Tax revenue trends of Jianghai Yangguan, 1844–1861*

Figure 6.2 shows that initially tax revenues from Janghai Yangguan increased. When in 1850 the Taiping Rebellion broke out, however, tax income began to decline quickly. Under the control of the Western powers tax revenues increased once again. Nonetheless, tax income in 1861 was far too low, not because of economic factors but because the period of taxation comprised only 50 days (from 26 July to 17 August).[10]

As from 1861, the administration of all *Yangguan* ports passed into the hands of the Western powers. Being located at Shanghai, the most important city in China during the late Qing, Janghai Yangguan quickly surpassed Yuehai Guan in terms of customs revenues, and it rapidly became the largest port for foreign trade of the period.

6.3 Zhehai Yangguan (1844–1861)

Zhehai Yangguan was located at Ningbo prefecture. Ningbo was one of the treaty ports opened to trade with the West under the strictures of the Sino-British Treaty of Nanjing. Zhehai Yangguan was opened in January 1844. As it adopted the same periods of taxation as Yuehai Guan, two entries of tax data were also recorded for Zhehai Yangguan in 1846.

As can be seen in Figure 6.3, before 1860 the tax revenues were very small. Only after it came under Western management did tax figures begin to increase.

10 LFZZ of FHAC: 3-4873-73. In Appendix 3, I have combined these revenues with Tang's data.

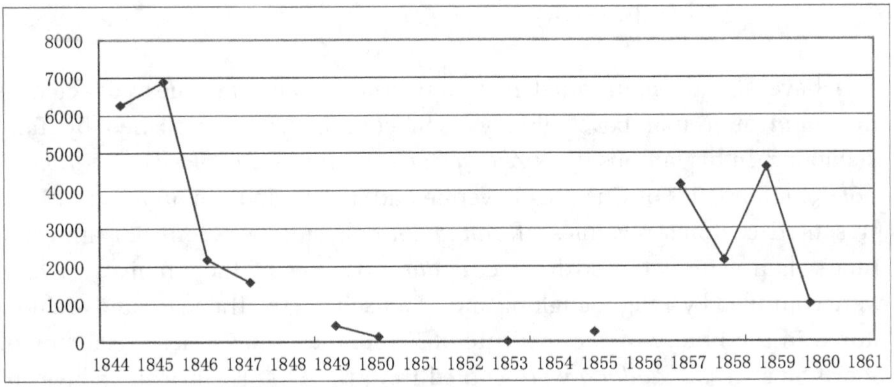

FIGURE 6.3 *Tax revenue trends of Zhehai Yangguan, 1844–1861*

6.4 Xiamen and Fuzhou Yangguan (1844–1861)

Under the provisions of the Sino-British Treaty of Nanjing, Xiamen and Fuzhou were opened to trade with the West in 1844. As in the case of Zhehai Yangguan, these two treaty ports adopted the same periods of taxation as Yuehai Guan. Consequently, two entries of tax data were made for 1846.

As one can see in Figure 6.4, customs duties colleceted at Xianmen and Fuzhou Yangguan enjoyed an extremely steep increase from 1853 onwards.

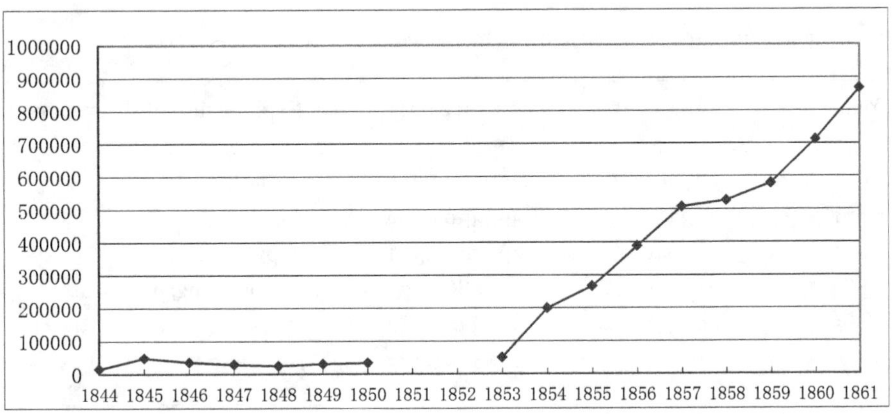

FIGURE 6.4 *Tax revenue trends of Xianmen and Fuzhou Yangguan, 1844–1861*

6.5 *Yangguan* (after 1861)

As I have already mentioned in Chapter 1, customs revenues collected at *Yangguan* after 1861 have already been compiled and published by Tang Xianglong. In his famous book *Zhong Guo Jin Dai Hai Guan He Fen Pei Tong Ji: 1861–1910* (Statistics of Customs Revenue and its Distribution: 1861–1910), Tang presented customs revenues of *Yangguan* collected between 1861 and 1910. Tang's data were gathered from *Chaodang* (Copies of the Archives), which were compiled by Tang Xianglong and other scholars in the 1930s and are now stored in the library of the Institute of Economics, the Chinese Academy of Social Sciences. *Chaodang* were copied from the First Historical Archives of China (Beijing), including Palace Midrange Rescript Memorials (ZPZZ), and Extra Copies of Grand Council Memorials (LFZZ). Somehow some of the original documents have been lost and *Chaodang* have become an "original" source in themselves. Nonetheless, for a variety of reasons there are still some mistakes in the data published in Tang's book.

Tang's book lists 30 *Yangguan* for the period 1861 to 1910, and since the volume of data is so huge, I cannot discuss the mistakes in his book one by one. Here I will use data for Jianghai Yangguan to illustrate the sorts of inaccuracies I have come across.

Jianghai Yangguan was the first and the biggest *Yangguan* that Tang treated in his book. The sources in the archive 3-4873-73 in LFZZ of FHAC contain its tax data for the period 17 August 1861 to 22 August 1866.

TABLE 6.2 *Tax revenue data of Jianghai Yangguan, 1861–1866 (in taels of silver)*

Year	Tang's data	Archive data	Explanation of discrepancy
1861	2072603	2072603.313	rounding
1862	3933305	3933304.704	rounding
1863	2926402	2927402.511	copying error
1864	2150662	2150662.993	no rounding, just omitted
1865	2233487	2233486.532	rounding
1866	2164052	2164051.573	rounding

Sources: archive 3-4873-73 in LFZZ of FHAC.

From Table 6.2 one can see that Tang's data for 1861–1862 and 1865–1866 are correct. The amount for 1864 would be higher by one tael if it was rounded up, while the data for 1863 should be 1,000 taels of silver higher to correct the copying error; if rounding up had been done properly the total amount would also be one tael higher.

Sources in the archive of 3-6330-26 in LFZZ contain data from the period 1873–1875.

TABLE 6.3 *Tax revenue data of Jianghai Yangguan, 1873–1875 (in taels of silver)*

Year	Tang's data	Archive data	Explanation of discrepancy
1873	3,294,165	3,294,164.507	rounding
1874	3,607,757	3,607,757.843	No rounding, just omitted
1875	3,610,700	3,608,000.269	copying mistake

Sources: archive 3-6330-26 in LFZZ of FHAC.

Sources in the archive 3-6339-40 in LFZZ contain revenue data from 1876, which in that year totalled 3,691,491.396 taels, but Tang's book reports an amount of 3,690,861 taels. The difference is so unusual that a rounding error cannot be the cause. The data for that year can be split up into seven parts, each one accounting for a different source of duty: Chinese import and export duties (CIED); foreign import and export duties (FIED); foreign traders' reimport half duties (FTRHD); mainland half duties (MHD); Chinese ship tax (CST); foreign ship tax (FST); and foreign traders' opium tax (FTOT).

TABLE 6.4 *Tax revenue data of Jianghai Yangguan in 1876 (in taels of silver)*

Name	Tang's data	Archive data	Explanation of discrepancy
CIED	12,550	12,550.199	rounding
FIED	2,193,325	2,193,325.161	rounding
TTRHD	163,362	163,361.858	rounding
MHD	349,848	349,848.032	rounding
CST	2,185	2,815.216	copying error
FST	105,968	105,967.502	rounding
FTOT	750,623	750,623.428	rounding

Sources: archive 3-6339-40 in LFZZ of FHAC.

The overview provided by Table 6.4 offers a clue to the unusal discrepancy for 1876: the difference between 3,691,491.396 taels (correct amount) and 3,690,861 taels (incorrect amount) arose because the actual CST of 2,815 taels was incorrectly copied as 2,185 taels of silver.

A similar mistake affects the revenue data of 1882. The archive (3-6349-78, LFZZ) amount was 4,350,181.136 taels, but Tang reports this to be 4,349,682 taels. A mistake was made when copying Foreign Import and Export Duties (FIED): it should be 203,941.274 taels, while Tang's book shows it to be 203,441 taels of silver. This mistake is reflected as a discrepancy in the total.

According to the archive's records (3-6353-35, LFZZ), revenue data for 1884 should be 3,819,202.223 taels, while Tang reports it to be 3,819,195, a difference of 7 taels. How could that be? After checking the sources in the archive, I found that foreign trader's opium tax (FTOT) should be 966,086.126 taels, but in Tang's book it is incorrectly put at 966,081 taels, a difference of 5 taels of silver. At the same time, Chinese ship tax (CST) was 10,801.558 taels, which Tang omitted completely. Foreign import and export duties (FIED) were 123,710.67, but Tang omitted to round it up altogether. When all these errors are taken into account, the 7 taels of silver can be explained.

Some other cases of discrepancies between Tang's and archive data can be found in Table 6.5.

TABLE 6.5 *Tax revenue data of Jianghai Yangguan, 1879–1886 (in taels of silver)*

Year	Tang's data	Archive data	Explanation of discrepancy	Archive no.
1879	4,020,741	4,020,741.333	rounding	3-6346-64, LFZZ
1881	4,653,373	4,653,373.153	rounding	3-6349-78, LFZZ
1883	3,820,888	3,820,888.83	No rounding, just omitted	3-6351-30, LFZZ
1885	4,199,277	4,199,277.28	rounding	3-6357-55, LFZZ
1886	4,546,976	4,547,976.217	copying error	3-6361-13, LFZZ

These mistakes listed in Table 6.5 are similar to the ones I have just discussed. To summarize, analysis of revenue data from Jianghai Yangguan in Tang's book does contain several errors, mainly due to rounding, not rounding, omitting amounts or copying errors, or a combination of these.

With this approach in mind, I have revised the revenue data of other ports, in particular the data of Zhenjiang Yangguan (1875-188, 1882, 1884–1886),

Hangzhou Yangguan (1897–1898), Zhehai Yangguan (1865-68, 1871–1872, 1874–1876, 1878–1880, 1882, 1884–1886, 1897–1898), Minhai Yangguan (1872, 1875, 1877–1880, 1882–1887), Taiwan Yangguan (1871, 1875, 1877–1879, 1881–1886, 1888–1892), Yuehai Yangguan (1905), Yuezhou Yangguan (1906–1907), Shashi Yangguan (1897–1899, 1902, 1904–1907), Yichang Yangguan (1889–1890, 1892, 1894–1895, 1898–1900, 1902–1905), Chongqing Yangguan (1906), Wuzhou Yangguan (1898, 1901, 1903–1907), Zhennan Yangguan (1894–1895, 1897–1900, 1902, 1904–1906), Mengzi Yangguan (1891–1892, 1895, 1897–1901, 1903–1907), Simao Yangguan (1892, 1895, 1897–1901, 1903–1907), and Tengyue Yangguan (1902–1906).

Some of the differences between them are rather large. For example, customs revenues for Zhenjiang Yangguan in 1884 were 148,415.257 taels, but Tang copied this by mistake as 148,445. Similarly, customs revenues for Yuezhou Yangguan in 1907 should be 20,425 taels instead of the incorrect 20,465 taels; Yichang Yangguan in 1890 should be 207,418.098 taels instead of the incorrect 207,488; Minhai Yangguan in 1872 should be 2,293,308.047 taels instead of the incorrect 2,293,208; and Taiwan Yangguan in 1891 should be 1,089,846.438 taels instead of the incorrect 1,089,447.

The material in the archive (3-6418-16, LFZZ) suggests that the Chinese import and export duties (CIED) of Wuzhou Yangguan in 1901 should have been 192,658.522 taels, but Tang's book incorrectly reports them to have been 192,699 taels of silver. The data of Wuzhou Yangguan in 1901 of 336,033 taels should be 335,993.47.

Furthermore, according to the archives (3-6443-28, 3-6450-20, LFZZ), customs duties from Mengzi Yangguan in 1906 and 1907 were 288,976.484 and 225,466.683 taels, respectively, but in Tang's book they were incorrectly reported to be 289,046 and 225,967 taels of silver. After closer examination I found that Tang had counted the native opium tax of 70 taels and 500 taels twice for these two respective years.

According to the reports in the archives *Guang Xu Chao Zhu Pi Zou Zhe* [Palace Midrange Rescript Memorials of the Guangxu Reign, edited by the First Historical Archives of China (Beijing), Beijing: Zhonghua Bookstore, 1995, page 854], tax revenues for Zhehai Yangguan in 1897 and 1898 were 1,022,547 and 702,028 taels of silver, respectively, but Tang's book reports these to be 1,022,908 and 702,029 taels.

Table 6.6 presents an overview of the differences between customs revenues as reported in archived material and the amounts noted by Tang in his book.

TABLE 6.6 *Tax revenue data of* Yangguan, *1861–1910 (in taels of silver)*

Year	Tang's book	Archives	Discrepancy	Year	Tang's book	Archives'	Discrepancy
1861	5,036,371	5,036,371	0	1886	15,263,475	15,263,475	0
1862	7,559,870	7,559,870	0	1887	20,081,682	18,447,644	1,634,038
1863	8,556,476	8,557,477	-1,001	1888	23,094,267	23,094,267	0
1864	8,377,014	8,377,015	-1	1889	21,929,723	21,929,721	2
1865	7,937,975	7,937,974	1	1890	21,984,309	21,984,239	70
1866	8,906,692	8,906,691	1	1891	23,126,136	23,126,536	-400
1867	8,927,309	8,927,310	-1	1892	22,808,391	22,808,397	-6
1868	9,887,484	9,887,485	-1	1893	22,066,185	22,066,185	0
1869	9,631,531	9,631,531	0	1894	22,797,364	22,797,028	336
1870	9,760,247	9,760,247	0	1895	20,984,970	20,985,110	-140
1871	10,717,471	10,717,470	1	1896	22,040,654	22,040,654	0
1872	11,605,818	11,605,919	-101	1897	22,672,911	22,672,550	361
1873	11,181,872	11,181,872	0	1898	21,828,055	21,828,054	1
1874	11,910,223	11,910,224	-1	1899	26,015,231	26,015,232	-1
1875	12,171,811	12,169,112	2,699	1900	24,090,590	24,090,590	0
1876	12,572,216	12,572,847	-631	1901	23,923,670	23,923,631	39
1877	12,293,699	12,293,700	-1	1902	28,377,186	28,377,190	-4
1878	12,455,213	12,455,212	1	1903	30,423,243	30,423,205	38
1879	13,196,197	13,196,197	0	1904	30,206,504	30,206,506	-2
1880	14,346,406	14,346,406	0	1905	32,675,574	32,675,574	0
1881	15,052,722	15,052,722		1906	34,968,046	34,967,986	60
1882	14,488,272	14,488,772	-500	1907	33,198,319	33,197,778	541
1883	13,603,926	13,603,925	1	1908	32,930,162	32,930,162	0
1884	13,738,336	13,738,314	22	1909	33,205,087	33,205,087	0
1885	14,178,227	14,178,229	-2	1910	34,518,859	34,518,859	0

Although, as Table 6.6 shows, Tang's book does contain some errors, it is still reliable and by and large useful. I have supplemented his data with my corrected data to arrive at amounts of tax revenues.

6.6 Brief Summary

Tang's research demonstrates that during the late Qing *Yangguan* levied seven different kinds of duty. Chinese import and export duties (CIED), for example, was a category of duty that had its origins in the Sino-British Treaty of Nanjing, signed in 1842. It stipulated that all taxable goods would attract customs duty of 5 of their value. Later, several adjustments were made to this, bringing the real rate of taxation down to about 3—among the lowest rates of taxation in the world. This lasted until 1901, when as a result of the Boxer Protocol the real rate of taxation increased to 5.[11]

A second kind of duty was the Foreign Opium Tax (FOT). Originating from the Treaty of Tianjin in 1858, it required that all imported opium was to attract a duty of 30 taels of silver per 50 kg of opium.[12] Mainland Half Duties (MHD), a third kind of duty, was created to counterbalance the effects of Likin. After the introduction of Likin in the late Qing it became difficult for foreigners to trade in China since many different kinds of Likin could be levied and they could be imposed anywhere and everywhere. In order to reduce the tax burden this created, the Treaty of Tianjin stipulated that foreign goods were to be taxed at a rate of 2.5% of the value, but after that they would not have to pay Likin.[13]

Another, fourth, kind of duty was Foreign Trader's Reimport Half Duties (FTRHD), which was introduced in 1861. In general, only Chinese citizens could trade on the mainland. If after importation a foreigner's goods were transported within China they would attract FTRHD, which like MHD was 2.5% of the value.[14]

A fifth kind of duty was Foreign Opium Likin Duties (FOLD), which was introduced in 1858: in addition to the 30 taels of silver levied as FOT, all imported opium was to be taxed a further 80 taels of silver per 50 kg.[15] Native Opium Duties and Likin Duties (NODLD), a sixth kind, which was introduced in 1887, levied duty on native (non-imported) opium at the rate of 110 taels of silver per 50 kg, i.e. the same combined rate as for imported (foreign) opium.[16]

Finally, the seventh kind of duty was Chinese Ship Tax (CST), which was based on the draft of a ship's hull. Originating from the Sino-British Treaty of Nanjing in 1842, for ships of 150 tons or more it was levied at the rate of 0.5 taels of silver per ton, and for ships lighter than 150 tons at the rate of 1 tael per ton. In 1858 the rate was changed to 0.4 taels of silver for ships of 150 tons or more; the rate for lighter ships remained at 1 tael per ton.[17]

---

11 Tang (2005), p. 14.
12 Tang (2005), p. 15.
13 Tang (2005), p. 15.
14 Tang (2005), p. 16.
15 Tang (2005), p. 17.
16 Tang (2005), p. 17.
17 Tang (2005), p. 18.

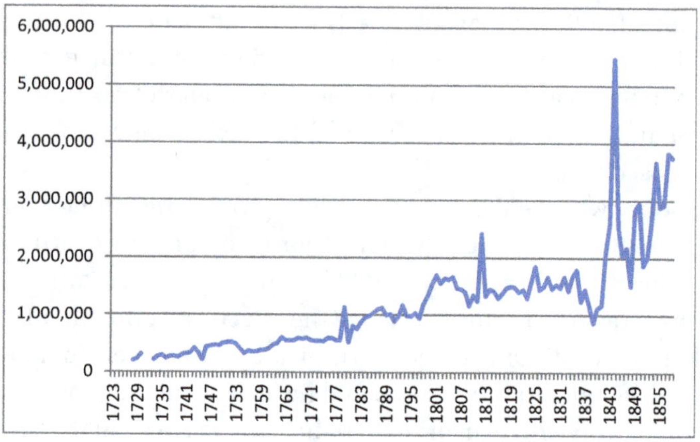

FIGURE 6.5a
Tax revenue trends of Yangguan, 1723–1860

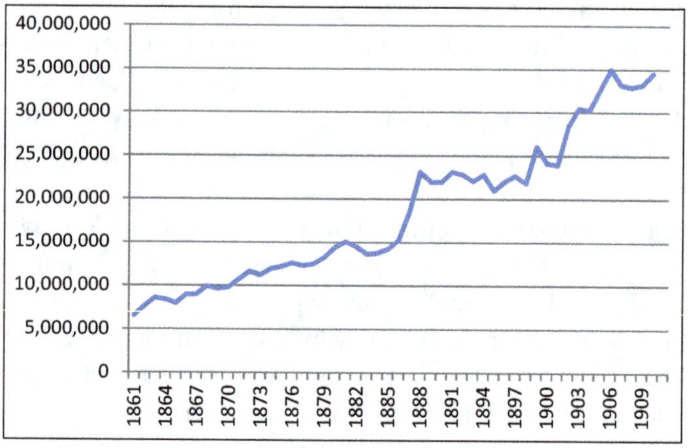

FIGURE 6.5b
Tax revenue trends of Yangguan 1861–1911

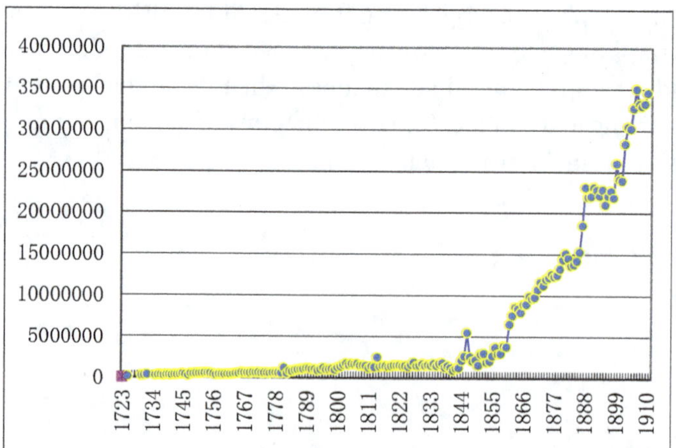

FIGURE 6.5c
Tax revenue trends of Yangguan, 1723–1911

The trends in tax revenues collected at *Yangguan* throughout the Qing dynasty are shown in Figures 6.5a, 6.5b, and 6.5c.

One can see from Figure 6.5a that there was a sharp increase in annual tax revenues before 1861, growing from less than 1,000,000 to 4,000,000 taels of silver. And, of course, the highest point was reached in 1846, the year in which there were two entries of tax data. Tax revenues were also a little higher in 1781 and 1814 as there were two entries of tax data for Yuehai Guan in those years. After 1861, annual customs revenues increased even faster than before, growing from 5,000,000 to 35,000,000 taels of silver. Such growth was, of course, to have a profound impact on the fiscal structure of Qing finances.

CHAPTER 7

Customs Duties and the Economy

7.1 *Changguan* and *Yangguan*

As I explained in the Introduction, in my study I have divided customs duties into two sorts: those collected at *Changguan* (ports and gates serving domestic trade); and those collected at *Yangguan* (ports serving foreign trade). Drawing on the revenue data presented in the Appendices, I have compiled Table 7.1, which summarizes the data on customs revenues collected during the Qing dynasty.

TABLE 7.1 *Customs revenues collected at* Changguan *and* Yangguan *during the Qing dynasty (in taels of silver)*

Year	*Changguan* Taxed amount	*Changguan* with missing	*Yangguan* Taxed amount data added[a]	Total taxed amount	Total with missing data added[a]
1723	175,095	3,211,753.6	–	175,095	3,211,754
1724	439,454.1	3,135,668.8	–	439,454.1	3,135,669
1725	779,876.8	3,236,678.5	97,294.56	877,171.3	3,333,973
1726	802,846.2	3,249,121.3	–	802,846.2	3,249,121
1727	847,448.5	3,423,694	–	847,448.5	3,423,694
1728	1,157,390	3,278,724.4	–	1,157,390	3,278,724
1729	861,575.9	3,375,394.7	–	861,575.9	3,375,395
1730	1,429,467	3,373,984.5	198,062.09	1,627,529	3,572,047
1731	787,349.8	3,390,198.7	228,659.7	1,016,009	3,618,858
1732	1,270,733	3,524,056.2	309,107.92	1,579,841	3,833,164
1733	1,768,135	3,803,698.3	–	1,768,135	3,803,698
1734	1,776,623	3,959,971.5	–	1,776,623	3,959,972
1735	3,476,388	3,905,231.3	216,000	3,692,388	4,121,231
1736	3,359,946	3,867,597.2	271,953.53	3,631,900	4,139,551
1737	3,153,387	3,942,507.7	285,154.91	3,438,542	4,227,663
1738	2,854,240	3,672,099.6	234,059.5	3,088,300	3,906,159
1739	3,089,173	3,642,089	270,620.84	3,359,794	3,912,710
1740	2,797,761	3,939,307.4	269,454.96	3,067,216	4,208,762
1741	3,265,201	3,919,456.1	252,606.05	3,517,807	4,172,062

 | DOI 10.1163/9789004324886_009

Year	*Changguan* Taxed amount	*Changguan* with missing data added[a]	*Yangguan* Taxed amount	Total taxed amount	Total with missing data added[a]
1742	3,450,161	3,964,822.7	296,920.9	3,747,082	4,261,744
1743	3,326,543	3,973,903	317,168.68	3,643,712	4,291,072
1744	3,584,946	4,019,034.6	328,776	3,913,722	4,347,811
1745	3,826,590	4,196,302.2	415,143	4,241,733	4,611,445
1746	3,374,869	3,840,106	339,618	3,714,487	4,179,724
1747	3,272,534	3,688,489.8	216,023	3,488,557	3,904,513
1748	4,610,790	5,034,433.4	435,080	5,045,870	5,469,513
1749	3,687,158	4,208,385.1	447,420.2	4,134,579	4,655,805
1750	3,854,776	4,469,334.8	467,562.5	4,322,339	4,936,897
1751	3,412,734	4,262,770.5	461,795	3,874,529	4,724,566
1752	4,258,399	4,609,154.8	503,303.8	4,761,703	5,112,459
1753	4,223,374	4,469,623.5	514,800	4,738,174	4,984,423
1754	3,841,688	4,196,768.5	515,300	4,356,988	4,712,068
1755	4,111,807	4,506,797.6	486,285.8	4,598,092	4,993,083
1756	4,271,902	4,509,537.6	405,009	4,676,911	4,914,547
1757	3,422,668	3,981,974.9	320,551	3,743,219	4,302,526
1758	3,551,367	4,014,685.8	370,071.31	3,921,438	4,384,757
1759	4,361,586	4,498,307.5	354,694.72	4,716,281	4,853,002
1760	4,284,768	4,531,262.7	356,266.54	4,641,035	4,887,529
1761	4,048,835	4,530,726.6	382,634.39	4,431,470	4,913,361
1762	4,283,958	4,498,885.8	382,652.51	4,666,610	4,881,538
1763	4,408,474	4,632,942.7	411,636.51	4,820,110	5,044,579
1764	4,485,854	4,734,194	474,412.79	4,960,267	5,208,607
1765	4,824,377	4,976,632.1	505,138.77	5,329,516	5,481,771
1766	4,443,153	4,753,434.2	600,120.81	5,043,274	5,353,555
1767	5,361,170	5,744,811.6	546,930.69	5,908,100	6,291,742
1768	4,027,854	4,520,327.5	547,737.68	4,575,591	5,068,065
1769	4,322,051	4,576,179.9	549,194.82	4,871,245	5,125,375
1770	4,942,461	5,399,645.2	591,067.35	5,533,528	5,990,713
1771	4,489,058	4,703,321.5	579,935.97	5,068,994	5,283,257
1772	4,459,563	4,668,252.5	593,869.71	5,053,433	5,262,122
1773	4,868,521	5,096,592.5	554,903.08	5,423,424	5,651,496
1774	4,909,152	5,018,753.2	541,553.19	5,450,706	5,560,306
1775	4,573,637	4,712,744.7	541,863.7	5,115,501	5,254,608
1776	4,530,297	4,886,863.9	533,178.41	5,063,475	5,420,042
1777	4,854,315	4,988,264.5	588,407.97	5,442,723	5,576,672

TABLE 7.1 *Customs revenues collected at Changguan and Yangguan* (cont.)

Year	*Changguan* Taxed amount	*Changguan* with missing data added[a]	*Yangguan* Taxed amount	Total taxed amount	Total with missing data added[a]
1778	4,496,971	4,714,477.8	588,453.97	5,085,425	5,302,932
1779	4,525,366	4,597,389.6	556,185.1	5,081,551	5,153,575
1780	4,494,464	4,929,295.8	556,233.94	5,050,698	5,485,530
1781	5,683,362	5,791,801	1130,684.5	6,814,047	6,922,485
1782	4,210,507	4,776,014.9	521,110.55	4,731,617	5,297,125
1783	4,402,590	4,803,335.8	797,861.57	5,200,451	5,601,197
1784	4,401,898	4,941,700.4	748,125.72	5,150,024	5,689,826
1785	4,045,273	4,601,567.6	872,150.91	4,917,424	5,473,718
1786	3,781,426	4,336,708.3	953,960.66	4,735,387	5,290,669
1787	4,062,671	4,349,315.4	981,686.31	5,044,358	5,331,002
1788	4,429,020	4,609,040.4	1,036,999.3	5,466,019	5,646,040
1789	4,883,279	5,444,405.3	1,101,362	5,984,641	6,545,767
1790	4,471,226	4,906,151.2	1,127,562.9	5,598,789	6,033,714
1791	4,649,298	4,812,745	995,882.52	5,645,181	5,808,628
1792	4,922,088	5,053,514.4	1,011,426.3	5,933,514	6,064,941
1793	4,429,746	4,548,191.5	885,612.8	5,315,359	5,433,804
1794	4,385,120	4,534,930.1	972,948.5	5,358,069	5,507,879
1795	3,889,343	4,541,496.8	1,171,911	5,061,254	5,713,408
1796	4,105,194	4,279,912.8	981,186.69	5,086,380	5,261,099
1797	4,142,212	4,315,003.7	973,172.98	5,115,385	5,288,177
1798	3,808,441	4,074,699.5	1,035,757.5	4,844,198	5,110,457
1799	3,934,494	4,247,623	937,073	4,871,567	5,184,696
1800	4,692,430	5,111,177.7	1,201,246.5	5,893,676	6,312,424
1801	3,331,307	4,258,902.8	1,336,171.8	4,667,479	5,595,075
1802	3,934,812	4,287,650.5	1,540,773.1	5,475,585	5,828,424
1803	4,143,604	4,647,897.1	1,695,389	5,838,993	6,343,286
1804	4,224,830	4,276,438	1,555,586.4	5,780,416	5,832,024
1805	4,309,959	4,431,512.9	1,641,971.8	5,951,931	6,073,485
1806	3,725,495	3,953,921	1,621,376	5,346,871	5,575,297
1807	3,824,203	4,073,611.1	1,663,830	5,488,033	5,737,441
1808	4,394,359	4,411,767.8	1,470,460.2	5,864,819	5,882,228
1809	4,097,684	4,300,111	1,457,201.8	5,554,886	5,757,313
1810	4,198,343	4,295,398.8	1,408,641.9	5,606,985	5,704,041
1811	3,823,611	4,066,343.6	1,165,263.1	4,988,874	5,231,607

Year	*Changguan* Taxed amount	*Changguan* with missing	*Yangguan* Taxed amount data added[a]	Total taxed amount	Total with missing data added[a]
1812	3,802,296	4,026,879.3	1,347,936.9	5,150,233	5,374,816
1813	3,834,350	4,160,078.9	1,246,708.2	5,081,058	5,406,787
1814	4,552,177	4,602,858.4	2,420,719.5	6,972,896	7,023,578
1815	3,872,834	4,105,222.8	1,331,239.9	5,204,074	5,436,463
1816	3,608,316	4,226,404.8	1,446,980	5,055,296	5,673,385
1817	3,850,449	4,265,727.9	1,421,303.8	5,271,753	5,687,032
1818	4,061,151	4,202,527	1,302,911	5,364,062	5,505,438
1819	4,381,216	4,478,290.7	1,380,097.1	5,761,313	5,858,388
1820	3,957,579	4,027,618.1	1,479,820.1	5,437,399	5,507,438
1821	3,707,677	4,045,148	1,497,022.5	5,204,699	5,542,171
1822	4,582,059	4,720,638.3	1,485,146.8	6,067,206	6,205,785
1823	3,809,708	3,981,066.6	1,404,913.2	5,214,621	5,385,980
1824	4,012,056	4,367,917.8	1,444,322.6	5,456,378	5,812,240
1825	3,800,705	4,033,414.7	1,298,829	5,099,534	5,332,244
1826	3,387,753	4,068,137.6	1,576,637.2	4,964,390	5,644,775
1827	3,395,334	4,178,583.3	1,850,046	5,245,380	6,028,629
1828	3,945,040	4,167,454.3	1,441,924.6	5,386,965	5,609,379
1829	4,001,500	4,194,929.6	1,499,580.7	5,501,080	5,694,510
1830	4,002,701	4,343,302.7	1,663,635	5,666,335	6,006,938
1831	3,401,558	3,953,880.7	1,461,806.2	4,863,364	5,415,687
1832	4,267,347	4,821,474.5	1,532,933.2	5,800,280	6,354,408
1833	3,383,615	3,697,609.9	1,477,846.3	4,861,461	5,175,456
1834	3,729,903	3,837,796.5	1,669,712.6	5,399,615	5,507,509
1835	4,100,031	4,392,103.8	1,424,944.2	5,524,976	5,817,048
1836	3,533,896	4,082,922	1,674,851.7	5,208,747	5,757,774
1837	3,642,313	4,060,062.9	1,789,424.3	5,431,737	5,849,487
1838	4,086,221	4,194,119.8	1,242,044.2	5,328,265	5,436,164
1839	3,826,262	3,929,040.2	1,448,559	5,274,821	5,377,599
1840	3,883,113	3,989,197.5	1,186,551.9	5,069,665	5,175,749
1841	3,918,769	4,045,066.5	864,232.17	4,783,001	4,909,299
1842	3,187,345	3,474,314.4	1,115,742.4	4,303,088	4,590,057
1843	3,076,397	3,483,898.7	1,182,489	4,258,886	4,666,388
1844	3,396,893	3,669,176.5	2,094,559.3	5,491,452	5,763,736
1845	3,333,729	3,847,870.5	2,603,953.9	5,937,683	6,451,824
1846	3,880,028	4,277,447.4	5,463,200.3	9,343,229	9,740,648
1847	2,657,012	3,747,617.5	2,536,226.4	5,193,238	6,283,844

TABLE 7.1 *Customs revenues collected at Changguan and Yangguan* (cont.)

Year	*Changguan* Taxed amount	*Changguan* with missing	*Yangguan* Taxed amount data added[a]	Total taxed amount	Total with missing data added[a]
1848	3,225,211	3,870,426.3	2,036,630.6	5,261,842	5,907,057
1849	3,888,043	3,987,041.3	2,172,997	6,061,040	6,160,038
1850	3,001,639	3,898,583.2	1,510,670	4,512,309	5,409,253
1851	3,433,436	3,819,654	2,836,574.1	6,270,010	6,656,228
1852	2,891,320	3,494,146.8	2,950,189.6	5,841,509	6,444,336
1853	2,382,813	2,653,691.8	1,869,407.9	4,252,221	4,523,100
1854	1,445,569	1,794,557.2	2,012,310.4	3,457,879	3,806,868
1855	1,564,027	1,876,696.4	2,647,440.9	4,211,468	4,524,137
1856	1,783,961	2,197,318.1	3,671,426.1	5,455,387	5,868,744
1857	1,650,652	1,883,510	2,886,398.6	4,537,050	4,769,909
1858	1,666,072	1,950,502.7	2,917,287.8	4,583,360	4,867,790
1859	1,680,141	2,057,870.2	3,831,183.8	5,511,325	5,889,054
1860	2,005,045	2,350,975.8	3,752,330.5	5,757,375	6,103,306
1861	1,375,014	1,576,966.1	6,510,065.6	7,885,080	8,087,032
1862	1,369,924	1,572,975.3	7,559,870	8,929,794	9,132,845
1863	1,562,564	1,868,521.4	8,557,477	10,120,041	10,425,998
1864	1,827,799	2,053,881	8,377,015	10,204,814	10,430,896
1865	1,867,277	2,079,909.2	7,937,974	9,805,251	10,017,883
1866	1,862,089	2,056,248.3	8,906,691	10,768,780	10,962,939
1867	1,891,568	2,171,095.4	8,927,310	10,818,878	11,098,405
1868	2,173,452	2,403,405.3	9,887,485	12,060,937	12,290,890
1869	2,060,005	2,339,699.1	9,631,531	11,691,536	11,971,230
1870	1,777,884	2,293,947.1	9,760,247	11,538,131	12,054,194
1871	2,007,061	2,331,883.6	10,717,470	12,724,531	13,049,354
1872	2,200,618	2,403,440.8	11,605,919	13,806,537	14,009,360
1873	2,157,054	2,396,488.5	11,181,872	13,338,926	13,578,360
1874	1,978,120	2,373,542.4	11,910,224	13,888,344	14,283,766
1875	1,958,529	2,393,919.9	12,169,112	14,127,641	14,563,032
1876	2,290,617	2,530,101.1	12,572,847	14,863,464	15,102,948
1877	2,343,364	2,541,450.2	12,293,700	14,637,064	14,835,150
1878	2,232,407	2,435,614.4	12,455,212	14,687,619	14,890,826
1879	2,858,386	3,101,585	13,196,197	16,054,583	16,297,782
1880	2,329,924	2,550,481.9	14,346,406	16,676,330	16,896,888
1881	2,308,991	2,552,189.5	15,052,722	17,361,713	17,604,912

Year	*Changguan* Taxed amount	*Changguan* with missing	*Yangguan* Taxed amount data added[a]	Total taxed amount	Total with missing data added[a]
1882	2,320,521	2,563,720	14,488,772	16,809,293	17,052,492
1883	2,295,812	2,499,019.3	13,603,925	15,899,737	16,102,944
1884	2,448,123	2,651,329.9	13,738,314	16,186,437	16,389,644
1885	2,193,896	2,477,791.2	14,178,229	16,372,125	16,656,020
1886	2,266,249	2,614,431.8	15,264,476	17,530,725	17,878,908
1887	2,368,705	2,672,883.2	18,447,644	20,816,349	21,120,527
1888	2,437,561	2,620,768.1	23,094,267	25,531,828	25,715,035
1889	2,378,190	2,585,903.2	21,929,721	24,307911	24,515,624
1890	2,818,237	3,170,016.2	21,984,239	24,802,476	25,154,255
1891	2,271,314	2,522,696.2	23,126,536	25,397,850	25,649,232
1892	2,556,720	2,757,912.2	22,808,397	25,365,117	25,566,309
1893	1,875,289	2,416,045.8	22,066,185	23,941,474	24,482,231
1894	2,237,431	2,443,221	22,797,028	25,034,459	25,240,249
1895	2,068,088	2,273,878	20,985,110	23,053,198	23,258,988
1896	2,138,192	2,381,577.8	22,040,654	24,178,846	24,422,232
1897	2,207,742	2,433,566.4	22,672,550	24,880,292	25,106,116
1898	2,128,385	2,462,763.1	21,828,054	23,956,439	24,290,817
1899	2,071,633	2,418,037.6	26,015,232	28,086,865	28,433,270
1900	2,293,039	2,580,640.1	24,090,590	26,383,629	26,671,230
1901	1,719,953	2,274,796.7	23,923,631	25,643,584	26,198,428
1902	2,269,038	2,956,632	28,377,190	30,646,228	31,333,822
1903	2,618,226	3,691,562.2	30,423,205	33,041,431	34,114,767
1904	2,561,707	3,614,061.6	30,206,506	32,768,213	33,820,568
1905	3,661,895	4,701,375.7	32,675,574	36,337,469	37,376,950
1906	2,912,488	4,142,801.3	34,967,986	37,880,474	39,110,787
1907	2,473,818	3,990,568.2	33,197,778	35,671,596	37,188,346
1908	2,335,880	4,196,506.5	32,930,162	35,266,042	37,126,668
1909	1,831,971	4,615,162.4	33,205,087	35,037,058	37,820,249
1910	169,413	4,519,541.6	34,518,859	34,688,272	39,038,401
1911	–	4,519,541.6	–	–	–

[a] Missing revenue data for *Changguan* calculated by extrapolating missing values from surrounding data points.

I have used the data summarized in Table 7.1 to plot customs revenues collected during the Qing against the dimension of time. Figures 7.1a to 7.1d show revenues collected at *Changguan* during the Qing; note that customs revenues collected at Yuehai Guan before 1861 are not included in these figures.

In general, these figures show that customs revenues at *Changguan* increased steeply during the reigns of Yongzheng and Qianlong, in step with the development of economic activity and expansion of the population. During the reigns of Jiaqing and Daoguang, however, revenue levels at *Changguan* were very stable, only dropping during the First Opium War. In the late Qing, revenues collected at *Changguan* dropped sharply during the Taiping Rebellion and recovered only gradually in the years that followed. In 1905 they reached a peak as a result of policy adjustments to customs policy that were

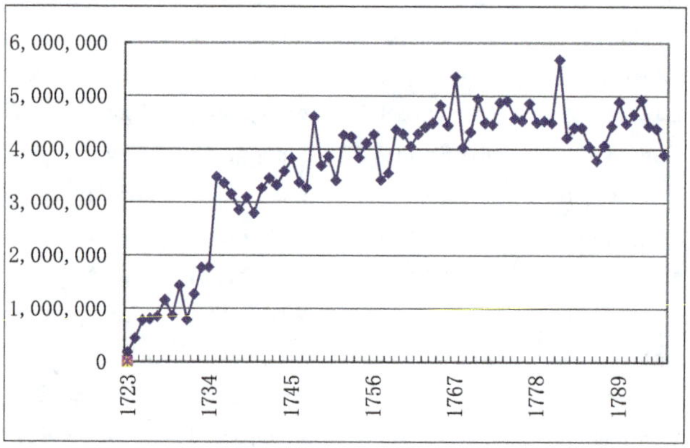

FIGURE 7.1a *Tax revenue trends of Changguan, 1723–1795*

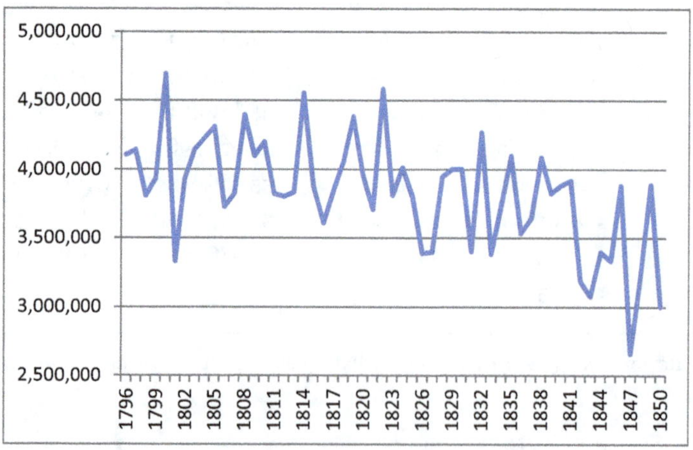

FIGURE 7.1b *Tax revenue trends of Changguan, 1795–1850*

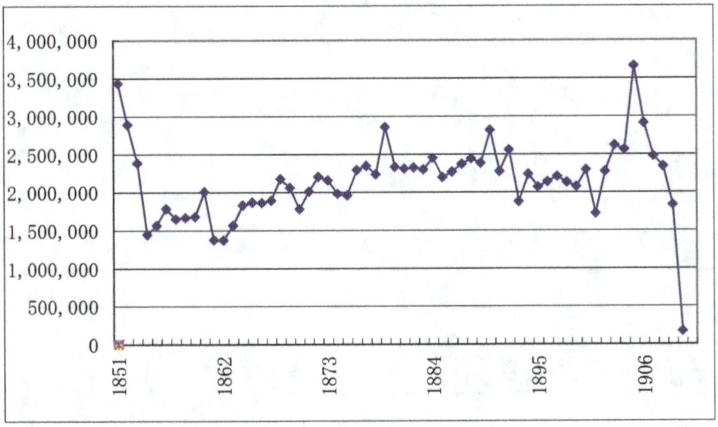

FIGURE 7.1c *Tax revenue trends of Changguan, 1851–1911*

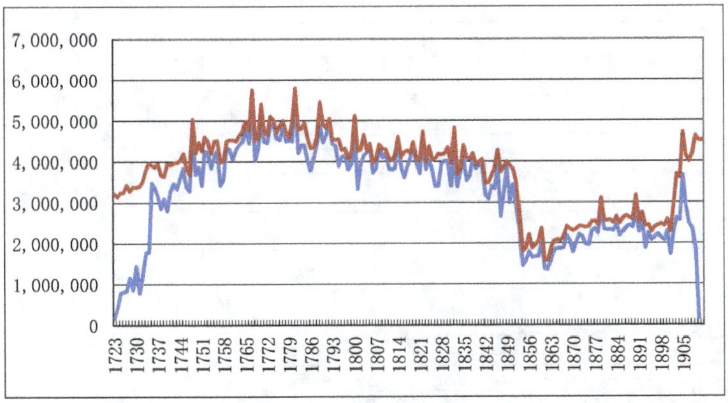

Note: The blue line represents data points reported in the archives; the red line represents data points from the archives to which have been added data for years that are missing.

FIGURE 7.1d *Tax revenue trends of Changguan, 1723–1911*

introduced. It is due to the Boxer Protocol that many data are missing after 1902. The drop shown in the figures at this time is most likely spurious: if the data were available, the figure would probably show that *Changguan* had increased further still. Nevertheless, on the whole, from 1850 onwards there was a decline, for the most part strongly connected to the rising influence of *Yangguan*.

In Chapter 6, I have discussed the trends of Yangguan in detail between 1723–1911 and before 1840, when Yuehai Guan was the only port to tax foreign goods. In Figre 7.2 I plot the trend after 1840 when more new ports were established allowed to tax foreign imports.

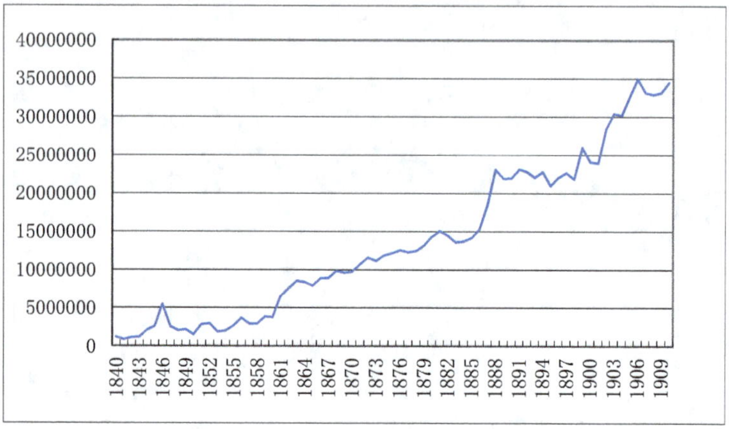

FIGURE 7.2 *Tax revenue trends of Yangguan, 1840–1911*

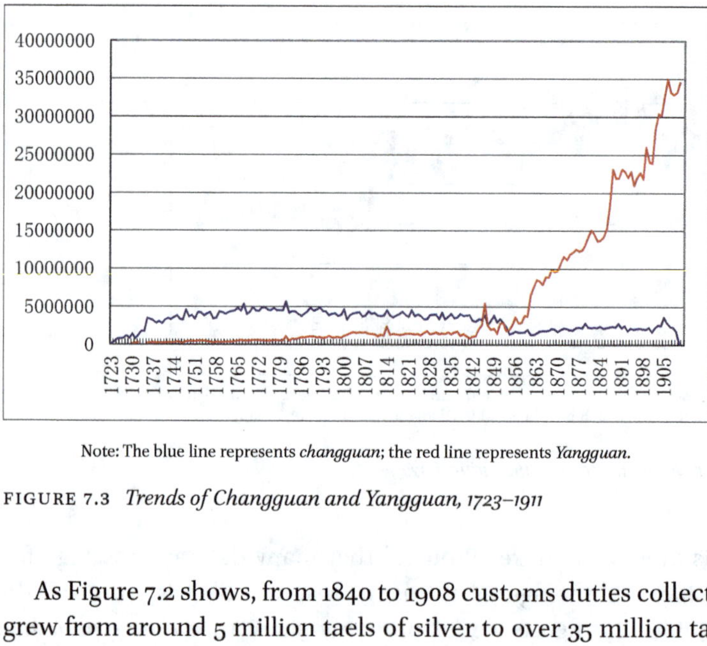

Note: The blue line represents *changguan*; the red line represents *Yangguan*.

FIGURE 7.3 *Trends of Changguan and Yangguan, 1723–1911*

As Figure 7.2 shows, from 1840 to 1908 customs duties collected at *Yangguan* grew from around 5 million taels of silver to over 35 million taels, i.e. a seven-fold increase.

A comparison of *Changguan* and *Yangguan* revenues with the data I collected from the archives is shown in Figure 7.3.

As the plotted data in Figure 7.3 clearly show, the period 1840–1850 was a turning point for customs revenues. Before then, revenues from *Changguan* (i.e. *Changguan*) were higher than those from *Yangguan*, while afterwards revenues from *Yangguan* (i.e. *Yangguan*) were higher. Figure 7-4 compares customs revenues from *Changguan* and *Yangguan* for the period before 1850.

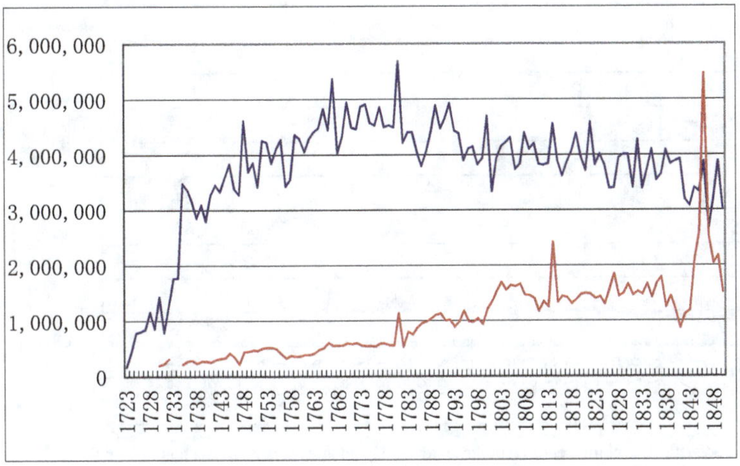

Note: The blue line represents *changguan*; the red line represents *Yangguan*.

FIGURE 7.4 *Trends of Changguan and Yangguan, 1723–1850*

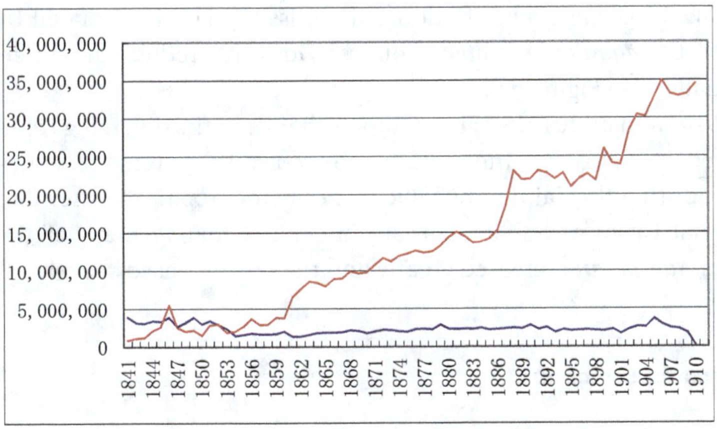

Note: The blue line represents *changguan*; the red line represents *Yangguan*.

FIGURE 7.5 *Trends of Changguan and Yangguan, 1841–1911*

Clearly, before 1840 tax revenues were for the most part derived from *Changguan*. Although a gradual increase in revenues from *Yangguan* was underway, taken over the whole period *Changguan* was still much larger than *Yangguan*, except in 1846, when owing to use of the Chinese lunar year there were two data entries at Yuhei Guan.

Figure 7.5 clearly illustrates how, after 1850, *Yangguan* overshadowed *Changguan* and that the differences between the two became larger and larger

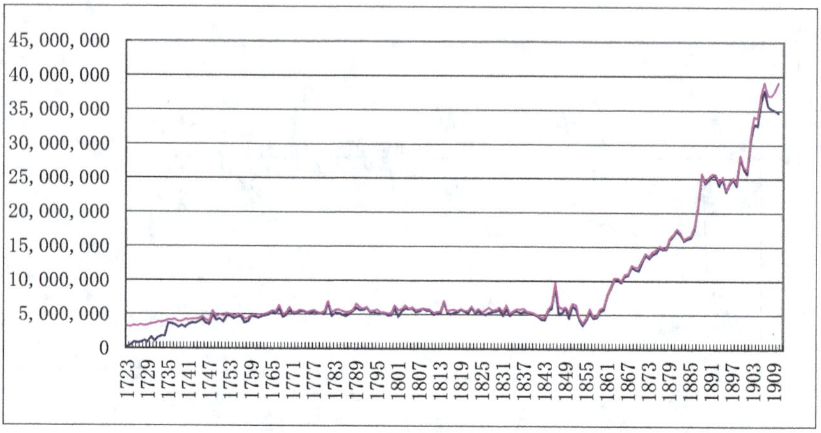

Note: The blue line represents data points reported in the archives; the red line represents data points from the archives to which have been added data for years that are missing.

FIGURE 7.6 *Trends of estimated Changguan with Yangguan, 1723–1911*

with time. But what is the effect of adding the missing data I estimated by extrapolation to *Changguan* customs revenues? Does this reduce the differences substantially? See Figure 7.6.

As Figure 7.6 demonstrates, there is not much change in the diverging trend already observed in Figure 7.5: the enormous increase in customs revenues after 1850, even during the Taiping Rebellion, is only too apparent. After 1861 with the Imperial Customs Service coming under the management of the Western Powers, *Yangguan* increased greatly and the tax increased sharply.

7.2 *Huguan* and *Gongguan*

Changguan were were either *Huguan* and *Gongguan*, i.e. ports belonging to either the Ministry of Revenue (*Hubu*) or the Ministry of Works (*Gongbu*), respectively. In terms of revenue collected, was there a difference in performance between ports run by *Hubu* and those run by *Gongbu*?

In fact, *Hubu* clearly played a dominant role in the collection of customs duties. There were more than 46 customs ports in Qing China before 1850, and of these, only 16 of them were administered by *Gongbu*. According to *Daqing Huidian Shili* (Explanation of the rules of the Qing dynasty), *Gongguan* included Linqing in Sandong province, Longjiang in Jiangsu province, Wuhu in Anhui province, Nanxin in Zhejiang province, Jinzhou Guan in Hubei province, Chen Guan in Hu'nan province, and Yu Guan in Sichuan province;

the other *Gongguan* included Suqian (belonging to Huai'an Guan), Youzha (belonging to Yangzhou Guan), Tongyongdao, Pantaokou, Guobeikou in Zhili province and Shahukou Mushui, Shengjin Mushui, Jilin Mushui and Yili Mushui. In contrast, *Hubu* had more than 30 ports.

From records in the archives I have inspected, it is possible to estimate the contribution of *Huguan* and *Gongguan* to total customs revenue collected; see Table 7.2.

TABLE 7.2 *Customs revenues collected at* Huguan *and* Gongguan, *1723–1910* (*in taels of silver*)

Year	Huguan	Gongguan	Total Changguan	Contribution Huguan (%)	Contribution Gongguan (%)
1723	163,053.65	12,041.30	175,094.95	93	7
1724	439,454.08	–	439,454.08	100	–
1725	655,984.25	123,892.50	779,876.75	84	16
1726	668,862.67	133,983.52	802,846.19	83	17
1727	838,148.46	9,300.00	847,448.46	99	1
1728	1,144,989.60	12,400.00	1,157,389.60	99	1
1729	849,075.90	12,500.00	861,575.90	99	1
1730	1,246,442.60	183,024.49	1,429,467.10	87	13
1731	787,349.79	–	787,349.79	100	–
1732	1,242,497.60	28,235.73	1,270,733.30	98	2
1733	1,742,067.70	26,067.61	1,768,135.30	99	1
1734	1,732,425.40	44,198.07	1,776,623.40	98	2
1735	3,130,138.70	346,249.03	3,476,387.70	90	10
1736	3,066,973.80	292,972.53	3,359,946.40	91	9
1737	2,924,513.30	228,873.75	3,153,387.10	93	7
1738	2,644,698.20	209,541.86	2,854,240.10	93	7
1739	2,779,954.10	309,219.13	3,089,173.30	90	10
1740	2,448,295.50	349,465.92	2,797,761.50	88	12
1741	2,915,625.10	349,576.23	3,265,201.40	89	11
1742	3,053,472.00	396,689.10	3,450,161.10	89	11
1743	2,945,627.70	380,915.48	3,326,543.10	89	11
1744	3,209,707.30	375,238.25	3,584,945.50	90	10
1745	3,404,151.90	422,438.54	3,826,590.40	89	11
1746	2,970,923.90	403,945.40	3,374,869.30	88	12
1747	2,844,351.20	428,182.87	3,272,534.10	87	13
1748	4,051,041.70	559,748.09	4,610,789.80	88	12
1749	3,278,503.10	408,655.31	3,687,158.40	89	11

TABLE 7.2 *Customs revenues collected at* Huguan *and* Gongguan, *1723–1910* (cont.)

Year	Huguan	Gongguan	Total Changguan	Contribution Huguan (%)	Contribution Gongguan (%)
1750	3,540,930.90	313,845.46	3,854,776.30	92	8
1751	3,022,977.00	389,756.84	3,412,733.80	89	11
1752	3,855,767.60	402,631.68	4,258,399.30	91	9
1753	3,857,165.00	366,208.59	4,223,373.60	91	9
1754	3,461,026.70	380,661.40	3,841,688.10	90	10
1755	3,744,999.30	366,807.24	4,111,806.60	91	9
1756	3,890,292.90	381,608.88	4,271,901.70	91	9
1757	3,107,094.70	315,573.31	3,422,668.00	91	9
1758	3,235,226.40	316,140.61	3,551,367.00	91	9
1759	3,804,050.30	557,535.78	4,361,586.10	87	13
1760	3,853,507.40	431,261.00	4,284,768.40	90	10
1761	3,635,708.60	413,126.75	4,048,835.30	90	10
1762	3,847,651.10	436,306.48	4,283,957.50	90	10
1763	3,962,639.50	445,834.06	4,408,473.60	90	10
1764	4,101,109.20	384,745.19	4,485,854.40	91	9
1765	4,407,818.50	416,558.29	4,824,376.80	91	9
1766	4,011,465.00	431,688.21	4,443,153.20	90	10
1767	4,784,725.50	576,444.21	5,361,169.70	89	11
1768	3,635,221.80	392,631.90	4,027,853.70	90	10
1769	3,931,442.50	390,608.03	4,322,050.50	91	9
1770	4,552,038.80	390,422.17	4,942,461.00	92	8
1771	4,106,275.00	382,782.76	4,489,057.80	91	9
1772	4,060,411.80	399,151.40	4,459,563.20	91	9
1773	4,463,986.00	404,535.15	4,868,521.10	92	8
1774	4,484,077.10	425,075.30	4,909,152.40	91	9
1775	4,145,466.30	428,171.08	4,573,637.40	91	9
1776	4,115,062.60	415,234.37	4,530,296.90	91	9
1777	4,423,427.00	430,887.59	4,854,314.60	91	9
1778	4,064,272.70	432,698.28	4,496,971.00	90	10
1779	4,119,254.30	406,111.66	4,525,366.00	91	9
1780	4,083,779.50	410,684.93	4,494,464.50	91	9
1781	5,271,184.00	412,178.50	5,683,362.50	93	7
1782	3,790,082.70	420,423.89	4,210,506.50	90	10
1783	3,978,575.50	424,014.32	4,402,589.90	90	10
1784	3,960,913.60	440,984.26	4,401,897.90	90	10

Year	Huguan	Gongguan	Total Changguan	Contribution Huguan (%)	Contribution Gongguan (%)
1785	3,621,575.20	423,697.60	4,045,272.80	90	10
1786	3,398,462.30	382,963.80	3,781,426.10	90	10
1787	3,734,224.70	328,446.71	4,062,671.40	92	8
1788	4,097,062.60	331,957.25	4,429,019.90	93	7
1789	4,503,465.50	379,813.06	4,883,278.60	92	8
1790	4,039,779.70	431,446.15	4,471,225.90	90	10
1791	4,225,400.40	423,897.79	4,649,298.20	91	9
1792	4,360,197.90	561,890.21	4,922,088.10	89	11
1793	4,016,172.30	413,574.12	4,429,746.40	91	9
1794	4,019,107.40	366,012.89	4,385,120.30	92	8
1795	3,558,322.90	331,020.55	3,889,343.40	91	9
1796	3,802,087.10	303,106.45	4,105,193.60	93	7
1797	3,813,762.60	328,449.35	4,142,211.90	92	8
1798	3,455,019.50	353,421.15	3,808,440.60	91	9
1799	3,570,475.40	364,018.43	3,934,493.90	91	9
1800	4,204,851.10	487,578.71	4,692,429.90	90	10
1801	3,096,522.80	234,783.93	3,331,306.80	93	7
1802	3,558,998.50	375,813.57	3,934,812.00	90	10
1803	3,834,140.70	309,463.08	4,143,603.80	93	7
1804	3,847,532.10	377,297.68	4,224,829.80	91	9
1805	3,949,419.30	360,539.84	4,309,959.20	92	8
1806	3,373,276.20	352,218.61	3,725,494.80	91	9
1807	3,441,067.70	383,134.83	3,824,202.50	90	10
1808	4,010,150.60	384,208.30	4,394,358.90	91	9
1809	3,727,916.50	369,768.02	4,097,684.50	91	9
1810	3,802,083.80	396,259.17	4,198,343.00	91	9
1811	3,434,136.60	389,474.54	3,823,611.10	90	10
1812	3,415,174.90	387,121.14	3,802,296.10	90	10
1813	3,446,170.50	388,179.35	3,834,349.80	90	10
1814	4,165,858.70	386,317.92	4,552,176.60	92	8
1815	3,497,905.00	374,928.65	3,872,833.60	90	10
1816	3,271,269.30	337,046.81	3,608,316.10	91	9
1817	3,463,319.10	387,129.80	3,850,448.90	90	10
1818	3,675,263.40	385,887.86	4,061,151.20	90	10
1819	3,982,379.70	398,836.06	4,381,215.80	91	9
1820	3,585,762.50	371,816.70	3,957,579.20	91	9
1821	3,307,862.50	399,814.07	3,707,676.60	89	11

TABLE 7.2 *Customs revenues collected at* Huguan *and* Gongguan, *1723–1910* (cont.)

Year	Huguan	Gongguan	Total Changguan	Contribution Huguan (%)	Contribution Gongguan (%)
1822	4,183,104.30	398,954.87	4,582,059.10	91	9
1823	3,407,721.40	401,986.92	3,809,708.30	89	11
1824	3,534,841.60	477,214.09	4,012,055.70	88	12
1825	3,465,548.20	335,157.06	3,800,705.30	91	9
1826	3,062,308.20	325,444.62	3,387,752.80	90	10
1827	3,082,212.00	313,121.74	3,395,333.80	91	9
1828	3,602,644.70	342,395.61	3,945,040.30	91	9
1829	3,663,017.50	338,482.05	4,001,499.60	92	8
1830	3,596,042.90	406,657.65	4,002,700.50	90	10
1831	3,083,702.00	317,855.61	3,401,557.70	91	9
1832	3,861,443.70	405,903.04	4,267,346.70	90	10
1833	3,095,520.00	288,094.99	3,383,614.90	91	9
1834	3,469,384.20	260,518.44	3,729,902.60	93	7
1835	3,794,235.70	305,795.83	4,100,031.50	93	7
1836	3,219,531.90	314,363.67	3,533,895.60	91	9
1837	3,304,516.50	337,796.07	3,642,312.60	91	9
1838	3,789,788.80	296,432.02	4,086,220.80	93	7
1839	3,559,781.50	266,480.83	3,826,262.30	93	7
1840	3,603,874.80	279,238.18	3,883,113.00	93	7
1841	3,678,229.20	240,540.01	3,918,769.20	94	6
1842	2,942,739.20	244,606.31	3,187,345.50	92	8
1843	2,786,584.80	289,812.08	3,076,396.90	91	9
1844	3,099,378.10	297,514.48	3,396,892.60	91	9
1845	3,013,429.80	320,299.06	3,333,728.90	90	10
1846	3,546,130.80	333,897.68	3,880,028.50	91	9
1847	2,480,381.20	176,630.57	2,657,011.80	93	7
1848	2,892,328.10	332,883.27	3,225,211.40	90	10
1849	3,584,283.80	303,759.27	3,888,043.00	92	8
1850	2,835,966.30	165,672.42	3,001,638.70	94	6
1851	3,172,572.90	260,863.30	3,433,436.20	92	8
1852	2,730,898.30	160,421.58	2,891,319.90	94	6
1853	2,311,280.80	71,532.41	2,382,813.20	97	3
1854	1,403,960.30	41,608.19	1,445,568.50	97	3
1855	1,505,321.80	58,705.14	1,564,026.90	96	4
1856	1,712,435.60	71,525.72	1,783,961.30	96	4

Year	Huguan	Gongguan	Total Changguan	Contribution Huguan (%)	Contribution Gongguan (%)
1857	1,573,992.80	76,659.03	1,650,651.80	95	5
1858	1,586,033.70	80,038.04	1,666,071.70	95	5
1859	1,597,909.30	82,231.84	1,680,141.10	95	5
1860	1,950,775.20	54,269.65	2,005,044.80	97	3
1861	1,322,477.10	52,537.11	1,375,014.20	96	4
1862	1,319,518.90	50,404.65	1,369,923.50	96	4
1863	1,515,118.90	47,445.19	1,562,564.10	97	3
1864	1,753,299.60	74,499.12	1,827,798.70	96	4
1865	1,793,553.60	73,723.31	1,867,276.90	96	4
1866	1,812,695.00	49,393.98	1,862,089.00	97	3
1867	1,841,394.40	50,173.79	1,891,568.20	97	3
1868	2,081,503.20	91,948.69	2,173,451.90	96	4
1869	2,010,424.90	49,579.86	2,060,004.80	98	2
1870	1,694,905.90	82,978.35	1,777,884.20	95	5
1871	1,956,521.60	50,539.53	2,007,061.20	97	3
1872	2,148,344.30	52,274.01	2,200,618.30	98	2
1873	2,107,651.30	49,403.21	2,157,054.50	98	2
1874	1,930,212.90	47,906.63	1,978,119.50	98	2
1875	1,908,573.40	49,955.57	1,958,528.90	97	3
1876	2,241,687.20	48,929.68	2,290,616.90	98	2
1877	2,221,041.70	122,322.47	2,343,364.20	95	5
1878	2,128,278.20	104,129.07	2,232,407.20	95	5
1879	2,734,774.30	123,611.91	2,858,386.20	96	4
1880	2,184,731.70	145,191.78	2,329,923.50	94	6
1881	2,183,987.50	125,003.27	2,308,990.70	95	5
1882	2,205,545.90	114,975.32	2,320,521.20	95	5
1883	2,177,776.50	118,035.56	2,295,812.10	95	5
1884	2,339,751.20	108,371.57	2,448,122.70	96	4
1885	2,118,891.80	75,004.58	2,193,896.40	97	3
1886	2,154,533.80	111,715.55	2,266,249.40	95	5
1887	2,256,321.00	112,384.30	2,368,705.30	95	5
1888	2,300,440.10	137,121.12	2,437,561.20	94	6
1889	2,263,699.30	114,490.68	2,378,190.00	95	5
1890	2,632,507.50	185,729.00	2,818,236.50	93	7
1891	2,152,703.00	118,611.06	2,271,314.00	95	5
1892	2,443,864.10	112,856.34	2,556,720.40	96	4
1893	1,851,942.10	23,347.14	1,875,289.30	99	1

TABLE 7.2 *Customs revenues collected at* Huguan *and* Gongguan, *1723–1910* (cont.)

Year	Huguan	Gongguan	Total Changguan	Contribution Huguan (%)	Contribution Gongguan (%)
1894	2,140,928.30	96,502.46	2,237,430.80	96	4
1895	1,959,991.70	108,096.03	2,068,087.80	95	5
1896	2,038,258.80	99,933.65	2,138,192.50	95	5
1897	2,110,049.10	97,692.46	2,207,741.60	96	4
1898	2,028,895.60	99,489.77	2,128,385.30	95	5
1899	2,001,774.40	69,858.23	2,071,632.60	97	3
1900	2,148,719.90	144,319.03	2,293,039.00	94	6
1901	1,645,207.10	74,745.83	1,719,952.90	96	4
1902	2,154,854.60	114,183.05	2,269,037.60	95	5
1903	2,527,892.50	90,333.44	2,618,226.00	97	3
1904	2,421,426.20	140,280.41	2,561,706.70	95	5
1905	3,480,977.70	180,916.86	3,661,894.50	95	5
1906	2,737,006.30	175,481.23	2,912,487.60	94	6
1907	2,227,509.60	246,308.59	2,473,818.20	90	10
1908	2,189,308.80	146,571.42	2,335,880.20	94	6
1909	1,681,805.30	150,166.18	1,831,971.50	92	8
1910	169,413.02		169,413.02	100	

Source: see Appendix A.

Even though there are some data missing, it remains clear that *Huguan* contributed most to customs revenues: the lowest proportion was 83%, but for most years they were responsible for more than 90% of total revenue. If we were to insert data on customs revenues from Yuehai Guan before 1861, the contribution of *Huguan* to total revenues would be even higher. This demonstrates convincingly that *Hubu* played a more significant role than *Gongbu* in the fiscal system of the Qing dynasty.

It is also worthwhile to compare customs revenues that came from the three main branches of customs at *Changguan* in Qing China, i.e. Land Border customs, Canal and Yangtze River customs, and Coastal customs.

TABLE 7.3 *Customs revenues collected at* Changguan, *as reported in archived records* (*in taels of silver*)

Year	Land border	Canal & Yangtze River	Coastal (1)a	Coastal (2)b	Land Border estimatesc	Canal & Yangtze River estimatesc	Coastal (2) estimatesc
1723	12,041.30	163,053.70	–	–	242,558.20	2,598,428.70	468,061.36
1724	–	332,798.10	106,656.00	106,656.00	242,558.20	2,522,343.80	468,061.36
1725	–	663,457.80	116,419.00	213,713.60	242,558.20	2,613,590.60	477,824.36
1726	87,759.39	598,975.30	116,111.50	116,111.50	242,558.20	2,626,340.80	477,516.86
1727	9,300.00	714,544.90	123,603.50	123,603.50	240,557.80	2,795,421.90	485,008.86
1728	12,400.00	1,002,549.00	142,440.50	142,440.50	243,657.80	2,628,515.30	503,845.86
1729	12,500.00	687,046.90	162,029.00	162,029.00	243,757.80	2,705,497.10	523,434.36
1730	95,387.89	1,155,065.00	179,013.70	377,075.80	244,674.70	2,686,185.30	641,186.59
1731	–	787,349.80	–	228,659.70	244,674.70	2,702,399.40	671,784.20
1732	–	1,270,733.00	–	309,107.90	244,674.70	2,836,257.00	752,232.42
1733	–	1,601,536.00	166,598.80	166,598.80	244,674.70	3,128,314.00	739,817.52
1734	12,955.41	1,582,843.00	180,825.40	180,825.40	243,201.20	3,271,834.20	754,044.12
1735	148,296.60	2,984,062.00	344,029.30	560,029.30	263,043.40	3,196,943.70	661,244.17
1736	62,557.39	2,963,501.00	333,887.70	605,841.30	269,386.90	3,163,107.70	707,056.11
1737	185,716.70	2,593,012.00	374,658.60	659,813.50	270,567.20	3,196,067.10	761,028.38
1738	127,338.80	2,350,406.00	376,495.60	610,555.10	275,341.40	2,919,047.70	711,769.96
1739	120,545.90	2,556,917.00	411,710.70	682,331.50	276,835.30	2,852,328.20	783,546.35
1740	42,585.35	2,333,770.00	421,406.10	690,861.10	276,100.20	3,140,586.20	792,075.95
1741	42,175.37	2,791,160.00	431,866.40	684,472.50	275,690.20	3,110,684.70	785,687.30
1742	146,176.10	2,849,584.00	454,400.80	751,321.70	270,345.30	3,138,861.80	852,536.54
1743	154,058.00	2,742,328.00	430,157.50	747,326.20	278,227.20	3,164,303.40	848,541.05
1744	161,795.10	3,006,661.00	416,489.70	745,265.70	285,964.20	3,215,365.80	846,480.56
1745	264,391.80	3,158,434.00	403,764.90	818,907.90	324,183.70	3,367,138.80	920,122.77
1746	171,150.70	2,793,353.00	410,365.30	749,983.30	326,467.60	3,002,058.30	851,198.15
1747	219,136.50	2,628,864.00	424,533.80	640,556.80	325,172.30	2,837,568.90	741,771.65
1748	229,359.70	3,618,089.00	763,341.30	1,198,421.00	331,651.10	3,838,226.20	1,299,636.11
1749	286,372.70	2,931,483.00	469,303.10	916,723.30	344,820.60	3,293,046.50	1,017,938.20
1750	282,553.40	3,068,581.00	503,641.70	971,204.20	339,127.70	3,525,350.70	1,072,419.00
1751	183,311.30	2,756,344.00	473,078.70	934,873.70	344,939.90	3,343,537.10	1,036,088.50
1752	180,259.10	3,573,123.00	505,017.20	1,008,321.00	353,792.90	3,649,129.80	1,109,535.85
1753	184,337.10	3,458,210.00	580,826.20	1,095,626.00	354,580.20	3,534,217.10	1,095,626.24
1754	75,129.47	3,176,956.00	589,603.00	1,104,903.00	354,203.10	3,252,962.40	1,104,903.01

TABLE 7.3 *Customs revenues collected at* Changguan, *as reported in archived records* (cont.)

Year	Land border	Canal & Yangtze River	Coastal (1)a	Coastal (2)b	Land Border estimatesc	Canal & Yangtze River estimatesc	Coastal (2) estimatesc
1755	48,626.50	3,459,874.00	603,305.60	1,089,591.00	354,961.70	3,548,530.20	1,089,591.42
1756	191,601.10	3,497,993.00	582,307.30	987,316.30	353,230.20	3,574,000.10	987,316.27
1757	88,880.34	2,746,141.00	587,646.60	908,197.60	360,545.20	3,033,783.10	908,197.58
1758	178,555.70	2,774,521.00	598,290.40	968,361.70	354,232.40	3,062,162.90	968,361.74
1759	246,568.10	3,524,217.00	590,801.50	945,496.20	355,099.70	3,552,406.20	945,496.21
1760	140,827.10	3,540,975.00	602,965.80	959,232.30	359,131.70	3,569,165.20	959,232.32
1761	216,582.80	3,204,878.00	627,374.30	1,010,009.00	379,056.40	3,524,295.90	1,010,008.69
1762	246,596.80	3,298,861.00	738,500.10	1,121,153.00	383,180.40	3,377,205.30	1,121,152.62
1763	238,118.50	3,535,105.00	635,250.20	1,046,887.00	371,662.70	3,626,029.80	1,046,886.76
1764	211,442.90	3,630,726.00	643,686.10	1,118,099.00	368,857.50	3,721,650.40	1,118,098.84
1765	251,465.50	3,928,663.00	644,247.80	1,149,387.00	375,531.10	3,956,853.10	1,149,386.60
1766	330,573.80	3,472,819.00	639,760.80	1,239,882.00	395,156.20	3,718,517.20	1,239,881.59
1767	358,778.80	4,361,862.00	640,529.10	1,187,460.00	496,722.00	4,607,560.50	1,187,459.79
1768	144,942.80	3,251,875.00	631,035.90	1,178,774.00	391,718.00	3,497,573.60	1,178,773.60
1769	194,947.70	3,543,793.00	583,309.90	1,132,505.00	382,025.50	3,610,844.60	1,132,504.71
1770	165,340.90	4,080,867.00	696,253.20	1,287,321.00	396,583.30	4,306,808.80	1,287,320.51
1771	226,558.70	3,627,370.00	635,129.10	1,215,065.00	400,857.00	3,667,335.40	1,215,065.07
1772	231,521.20	3,586,698.00	641,343.90	1,235,214.00	400,245.10	3,626,663.50	1,235,213.56
1773	230,968.90	3,989,807.00	647,745.30	1,202,648.00	401,975.30	4,046,871.90	1,202,648.35
1774	336,520.40	3,926,682.00	645,949.90	1,187,503.00	406,155.80	3,966,647.50	1,187,503.12
1775	266,359.10	3,665,699.00	641,579.60	1,183,443.00	405,466.40	3,665,698.70	1,183,443.34
1776	107,348.90	3,791,563.00	631,385.20	1,164,564.00	406,741.00	3,848,737.70	1,164,563.60
1777	284,903.60	3,941,950.00	627,461.30	1,215,869.00	418,853.60	3,941,949.60	1,215,869.32
1778	308,779.30	3,547,917.00	640,274.70	1,228,729.00	450,612.60	3,623,590.50	1,228,728.70
1779	358,931.70	3,520,317.00	646,117.30	1,202,302.00	430,955.30	3,520,316.90	1,202,302.45
1780	359,740.50	3,464,373.00	670,350.70	1,226,585.00	431,764.00	3,827,181.00	1,226,584.65
1781	493,869.40	4,032,281.00	1,157,212.00	2,287,896.00	569,196.40	4,065,392.90	2,287,896.20
1782	235,163.60	3,337,556.00	637,786.70	1,158,897.00	438,838.00	3,699,390.30	1,158,897.20
1783	365,537.70	3,418,250.00	618,802.20	1,416,664.00	437,561.20	3,746,972.40	1,416,663.78
1784	243,620.80	3,529,793.00	628,483.70	1,376,609.00	438,996.90	3,874,219.90	1,376,609.41
1785	239,356.60	3,178,890.00	627,026.10	1,499,177.00	438,078.40	3,536,463.10	1,499,177.05
1786	240,883.70	2,910,010.00	630,532.60	1,584,493.00	438,592.90	3,267,582.80	1,584,493.30
1787	241,907.00	3,284,709.00	536,055.20	1,517,742.00	440,713.10	3,372,547.10	1,517,741.50

Year	Land border	Canal & Yangtze River	Coastal (1)a	Coastal (2)b	Land Border estimatesc	Canal & Yangtze River estimatesc	Coastal (2) estimatesc
1788	349,525.80	3,505,080.00	574,413.90	1,611,413.00	441,708.40	3,592,918.10	1,611,413.23
1789	205,698.90	4,085,925.00	591,655.10	1,693,017.00	390,858.90	4,461,891.20	1,693,017.09
1790	319,449.90	3,550,949.00	600,827.30	1,728,390.00	391,555.10	3,913,768.90	1,728,390.14
1791	324,742.50	3,723,337.00	601,218.70	1,597,101.00	400,351.40	3,811,174.90	1,597,101.26
1792	323,159.10	4,029,936.00	568,993.40	1,580,420.00	408,466.10	4,076,054.90	1,580,419.73
1793	373,644.30	3,455,307.00	600,795.00	1,486,408.00	445,970.00	3,501,426.40	1,486,407.84
1794	325,084.00	3,461,120.00	598,916.70	1,571,865.00	415,623.80	3,520,389.60	1,571,865.23
1795	360,682.60	3,116,660.00	412,001.30	1,583,912.00	451,222.40	3,462,425.70	1,799,759.70
1796	361,697.70	3,315,203.00	428,292.50	1,409,479.00	450,967.50	3,400,652.70	1,409,479.24
1797	360,376.90	3,345,932.00	435,903.20	1,409,076.00	447,719.30	3,431,381.20	1,409,076.16
1798	350,378.30	3,105,584.00	352,478.00	1,388,236.00	423,195.60	3,191,033.70	1,496,227.71
1799	271,204.00	3,287,573.00	375,717.20	1,312,790.00	434,816.00	3,329,097.60	1,420,782.45
1800	179,354.90	4,062,570.00	450,504.80	1,651,751.00	434,864.00	4,225,808.90	1,651,751.35
1801	303,190.00	2,677,820.00	350,296.80	1,686,469.00	436,392.40	3,357,338.90	1,801,343.26
1802	261,329.90	3,305,768.00	367,714.00	1,908,487.00	457,768.70	3,347,293.10	2,023,361.70
1803	374,629.30	3,244,180.00	524,794.40	2,220,183.00	459,696.10	3,663,406.70	2,220,183.40
1804	410,565.50	3,362,561.00	451,702.80	2,007,289.00	455,903.20	3,368,832.00	2,007,289.20
1805	410,624.70	3,475,174.00	424,160.20	2,066,132.00	450,623.70	3,556,729.00	2,066,131.98
1806	293,594.70	3,008,701.00	423,199.60	2,044,576.00	450,959.60	3,079,761.80	2,044,575.57
1807	419,071.50	2,950,656.00	454,474.70	2,118,305.00	436,441.90	3,182,694.50	2,118,304.71
1808	449,144.90	3,455,533.00	489,681.60	1,960,142.00	461,432.70	3,460,653.60	1,960,141.81
1809	317,992.70	3,273,513.00	506,178.70	1,963,380.00	440,440.60	3,353,491.80	1,963,380.47
1810	406,943.60	3,289,990.00	501,408.90	1,910,051.00	440,165.00	3,353,824.90	1,910,050.75
1811	331,098.40	3,007,810.00	484,702.80	1,649,966.00	467,670.60	3,113,970.10	1,649,965.96
1812	416,759.20	2,992,314.00	393,223.20	1,741,160.00	438,590.10	3,098,473.90	1,837,752.18
1813	302,059.80	3,018,872.00	513,417.80	1,760,126.00	438,633.00	3,208,028.10	1,760,125.93
1814	503,664.10	3,236,721.00	811,791.30	3,232,511.00	549,224.80	3,241,842.30	3,232,510.84
1815	306,083.40	3,164,349.00	402,401.10	1,733,641.00	437,568.20	3,169,470.30	1,829,424.21
1816	195,362.30	3,017,815.00	395,139.00	1,842,119.00	438,277.30	3,297,205.20	1,937,902.29
1817	191,578.30	3,230,188.00	428,682.40	1,849,986.00	437,799.00	3,303,463.30	1,945,769.45
1818	398,641.70	3,268,322.00	394,187.80	1,697,099.00	439,113.10	3,273,442.80	1,792,882.11
1819	404,810.30	3,489,333.00	487,072.80	1,867,170.00	438,043.30	3,553,174.60	1,867,169.87
1820	430,455.00	3,041,398.00	485,726.30	1,965,546.00	436,652.00	3,105,239.90	1,965,546.40
1821	301,117.00	2,923,148.00	483,411.40	1,980,434.00	437,010.80	3,124,725.80	1,980,433.85
1822	485,260.60	3,615,454.00	481,344.70	1,966,492.00	498,002.90	3,741,290.70	1,966,491.52

TABLE 7.3 *Customs revenues collected at* Changguan*, as reported in archived records* (cont.)

Year	Land border	Canal & Yangtze River	Coastal (1)[a]	Coastal (2)[b]	Land Border estimates[c]	Canal & Yangtze River estimates[c]	Coastal (2) estimates[c]
1823	270,209.40	3,059,058.00	480,440.40	1,885,354.00	436,446.70	3,064,179.60	1,885,353.54
1824	269,936.40	3,262,684.00	479,435.40	1,923,758.00	436,558.40	3,451,924.00	1,923,757.99
1825	393,240.00	2,930,694.00	476,771.60	1,775,601.00	436,709.30	3,119,933.80	1,775,600.53
1826	383,339.30	2,529,384.00	475,030.00	2,051,667.00	435,216.50	3,157,891.20	2,051,667.12
1827	250,999.40	2,569,608.00	574,726.70	2,424,773.00	436,588.60	3,167,268.00	2,424,772.67
1828	248,831.60	3,216,395.00	479,814.10	1,921,739.00	435,437.20	3,252,203.00	1,921,738.71
1829	336,865.60	3,188,226.00	476,407.90	1,975,989.00	435,761.90	3,282,759.80	1,975,988.65
1830	438,406.70	3,184,351.00	379,943.10	2,043,578.00	485,163.30	3,382,455.40	2,139,318.95
1831	250,997.90	2,674,270.00	476,290.10	1,938,096.00	439,329.00	3,038,261.60	1,938,096.24
1832	249,592.70	3,561,227.00	456,526.60	1,989,460.00	439,728.40	3,925,219.40	1,989,459.88
1833	345,428.50	2,616,213.00	421,973.50	1,899,820.00	439,436.60	2,836,199.80	1,899,819.74
1834	367,467.20	2,887,341.00	475,094.00	2,144,807.00	439,552.70	2,923,149.90	2,144,806.63
1835	414,188.10	3,136,086.00	549,757.80	1,974,702.00	486,273.60	3,356,072.40	1,974,701.96
1836	255,004.20	2,805,518.00	473,373.40	2,148,225.00	440,031.70	3,169,516.90	2,148,225.11
1837	368,096.40	2,795,014.00	479,202.60	2,268,627.00	440,186.90	3,140,673.40	2,268,626.93
1838	368,224.70	3,237,025.00	480,970.90	1,723,015.00	440,315.20	3,272,833.60	1,723,015.14
1839	368,486.20	2,992,737.00	465,039.10	1,913,598.00	440,576.70	3,023,424.40	1,913,598.07
1840	370,245.20	3,072,647.00	440,220.40	1,626,772.00	440,521.20	3,108,455.90	1,626,772.28
1841	372,686.70	3,090,773.00	455,309.80	1,319,542.00	463,175.40	3,126,581.30	1,319,541.98
1842	399,079.30	2,565,688.00	222,577.80	1,338,320.00	466,049.20	2,785,687.40	1,338,320.14
1843	215,760.30	2,518,861.00	341,775.50	1,524,264.00	403,263.10	2,738,860.10	1,524,264.49
1844	248,996.10	2,740,513.00	407,383.30	2,437,926.00	426,744.30	2,835,048.90	2,437,926.43
1845	191,350.40	2,769,063.00	373,315.80	2,734,148.00	426,754.60	3,047,800.10	2,734,147.96
1846	330,330.20	2,966,119.00	583,579.40	4,742,200.00	538,426.20	3,155,441.80	4,742,199.62
1847	228,964.20	1,994,489.00	433,558.60	2,258,782.00	428,627.60	2,885,431.30	2,258,781.71
1848	235,529.30	2,586,312.00	403,369.60	1,827,415.00	428,679.30	3,004,514.30	1,861,278.67
1849	367,316.50	3,080,957.00	439,769.20	1,911,088.00	430,506.20	3,116,765.80	1,911,087.72
1850	271,184.20	2,289,160.00	441,294.40	1,918,162.00	425,612.50	3,031,676.40	1,918,162.33
1851	274,892.90	2,717,964.00	440,578.80	2,077,153.00	417,485.50	2,961,589.70	2,077,152.93
1852	195,657.90	2,321,833.00	373,829.30	2,040,641.00	423,167.20	2,697,150.30	2,040,641.27
1853	277,269.90	1,793,060.00	312,483.40	1,586,613.00	419,862.40	1,847,335.00	1,660,623.83
1854	256,815.30	906,380.90	282,372.30	1,448,864.00	400,481.00	1,111,703.90	1,448,864.47
1855	234,961.80	1,010,239.00	318,826.40	723,585.10	377,554.40	1,180,315.60	723,585.13

Year	Land border	Canal & Yangtze River	Coastal (1)a	Coastal (2)b	Land Border estimatesc	Canal & Yangtze River estimatesc	Coastal(2) estimatesc
1856	282,184.90	1,126,289.00	375,487.90	1,532,294.00	444,780.00	1,377,050.20	1,532,293.73
1857	267,543.60	980,600.90	402,507.40	503,629.00	414,514.80	1,066,487.90	503,628.98
1858	251,543.00	995,857.10	418,671.60	852,943.80	416,878.90	1,114,952.10	852,943.80
1859	148,637.00	1,093,634.00	437,869.90	1,319,888.00	408,463.20	1,211,537.20	1,319,887.55
1860	131,312.40	1,356,889.00	516,842.90	1,508,731.00	393,372.20	1,440,760.70	1,508,731.46
1861	328,991.30	616,120.50	429,902.40	429,902.40	471,583.90	675,479.79	429,902.41
1862	289,978.70	645,856.20	434,088.50	434,088.50	433,671.20	705,215.52	434,088.54
1863	211,572.10	912,929.10	438,062.80	438,062.80	437,813.00	992,645.58	438,062.81
1864	258,077.90	1,170,538.00	399,182.30	399,182.30	427,565.00	1,198,138.40	428,177.51
1865	242,201.60	1,169,800.00	455,275.60	455,275.60	431,722.10	1,192,911.50	455,275.62
1866	243,601.50	1,126,210.00	492,277.10	492,277.10	413,088.60	1,150,882.50	492,277.14
1867	262,160.80	1,178,062.00	451,345.70	451,345.70	431,647.90	1,288,101.80	451,345.71
1868	346,390.40	1,232,290.00	594,771.10	594,771.10	515,877.50	1,292,756.60	594,771.14
1869	300,420.40	1,282,224.00	477,360.60	477,360.60	469,907.50	1,306,895.90	562,895.67
1870	295,386.60	980,492.00	502,005.70	502,005.70	489,139.60	1,217,266.80	587,540.69
1871	274,306.60	1,240,850.00	491,904.50	491,904.50	449,150.40	1,305,293.60	577,439.52
1872	274,299.60	1,264,770.00	661,548.50	661,548.50	452,449.90	1,289,442.40	661,548.46
1873	280,379.70	1,280,361.00	596,313.40	596,313.40	455,223.50	1,344,951.50	596,313.43
1874	288,805.40	1,088,217.00	601,097.40	601,097.40	463,649.20	1,308,795.80	601,097.37
1875	277,269.50	1,075,425.00	605,834.90	605,834.90	452,113.30	1,335,971.70	605,834.91
1876	281,228.70	1,332,572.00	676,816.20	676,816.20	456,072.60	1,397,212.30	676,816.22
1877	280,114.40	1,454,474.00	608,775.70	608,775.70	454,958.30	1,477,716.20	608,775.74
1878	263,050.60	1,359,391.00	609,965.50	609,965.50	437,894.40	1,387,754.60	609,965.45
1879	471,107.00	1,394,209.00	993,070.60	993,070.60	645,950.80	1,462,563.60	993,070.56
1880	298,663.50	1,358,460.00	672,800.00	672,800.00	450,866.90	1,426,815.00	672,800.02
1881	300,327.40	1,318,362.00	690,301.10	690,301.10	475,171.30	1,386,717.10	690,301.15
1882	288,255.50	1,344,231.00	688,035.10	688,035.10	463,099.40	1,412,585.50	688,035.14
1883	218,548.50	1,394,253.00	683,010.60	683,010.60	393,392.30	1,422,616.40	683,010.56
1884	321,230.50	1,469,271.00	657,621.60	657,621.60	496,074.40	1,497,633.90	657,621.62
1885	275,717.50	1,306,741.00	611,438.10	611,438.10	494,565.90	1,371,787.20	611,438.06
1886	221,117.50	1,360,391.00	684,741.10	684,741.10	513,031.50	1,416,659.20	684,741.11
1887	261,145.40	1,417,069.00	690,490.60	690,490.60	509,055.00	1,473,337.70	690,490.58
1888	326,551.00	1,392,998.00	718,012.00	718,012.00	453,489.50	1,449,266.60	718,011.99
1889	279,604.00	1,373,117.00	725,469.00	725,469.00	431,048.80	1,429,385.40	725,468.99
1890	121,549.80	2,025,830.00	670,857.10	670,857.10	417,061.10	2,082,098.00	670,857.13

TABLE 7.3 *Customs revenues collected at* Changguan, *as reported in archived records* (cont.)

Year	Land border	Canal & Yangtze River	Coastal (1)a	Coastal (2)b	Land Border estimatesc	Canal & Yangtze River estimatesc	Coastal (2) estimatesc
1891	320,657.30	1,289,554.00	661,102.90	661,102.90	470,998.50	1,390,594.80	661,102.92
1892	304,176.10	1,483,742.00	768,802.50	768,802.50	449,099.40	1,540,010.30	768,802.45
1893	84,212.00	1,131,332.00	659,745.10	659,745.10	420,264.70	1,336,036.10	659,745.07
1894	277,888.80	1,320,889.00	638,653.50	638,653.50	427,410.60	1,377,156.90	638,653.45
1895	136,175.30	1,325,343.00	606,569.30	606,569.30	285,697.10	1,381,611.60	606,569.30
1896	263,585.10	1,241,080.00	633,527.40	633,527.40	413,107.00	1,334,943.40	633,527.43
1897	269,601.20	1,275,569.00	662,571.70	662,571.70	439,157.60	1,331,837.10	662,571.69
1898	271,463.80	1,167,107.00	689,814.50	689,814.50	441,020.20	1,331,928.30	689,814.52
1899	241,625.60	1,166,563.00	663,444.40	663,444.40	442,027.20	1,312,566.00	663,444.39
1900	323,081.40	1,346,300.00	623,657.60	623,657.60	454,618.40	1,408,293.20	717,728.54
1901	38,483.89	1,074,926.00	606,542.60	606,542.60	234,482.50	1,299,632.10	740,682.04
1902	65,212.22	1,270,647.00	933,178.60	933,178.60	235,418.40	1,653,895.50	1,067,318.10
1903	54,940.82	859,398.30	1,703,887.00	1,703,887.00	250,939.40	1,736,735.90	1,703,886.80
1904	99,492.77	853,360.00	1,608,854.00	1,608,854.00	262,232.50	1,742,975.20	1,608,853.90
1905	135,615.00	1,051,776.00	2,474,504.00	2,474,504.00	298,354.60	1,928,517.10	2,474,504.00
1906	121,135.30	1,026,859.00	1,764,493.00	1,764,493.00	283,875.00	1,968,655.70	1,890,270.60
1907	292,184.50	885,487.30	1,296,146.00	1,296,146.00	423,721.50	1,762,152.60	1,804,694.10
1908	381,902.00	473,668.70	1,480,310.00	1,480,310.00	610,003.00	1,980,416.70	1,606,086.70
1909	325,864.50	488,395.30	1,017,712.00	1,017,712.00	717,901.70	2,049,900.20	1,847,360.50
1910	–	169,413.00	–	–	752,901.70	1,919,279.30	1,847,360.50
1911	–	–	–	–	752,901.70	1,919,279.30	1,847,360.50

a Coastal (1) = customs revenue data excluding revenues collected at Yuehai Guan from before 1861.
b Coastal (2): customs revenue data including revenues collected at Yuehai Guan's from before 1861.
c Revenues to which extrapolated (hence estimates) missing data for *Changguan* have been added.

As can be seen in Figure 7.7, customs revenues collected by Canal and Yangtze River customs were generally much larger than the other two branches, but this trend began to change from 1850 onwards, when the impact of Coastal customs grew stronger.

If customs data of Yuehai Guan from before 1861 are added to Coastal customs revenues, the data trend steepens substantially (see Figure 7.8).

As Figure 7.8 demonstrates, Coastal customs with revenues from Yuhei

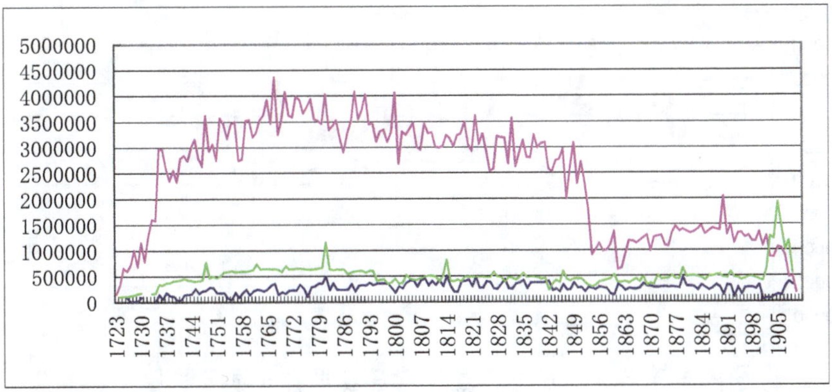

FIGURE 7.7 *Tax revenue for the three types*[a] *of Changguan, 1723–1911*

[a] Land Border customs = blue line; Canal and Yangtze River customs = red line; Coastal customs = green line.
Source: Table 7.3.

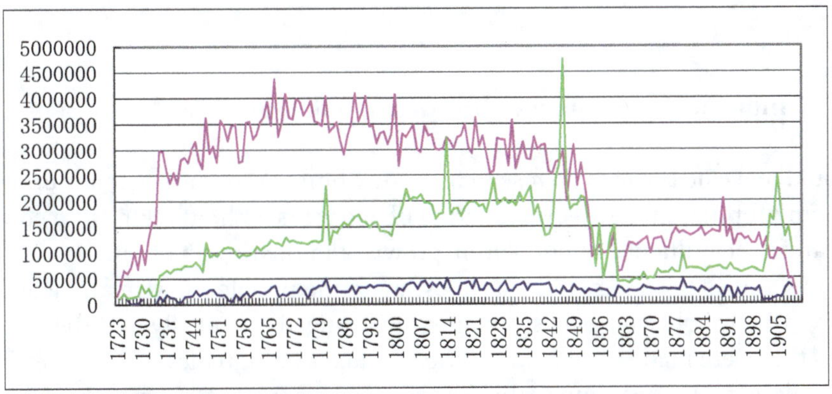

FIGURE 7.8 *Tax revenue trends for the three types*[a] *of Changguan with data from Yuehai Guan added, 1723–1911*

[a] Blue = data points for revenue of Land Border customs; red = data points for revenue of Canal and Yangtze River customs; green = data points for revenue of Coastal customs.

Guan added experienced its largest increases before 1850, even seriously challenging Canal and Yangtze River customs in the first half of the nineteenth century as the most important source of tax revenues.

The impact of adding my extrapolated estimates of missing data to recorded *Changguan* customs revenue data can be seen in Figure 7.9.

As Figure 7.9 shows, even with the missing data added, the general trends for revenues collected by the three branches of customs remain much the same.

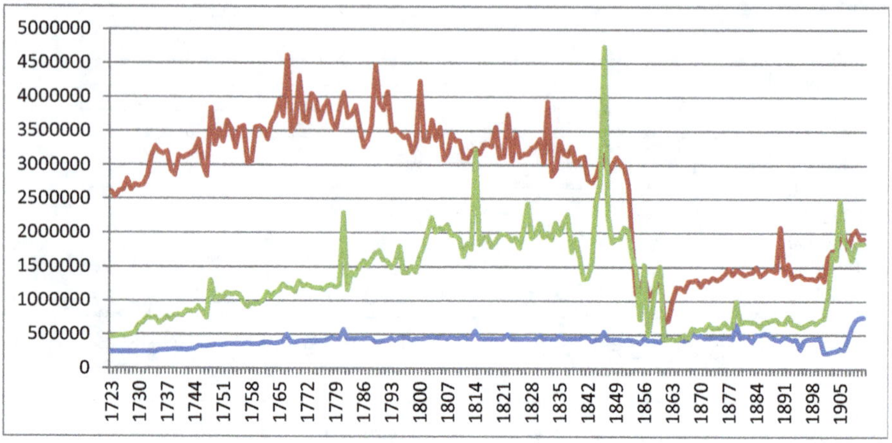

Note: Blue = land estimate; Red = canal estimate; green = coastal estimate

FIGURE 7.9 *Tax revenue trends including estimates (extrapolated) of missing data for Changguan, 1723–1911*

7.3 Influence of Population Growth and Inflation

It would make no sense to do research on the Chinese economy—or any other economy, for that matter—over a period of 200 years without taking into consideration the influence of population growth and the impact of inflation.

It has always been very difficult to estimate the population size of ancient China, primarily because census standards changed repeatedly and the estimates that were made were mainly based on taxation statistics.

Population size was, nevertheless, relatively constant during the Qing dynasty, and government publications such as the *Da Qing Li Chao Shi Lu*, *Qing Chao Xu Wen Xian Tong Kao* provide annual census figures for the Qing dynasty, once again for taxation purposes, which immediately introduces sources of error. For example, not only were taxes frozen in the early Qing, also women and children were not subject to taxation and were, therefore, not included in the appropriate registers. The same applied to immigrants, and even to those who had migrated into a region generations prior to the censuses, but who, as a rule, remained registered in their region of origin rather than that of their actual residence. Thanks to the hard and impressive work of many scholars, population size estimates for Qing China have become increasingly accurate. In particular, data published by Cao Shuji (see Table 7.4) have gained the greatest authority.

TABLE 7.4 *Population sizes during the Qing dynasty (millions)*

Year	1644	1776	1820	1851	1880	1910
population	152.5	311.4	383.1	436.1	364.4	436

Sources: Cao Shuji: "Population history", Volume 4, pp. 451-452; Volume 5, pp. 703-704.

Figure 7.10 presents these figures in graphical form:

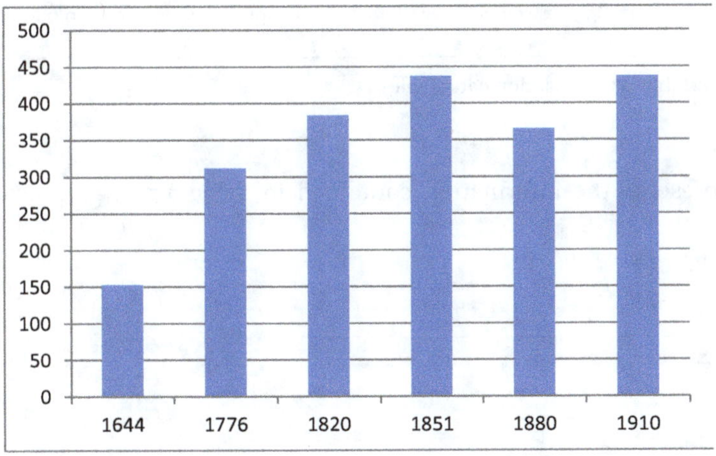

FIGURE 7.10 *Population sizes during the Qing dynasty (millions)*

Because it is impossible to obtain population estimates year by year, I only use population data from 1776, 1820, 1851, 1880, and 1910 to calculate the value of customs duties per capita (see Table 7.5).

TABLE 7.5 *Customs duties per capita during the Qing dynasty (in taels of silver)*

Year	Changguan		Yangguan		Combined		Missing data included	
	Total	Per capita	Total	Per capita	Total	Per capita	Total	Per capita
1776	4,530,297	0.0145	533,178.41	0.0017	5,063,475	0.0163	5,420,042	0.0174
1820	3,957,579	0.0103	1,479,820.10	0.0039	5,437,399	0.0142	5,507,438	0.0144

TABLE 7.5 *Customs duties per capita during the Qing dynasty (in taels of silver)* (cont.)

Year	Changguan		Yangguan		Combined		Missing data included	
	Total	Per capita	Total	Per capita	Total	Per capita	Total	Per capita
1851	3,433,436	0.0079	2,836,574.10	0.0065	6,270,010	0.0144	6,656,228	0.0153
1880	2,329,924	0.0064	14,346,406	0.0394	16,676,330	0.0458	16,896,888	0.0464
1910	169,413	0.0004	34,518,859	0.0792	34,688,272	0.0796	39,038,401	0.0895

Source: Customs duties data: Table 7.1, Population data: Table 7.3.

Figure 7.11 presents the information contained in Table 7.5 in graphical form:

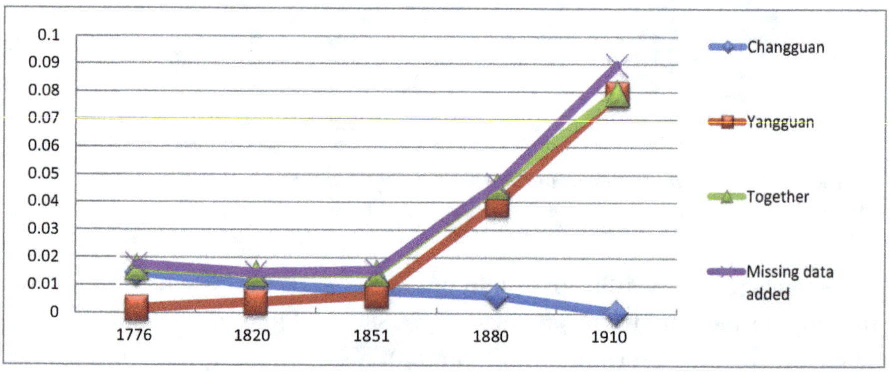

FIGURE 7.11 *Trends of customs duties per capita during the Qing dynasty, 1776–1910*

There is much to be learned from Figure 7.11. First of all, it shows that the level of taxation per capita before 1851 was fairly stable. Its slightly declining trend indicates that over a period of almost 100 years, during which time the population expanded, the tax burden became a little lighter for the individual inhabitant. Second, after 1851, per capita levels of *Changguan* declined, while *Yangguan* per capita increased, which indicates that *Yangguan* revenues had already surpassed those from *Changguan* to become the major source of customs revenue. Third, and finally, the trend of combined customs revenues

(*Changguan* plus *Yangguan*) is similar whether or not missing *Changguan* data are included: i.e. stability before 1851, followed by a great, steep increase in the 1880–1911. Obviously, the year 1851 (early on in the Taiping Rebellion) was the fiscal tipping point of the Qing dynasty.

In addition to population growth, inflation is another aspect of the Qing economy to be taken into account. Exact figures for inflation during the Qing dynasty are perhaps even more difficult to come by than population estimates. The easiest way of getting an idea of inflation during the Qing is to compare the various published estimates of changing price levels; see Figure 7.12.

Opinions differ about the extent of inflation during the Qing, and it is impossible to arrive at an index that is widely accepted. Table 7.6 gives an indication of the levels of inflation that occurred in the Qing economy: I show annual customs revenues for the period 1723–1910 (revenue for 1911 is missing), whereby revenue collected in 1910 is indexed to be equal to 100. Of course, in doing this I am assuming that developments in revenues collected are indicative of price movement.

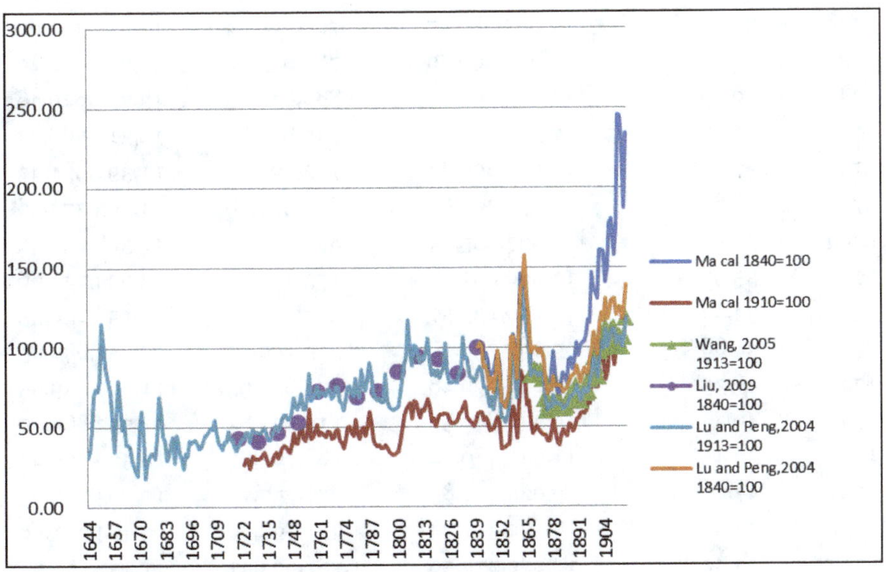

FIGURE 7.12 *Estimates of price trends for the period 1644–1911*
Source: Ma, Y., de Jong, H. J. & Chu, T. 2014, "Living standards in China between 1840 and 1912: A new estimate of Gross Domestic Product per capita", GGDC Research Memorandum No. 147, Appendix B, Table B. 12.

TABLE 7.6 *Customs duties in real terms (index 1910 = 100) collected at* Changguan *and* Yangguan *(taels of silver)*

Year	Price index[a]	*Changguan*	*Yangguan*	Total *guanshui*
1723	26.27	12,225,936.81	–	12,225,938.33
1724	30.12	10,410,586.99	–	10,410,587.65
1725	30.12	10,745,944.56	323,023.11	11,068,967.46
1726	24.28	13,381,883.44	–	13,381,882.21
1727	31.98	10,705,734.83	–	10,705,734.83
1728	30.12	10,885,539.18	–	10,885,537.85
1729	30.12	11,206,489.71	–	11,206,490.70
1730	30.12	11,201,807.77	657,576.66	11,859,385.79
1731	30.59	11,082,702.52	747,498.20	11,830,199.41
1732	32.48	10,849,926.72	951,686.95	11,801,613.30
1733	34.34	11,076,582.12	–	11,076,581.25
1734	30.59	12,945,313.83	–	12,945,315.46
1735	26.68	14,637,298.73	809,595.20	15,446,892.80
1736	26.68	14,496,241.38	1,019,316.08	15,515,558.47
1737	28.66	13,756,132.94	994,957.82	14,751,092.11
1738	32.48	11,305,725.37	720,626.54	12,026,351.60
1739	34.34	10,605,966.80	788,063.02	11,394,030.29
1740	30.59	12,877,762.01	880,859.63	13,758,620.46
1741	33.87	11,572,058.16	745,810.60	12,317,868.32
1742	37.41	10,598,296.44	793,693.93	11,391,991.45
1743	38.68	10,273,792.66	819,981.08	11,093,774.56
1744	37.78	10,637,995.24	870,238.22	11,508,234.52
1745	35.38	11,860,661.96	1,173,383.27	13,034,044.66
1746	34.44	11,150,133.57	986,114.98	12,136,248.55
1747	38.86	9,491,739.06	555,900.67	10,047,640.25
1748	46.35	10,861,776.48	938,683.93	11,800,459.55
1749	40.3	10,442,642.93	1,110,223.82	11,552,866.00
1750	39.4	11,343,489.34	1,186,706.85	12,530,195.43
1751	47.23	9,025,556.85	977,757.78	10,003,315.69
1752	54.02	8,532,311.74	931,699.00	9,464,011.48
1753	43.52	10,270,274.59	1,182,904.41	11,453,177.85
1754	41.81	10,037,714.66	1,232,480.27	11,270,193.73
1755	46.5	9,692,037.85	1,045,775.91	10,737,812.90
1756	61.13	7,376,963.19	662,537.22	8,039,501.06
1757	42.95	9,271,187.19	746,335.27	10,017,522.70

Year	Price index[a]	*Changguan*	*Yangguan*	Total *guanshui*
1758	43.89	9,147,153.79	843,179.11	9,990,332.65
1759	47.6	9,450,225.84	745,156.97	10,195,382.35
1760	51.73	8,759,448.48	688,703.92	9,448,151.94
1761	45.28	10,006,021.64	845,040.61	10,851,062.28
1762	46.95	9,582,291.37	815,021.32	10,397,312.03
1763	45.28	10,231,763.91	909,091.23	11,140,854.68
1764	43.78	10,813,599.82	1,083,629.03	11,897,229.33
1765	47.31	10,519,197.00	1,067,720.93	11,586,918.20
1766	47.13	10,085,792.91	1,273,330.81	11,359,123.70
1767	42.45	13,533,125.09	1,288,411.52	14,821,535.92
1768	43.59	10,370,102.09	1,256,567.29	11,626,668.96
1769	48.05	9,523,787.51	1,142,965.29	10,666,753.38
1770	48.59	11,112,667.63	1,216,438.26	12,329,106.81
1771	41.81	11,249,274.10	1,387,074.79	12,636,347.76
1772	40.45	11,540,797.28	1,468,157.50	13,008,954.26
1773	36.68	13,894,745.09	1,512,821.92	15,407,568.16
1774	42.01	11,946,567.96	1,289,105.43	13,235,672.46
1775	49.88	9,448,165.00	1,086,334.60	10,534,498.80
1776	50.61	9,655,925.51	1,053,504.07	10,709,428.97
1777	46.57	10,711,325.96	1,263,491.45	11,974,816.41
1778	44.31	10,639,760.32	1,328,038.75	11,967,799.59
1779	54.89	8,375,641.46	1,013,272.18	9,388,914.19
1780	46.57	10,584,702.17	1,194,403.99	11,779,106.72
1781	42.8	13,532,245.33	2,641,786.21	16,174,030.37
1782	48.41	9,865,761.00	1,076,452.28	10,942,212.35
1783	49.69	9,666,604.55	1,605,678.35	11,272,282.15
1784	44.51	11,102,449.79	1,680,803.68	12,783,253.20
1785	50.41	9,128,283.28	1,730,114.88	10,858,397.14
1786	59.81	7,250,808.06	1,594,985.22	8,845,793.35
1787	52.2	8,332,021.84	1,880,625.11	10,212,647.51
1788	41.65	11,066,123.41	2,489,794.24	13,555,918.37
1789	39.12	13,917,191.46	2,815,342.54	16,732,533.23
1790	37.73	13,003,316.19	2,988,504.90	15,991,820.83
1791	38.64	12,455,344.20	2,577,335.71	15,032,681.16
1792	36.84	13,717,465.80	2,745,456.84	16,462,923.45
1793	36.64	12,413,186.41	2,417,065.50	14,830,251.09
1794	38.24	11,859,126.83	2,544,321.39	14,403,449.27

TABLE 7.6 *Customs duties in real terms (index 1910 = 100) collected at* Changguan *and* Yangguan (*taels of silver*) (cont.)

Year	Price index[a]	*Changguan*	*Yangguan*	Total *guanshui*
1795	36.84	12,327,624.32	3,181,083.06	15,508,707.93
1796	33.99	12,591,682.26	2,886,692.23	15,478,373.05
1797	32.95	13,095,610.62	2,953,484.01	16,049,095.60
1798	32.54	12,522,125.08	3,183,028.58	15,705,153.66
1799	33.37	12,728,867.25	2,808,130.06	15,536,997.30
1800	34.6	14,772,189.88	3,471,810.69	18,244,000.00
1801	40.84	10,428,263.47	3,271,723.31	13,699,987.76
1802	48.8	8,786,169.06	3,157,321.93	11,943,491.80
1803	57.44	8,091,742.86	2,951,582.52	11,043,325.21
1804	61.01	7,009,405.02	2,549,723.65	9,559,128.01
1805	63.07	7,026,340.42	2,603,411.76	9,629,752.66
1806	64.94	6,088,575.61	2,496,729.29	8,585,304.90
1807	55.2	7,379,730.25	3,014,184.78	10,393,914.86
1808	66.53	6,631,245.75	2,210,221.25	8,841,467.01
1809	65.91	6,524,216.36	2,210,896.37	8,735,113.03
1810	60.36	7,116,300.20	2,333,734.10	9,450,034.79
1811	56.15	7,241,929.83	2,075,268.21	9,317,198.58
1812	60.86	6,616,627.18	2,214,815.81	8,831,442.66
1813	60.48	6,878,437.33	2,061,356.15	8,939,793.32
1814	64.07	7,184,108.63	3,778,241.77	10,962,350.55
1815	67.39	6,091,738.83	1,975,426.47	8,067,165.75
1816	62.37	6,776,342.47	2,319,993.59	9,096,336.38
1817	53.51	7,971,833.12	2,656,146.14	10,627,979.82
1818	55.48	7,574,850.40	2,348,433.67	9,923,284.07
1819	50.85	8,806,864.70	2,714,055.26	11,520,920.35
1820	55.02	7,320,280.08	2,689,603.96	10,009,883.68
1821	57.95	6,980,410.70	2,583,300.26	9,563,711.82
1822	57.98	8,141,839.08	2,561,481.20	10,703,320.11
1823	58.19	6,841,496.13	2,414,355.04	9,255,851.52
1824	58.17	7,508,883.96	2,482,933.81	9,991,817.09
1825	58.06	6,946,976.75	2,237,046.16	9,184,023.42
1826	54.26	7,497,489.13	2,905,708.07	10,403,197.57
1827	52.28	7,992,699.50	3,538,726.09	11,531,425.02
1828	52.49	7,939,520.48	2,747,046.29	10,686,566.97
1829	53.21	7,883,724.11	2,818,230.97	10,701,954.52

Year	Price index[a]	*Changguan*	*Yangguan*	Total *guanshui*
1830	54.32	7,995,770.80	3,062,656.48	11,058,427.84
1831	58.25	6,787,778.03	2,509,538.54	9,297,316.74
1832	59.81	8,061,318.34	2,563,004.85	10,624,323.69
1833	62.88	5,880,422.87	2,350,264.47	8,230,687.02
1834	65.82	5,830,745.21	2,536,786.08	8,367,531.15
1835	55.89	7,858,478.80	2,549,551.26	10,408,030.06
1836	53.69	7,604,622.83	3,119,485.38	10,724,108.77
1837	52.35	7,755,612.03	3,418,193.51	11,173,805.16
1838	50.74	8,265,904.22	2,447,860.07	10,713,764.29
1839	53.43	7,353,621.94	2,711,134.19	10,064,755.76
1840	58.16	6,859,005.33	2,040,151.13	8,899,155.78
1841	59.26	6,825,964.39	1,458,373.56	8,284,338.51
1842	59.08	5,880,694.65	1,888,528.10	7,769,223.09
1843	54.05	6,445,696.02	2,187,768.73	8,633,465.31
1844	56.11	6,539,255.93	3,732,951.88	10,272,208.16
1845	53.69	7,166,829.02	4,849,979.33	12,016,807.60
1846	47.64	8,978,688.92	11,467,674.85	20,446,364.40
1847	48.31	7,757,436.35	5,249,899.40	13,007,335.96
1848	48.9	7,914,982.21	4,164,888.75	12,079,871.17
1849	52.85	7,544,070.58	4,111,631.03	11,655,701.04
1850	56.15	6,943,157.97	2,690,418.52	9,633,576.14
1851	52.14	7,325,765.25	5,440,303.22	12,766,068.28
1852	35.8	9,760,186.59	8,240,753.07	18,000,938.55
1853	36.41	7,288,359.79	5,134,325.46	12,422,686.08
1854	37.01	4,848,844.10	5,437,207.24	10,286,052.42
1855	38.61	4,860,648.54	6,856,878.79	11,717,526.55
1856	39.01	5,632,704.69	9,411,499.87	15,044,204.05
1857	60.45	3,115,814.72	4,774,852.94	7,890,668.32
1858	62.62	3,114,823.86	4,658,715.75	7,773,538.81
1859	55.49	3,708,542.44	6,904,277.89	10,612,820.33
1860	42.89	5,481,407.79	8,748,730.47	14,230,137.56
1861	65.54	2,406,112.45	9,932,965.52	12,339,078.43
1862	85.05	1,849,471.25	8,888,736.04	10,738,206.94
1863	78.93	2,367,314.58	10,841,856.08	13,209,170.15
1864	81	2,535,655.56	10,341,993.83	12,877,649.38
1865	63.58	3,271,326.20	12,485,017.30	15,756,343.19
1866	66.19	3,106,584.53	13,456,248.68	16,562,832.75

TABLE 7.6 *Customs duties in real terms (index 1910 = 100) collected at* Changguan *and* Yangguan (*taels of silver*) (cont.)

Year	Price index[a]	*Changguan*	*Yangguan*	Total *guanshui*
1867	53.66	4,046,021.99	16,636,805.81	20,682,827.06
1868	45.45	5,288,020.46	21,754,642.46	27,042,662.27
1869	48.24	4,850,122.51	19,965,860.28	24,815,982.59
1870	50.44	4,547,872.92	19,350,212.13	23,898,084.85
1871	48.19	4,838,936.71	22,240,029.05	27,078,966.59
1872	46.09	5,214,668.69	25,180,991.54	30,395,660.66
1873	44.73	5,357,676.06	24,998,596.02	30,356,270.96
1874	44.73	5,306,376.93	26,626,926.00	31,933,302.03
1875	40.97	5,843,104.47	29,702,494.51	35,545,599.22
1876	40.97	6,175,496.95	30,687,935.07	36,863,431.78
1877	46.86	5,423,495.95	26,234,955.19	31,658,450.70
1878	55.07	4,422,760.85	22,617,054.66	27,039,814.78
1879	46.47	6,674,381.32	28,397,239.08	35,071,620.40
1880	40.37	6,317,765.42	35,537,295.02	41,855,060.69
1881	38.47	6,634,233.17	39,128,468.94	45,762,703.41
1882	44.74	5,730,263.75	32,384,380.87	38,114,644.61
1883	47.99	5,207,375.08	28,347,416.13	33,554,790.58
1884	45.97	5,767,522.08	29,885,390.47	35,652,912.77
1885	43.92	5,641,601.09	32,281,942.17	37,923,542.81
1886	51.56	5,070,659.04	29,605,267.65	34,675,927.08
1887	51.36	5,204,211.84	35,918,309.97	41,122,521.42
1888	46.78	5,602,325.99	49,367,821.72	54,970,147.50
1889	49.58	5,215,617.59	44,230,982.25	49,446,599.44
1890	54.86	5,778,374.41	40,073,348.52	45,851,722.57
1891	55.45	4,549,497.20	41,707,008.12	46,256,504.96
1892	58.25	4,734,613.22	39,156,046.35	43,890,659.23
1893	58.89	4,102,641.87	37,470,173.20	41,572,815.42
1894	58.47	4,178,589.02	38,989,273.13	43,167,862.15
1895	60.38	3,765,945.68	34,755,067.90	38,521,013.58
1896	65.62	3,629,347.46	33,588,317.59	37,217,665.35
1897	64.17	3,792,374.01	35,332,008.73	39,124,382.11
1898	82.41	2,988,427.50	26,487,142.34	29,475,569.71
1899	75.56	3,200,155.64	34,429,899.42	37,630,055.58
1900	74.56	3,461,158.93	32,310,340.67	35,771,499.46
1901	74.76	3,042,799.22	32,000,576.51	35,043,376.14
1902	92.82	3,185,339.37	30,572,279.68	33,757,619.05

Year	Price index[a]	*Changguan*	*Yangguan*	Total *guanshui*
1903	92.42	3,994,332.61	32,918,421.34	36,912,753.73
1904	91.44	3,952,385.83	33,034,236.66	36,986,622.92
1905	79.34	5,925,605.87	41,184,237.46	47,109,843.71
1906	84.44	4,906,207.13	41,411,636.67	46,317,843.44
1907	101.34	3,937,801.66	32,758,809.95	36,696,611.41
1908	102.86	4,079,823.55	32,014,545.98	36,094,369.05
1909	88.86	5,193,745.67	37,367,867.43	42,561,612.65
1910	100	4,519,541.60	34,518,859.00	39,038,401.00

Source: [a] Price index is from Ma, Y., de Jong, H. J. & Chu, T., 2014; other data from own research, see appendices.

To present a clearer idea of how inflation developed, I have divided the period into three parts: 1723–1795, 1796–1850, and 1850–1910.

For 1723–1795, the trend line for *Changguan* is more or less flat, while that of *Yangguan* shows an increase.

During the reigns of Jiaqing and Daoguang, both *Changguan* and total *guanshui* experienced a slight decline, while *Yangguan* enjoyed a slight increase.

In the late Qing, *Changguan* was stable, while *Yangguan,* and thus total customs revenues (Total *guanshui*), increased very quickly, especially up until the 1880s.

Figure 7.16 shows that changes of customs revenues in real terms was not as sharp as the changes in nominal tax revenues in Figure 7.3. In general, *Changguan*'s trend is declining, while *Yangguan*'s trend is increasing, with the largest real increase occurring after 1850. Also, there was a very obvious decline during the reigns of Jiaqing and Daoguang when compared with that of the Qianlong, which shows that economic development in the first half of 19th century was not without its problems. Only in this sense does the "Daoguang Depression" theory make sense.[1]

There are two methods for estimating the commercial value of economic activity. One is to estimate the value of the quantity of commodities in circulation, and the other is to estimate the value of customs revenues collected and calculate the equivalent value of commercial/economic activity. In theory both approaches should lead to the same outcome. As I have already indicated, customs tariffs at *Changguan* were about 2–5% of the value of the goods.

1 Ni Yuping (2013 A), p. 78.

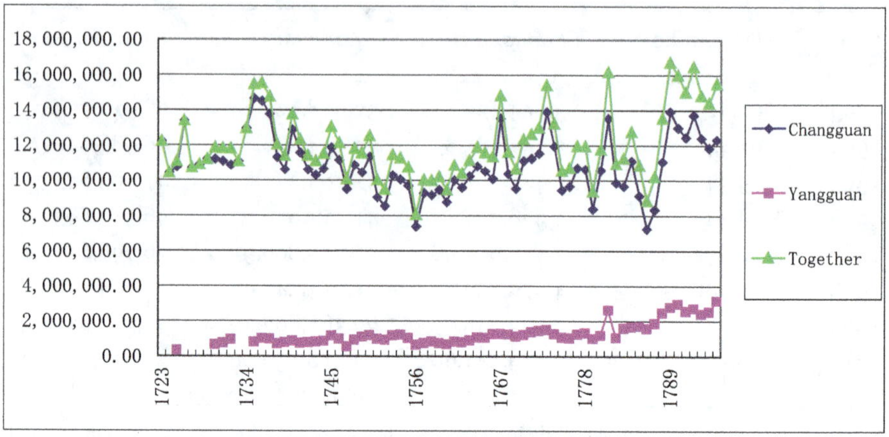

FIGURE 7.13 *Trends in real customs duties, 1723–1795*

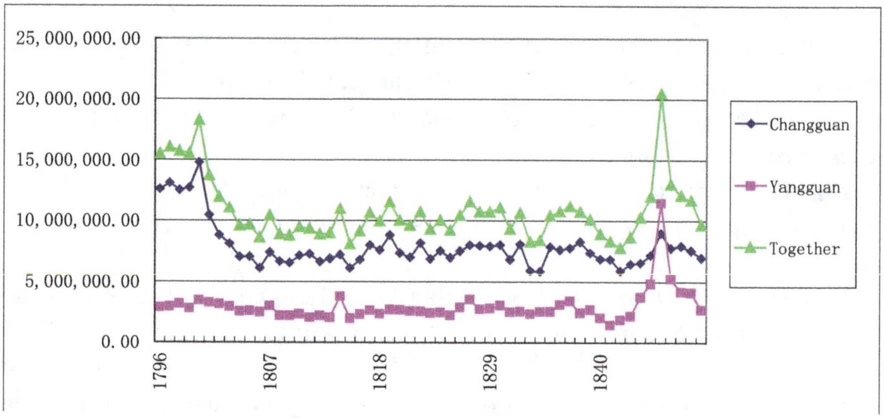

FIGURE 7.14 *Trends in real customs duties, 1796–1850*

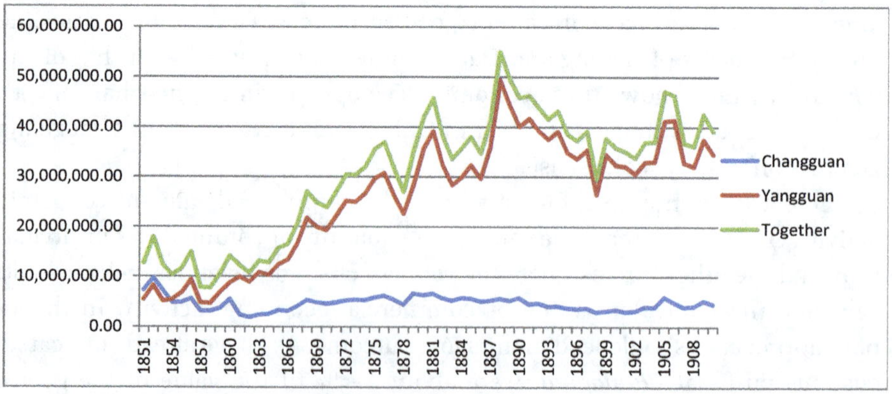

FIGURE 7.15 *Trends in real customs duties, 1851–1910*

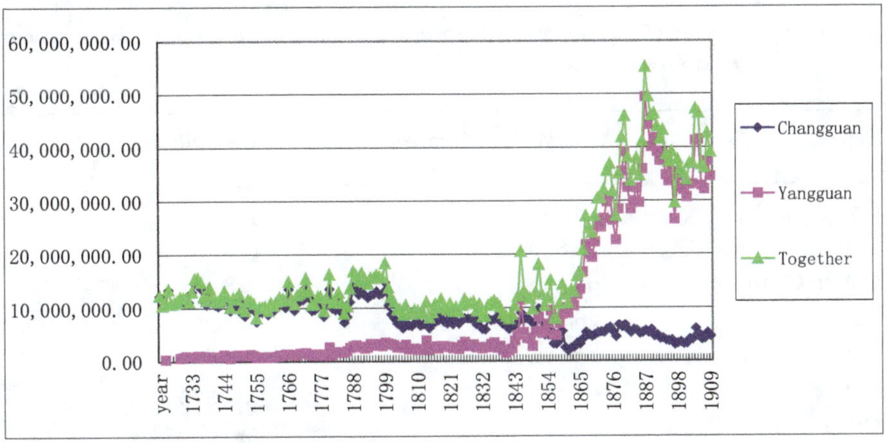

FIGURE 7.16 *Trends in real customs duties, 1723–1910*

However, at the same time we know that evasion of customs duties was widespread. In addition, customs duties were only levied on a certain varieties of goods circulating in each county—usually no more than half of sort of goods traded. Nevertheless, using customs revenues to estimate the total value of underlying commercial activity is a new way of doing this kind of research, and it has the advantage that time series of revenue data over long periods are available, rather than just for single years. However, how do they compare in years when both estimates are available?

To start with the first method, I have estimated the value of the quantity of grain, cotton, salt, and tea being traded in the year 1840. Although this has already been thoroughly researched by Xu Dixing and Wu Chengming, I have made some adjustments to the value of grain and cotton, to take into account new research done by Shi Zhihong, Xu Yi and myself. In this way, I have estimated that the commercial value of these products in 1840 was about 750 million taels of silver.

I then used customs revenue data to estimate the equivalent commercial value of these same products in 1840. As I have already stated, during the Qing dynasty customs tariffs were about 2%– 5%. To take into account corruption by officials and tax evasion by the merchants, I have used a rate of 2% to estimate the value of commerce, which I have calculated to be 250 million taels from domestic production and 150 million taels from international trade. There was also 58.529 million taels worth of salt production at that time.[2] So, together there was about 460 million taels of long-distance trade—customs duties were only levied on long-distance transport and not on local or short-distance

2 Xu Dixing and Wu Chengming (1985), Volume 1, p. 252.

TABLE 7.7 *Estimates of the value of commerce in grain, cotton, salt, and tea in 1840 (in million taels of silver)*

Type	Xu & Wu's estimate[a]	My estimate[b]
Grain	138.833	385.8
Cotton	10.859	149
Cotton Cloth	94.553	48.135
Silk	26.573	17.325
Tea	27.082	24.6
Salt	58.529	58.529
Other[c]		
> 60		
Total	387.624	750

Sources: [a] Xu Dixing and Wu Chengming (1985), Volume 1, p. 284; [b] Shi Zhihong, Xu Yi and Ni Yuping (forthcoming). [c] including, for example, fibre, mulberries, cane, tobacco, timber.

transport, which was even greater than the former. Since only about half of the goods were subject to taxation, I estimate that the total value of goods was the double of the value reflected in customs duties statistics. A total value of 750 million taels seems to be a reasonable figure for 1840, thus showing that one can estimate the value of economic activity using customs revenues.

Unfortunately, it is impossible to get production data for grain, cotton, salt, and tea in any other benchmark years. Customs revenues, however, are available for all these years. Thus, I use customs revenue data as a standard to estimate the value of commerce in benchmark years other than 1840.

TABLE 7.8 *Estimates of the value of commerce during the Qing dynasty (in million taels of silver)*

Year	1724	1766	1812	1840	1850	1887	1910
Value	241	966	850	750	840	3,710	4,173

Sources: Xu Dixing and Wu Chengming (1985), Volume 1; Ni Yuping (2010); H.B. Morse (1908); Li Hongzhang (1908); Liu Yueyun (1901).

How does population size at various times during the Qing dynasty affect these estimates? As I said earlier in this chapter, there is debate about Chinese population sizes during the Qing. I have applied several corrections to the official figures by using the data from various authors (e.g. Deng 2004; Liang 1980; Maddison 1998). Most recently, in a highly detailed analysis of the Chinese population, these numbers were further refined by Cao (2001) and Shi (2012). I get the benchmarks years' data based the population growth rates of Cao (2001).

TABLE 7.9 *Adjusted population figures in the Qing dynasty (in millions).*

Year	1724	1766	1812	1840	1850	1887	1910
Population size	202	286	369	410	436	436	439

An estimate of the value of the per capita commerce in real terms in these benchmark years can be obtained from a combination of the price index data and population figures.

TABLE 7.10 *Real capita and real per capita value of commerce during the Qing dynasty*

Benchmark year	**1724**	**1766**	**1812**	**1840**	**1850**	**1887**	**1910**
Index (1910 = 100)	30.12	47.13	60.86	58.16	56.15	51.36	100
Real value (in millions)	800	2,050	1,397	1,290	1,496	7,224	4,173
Real per capita value (in silver taels)	3.96	7.17	3.79	3.15	3.43	16.57	9.51

Table 7.10 can also be graphed; see Figure 7.17.

Figure 7.17 clearly shows that before 1850, in real terms the highest value of commerce per capita was achieved in the mid-Qianlong, a period regarded as the peak of *Kang Qian Sheng Shi* (Flourishing ages between Kangxi and Qianlong emperors). Following that, with the expansion of the population the per capita commerce entered the period of slight decline. After 1850, as a result of the modernization of industry, per capita commerce recovered, climbing to reach its highest point in 1887, several years before the First Sino-Japanese war and the Boxer Rebellion. Under the influence of war, the subsequent fall in per capita value of commerce is, of course, to be expected.

From recent research on Chinese GDP per capita between 1661 and 1933, it appears that the trend of per capita commerce closely follows that of per

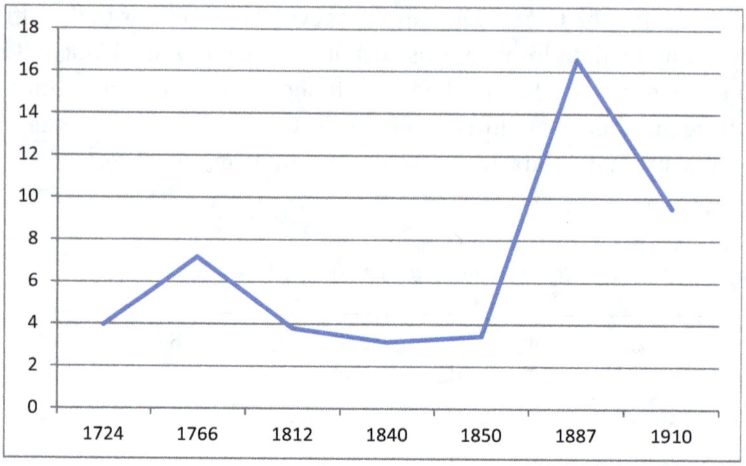

FIGURE 7.17 *Value of commerce per capita in real terms during the Qing dynasty*

capita gross domestic product[3], the lowest point of the latter occurring between 1812 and 1850. Although per capita GDP was higher before and after that period, its rise after 1850 was not as sharp as that of per capita commerce. Of course, this is only a very simple estimate based on customs revenues collected. Nevertheless, in the future it may help to estimate historical GDP more precisely.

3 Yixu, Zhihong Shi, Bas van Leeuwen, Yuping Ni, Zipeng Zhang, Ye Ma: *Chinese National Income, ca. 1661–1933*, forthcoming.

CHAPTER 8

Conclusion

Through the material I have presented in this book I have shown that the history of customs revenues collected during the Qing dynasty reflects the development of the Qing fiscal system, especially in its transition from a rather traditional to a more modern economy, and how the Qing state changed from a state with a tax system to become a fiscal state.

I readily admit that the data in the records I have accessed may be imperfect, for example because customs officials were sometimes corrupt or, more simply, because of reporting errors. However, since the reported amounts of money had to be sent to Imperial Court, the data can be interpreted as representing, at the very least, minimum amounts of revenue, and the errors can be treated as unsystematic and thus of no great influence on the general picture.

For the period before 1795, it is useful to consider customs duties of the early Qing in two parts. The first concerns the years before 1723 (which includes the reigns of Shunzhi and Kangxi), for which many data points are missing. The second part concerns the period from 1723 to 1795 (which includes the reigns of Yongzheng and Qianlong). Results from former research on the fiscal revenue of the early and middle Qing periods, are summarized in Table 8.1.

As the table shows, customs duties before 1850 still accounted for only a very small part of fiscal revenues. They represented no more than 15 of total revenues and were even smaller than the Salt Tax; the major contributor to fiscal revenues was Land Tax. The figures clearly demonstrate that Qing society before 1850 was still agricultural in its nature, with an agricultural fiscal structure. With this point of view in mind, it is easy to see that the Qing fiscal system could be typified as traditional and conservative.

From the end of the 17th century until 1840, the function of levying customs changed substantially in the West, aiming to ensure the stimulation of manufacturing and commerce. The Qing government, however, still wanted to use customs duties to safeguard the political system and stimulate its agricultural sector.

From 1840 to 1860, the Qing customs system underwent a process of change, especially due to the Taiping Rebellion, which had a unmistakable negative impact on trade and hence customs revenues. The rebellion forced the Qing government to find all kinds of ways of generating tax revenues: one by one, fiscal innovations were created, including the system of *Likin* and *Yangguan* ports. Among the domestic turmoil and foreign threats the dynasty was facing,

 | DOI 10.1163/9789004324886_010

TABLE 8.1 *Fiscal revenue of the early and middle Qing (in million taels of silver)*

Year	Total	Land Tax		Salt Tax		Customs duties		Miscellaneous taxes	
		Amount	Proportion of total (%)	Amount	Proportion of total (%)	Amount	Proportion of total (%)	Amount	Proportion of total (%)
1652	24.38	21.26	87	2.12	9	0.642	2.6	0.358	1.55
1685	31.90	27.27	85	2.76	9	1.20	3.78	0.67	2.1
1725	36.53	30.07	82	4.43	12	1.35	3.7	0.68	1.9
1753	41.74	29.38	70	7.01	17	4.30	10.3	1.05	2.5
1766	42.25	29.91	71	5.74	14	5.40	12.8	1.20	2.8
1812	40.13	28.33	71	5.79	14	4.81	11.9	1.20	3
1841	42.45	29.43	69	7.47	18	4.35	10.2	1.20	2.8

Source: He Benfang (1987), pp. 78–81.

its officials came to realize more and more the potential benefits a comprehensive system of customs duties offered.

Finally, from 1860 through to the early 20th century the Qing customs system gradually—step by step—came under the control of Western powers.

Table 8.2 illustrates how the fiscal structure underwent great change in the 19th century. Customs duties, together with *Likin* and Salt Taxes, were almost three times as large as Land Tax. At the same time, customs duties had become one of the most powerful fiscal instruments at the Qing government's disposal and it was to be an indispensable tool in the struggle to keep the government alive in the late Qing. Thus, we are able to say that in the late Qing, China was in the process of changing from a traditional agricultural society that depended on a mainly land-based system of taxation to a modern commercially-based society with a complementary fiscal system. Understanding about the function of customs systems evolved rapidly, and people began to accept Western ideas about its value.

However, due to insufficient development of the production of handicrafts and manufacturing, and in the face of great difficulties in maintaining an agriculture-based fiscal system, the government had little choice but to embrace a commercial fiscal system. Regarding *Yangguan*, Tang's book offers a detailed explanation. Of the income sourced from *Yangguan*, between two-thirds and four-fifths would be sent to the central government and used to pay

TABLE 8.2 *Sources of fiscal revenue in the late Qing (in taels of silver)*

Year	Land tax		Salt tax		Customs duties		Miscellaneous taxes	
	Amount	Proportion of total (%)	Amount	Proportion of total (%)	Amount	Proportion of total (%)	Amount Amount	Proportion of total (%)
1842	29,575,722	76	4,981,845	13	–	–	4,130,455	11
1885	32,356,768	48	7,394,228	11	12,811,708	19	14,472,766	22
1888	33,243,437	42	7,507,128	10	13,600,733	18	23,167,892	30
1894	32,669,086	43	6,737,469	9	13,286,816	18	22,523,605	30
1903	37,187,788	38	13,050,000	13	16,252,692	17	30,530,699	32
1911	48,101,346	27	46,312,355	26	43,187,097	24	43,139,287	23

Source: Deng Shaohui (1997).

government salaries, military expenditures, indemnities and external debt (Tang (2005): 25-43).

A second part was sent to the local province. Tang writes that before 1867 the proportion would be 20-30, while after 1867 it declined quickly: "From 1861 to 1910 provincial expenditures were 72,260,204 taels, which represented about 7.94 of all the *Yangguan*" (Tang (2005): 44).

A third, smaller part, amounting to no more than 15 of total revenues, was set aside to meet administrative overheads and agency expenses (a 63.2 share), which were mainly the salaries (including the Western administrator's fee) and daily working expenses of the Customs Revenue Division. From 1861 to 1910 this part totalled 127,713,615 taels of silver, representing 14.03 of all expenditure. Tang also writes that there were 910,000 000 taels of income from *Yangguan*, of which the central government took 694,717,188 taels, which was used to meet a variety of expenses including military expenditures, indemnities and external debt.

As a result of his research, Tang arrived at the conclusion that "From these figures, we can see clearly the areas in which the Chinese Customs Service was mainly used and whom it serviced. These fifty years of data of the distribution of customs revenues prove that Chinese customs system had a semi-feudal nature" (Tang (2005): 47).

As I have already mentioned, the development of the customs system during the Qing dynasty possessed peculiar characteristics. Sometimes it remained so stable that one cannot directly estimate economic development from the data, which merely demonstrate the fiscal ability of the country without saying much about its economic and social development. However, in the long run the data do, in fact, reflect changes taking place in economic development and the social system. They clearly show that traditional Qing China still followed the rule of the "natural economy" and that nobody had the power to challenge the rule of nature.

Postscript

It was more than ten years ago that I began my research on the customs duties of the Jiaqing and Daoguang periods (1796–1850) of the Qing China. At the beginning, I mainly focused on the debate of "Daoguang Depression" which was initiated by Prof. Wu Chengming (1917.1.3-2011.7.8). My monograph titled *Qing Chao Jia Dao Guan Shui Yan Jiu* (Research on the Customs Duties in the Jiaqing and Daoguang Reigns of the Qing Dynasty) (Beijing: Beijing Normal University Press, 2010) summarized my initial results. After that, I continued to collected archives and other material of customs duties during the whole Qing Dynasty. This book is the result of that archival research.

I wish to express gratitude and great respect to Prof. Wu Chengming, without his assistance, I could not have pursued this research in such detail. I am also grateful to Prof. Tang Xianglong. I revised his data published in his classical book *Zhong Guo Jin Dai Hai Guan Shui Shou He Fen Pei Tong Ji: 1861–1910* (Statistics of Customs Revenue and Its Distribution: 1861–1910) (Beijing: Zhonghua Shuju, 2005).

I am very grateful to Prof. Bozhong Li of Tsinghua University, for him wiritng a foreword for this book. As the most outstanding scholar in Chinese economic historian, he has always given me advice and encouragement. I feel especially lucky that we are now colleagues and neighbours. My thanks go to Prof. Maaten Duijvendak of Groningen University, who wrote the second forword for this book. When I stayed in Groningen, he spent much time to help me to adapt to the new circumstances and he was always ready to discuss my research. It was a wonderful experience.

I do not know how to express my thanks to Prof. Martin Uebele of Groningen University, who helped me to have the cooperation with Dutch historians. As guest researcher at Groningen University from January to August of 2015, I really enjoyed the time to teach a course "Fiscal and Economic History of China and Europe" in Groningen University with him. We discussed this book for many hours in our office, in emails or in other ways. Under his influence, I began to treat Chinese historical data in a more economic way. He helped me to revise this book chapter after chapter, in terms of language and contents.

My sincere thanks to Prof. Bas van Leeuwen of Utrecht University, Prof. Yi Xu of Guangxi Normal University. They encouraged me to join the program of the Quantitative Economic History of China, which pushed me to write such a book in English directly. It is a great challenge but also a memorable experience for me.

 | DOI 10.1163/9789004324886_011

The research for this book was made possible by the generous support from Prof. Dwight. H. Perkins (Harvard University), Prof. Zhihong Shi (Chinese Academy of Social Sciences, Weimin Zhong (Tsinghua University), James Kung (The Hong Kong University of Science and Technology) and Yibin Deng (Beijing Academy of Social Sciences). Many people have read and provided helpful comments on this manuscript: Peter Foldvari (editor of the series Quantitative Economic History of China, International Institute of Social History), Patrick Wallis (London School of Economic and Political Science), Guillaume Daudin (Paris Dauphine University). Especially Peter Foldvari spent a lot of time to help me improve the language of this book.I have also benefited from considerable support from Manhong Lin (Taiwan Academia Sinica), Kishimoto Mio (Ochanomizu University) and Bin Yang (National Singapore University). During my stay in Groningen, I learned a lot from Prof. Anjana Singh, Geurt Collenteur, Richard Paping, Erwin Karel, H.J.de.Jong, and Ye Ma, either in lunch time or from our chats in the corridor.

I gratefully acknowledge the financial support by the Confucius Understanding China Program, the Netherlands Organization for Scientific Research NWO, and the Graduate School for the Humanities at the University of Groningen. This book was mainly finished in Groningen, with the support by Hanban of China government. I also would like to express my thanks to Ms. Jinyi Li, Xuefei Cao and Yingying Xiao of Groningen Confucius Institute. I hope I will have the chance to get in touch with them in the future.

Last but not least, I would like to express my gratitude to my family who have shown remarkable strength during these years. They are always the driving force of my work and, at last, they can now see what I have been up to during the recent years.

APPENDIX A

Customs Revenues Collected at *Changguan*, 1723–1910

TABLE A.1 *Customs revenues collected at selected* Changguan, *1723–1909 (taels of silver)*

Year	Shanhai Guan	Zhangjiakou	Shahukou	Guihuacheng	Dajianlu	Chen Guan	Zhongjiang
1723	–	–	12,041.30	–	–	–	–
1724	–	–	–	–	–	–	–
1725	–	–	–	–	–	–	–
1726	–	–	–	–	–	–	4,800.00
1727	–	–	–	–	–	9,300.00	–
1728	–	–	–	–	–	12,400.00	–
1729	–	–	–	–	–	12,500.00	–
1730	–	–	–	–	–	13,416.89	–
1731	–	–	–	–	–	–	–
1732	–	–	–	–	–	–	–
1733	–	–	–	–	–	–	–
1734	–	–	–	–	–	12,553.34	–
1735	–	–	19,323.17	–	19,368.00	13,427.66	4,095.10
1736	–	–	25,929.00	–	19,324.76	12,500.00	4,803.63
1737	59,329.68	–	28,216.35	–		12,535.98	3,822.44
1738	–	–	31,433.92	–		13,429.24	–
1739	–	–	–	–	20,246.59	12,533.95	4,806.00
1740	–	–	–	–	20,319.44	12,527.60	4,004.40
1741	–	–	–	–	20,478.64	13,438.92	3,210.20
1742	–	–	27,638.41	–	20,092.02	12,552.20	3,158.38
1743	–	–	38,358.06	–	19,585.60	13,400.00	3,313.60
1744	–	–	38,093.52	–	20,115.68	12,544.98	4,395.30
1745	95,525.03	–	37,315.88	–	19,699.86	12,542.73	3,050.00
1746	–	–	37,415.88	–	18,684.75	13,476.36	3,537.00
1747	–	48,013.89	34,515.85	–	20,008.88	12,565.50	4,364.33
1748	–	52,083.62	34,752.11	–	18,147.15	12,928.81	4,610.71
1749	102,132.22	–	37,999.56	–	19,504.52	13,801.05	3,477.31
1750	103,026.28	–	36,968.36	–	20,504.47	12,936.56	–
1751	–	–	36,390.44	–	19,371.68	16,336.71	4,304.49
1752	–	–	36,910.76	–	19,401.30	14,619.41	–

 | DOI 10.1163/9789004324886_012

TABLE A.1 *Customs revenues collected at selected* Changguan, *1723–1909* (*taels of silver*) (cont.)

Year	Shanhai Guan	Zhangjiakou	Shahukou	Guihuacheng	Dajianlu	Chen Guan	Zhongjiang
1753	–	–	36,427.55	–	19,702.35	14,620.62	4,756.05
1754	–	–	35,875.64	–	19,675.13	16,322.50	3,256.20
1755	–	–	–	–	19,779.62	14,618.76	3,447.85
1756	–	–	33,318.97	–	19,416.63	14,621.46	2,295.24
1757	–	–	35,807.27	–	21,673.69	16,337.92	–
1758	–	–	32,626.54	–	19,805.62	14,644.83	2,720.27
1759	–	47,429.44	34,600.54	–	21,044.09	15,691.49	3,081.85
1760	–	49,890.05	30,146.16	–	22,598.82	20,051.40	3,039.37
1761	–	–	30,740.70	24,000.00	20,146.12	18,191.22	–
1762	–	47,059.08	34,181.56	–	20,180.63	20,053.70	–
1763	–	37,491.61	33,349.04	–	22,504.71	18,196.23	3,255.64
1764	–	40,849.39	–	17,569.78	22,923.56	18,196.28	3,095.55
1765	–	43,543.04	36,639.08	17,752.23	22,521.53	20,054.21	2,137.62
1766	107,163.45	–	52,236.53	17,958.06	23,021.76	18,198.34	3,166.30
1767	98,424.05	–	–	–	23,506.45	19,154.29	–
1768	101,371.09	–	–	–	23,506.45	20,065.29	–
1769	–	–	44,405.50	–	23,506.45	18,203.79	–
1770	–	48,593.30	44,479.33	25,686.40	23,216.45	20,070.82	3,294.62
1771	–	–	34,988.82	25,889.24	24,180.88	18,204.67	–
1772	–	–	35,121.66	25,960.08	23,352.44	18,205.64	3,295.47
1773	–	–	35,384.49	25,983.41	22,923.27	20,071.96	3,296.08
1774	106,709.17	–	35,437.82	25,987.50	23,564.37	18,207.29	3,298.34
1775	101,310.16	50,623.28	35,556.16	25,990.98	25,221.13	18,209.00	3,339.28
1776	–	–	35,860.79	25,169.06	25,233.87	20,072.51	–
1777	120,058.94	53,187.43	36,009.37	26,853.15	19,362.08	18,210.05	–
1778	124,022.10	53,506.23	36,160.53	53,712.60	19,828.81	18,210.57	3,338.48
1779	127,558.56	–	36,273.35	26,860.44	21,458.52	20,073.19	3,368.40
1780	130,176.00	–	36,376.33	26,864.64	21,464.57	18,211.02	3,303.44
1781	261,631.50	–	36,622.15	26,873.15	25,221.13	20,073.79	–
1782	–	–	37,021.96	26,882.97	25,234.89	18,211.62	4,461.81
1783	131,650.85	–	36,893.52	26,889.49	25,235.02	18,212.28	3,303.95
1784	132,199.90	–	37,053.66	26,898.98	24,048.02	20,074.51	3,345.69
1785	134,203.90	–	37,283.81	26,910.58	22,745.51	18,212.80	–
1786	135,755.90	–	37,584.95	26,961.33	21,271.51	18,213.04	–
1787	136,129.90	–	38,023.39	26,972.94	20,706.02	20,074.74	–

Year	Shanhai Guan	Zhangjiakou	Shahukou	Guihuacheng	Dajianlu	Chen Guan	Zhongjiang
1788	136,633.33	–	38,633.73	26,984.83	19,694.32	–	3,304.78
1789	86,753.33	–	39,436.08	26,991.58	19,723.39	18,213.00	3,361.52
1790	85,788.35	–	40,278.78	26,997.36	20,389.52	18,213.00	3,503.63
1791	94,149.85	–	40,840.03	26,999.11	20,258.41	18,213.85	–
1792	102,203.19	–	40,873.37	27,003.70	20,258.41	–	3,304.98
1793	137,029.90	–	41,162.51	27,007.38	22,641.09	18,214.06	3,305.02
1794	103,345.97	–	43,126.77	27,013.60	24,007.01	–	3,305.04
1795	137,542.20	–	43,396.77	27,019.45	25,131.87	–	3,305.06
1796	137,615.80	–	43,640.06	27,023.63	24,591.12	–	3,305.10
1797	137,702.19	–	43,769.75	27,028.88	21,296.78	–	–
1798	110,642.38	–	43,972.61	27,032.15	23,409.15	–	3,305.14
1799	115,624.16	60,906.17	44,199.30	–	22,460.15	18,215.42	3,305.17
1800	–	60,937.60	44,340.03	27,032.14	22,306.15	18,215.55	–
1801	–	60,820.09	45,047.93	27,032.15	20,000.00	27,711.08	3,305.25
1802	135,568.17	–	45,067.88	27,033.28	21,341.52	27,711.14	3,338.37
1803	136,149.27	61,001.07	–	27,033.37	21,847.11	–	3,305.30
1804	131,938.73	60,994.62	45,162.81	–	22,139.14	27,711.16	3,305.32
1805	127,550.15	61,003.40	45,229.98	27,033.81	22,145.61	–	3,305.35
1806	127,643.55	61,005.62	45,302.81	–	22,289.14	27,711.19	3,326.81
1807	115,389.90	61,008.71	45,344.36	27,034.09	20,000.00	27,711.19	3,305.39
1808	113,429.42	61,018.12	45,417.98	27,034.21	44,881.49	29,692.00	3,305.45
1809	113,657.63	61,015.80	45,492.80	27,034.38	22,223.46	29,692.00	–
1810	114,138.55	61,018.71	45,580.69	–	21,590.00	29,692.00	3,305.49
1811	114,231.41	61,021.04	45,677.41	54,069.39	21,868.64	29,692.00	3,305.52
1812	111,598.09	61,025.44	45,755.34	27,035.01	22,372.57	29,692.00	–
1813	111,551.04	61,028.97	45,780.69	27,035.20	22,433.41	29,692.00	3,305.54
1814	223,063.10	61,034.93	45,795.27	–	21,490.86	29,692.00	3,305.57
1815	111,430.24	61,041.41	45,845.40	27,035.04	21,407.71	29,692.00	3,305.59
1816	–	61,043.65	45,848.12	27,035.81	22,104.28	29,692.19	3,305.61
1817	–	61,045.43	45,887.27	27,036.01	21,584.86	29,692.00	–
1818	111,966.80	61,047.63	45,895.13	–	22,350.60	29,692.00	3,305.66
1819	112,325.50	60,966.73	45,898.27	–	22,157.00	29,692.00	3,305.69
1820	112,601.34	60,980.75	45,908.94	27,036.36	20,000.00	29,692.00	3,305.71
1821	112,940.44	60,979.51	45,929.13	27,036.65	20,000.00	29,692.50	3,305.74
1822	112,460.96	121,972.13	45,946.50	27,036.46	20,460.60	29,692.52	3,305.75
1823	112,554.41	60,992.16	45,960.37	–	19,975.49	29,692.00	–
1824	112,622.93	60,998.72	45,971.91	27,037.07	20,000.00	–	3,305.80

TABLE A.1 *Customs revenues collected at selected* Changguan, *1723–1909* (*taels of silver*) (cont.)

Year	Shanhai Guan	Zhangjiakou	Shahukou	Guihuacheng	Dajianlu	Chen Guan	Zhongjiang
1825	112,755.16	61,004.83	45,982.40	27,037.19	20,000.00	–	3,305.82
1826	111,245.24	61,000.95	46,002.96	27,037.33	20,000.00	–	–
1827	112,611.97	61,006.53	46,021.16	27,037.48	–	–	3,305.89
1828	111,446.99	61,011.11	46,029.97	27,037.62	–	–	3,305.90
1829	111,738.15	61,013.88	46,058.53	–	–	–	–
1830	111,457.15	61,095.93	92,131.27	27,037.93	23,519.19	–	–
1831	111,751.75	61,008.41	46,088.99	27,038.16	–	–	–
1832	112,203.78	60,950.63	46,094.09	27,038.22	–	–	3,305.94
1833	111,887.37	60,953.02	46,109.42	–	–	–	3,305.95
1834	112,291.38	60,953.12	46,125.67	27,038.53	–	–	3,305.98
1835	112,514.77	60,966.58	92,304.47	27,038.69	–	–	3,305.99
1836	112,381.28	60,980.92	46,176.56	27,038.85	–	–	3,305.99
1837	112,429.88	61,076.25	46,187.01	27,039.00	–	–	3,306.00
1838	112,626.53	60,996.24	46,198.16	27,039.15	–	–	3,306.01
1839	112,890.64	60,985.10	46,206.21	27,039.30	–	–	3,306.01
1840	112,836.25	60,970.68	46,215.26	27,039.45	–	–	–
1841	111,969.29	60,964.98	46,221.86	27,039.60	–	–	3,306.03
1842	111,326.84	60,951.05	46,229.11	54,079.70	–	–	3,306.04
1843	87,979.13	60,956.12	46,235.42	–	–	17,283.63	3,306.05
1844	111,441.78	60,968.26	46,241.80	27,038.25	–	–	3,306.06
1845	–	–	46,248.52	27,040.45	–	–	–
1846	223,119.98	60,957.05	46,253.12	–	–	–	–
1847	111,997.77	62,270.71	46,257.77	–	–	–	3,306.07
1848	111,844.66	62,283.95	46,258.97	–	–	–	3,306.08
1849	111,862.96	62,285.69	46,263.37	28,840.74	–	–	–
1850	111,900.68	62,292.50	46,467.37	27,040.93	20,176.68	–	3,306.09
1851	111,970.38	62,297.78	46,271.87	27,040.59	21,544.29	–	4,693.29
1852	119,029.11	–	46,281.63	27,041.05	–	–	3,306.10
1853	117,233.92	62,303.30	46,278.57	27,041.12	20,033.72	–	3,306.11
1854	112,673.38	78,744.10	22,623.23	18,021.30	21,447.20	–	3,306.11
1855	112,331.86	43,680.12	28,935.32	25,636.00	20,002.62	–	3,306.12
1856	152,906.38	62,126.14	37,137.69	25,636.00	–	–	3,306.13
1857	116,160.38	62,143.93	41,774.10	25,794.29	21,670.86	–	–
1858	116,161.05	62,136.39	44,145.03	25,794.36	–	–	3,306.15
1859	–	55,175.34	44,356.48	25,794.44	20,004.62	–	3,306.17

Year	Shanhai Guan	Zhangjiakou	Shahukou	Guihuacheng	Dajianlu	Chen Guan	Zhongjiang
1860	–	38,514.57	44,363.93	25,794.51	21,629.44	–	–
1861	172,243.38	62,161.44	44,370.57	25,794.57	20,015.25	–	3,306.20
1862	139,416.09	56,753.77	43,150.21	25,794.63	21,557.82	–	3,306.22
1863	143,865.38	–	44,374.52	–	20,025.99	–	3,306.24
1864	131,234.88	59,124.05	44,379.32	–	20,033.42	–	3,306.27
1865	151,157.36	43,345.57	44,392.41	–	–	–	3,306.30
1866	132,475.88	43,392.05	44,396.87	–	20,030.41	–	3,306.33
1867	153,151.31	42,553.25	44,409.51	–	20,017.28	–	2,029.46
1868	191,129.38	43,420.50	88,842.97	–	21,631.35	–	1,366.22
1869	191,129.38	41,549.52	44,431.85	–	20,003.27	–	3,306.39
1870	191,129.38	–	44,436.59	–	21,662.26	34,851.95	3,306.42
1871	169,141.71	37,366.37	44,441.42	–	20,050.63	–	3,306.46
1872	172,335.12	37,474.38	44,446.52	–	20,043.63	–	–
1873	173,255.79	37,687.90	44,451.52	–	21,677.92	–	3,306.53
1874	183,178.06	37,829.30	44,456.02	–	20,035.43	–	3,306.59
1875	171,632.59	37,839.85	44,459.05	–	20,031.36	–	3,306.64
1876	173,904.68	37,891.69	44,463.10	–	21,662.57	–	3,306.69
1877	174,304.59	37,992.09	44,466.60	–	20,044.38	–	3,306.75
1878	173,661.81	38,156.60	27,886.21	–	20,039.14	–	3,306.80
1879	364,372.61	38,367.36	43,391.68	–	21,668.49	–	3,306.86
1880	173,243.23	38,623.87	43,391.80	–	17,457.25	22,640.38	3,306.92
1881	191,129.38	40,846.85	43,391.90	–	21,652.28	–	3,307.00
1882	191,129.38	38,923.11	34,892.71	–	20,003.27	–	3,307.07
1883	119,129.38	39,072.33	34,733.73	–	20,038.08	–	5,574.97
1884	191,129.38	39,174.79	25,267.74	–	21,654.08	–	44,004.54
1885	191,129.38	39,287.85	25,266.20	–	20,034.10	–	–
1886	–	39,408.00	43,542.13	–	20,037.26	–	–
1887	–	79,290.55	43,542.13	–	21,654.30	–	23,859.72
1888	191,129.38	40,121.16	43,542.13	–	20,043.02	24,506.30	7,209.04
1889	168,572.78	40,442.19	43,542.13	–	20,041.39	–	7,005.53
1890	–	41,456.98	35,042.08	–	21,648.00	17,984.81	5,417.94
1891	215,288.89	41,781.12	43,542.13	–	20,045.15	–	–
1892	191,129.38	42,104.72	43,542.13	–	21,661.37	–	5,738.51
1893	–	42,240.13	17,323.03	–	20,050.33	–	4,598.52
1894	191,129.38	40,384.81	26,323.34	–	20,051.25	–	–
1895	36,500.00	40,492.23	37,524.44	–	21,658.63	–	–
1896	171,675.59	42,149.41	29,725.54	–	20,034.58	–	–

TABLE A.1 *Customs revenues collected at selected* Changguan, *1723–1909* (*taels of silver*) (cont.)

Year	Shanhai Guan	Zhangjiakou	Shahukou	Guihuacheng	Dajianlu	Chen Guan	Zhongjiang
1897	199,646.74	42,303.68	27,650.77	–	–	–	–
1898	198,144.92	42,473.71	30,845.20	–	–	–	–
1899	198,235.25	43,390.34	–	–	–	–	–
1900	198,239.96	31,202.66	60,203.08	–	21,658.92	11,776.73	–
1901	7,466.53	–	–	–	20,039.25	10,978.11	–
1902	–	–	33,258.93	–	20,037.25	11,916.05	–
1903	24,157.76	–	–	–	21,659.92	9,123.14	–
1904	23,195.20	–	43,338.07	–	20,042.25	12,917.25	–
1905	46,795.35	–	43,338.07	–	20,040.25	25,441.28	–
1906	33,269.36	–	46,142.10	–	21,649.47	20,074.41	–
1907	34,743.29	96,564.05	114,208.30	–	20,034.57	26,634.27	–
1908	231,203.10	–	113,760.77	–	20,039.32	16,898.77	–
1909	–	–	131,939.43	–	28,928.25	18,226.76	–

TABLE A.2 *Customs revenues collected at selected* Changguan, *1723–1910* (*taels of silver*)

Year	Fengtian Niuma Shui	Wuchang and Xunchang	Pantaokou	Wuyuancheng	Gubeikou	Chongwenmen	Zuoyi
1723	–	–	–	–	–	–	–
1724	–	–	–	–	–	–	–
1725	–	–	–	–	–	–	–
1726	–	82,959.39	–	–	–	–	–
1727	–	–	–	–	–	–	–
1728	–	–	–	–	–	–	–
1729	–	–	–	–	–	–	–
1730	–	80,959.00	–	–	1,012.00	–	–
1731	–	–	–	–	–	–	–
1732	–	–	–	–	–	–	–
1733	–	–	–	–	–	–	–
1734	–	–	–	–	402.07	–	–
1735	–	81,974.04	10,108.67	–	–	237,058.51	–
1736	–	–	–	–	–	304,520.14	–
1737	–	81,812.23	–	–	–	–	–

Year	Fengtian Niuma Shui	Wuchang and Xunchang	Pantaokou	Wuyuancheng	Gubeikou	Chongwenmen	Zuoyi
1738	–	82,475.60	–	–	–	213,270.77	–
1739	–	82,959.39	–	–	–	–	–
1740	5,733.90	–	–	–	–	–	–
1741	5,047.61	–	–	–	–	–	–
1742	–	82,735.09	–	–	–	–	–
1743	–	79,400.78	–	–	–	–	–
1744	–	86,645.57	–	–	–	262,147.88	–
1745	5,070.61	91,187.69	–	–	–	154,280.18	–
1746	5,024.27	93,012.47	–	–	–	154,425.24	–
1747	5,097.06	93,303.76	–	1,267.22	–	157,003.67	–
1748	–	92,544.33	14,292.96	–	–	152,858.88	–
1749	–	92,919.45	15,525.25	–	1,013.32	–	–
1750	4,238.09	92,944.66	10,667.68	1,267.32	–	130,423.81	–
1751	–	98,293.95	8,614.00	–	–	–	–
1752	–	108,313.90	–	–	1,013.76	153,981.97	–
1753	–	108,830.53	–	–	–	149,558.15	–
1754	–	–	–	–	–	181,409.19	–
1755	–	–	10,780.27	–	–	193,117.57	–
1756	–	108,754.37	13,194.47	–	–	198,979.94	–
1757	–	–	14,048.92	–	1,012.53	–	–
1758	–	108,758.42	–	–	–	–	–
1759	–	108,760.31	14,947.81	–	1,012.53	199,947.44	47,817.07
1760	–	–	15,101.35	–	–	241,072.97	50,154.95
1761	–	108,775.16	14,729.60	–	–	–	–
1762	–	108,789.46	16,332.37	–	–	260,085.68	–
1763	–	108,799.86	14,521.37	–	–	172,139.56	–
1764	–	108,808.30	–	–	–	264,569.62	–
1765	–	108,817.84	–	–	–	204,917.56	38,739.15
1766	–	108,829.40	–	–	–	–	41,795.79
1767	–	217,693.98	–	–	–	–	41,140.16
1768	–	–	–	–	–	–	38,861.88
1769	–	108,831.94	–	–	–	197,752.17	–
1770	–	–	–	–	–	–	39,965.40
1771	–	123,295.09	–	–	–	201,926.70	–
1772	–	123,303.35	–	1,269.97	1,012.63	228,675.75	–
1773	–	123,309.67	–	–	–	264,768.21	–

TABLE A.2 *Customs revenues collected at selected* Changguan, *1723–1910* (*taels of silver*) (cont.)

Year	Fengtian Niuma Shui	Wuchang and Xunchang	Pantaokou	Wuyuancheng	Gubeikou	Chongwenmen	Zuoyi
1774	–	123,315.96	–	–	–	309,563.10	–
1775	5,012.07	–	–	–	1,097.01	309,339.46	44,567.70
1776	–	–	–	–	1,012.63	316,089.47	–
1777	–	–	11,222.64	–	–	309,673.28	43,949.93
1778	–	–	–	–	–	322,641.37	–
1779	–	123,339.29	–	–	–	316,834.95	46,916.62
1780	–	123,344.50	–	–	–	–	48,877.09
1781	–	123,447.70	–	–	–	269,735.04	46,119.30
1782	–	123,350.31	–	–	–	–	–
1783	–	123,352.55	–	–	–	–	–
1784	–	–	–	–	–	–	–
1785	–	–	–	–	–	–	–
1786	–	–	–	–	1,096.97	–	–
1787	–	–	–	–	–	287,303.17	–
1788	–	124,274.80	–	–	–	288,128.70	–
1789	–	–	11,219.98	–	–	–	–
1790	–	124,279.23	–	–	–	–	–
1791	–	124,281.26	–	–	–	285,397.38	–
1792	5,232.59	124,282.83	–	–	–	296,544.60	–
1793	–	124,284.32	–	–	–	286,893.56	–
1794	–	124,285.57	–	–	–	283,507.57	–
1795	–	124,287.22	–	–	–	–	41,525.00
1796	–	124,289.00	–	1,233.00	–	288,831.22	–
1797	5,059.73	124,286.61	–	1,233.00	–	294,029.97	–
1798	5,301.04	124,292.00	11,190.84	1,233.00	–	288,115.57	–
1799	5,260.66	–	–	1,233.00	–	299,914.50	–
1800	5,290.42	–	–	1,233.00	–	297,829.72	–
1801	–	118,040.49	–	1,233.00	–	–	–
1802	–	–	–	1,269.57	–	307,806.18	–
1803	6,016.50	118,043.64	–	1,233.00	–	316,729.32	–
1804	–	118,044.19	–	1,269.58	–	322,539.72	42,078.99
1805	5,080.16	118,043.26	–	1,233.00	–	313,564.82	–
1806	5,082.59	–	–	1,233.00	–	314,659.82	42,897.55
1807	–	118,044.84	–	1,233.00	–	322,501.30	–
1808	5,087.76	118,045.44	–	1,233.00	–	322,645.02	45,286.25

Year	Fengtian Niuma Shui	Wuchang and Xunchang	Pantaokou	Wuyuancheng	Gubeikou	Chongwenmen	Zuoyi
1809	5,090.05	–	12,553.61	1,233.00	–	264,387.06	–
1810	–	118,046.73	12,338.44	1,233.00	–	308,279.96	42,325.78
1811	–	–	–	1,233.00	–	322,655.34	–
1812	–	118,047.70	–	1,233.00	–	286,126.50	–
1813	–	–	–	1,233.00	–	297,142.85	37,911.14
1814	–	118,049.39	–	1,233.00	–	322,804.22	40,798.67
1815	5,093.02	–	–	1,233.00	–	314,871.92	41,532.53
1816	5,099.65	–	–	1,233.00	–	290,118.50	–
1817	5,099.76	–	–	1,233.00	–	314,871.24	–
1818	5,099.99	118,050.90	–	1,233.00	–	314,873.42	40,216.32
1819	–	118,051.27	11,180.90	1,233.00	–	322,891.58	39,099.30
1820	–	118,051.56	11,645.35	1,233.00	–	314,872.92	39,441.57
1821	–	–	–	1,233.00	–	290,229.52	40,115.12
1822	5,100.39	118,052.29	–	1,233.00	–	291,651.43	39,776.08
1823	–	–	–	1,035.00	–	320,317.04	39,421.86
1824	–	–	–	–	–	319,604.48	38,844.93
1825	5,102.01	118,052.58	–	–	–	319,008.69	39,642.83
1826	–	118,052.87	–	–	–	–	38,608.32
1827	–	–	–	1,016.42	–	–	78,920.22
1828	–	–	–	–	–	319,021.87	38,749.50
1829	–	118,055.06	–	–	–	319,039.47	38,858.72
1830	5,109.94	118,055.28	–	–	–	328,183.57	38,999.58
1831	5,110.58	–	–	–	–	–	38,055.08
1832	–	–	–	–	–	–	38,631.35
1833	5,115.56	118,057.16	–	–	–	323,381.18	37,981.70
1834	–	117,752.50	–	–	–	315,358.44	38,191.35
1835	–	118,057.63	–	–	–	328,190.47	39,498.89
1836	5,120.57	–	–	–	–	–	39,325.55
1837	–	118,058.30	–	–	–	–	39,196.64
1838	–	118,058.66	–	–	–	323,394.45	39,004.14
1839	–	118,058.96	–	–	–	315,380.25	38,483.54
1840	5,124.26	118,059.31	–	–	–	315,099.45	39,004.97
1841	5,125.26	118,059.65	–	–	–	323,112.42	38,214.62
1842	5,126.55	118,060.03	–	–	–	315,102.65	37,767.87
1843	–	–	–	–	–	323,114.62	37,814.72
1844	–	–	–	–	–	315,119.17	38,687.85

TABLE A.2 *Customs revenues collected at selected* Changguan, *1723–1910* (*taels of silver*) (cont.)

Year	Fengtian Niuma Shui	Wuchang and Xunchang	Pantaokou	Wuyuancheng	Gubeikou	Chongwenmen	Zuoyi
1845	–	118,061.46	–	–	–	315,627.00	38,025.89
1846	–	–	–	–	–	323,666.06	38,099.78
1847	5,131.84	–	–	–	–	–	37,680.81
1848	–	–	11,835.67	–	–	–	37,533.18
1849	–	118,063.70	–	–	–	323,739.00	37,557.84
1850	–	–	–	–	–	–	37,985.53
1851	–	–	1,074.70	–	–	314,976.72	37,728.31
1852	–	–	–	–	–	323,678.60	37,322.19
1853	–	–	1,073.14	–	–	314,976.72	38,193.77
1854	–	–	–	–	–	141,736.96	27,915.05
1855	–	–	1,069.78	–	–	174,010.62	27,432.29
1856	–	–	1,072.53	–	–	231,489.35	30,060.95
1857	–	–	–	–	–	216,339.97	32,015.93
1858	–	–	–	–	–	159,410.24	–
1859	–	–	–	–	–	201,275.85	–
1860	–	–	1,010.00	–	–	245,171.00	52,215.86
1861	–	–	1,099.91	–	–	145,980.30	27,459.24
1862	–	–	–	–	–	180,180.39	25,164.94
1863	–	–	–	–	–	182,023.89	25,284.56
1864	–	–	–	–	–	170,036.54	26,027.69
1865	–	–	–	–	–	190,650.76	22,968.17
1866	–	–	–	–	–	183,080.59	26,066.45
1867	–	–	–	–	–	185,078.59	22,949.68
1868	–	–	–	–	–	167,218.51	21,563.64
1869	–	–	–	–	–	187,078.59	23,797.08
1870	–	–	–	–	–	180,058.59	23,239.89
1871	–	–	–	–	–	180,061.11	19,848.84
1872	–	–	–	–	–	171,242.38	18,643.85
1873	–	–	–	–	–	178,468.83	18,707.12
1874	–	–	–	–	–	172,243.44	19,142.50
1875	–	–	–	–	–	172,616.14	30,036.22
1876	–	–	–	–	–	181,244.27	25,619.51
1877	–	–	–	–	–	174,400.07	21,076.21
1878	–	–	–	–	–	166,174.79	21,930.64
1879	–	–	–	–	–	175,193.50	23,161.48

Year	Fengtian Niuma Shui	Wuchang and Xunchang	Pantaokou	Wuyuancheng	Gubeikou	Chongwenmen	Zuoyi
1880	–	–	–	–	–	171,657.28	23,147.97
1881	–	–	–	–	–	181,097.09	20,813.18
1882	–	–	–	–	–	172,692.16	22,128.95
1883	–	–	–	–	–	172,801.25	24,505.88
1884	–	–	–	–	–	176,360.31	21,894.78
1885	–	–	–	–	–	172,914.88	23,085.90
1886	–	118,130.07	–	–	–	173,060.31	23,826.83
1887	–	92,798.74	–	–	–	181,658.69	20,349.78
1888	–	–	–	–	–	173,171.46	22,888.50
1889	–	–	–	–	–	173,296.12	21,986.74
1890	–	–	–	–	–	181,004.94	22,760.83
1891	–	–	–	–	–	160,715.14	24,457.29
1892	–	–	–	–	–	173,946.90	49,559.40
1893	–	–	–	–	–	164,831.66	23,852.56
1894	–	–	–	–	–	165,042.02	23,156.45
1895	–	–	–	–	–	164,950.55	21,693.20
1896	–	–	–	–	–	159,825.78	21,226.68
1897	–	–	–	–	–	162,200.04	22,925.59
1898	–	–	–	–	–	169,498.66	–
1899	–	–	–	–	–	176,558.43	–
1900	–	–	–	–	–	171,647.92	14,988.56
1901	–	–	–	–	–	–	–
1902	–	–	–	–	–	472,497.62	29,617.72
1903	–	–	–	–	–	–	26,565.60
1904	–	–	–	–	–	–	–
1905	–	–	–	–	–	–	–
1906	–	–	–	–	–	–	–
1907	–	–	–	–	–	–	–
1908	–	–	–	–	–	–	–
1909	–	146,770.05	–	–	–	–	34,958.59
1910	–	–	–	–	–	–	41,650.71

TABLE A.3 *Customs revenues collected at selected* Changguan, *1723–1910 (taels of silver)*

Year	Youyi	Zuoliangtin	Huai'an Guan	Hushu Guan	Yangzhou Guan	Wuhu Huguan	Wuhu Gongguan
1723	–	–	–	–	–	–	–
1724	–	–	–	–	–	–	–
1725	–	–	–	299,480.45	–	–	–
1726	–	–	–	–	–	–	–
1727	–	–	–	–	–	–	–
1728	–	–	398,956.00	353,218.19	–	–	–
1729	–	–	464,143.00	–	–	–	–
1730	–	–	414,657.00	–	–	–	–
1731	–	–	301,250.00	–	–	–	–
1732	–	12,815.26	428,800.00	–	145,512.35	–	–
1733	–	12,491.26	544,600.00	–	146,854.35	–	–
1734	–	14,002.26	566,300.00	–	193,658.57	–	–
1735	–	12,853.26	510,350.00	416,358.25	173,020.99	218,819.71	117,326.16
1736	–	15,531.04	496,046.60	458,732.98	217,361.00	214,790.05	117,328.10
1737	–	13,735.00	483,807.00	391,886.94	210,203.00	218,219.71	129,316.16
1738	–	11,460.00	295,479.00	381,701.15	133,354.00	–	–
1739	–	9,560.93	406,861.00	311,669.42	157,387.00	231,113.71	148,433.30
1740	–	6,352.81	–	333,115.45	115,359.16	247,202.71	165,220.30
1741	–	10,541.44	386,515.00	384,739.39	204,858.57	250,993.08	172,876.41
1742	–	11,021.20	351,351.00	375,348.00	183,110.35	241,229.52	161,826.68
1743	–	12,654.19	367,028.00	376,788.00	189,620.35	236,585.09	146,033.02
1744	–	11,414.82	467,849.00	166,442.89	167,813.35	316,190.04	119,707.52
1745	–	11,415.50	619,583.00	202,528.79	197,220.35	278,687.35	144,717.75
1746	–	11,420.39	237,213.00	242,544.83	189,897.35	260,610.09	149,148.76
1747	–	11,432.35	238,760.50	264,402.92	119,279.11	201,628.90	140,240.03
1748	–	–	262,137.10	407,276.31	230,041.32	201,905.51	140,286.71
1749	–	11,470.26	414,309.00	404,879.39	195,878.00	201,991.28	126,378.13
1750	–	12,643.39	626,085.00	545,294.00	210,831.00	258,098.09	126,506.29
1751	–	25,291.51	445,858.20	427,635.64	160,875.05	256,138.42	141,286.38
1752	–	12,647.34	464,621.90	544,804.61	221,429.00	271,033.00	141,993.68
1753	–	12,647.93	547,492.50	495,227.09	201,903.10	254,378.27	123,374.62
1754	–	12,648.98	331,893.90	410,182.00	168,770.35	246,680.38	132,506.02
1755	–	–	515,908.70	502,710.45	197,353.00	243,883.00	134,647.16
1756	–	12,655.26	375,907.20	353,592.92	150,859.35	224,110.20	133,737.20
1757	–	–	305,679.20	385,045.46	132,962.00	231,658.30	101,887.24

Year	Youyi	Zuoliangtin	Huai'an Guan	Hushu Guan	Yangzhou Guan	Wuhu Huguan	Wuhu Gongguan
1758	–	–	304,299.70	413,286.93	136,931.40	233,292.84	102,054.15
1759	–	12,566.61	374,241.00	462,932.52	162,467.00	255,159.22	125,533.15
1760	–	12,569.33	471,630.00	490,318.00	147,113.10	216,266.50	136,553.19
1761	–	12,571.00	525,368.00	451,381.30	148,583.80	217,408.20	119,483.19
1762	–	12,580.26	451,644.00	373,674.31	149,725.90	241,483.88	133,958.82
1763	–	–	462,631.00	567,928.89	150,731.00	247,587.48	133,261.41
1764	–	–	483,718.00	579,093.06	152,230.35	247,609.15	136,296.92
1765	–	12,591.35	522,127.00	541,896.09	153,357.00	247,635.61	131,576.45
1766	–	–	571,497.00	566,180.12	154,162.30	247,652.94	131,851.69
1767	–	–	1,106,705.00	566,409.47	155,045.70	495,867.83	265,450.90
1768	–	–	513,250.00	567,392.67	157,116.55	247,961.69	133,064.08
1769	–	12,601.59	556,703.00	543,255.27	159,178.80	220,110.54	113,759.98
1770	–	12,602.95	596,967.00	1,110,944.40	168,376.00	221,121.74	113,861.54
1771	28,189.73	12,603.59	502,054.00	564,384.40	165,948.60	232,110.08	113,973.16
1772	17,099.52	12,604.82	395,828.60	567,487.83	166,225.50	232,155.00	115,038.00
1773	–	12,606.19	556,548.00	571,992.07	166,842.30	232,189.88	115,092.26
1774	19,980.35	12,606.76	480,428.80	571,354.26	168,011.65	215,267.98	134,529.06
1775	29,705.36	12,607.14	382,955.20	535,262.23	168,748.70	215,371.96	134,541.64
1776	30,921.07	–	426,904.10	552,716.72	168,981.30	231,602.40	118,529.34
1777	31,723.60	12,854.49	496,990.20	560,167.09	184,678.30	223,886.76	126,553.55
1778	–	12,857.36	348,309.20	463,983.18	185,035.20	215,890.45	134,777.86
1779	33,111.52	12,861.30	313,361.70	471,824.65	158,365.62	231,908.91	118,871.30
1780	–	–	449,205.50	564,353.23	185,299.00	231,919.43	119,064.54
1781	–	12,868.08	460,771.00	575,368.20	371,376.00	232,022.87	119,265.93
1782	–	–	277,309.20	575,523.66	185,888.00	232,134.04	119,474.02
1783	28,572.12	–	343,158.20	576,190.95	185,938.35	232,265.82	119,691.88
1784	–	26,247.07	340,405.50	576,397.13	185,967.00	232,317.67	119,803.93
1785	–	–	329,978.10	456,079.18	126,904.51	232,332.30	119,839.29
1786	–	–	237,266.10	281,620.98	118,762.61	232,464.18	109,301.42
1787	–	–	259,265.30	527,997.76	120,283.29	214,507.98	75,154.37
1788	–	–	353,149.24	553,878.01	153,426.98	232,539.86	90,018.30
1789	–	–	483,473.90	561,254.01	176,027.00	232,577.25	101,627.27
1790	–	13,146.52	488,066.00	578,974.40	185,991.00	232,632.57	119,886.50
1791	–	–	418,268.50	582,842.37	186,013.00	232,672.49	119,954.45
1792	38,988.97	13,149.58	442,106.70	583,050.55	176,391.00	232,682.66	119,959.75
1793	37,930.60	13,150.69	358,585.80	505,324.06	140,205.00	232,687.89	119,962.29

TABLE A.3 *Customs revenues collected at selected* Changguan, *1723–1910* (*taels of silver*) (cont.)

Year	Youyi	Zuoliangtin	Huai'an Guan	Hushu Guan	Yangzhou Guan	Wuhu Huguan	Wuhu Gongguan
1794	33,851.60	–	423,631.27	543,596.79	168,511.00	232,691.38	119,963.73
1795	–	–	403,202.00	484,384.53	169,285.37	232,695.90	119,965.65
1796	–	13,157.62	365,399.76	486,429.87	172,313.54	232,699.05	82,453.65
1797	–	13,160.42	313,994.78	487,550.30	152,594.68	225,347.95	103,812.66
1798	–	13,162.26	291,340.89	421,285.31	164,461.00	232,754.35	119,994.20
1799	26,987.38	12,339.26	386,796.42	451,384.84	173,792.56	232,756.76	119,995.74
1800	26,740.69	12,339.26	854,170.27	456,585.38	167,262.84	460,401.86	234,638.00
1801	26,721.89	12,346.79	402,244.60	431,676.76	169,039.88	230,394.58	–
1802	26,081.08	12,348.30	366,484.41	423,921.38	168,143.00	230,176.38	117,294.76
1803	–	12,339.26	281,965.69	800,483.74	156,202.00	230,220.58	117,266.56
1804	27,123.44	12,352.29	336,703.47	431,436.19	154,810.00	230,164.38	117,273.66
1805	–	–	387,567.23	375,072.04	164,896.47	230,040.78	117,199.66
1806	27,441.43	–	286,564.85	329,115.08	164,086.70	230,037.68	117,202.26
1807	28,868.48	12,356.24	294,521.55	318,346.29	164,898.51	230,042.88	117,197.36
1808	29,713.54	12,350.62	388,487.63	360,103.53	164,047.79	230,039.58	117,200.96
1809	29,180.29	12,351.89	400,078.92	414,003.50	154,029.00	230,043.68	117,200.06
1810	26,487.51	12,348.39	363,959.37	403,498.86	156,215.00	230,049.68	117,202.46
1811	26,369.71	12,346.79	221,247.21	373,176.95	153,955.00	230,047.88	117,204.66
1812	26,764.11	12,344.62	272,400.97	392,801.95	144,360.00	230,049.58	117,201.86
1813	26,792.74	12,349.00	237,829.17	423,499.48	151,212.00	230,029.38	117,180.26
1814	22,121.63	12,340.74	155,729.67	297,090.64	303,816.00	230,034.18	117,177.06
1815	26,621.47	12,345.72	246,383.94	343,480.25	160,098.00	230,045.98	117,178.56
1816	–	24,687.67	386,136.60	413,526.13	146,868.85	229,932.08	117,133.16
1817	–	12,341.43	346,975.60	426,571.05	157,438.00	229,935.00	117,159.74
1818	25,176.45	12,343.99	408,830.62	428,437.49	165,427.34	230,079.92	117,991.15
1819	22,279.78	12,345.86	441,153.45	426,854.17	164,061.00	230,235.92	118,832.14
1820	25,386.18	12,342.33	253,648.93	386,390.79	144,479.00	240,030.36	117,562.93
1821	26,734.07	–	252,211.15	401,285.23	123,984.90	238,584.33	119,312.54
1822	26,077.46	12,345.79	275,389.96	362,485.99	129,201.20	231,159.18	118,006.46
1823	27,008.73	12,345.62	184,014.17	328,376.95	135,463.00	230,842.48	117,458.76
1824	26,165.60	12,344.89	248,007.88	474,989.18	143,711.30	210,434.08	101,220.26
1825	25,544.13	12,345.72	287,808.78	362,171.62	122,317.00	229,992.64	117,174.00
1826	25,617.30	12,339.26	301,615.26	371,440.09	156,884.00	229,938.58	97,258.55
1827	50,576.82	12,344.38	258,253.76	343,382.54	145,117.00	229,970.06	92,571.33
1828	26,154.91	12,347.00	307,983.71	374,691.18	162,635.00	230,027.50	117,182.94

Year	Youyi	Zuoliangtin	Huai'an Guan	Hushu Guan	Yangzhou Guan	Wuhu Huguan	Wuhu Gongguan
1829	25,748.53	12,344.34	301,802.60	376,531.02	149,607.00	230,019.08	117,176.16
1830	25,381.63	12,351.49	324,412.07	380,566.04	159,055.00	229,999.08	117,166.16
1831	26,408.09	12,351.90	309,549.38	391,310.14	123,319.00	229,989.08	117,186.16
1832	25,381.99	12,348.61	662,831.88	353,125.00	153,953.00	435,442.11	200,678.07
1833	24,714.30	12,352.62	146,987.85	371,407.03	113,886.30	155,501.56	113,412.22
1834	25,680.13	12,354.27	279,612.80	316,408.82	124,191.30	229,947.38	91,093.44
1835	25,772.21	12,347.82	266,716.33	679,851.15	163,895.30	230,943.42	87,248.66
1836	25,343.13	12,348.27	302,455.63	302,389.46	163,791.30	229,984.41	117,178.96
1837	25,698.57	–	271,789.27	300,302.54	163,828.00	231,426.31	115,747.61
1838	25,388.42	11,184.07	309,944.64	289,171.85	163,793.30	231,354.11	115,793.91
1839	25,132.39	12,356.81	296,786.64	276,177.94	163,803.00	223,919.08	89,146.16
1840	24,809.64	12,348.70	328,512.46	301,622.70	163,793.00	229,971.08	101,021.54
1841	24,334.62	12,387.00	309,612.67	296,767.76	163,808.00	208,943.75	70,547.84
1842	24,390.58	12,344.57	238,603.67	390,697.90	133,101.30	170,297.21	70,547.00
1843	24,905.81	12,339.26	189,425.67	274,174.92	132,550.30	230,120.42	117,248.73
1844	24,445.53	12,342.38	207,575.10	293,347.04	110,088.00	230,099.40	117,196.38
1845	24,409.81	12,342.31	269,278.94	288,863.26	111,049.30	230,042.70	117,218.02
1846	24,260.88	12,344.00	273,303.04	291,753.88	240,385.30	230,087.83	117,178.28
1847	24,423.99	12,344.62	246,920.69	313,311.53	115,069.30	–	–
1848	24,206.72	12,345.43	189,068.08	317,389.74	118,453.00	230,304.00	117,081.93
1849	24,013.90	23,366.13	304,859.44	279,990.66	129,861.00	223,810.34	123,223.48
1850	24,118.71	–	327,109.81	414,420.28	144,987.00	–	–
1851	24,262.46	12,347.28	324,661.13	334,416.76	123,921.38	235,326.05	103,015.99
1852	24,148.03	12,347.47	139,632.36	307,569.18	101,078.31	–	–
1853	24,158.35	10,115.35	100,120.69	279,868.71	0.00	0.00	0.00
1854	17,449.18	7,367.27	69,520.13	311,805.78	–	0.00	0.00
1855	17,431.98	7,761.92	153,950.15	326,850.89	31,612.00	0.00	0.00
1856	18,054.34	10,446.32	190,671.52	346,922.89	–	0.00	0.00
1857	18,187.49	9,998.58	110,103.31	168,793.63	–	0.00	0.00
1858	18,266.39	7,458.58	114,581.95	236,543.08	–	0.00	0.00
1859	16,286.75	9,880.17	116,057.69	287,595.83	–	0.00	0.00
1860	26,315.60	9,040.24	98,570.00	358,000.00	35,946.00	0.00	0.00
1861	19,543.53	6,354.86	44,975.06	0.00	15,236.47	0.00	0.00
1862	19,043.52	7,268.24	29,705.33	0.00	20,333.46	0.00	0.00
1863	16,704.27	6,387.81	37,615.80	0.00	35,558.45	0.00	0.00
1864	18,112.02	6,752.41	38,814.51	0.00	43,242.52	0.00	0.00

TABLE A.3 *Customs revenues collected at selected* Changguan, *1723–1910* (*taels of silver*) (cont.)

Year	Youyi	Zuoliangtin	Huai'an Guan	Hushu Guan	Yangzhou Guan	Wuhu Huguan	Wuhu Gongguan
1865	18,781.10	7,103.30	82,995.66	0.00	40,551.80	0.00	0.00
1866	18,158.21	7,011.48	35,754.17	0.00	44,217.00	0.00	0.00
1867	17,480.74	6,350.77	33,101.00	0.00	34,461.00	0.00	0.00
1868	16,778.66	6,812.01	34,118.99	0.00	31,365.00	0.00	0.00
1869	17,665.42	6,980.09	44,161.92	0.00	37,454.00	0.00	0.00
1870	17,530.40	7,183.69	52,798.14	0.00	56,996.00	0.00	0.00
1871	17,071.99	7,272.65	41,756.45	0.00	43,140.00	0.00	0.00
1872	16,370.16	7,617.58	51,121.39	0.00	42,188.00	0.00	0.00
1873	17,058.59	8,153.72	56,871.77	0.00	43,259.00	0.00	0.00
1874	16,266.00	6,370.06	32,210.85	0.00	43,379.00	0.00	0.00
1875	20,314.41	8,045.98	42,372.12	0.00	43,391.00	0.00	0.00
1876	20,408.10	8,128.15	38,391.85	0.00	86,956.00	0.00	0.00
1877	19,420.59	8,162.65	38,481.40	0.00	43,516.00	60,510.11	70,686.55
1878	19,334.15	8,163.48	41,006.98	0.00	43,591.00	60,257.46	74,744.91
1879	20,054.06	7,904.02	38,634.93	0.00	43,637.00	59,146.56	76,247.32
1880	23,905.09	8,185.48	74,129.35	0.00	43,664.00	61,934.29	73,823.55
1881	20,114.25	15,181.16	51,454.94	0.00	43,700.00	57,098.94	78,826.14
1882	20,039.12	8,814.97	62,650.44	0.00	43,806.00	61,558.30	75,418.59
1883	19,646.16	8,551.36	62,828.30	0.00	44,113.00	58,766.82	78,229.02
1884	18,855.61	8,777.98	47,381.77	0.00	44,125.00	59,072.61	78,157.03
1885	19,929.08	–	41,103.13	0.00	44,167.00	81,955.30	42,774.00
1886	18,106.17	7,827.51	51,525.54	0.00	44,212.00	75,663.74	61,637.79
1887	17,839.98	9,386.77	85,796.44	0.00	44,272.00	80,467.81	62,309.81
1888	20,449.93	8,822.03	66,951.29	0.00	44,331.00	76,102.38	63,054.84
1889	19,389.09	8,823.98	38,789.61	0.00	44,386.00	75,673.02	63,579.62
1890	19,084.13	8,823.73	41,811.06	0.00	44,398.00	151,454.31	127,439.26
1891	18,889.53	–	45,549.21	0.00	44,405.00	75,729.56	63,767.79
1892	38,069.46	8,823.13	53,326.24	0.00	44,426.00	76,353.79	63,235.75
1893	17,862.28	–	40,436.92	0.00	44,462.00	–	–
1894	19,437.30	7,864.23	55,224.90	0.00	44,457.00	75,211.04	64,426.30
1895	22,549.22	6,203.19	55,844.67	0.00	44,509.00	76,399.74	63,355.64
1896	18,852.76	8,170.47	41,881.07	0.00	44,520.00	75,421.65	64,446.64
1897	18,818.02	7,492.92	43,544.60	0.00	44,531.00	75,474.04	64,496.64
1898	–	–	96,786.47	0.00	44,541.00	76,505.35	63,466.54
1899	18,941.57	–	59,908.10	0.00	44,549.00	75,825.63	64,148.90
1900	7,334.15	–	47,429.24	0.00	44,558.00	75,580.51	64,395.34

Year	Youyi	Zuoliangtin	Huai'an Guan	Hushu Guan	Yangzhou Guan	Wuhu Huguan	Wuhu Gongguan
1901	–	–	44,647.48	0.00	44,500.00	75,274.05	59,581.30
1902	20,781.16	–	61,595.27	0.00	44,580.00	83,665.66	61,756.66
1903	21,433.06	–	62,828.01	0.00	44,591.00	86,283.71	63,213.35
1904	–	–	56,142.11	0.00	53,783.03	91,174.38	72,276.34
1905	–	–	174,349.06	0.00	86,493.00	95,125.54	70,338.47
1906	–	–	236,399.01	0.00	102,734.00	76,266.80	64,967.07
1907	–	–	81,127.48	0.00	95,446.00	77,054.03	59,909.45
1908	–	–	–	0.00	102,789.00	–	–
1909	–	–	200,666.34	0.00	102,818.00	–	–
1910	26,123.31	–	–	0.00	101,639.00	–	–

TABLE A.4 *Customs revenues collected at selected* Changguan, *1723–1908* (*taels of silver*)

Year	Fengyang Guan	Longjiang Guan	Xixing Guan	Jiujiang Guan	Gan Guan	Beixin Guan	Nanxin Guan
1723	–	–	–	–	–	163,053.65	–
1724	–	–	–	224,922.90	–	–	–
1725	–	123,892.50	–	240,084.80	–	–	–
1726	–	133,983.52	–	242,744.00	–	163,053.65	–
1727	174,000.00	–	–	431,132.41	–	–	–
1728	–	–	–	211,109.09	–	–	–
1729	–	–	–	222,903.90	–	–	–
1730	–	139,595.60	–	223,758.74	91,767.52	163,053.65	–
1731	150,000.00	–	–	252,122.63	–	–	–
1732	176,789.60	–	59,291.33	256,083.66	–	163,205.43	28,235.73
1733	208,551.00	–	78,988.33	325,311.31	–	165,710.59	26,067.61
1734	–	–	81,982.33	333,431.31	–	181,018.93	24,171.44
1735	164,439.60	120,393.86	81,052.58	367,123.00	107,734.50	194,020.76	54,324.89
1736	137,987.60	111,003.44	81,583.59	309,072.72	87,586.18	166,663.65	–
1737	159,544.60	–	–	340,292.52	77,580.71	179,053.65	34,611.86
1738	150,944.60	127,246.76	86,391.97	321,395.05	77,644.43	216,580.80	31,744.12
1739	112,591.60	95,797.23	80,316.33	324,934.64	80,430.12	214,895.79	30,247.50
1740	154,012.60	125,307.20	84,591.33	351,642.90	–	353,416.31	–
1741	182,585.66	120,807.20	80,446.33	352,940.40	89,213.79	178,246.09	–
1742	229,628.24	108,967.20	74,547.33	367,626.64	129,980.04	193,571.89	29,127.76

TABLE A.4 *Customs revenues collected at selected* Changguan, *1723–1908* (*taels of silver*) (cont.)

Year	Fengyang Guan	Longjiang Guan	Xixing Guan	Jiujiang Guan	Gan Guan	Beixin Guan	Nanxin Guan
1743	188,521.34	107,344.20	67,716.33	356,348.20	97,342.65	200,456.07	21,331.60
1744	283,766.13	105,238.26	85,258.91	358,084.67	92,429.07	214,904.48	31,723.96
1745	316,163.94	118,062.49	83,618.29	369,911.11	85,334.90	202,611.45	29,374.07
1746	394,619.53	102,846.45	52,437.70	372,742.52	89,102.51	205,326.96	29,669.85
1747	285,733.32	139,756.42	89,376.45	372,105.31	91,161.09	214,049.32	31,920.13
1748	335,523.64	241,074.06	168,153.55	787,797.23	91,410.76	221,316.91	29,292.09
1749	344,584.88	114,674.76	85,499.90	380,762.58	96,011.76	226,365.67	26,784.89
1750	301,296.00	35,815.14	33,503.98	–	101,035.58	196,055.55	23,694.36
1751	316,622.60	111,586.03	81,381.13	–	105,532.18	183,938.54	27,911.67
1752	381,175.47	122,540.46	73,983.09	390,242.29	105,674.10	221,284.89	27,935.08
1753	314,197.47	113,399.29	75,442.18	382,675.60	105,144.86	224,207.82	25,250.12
1754	287,930.14	110,668.84	72,307.58	354,228.40	196,825.00	214,458.59	25,963.91
1755	305,346.90	121,577.74	67,958.45	375,248.20	94,280.00	220,536.45	26,180.15
1756	342,449.41	109,563.70	64,256.36	754,754.50	91,988.00	204,735.43	17,184.08
1757	274,445.82	76,804.68	59,281.75	431,605.30	94,295.00	203,200.35	10,602.61
1758	244,317.13	87,174.76	59,478.47	419,470.92	94,886.00	201,382.08	22,200.53
1759	246,589.70	278,899.40	145,964.57	408,579.11	96,104.00	208,600.76	25,915.83
1760	308,500.23	139,748.10	79,140.77	444,106.37	96,659.00	210,496.72	26,589.82
1761	310,974.90	140,136.93	79,340.77	393,468.55	98,297.00	212,527.43	26,703.41
1762	238,482.50	141,287.00	79,591.00	394,000.41	98,679.00	218,637.99	26,814.64
1763	289,754.79	150,906.00	79,664.00	396,268.02	99,237.00	218,768.05	26,939.68
1764	298,708.48	144,947.00	79,739.00	398,451.45	99,810.00	223,880.82	22,985.55
1765	633,454.23	142,975.10	78,189.00	398,482.12	101,841.00	204,305.63	23,094.11
1766	331,561.76	143,798.80	77,810.50	390,100.52	101,991.00	208,129.45	23,673.69
1767	280,112.55	134,243.08	76,017.10	340,953.50	101,881.00	208,285.93	47,410.27
1768	220,589.49	150,685.44	66,069.67	332,856.30	101,908.00	208,394.65	23,801.24
1769	222,825.03	124,423.00	66,380.00	499,920.00	102,067.00	208,506.96	25,410.25
1770	261,589.32	123,507.02	65,484.80	547,853.00	102,589.00	192,746.46	23,775.22
1771	261,761.47	127,381.35	71,912.50	545,639.00	102,388.00	179,781.09	23,446.04
1772	190,422.84	134,390.94	79,346.41	639,438.00	102,374.00	180,703.87	30,076.72
1773	195,514.00	137,840.33	76,498.99	651,767.00	102,765.00	367,048.31	30,591.98
1774	187,617.43	140,420.00	79,984.72	659,657.00	102,866.00	185,045.06	30,600.50
1775	123,490.45	144,920.92	76,603.81	661,384.00	102,958.00	187,375.64	27,619.60
1776	240,696.29	145,709.66	76,664.30	662,129.00	102,981.00	190,017.06	28,221.74
1777	240,824.20	143,429.92	79,349.89	664,412.00	103,184.00	191,097.35	29,617.38
1778	126,032.06	147,136.57	76,863.64	681,289.42	103,189.52	192,276.87	30,371.25

Year	Fengyang Guan	Longjiang Guan	Xixing Guan	Jiujiang Guan	Gan Guan	Beixin Guan	Nanxin Guan
1779	101,283.56	156,613.83	68,705.31	684,722.59	103,266.98	192,772.07	29,881.94
1780	175,202.26	151,905.45	74,433.93	647,753.41	103,292.61	193,314.48	29,721.89
1781	200,117.23	146,942.72	80,121.10	633,386.76	103,322.77	193,739.46	29,847.34
1782	186,347.77	149,907.17	80,203.43	702,588.41	103,324.82	193,934.79	29,931.25
1783	136,571.01	153,335.30	80,686.80	733,332.27	103,330.90	194,042.14	29,988.66
1784	163,109.24	167,522.91	75,828.00	739,404.31	103,335.10	194,165.75	30,156.66
1785	144,641.51	166,747.61	76,713.81	743,103.54	103,341.70	171,550.71	18,677.22
1786	72,949.64	137,958.55	57,834.16	743,310.03	206,697.88	182,163.55	12,724.73
1787	112,925.48	118,920.61	55,377.26	701,885.02	103,354.23	194,200.84	18,733.19
1788	173,991.57	131,380.21	65,900.17	655,826.35	103,359.66	194,251.07	20,124.57
1789	174,402.46	134,844.52	77,126.84	1,322,435.37	103,365.16	194,281.92	22,507.88
1790	175,415.54	166,798.89	77,720.25	690,970.41	103,371.76	194,339.61	26,065.91
1791	133,454.67	163,787.27	81,255.43	703,304.61	103,373.60	194,485.18	24,927.83
1792	125,685.41	319,614.60	148,136.66	704,056.81	103,377.54	194,566.79	22,936.22
1793	118,858.61	141,344.51	58,967.83	612,990.73	103,380.92	194,623.69	30,205.34
1794	121,527.36	114,378.03	60,590.15	534,651.06	103,385.71	194,727.95	30,151.42
1795	122,193.61	104,295.95	70,822.34	546,347.83	103,389.49	194,879.43	25,274.06
1796	122,291.83	111,521.12	68,815.31	569,013.25	103,394.10	195,749.41	25,430.49
1797	214,522.50	122,393.47	71,513.60	607,087.04	103,398.23	195,931.09	26,128.87
1798	124,421.48	118,003.20	75,148.74	560,027.22	103,402.58	196,043.98	28,602.88
1799	115,001.58	118,462.76	75,637.22	567,054.04	103,401.20	196,182.44	28,765.64
1800	114,495.38	126,669.59	66,422.58	567,821.21	103,403.47	196,415.08	–
1801	102,019.52	123,025.57	66,087.07	565,973.43	105,621.33	208,371.93	–
1802	105,476.22	117,237.19	65,954.76	538,539.61	108,938.18	218,119.92	29,345.55
1803	105,669.76	120,694.13	64,589.83	513,948.16	–	248,571.27	29,414.35
1804	110,183.92	121,869.73	61,446.17	542,951.30	121,483.35	248,658.35	29,452.57
1805	107,366.91	124,778.30	53,343.05	561,520.40	121,497.52	429,960.44	29,509.17
1806	95,382.59	93,348.07	54,922.12	492,187.10	120,304.31	202,126.37	29,454.23
1807	110,005.40	128,258.72	59,752.80	528,760.31	120,964.86	202,638.25	29,344.34
1808	119,104.36	130,393.19	51,569.13	500,753.53	121,013.24	202,712.86	29,571.35
1809	125,534.18	133,207.23	54,291.90	544,401.10	121,027.23	192,147.59	–
1810	108,977.29	130,114.27	57,181.60	552,154.47	121,050.75	202,888.47	29,354.12
1811	107,227.10	134,428.55	52,888.58	514,948.26	120,933.12	203,362.28	29,444.94
1812	95,488.83	135,372.00	51,969.91	492,123.39	120,550.18	200,125.39	29,474.06
1813	111,570.73	133,984.46	53,234.93	582,486.95	120,701.78	194,343.27	29,485.16
1814	102,527.59	134,185.58	47,944.39	581,323.66	120,082.83	194,403.74	29,061.46
1815	102,301.49	122,827.92	45,177.50	570,105.22	120,178.75	194,435.59	28,844.88

TABLE A.4 *Customs revenues collected at selected* Changguan, *1723–1908* (*taels of silver*) (cont.)

Year	Fengyang Guan	Longjiang Guan	Xixing Guan	Jiujiang Guan	Gan Guan	Beixin Guan	Nanxin Guan
1816	102,506.59	109,624.01	47,745.96	496,809.99	120,279.37	194,377.26	28,864.84
1817	108,182.51	129,467.32	46,820.36	520,566.74	120,289.88	194,535.39	28,953.77
1818	117,258.80	132,861.06	56,161.12	403,372.40	120,291.12	194,372.80	28,725.97
1819	108,411.16	133,457.46	54,850.96	542,679.12	240,580.52	194,423.15	28,715.53
1820	104,273.39	106,428.79	52,922.02	521,924.26	120,268.71	194,451.28	28,757.54
1821	110,053.60	141,903.63	56,702.56	530,623.19	120,715.73	194,475.29	28,824.25
1822	107,391.51	140,463.17	51,640.21	1,169,252.30	–	194,487.69	30,215.48
1823	107,410.40	144,165.00	51,491.05	579,403.75	112,529.05	192,173.59	30,172.27
1824	107,861.77	262,909.94	98,737.94	584,127.28	120,258.78	190,076.52	29,444.95
1825	102,322.26	115,246.58	47,984.63	540,674.57	120,258.85	189,124.14	20,553.81
1826	102,461.13	115,021.54	52,702.08	523,121.57	–	189,215.51	30,056.31
1827	114,567.97	137,695.62	51,189.56	526,917.00	116,527.59	189,087.01	29,843.21
1828	127,197.32	142,936.39	45,382.22	539,493.43	116,356.85	188,170.83	30,059.32
1829	128,567.35	139,611.81	47,687.98	600,008.52	115,880.05	189,345.96	29,714.68
1830	247,938.59	127,073.00	45,628.16	541,493.92	114,428.06	190,153.47	30,014.68
1831	116,570.62	118,015.67	45,303.35	371,374.31	113,210.04	188,880.15	30,088.17
1832	108,504.25	91,605.90	41,448.75	463,842.09	102,022.40	188,284.65	60,153.81
1833	107,411.52	92,037.95	42,063.11	505,509.70	98,235.24	189,183.00	28,882.97
1834	107,431.24	88,549.65	42,511.56	522,468.63	97,156.45	162,581.98	30,095.94
1835	107,465.41	88,808.22	42,715.23	531,621.97	96,965.93	154,941.80	30,085.72
1836	116,205.52	114,645.11	41,449.94	599,670.30	96,965.93	169,143.15	29,798.18
1837	108,407.92	110,572.64	41,395.27	603,039.46	94,934.93	188,207.29	30,160.39
1838	108,490.73	99,188.17	41,571.76	589,476.17	94,944.66	337,611.41	29,885.57
1839	100,695.74	90,229.87	43,172.67	574,532.87	93,110.03	188,213.48	30,157.87
1840	107,382.82	95,740.12	42,612.44	562,932.17	92,198.53	188,566.59	30,072.09
1841	107,175.10	90,599.33	41,437.03	536,816.25	81,960.60	188,218.72	28,961.17
1842	96,431.10	95,291.18	41,815.35	424,927.99	92,251.54	170,147.31	28,435.18
1843	128,389.48	74,232.10	34,390.45	398,116.30	92,253.63	185,270.23	30,070.60
1844	116,044.56	100,900.42	41,481.44	451,740.57	92,252.55	188,525.61	28,568.22
1845	107,278.26	118,718.23	41,717.29	583,025.90	89,557.32	188,802.03	30,116.20
1846	109,844.92	106,086.67	41,515.20	545,004.28	83,753.77	188,487.50	29,910.39
1847	110,645.56	97,438.94	41,516.44	484,645.54	79,423.09	179,845.82	30,049.39
1848	99,484.75	120,937.10	41,892.12	585,089.78	78,953.75	188,498.86	30,157.93
1849	106,303.60	98,670.96	41,547.98	562,591.64	93,771.00	188,257.81	30,123.75
1850	109,852.95	86,885.61	41,493.27	469,351.02	79,329.18	188,292.15	28,935.60
1851	107,362.01	78,683.63	41,551.85	430,499.03	185,198.91	177,376.02	28,394.13

Year	Fengyang Guan	Longjiang Guan	Xixing Guan	Jiujiang Guan	Gan Guan	Beixin Guan	Nanxin Guan
1852	107,231.45	78,767.63	41,742.56	483,613.12	92,632.73	176,024.00	29,871.20
1853	84,172.56	0.00	0.00	450,314.61	58,853.99	151,048.00	18,688.47
1854	23,026.26	0.00	0.00	0.00	53,491.24	–	16,584.29
1855	32,651.74	0.00	0.00	0.00	0.00	164,874.65	24,166.61
1856	59,294.28	0.00	0.00	0.00	0.00	–	30,107.94
1857	32,283.64	0.00	0.00	0.00	0.00	124,991.58	29,622.67
1858	14,512.01	0.00	0.00	0.00	0.00	121,578.11	29,554.14
1859	6,650.98	0.00	0.00	0.00	0.00	123,580.68	25,583.92
1860	1,210.82	0.00	0.00	0.00	92,742.94	115,031.31	–
1861	5,764.22	0.00	0.00	0.00	92,404.38	0.00	3,312.98
1862	0.00	0.00	0.00	0.00	83,741.81	–	–
1863	0.00	0.00	0.00	253,374.72	92,399.61	–	–
1864	0.00	0.00	0.00	477,441.70	87,388.57	–	–
1865	0.00	0.00	0.00	429,865.88	53,943.45	14,429.79	1,445.83
1866	0.00	0.00	0.00	412,984.00	60,424.30	0.00	0.00
1867	0.00	0.00	0.00	409,517.00	57,123.69	0.00	0.00
1868	0.00	0.00	0.00	435,721.98	70,175.70	0.00	0.00
1869	0.00	0.00	0.00	439,017.08	75,231.06	0.00	0.00
1870	0.00	0.00	0.00	336,894.46	64,130.97	0.00	0.00
1871	0.00	0.00	0.00	455,661.07	62,206.23	0.00	0.00
1872	0.00	0.00	0.00	425,849.58	65,153.84	0.00	0.00
1873	0.00	0.00	0.00	427,474.02	75,728.61	0.00	0.00
1874	0.00	0.00	0.00	442,522.82	88,318.41	0.00	0.00
1875	0.00	0.00	0.00	450,368.83	92,458.03	0.00	0.00
1876	0.00	0.00	0.00	455,947.76	81,942.87	0.00	0.00
1877	24,404.48	0.00	0.00	457,324.16	89,613.41	0.00	0.00
1878	55,056.57	0.00	0.00	403,388.60	61,241.11	0.00	0.00
1879	49,870.29	0.00	0.00	442,061.34	101,130.12	0.00	0.00
1880	48,828.27	0.00	0.00	425,844.84	42,133.25	0.00	0.00
1881	49,826.59	0.00	0.00	426,122.53	57,681.42	0.00	0.00
1882	55,064.77	0.00	0.00	412,223.69	72,876.87	0.00	0.00
1883	52,942.78	0.00	0.00	425,028.59	67,439.83	0.00	0.00
1884	49,966.34	0.00	0.00	465,623.79	105,517.70	0.00	0.00
1885	38,177.52	0.00	0.00	449,679.73	52,653.98	0.00	0.00
1886	48,394.36	0.00	0.00	437,252.83	53,176.94	0.00	0.00
1887	62,631.50	0.00	0.00	445,534.29	46,471.06	0.00	0.00
1888	63,103.57	0.00	0.00	449,711.36	52,681.11	0.00	0.00

TABLE A.4 *Customs revenues collected at selected* Changguan, *1723–1908* (*taels of silver*) (cont.)

Year	Fengyang Guan	Longjiang Guan	Xixing Guan	Jiujiang Guan	Gan Guan	Beixin Guan	Nanxin Guan
1889	63,424.49	0.00	0.00	455,308.09	59,015.38	0.00	0.00
1890	136,224.99	0.00	0.00	916,311.00	52,721.88	0.00	0.00
1891	66,500.09	0.00	0.00	456,730.09	59,686.03	0.00	0.00
1892	54,593.09	0.00	0.00	414,375.88	60,046.25	0.00	0.00
1893	68,871.24	0.00	0.00	425,059.58	53,415.58	0.00	0.00
1894	70,930.74	0.00	0.00	426,192.13	52,781.85	0.00	0.00
1895	70,456.37	0.00	0.00	426,793.58	60,597.16	0.00	0.00
1896	70,021.58	0.00	0.00	427,384.07	52,607.73	0.00	0.00
1897	73,215.90	0.00	0.00	422,051.17	52,614.85	0.00	0.00
1898	60,442.04	0.00	0.00	396,584.59	52,600.27	0.00	0.00
1899	65,798.09	0.00	0.00	393,198.98	61,211.00	0.00	0.00
1900	104,263.73	0.00	0.00	430,120.71	52,609.88	0.00	0.00
1901	82,001.76	0.00	0.00	402,712.36	51,216.37	0.00	0.00
1902	84,388.74	0.00	0.00	–	52,599.19	0.00	0.00
1903	85,648.81	0.00	0.00	–	52,621.49	0.00	0.00
1904	95,271.24	0.00	0.00	–	46,063.80	0.00	0.00
1905	107,159.60	0.00	0.00	–	39,679.26	0.00	0.00
1906	103,888.48	0.00	0.00	–	–	0.00	0.00
1907	108,363.14	0.00	0.00	–	0.00	0.00	0.00
1908	–	0.00	0.00	–	72,103.42	0.00	0.00

TABLE A.5 *Customs revenues collected at selected* Changguan, *1723–1909* (*taels of silver*)

Year	Linqin Huguan	Linqin Gongguan	Taiping Guan	Wuchang Guan	Jingzhou Guan	Hubei Xinguan	Kui Guan
1723	–	–	–	–	–	–	–
1724	–	–	107,875.18	–	–	–	–
1725	–	–	–	–	–	–	–
1726	59,194.09	–	–	–	–	–	–
1727	39,886.80	–	–	–	–	–	69,525.70
1728	39,265.78	–	–	–	–	–	–
1729	–	–	–	–	–	–	–
1730	–	–	–	–	29,000.00	–	93,232.94
1731	–	–	–	–	–	–	83,977.16

Year	Linqin Huguan	Linqin Gongguan	Taiping Guan	Wuchang Guan	Jingzhou Guan	Hubei Xinguan	Kui Guan
1732	–	–	–	–	–	–	–
1733	–	–	–	–	–	–	92,962.04
1734	78,781.12	–	–	–	–	–	102,425.46
1735	42,218.36	6,134.00	–	40,635.49	–	–	114,987.19
1736	–	–	124,713.90	–	22,738.27	–	94,368.24
1737	73,347.41	–	109,480.18	36,407.85	24,193.41	–	111,331.81
1738	73,439.40	–	107,952.61	–	–	–	116,113.20
1739	46,518.10	–	109,944.27	42,951.60	17,019.77	–	131,056.99
1740	53,317.77	7,516.06	116,856.00	39,589.88	30,068.77	–	141,374.73
1741	46,080.14	5,546.84	113,445.48	40,518.63	31,774.77	–	133,898.28
1742	38,468.93	5,676.81	119,830.13	44,674.27	44,591.35	–	132,698.25
1743	38,329.78	8,750.46	240,169.36	41,610.80	40,686.42	–	–
1744	79,322.51	16,094.52	124,773.03	51,664.27	46,668.92	–	–
1745	84,025.50	8,933.50	126,891.73	53,581.71	66,314.13	–	–
1746	48,963.39	10,994.12	128,485.58	52,510.99	55,215.69	–	–
1747	24,929.53	12,816.53	128,816.06	49,083.76	51,103.14	–	–
1748	80,496.89	9,370.24	132,055.17	49,341.35	72,512.63	–	–
1749	42,433.97	6,249.15	136,040.81	50,938.93	61,011.91	–	–
1750	55,896.79	8,449.35	138,842.31	53,288.70	55,285.16	–	152,014.22
1751	40,834.82	7,316.32	137,186.38	109,535.91	37,269.29	–	137,097.84
1752	42,499.70	6,043.54	137,186.38	55,104.86	48,245.00	–	147,366.64
1753	42,606.77	7,078.39	137,947.62	56,234.47	41,617.00	–	143,386.06
1754	42,653.80	7,081.32	124,107.02	56,776.76	45,926.00	–	147,620.29
1755	42,690.89	7,088.70	135,880.50	56,979.67	44,953.90	–	166,572.47
1756	42,705.96	7,173.37	129,902.71	57,526.81	46,271.90	–	173,095.30
1757	43,672.75	7,171.40	130,302.25	57,820.86	46,685.40	–	147,805.40
1758	44,385.55	8,201.70	127,385.75	57,996.91	42,754.00	–	168,537.95
1759	48,191.20	9,733.88	128,607.62	58,196.03	44,341.91	–	176,969.27
1760	50,349.40	10,435.59	128,171.17	58,363.92	46,134.00	–	170,100.98
1761	50,408.70	10,440.00	128,276.74	56,666.39	46,183.00	–	170,140.23
1762	50,492.60	10,614.65	128,409.02	58,371.50	46,202.40	–	177,263.74
1763	101,703.90	17,013.80	128,506.07	58,376.70	46,230.40	–	182,040.98
1764	67,182.30	9,905.60	128,586.34	58,378.30	46,412.90	–	182,219.73
1765	50,684.00	9,915.80	128,768.95	58,487.06	46,421.20	–	193,322.65
1766	50,706.00	9,922.60	129,143.23	58,491.49	46,742.70	–	182,343.17
1767	50,726.20	9,951.50	129,248.62	58,493.52	94,401.60	–	193,685.34
1768	50,763.30	9,955.20	129,283.88	58,494.64	49,021.00	–	186,365.62

TABLE A.5 *Customs revenues collected at selected* Changguan, *1723–1909* (*taels of silver*) (cont.)

Year	Linqin Huguan	Linqin Gongguan	Taiping Guan	Wuchang Guan	Jingzhou Guan	Hubei Xinguan	Kui Guan
1769	51,992.30	9,961.80	129,591.49	58,532.06	49,046.70	–	186,378.01
1770	52,002.39	9,964.34	129,865.54	58,572.91	49,077.00	–	194,314.02
1771	52,016.30	9,967.20	131,697.98	58,590.78	49,385.60	–	186,776.50
1772	52,228.10	9,971.10	131,882.08	58,598.46	49,896.70	–	186,815.89
1773	52,038.50	9,975.64	132,179.17	58,604.27	49,921.90	–	199,366.41
1774	52,041.30	9,978.90	264,851.48	58,605.35	50,616.20	–	187,370.67
1775	52,047.20	9,987.80	131,324.12	58,607.40	50,639.95	–	200,041.46
1776	55,069.40	9,990.50	132,518.45	58,609.61	50,656.18	–	187,374.29
1777	55,073.00	9,994.00	132,647.32	58,612.38	50,669.43	–	187,380.25
1778	55,077.80	9,998.14	132,621.49	58,615.56	50,685.18	–	194,906.67
1779	55,081.40	10,000.70	132,709.36	58,619.36	29,215.62	–	188,205.91
1780	55,083.80	10,002.40	132,709.90	58,623.77	40,221.36	–	188,207.28
1781	110,173.30	10,003.10	132,795.55	58,628.57	44,065.18	–	196,253.57
1782	55,089.80	10,006.20	132,814.19	58,633.57	50,688.94	–	188,574.35
1783	55,091.50	10,007.64	132,818.36	58,638.74	50,702.36	–	188,704.32
1784	55,092.77	10,009.00	134,858.28	117,295.84	50,706.99	–	201,513.70
1785	43,090.71	7,042.62	135,470.98	58,658.91	50,711.11	–	188,823.15
1786	55,096.40	10,010.80	135,525.86	58,667.41	50,714.17	–	201,582.18
1787	55,458.30	10,015.60	134,241.55	58,673.28	42,341.57	–	188,887.16
1788	55,485.20	10,028.70	134,247.57	58,677.39	36,588.37	–	188,894.86
1789	55,490.90	10,034.50	134,261.06	58,680.91	36,272.32	–	201,603.82
1790	55,498.40	10,042.30	134,278.81	58,684.85	44,977.36	–	188,904.25
1791	55,504.60	10,051.60	134,317.82	58,690.18	40,939.29	–	188,913.25
1792	55,514.20	10,060.40	134,345.91	58,695.33	42,788.36	–	201,626.06
1793	55,521.80	10,068.00	134,360.64	58,699.92	47,433.92	–	188,927.82
1794	55,525.30	10,072.80	134,394.11	58,702.93	43,136.64	–	188,939.32
1795	55,532.66	–	134,414.21	58,705.54	38,088.13	–	211,657.84
1796	55,536.04	–	134,436.36	58,707.85	34,877.60	–	188,961.70
1797	55,538.32	–	134,447.05	58,710.75	27,224.60	–	133,425.54
1798	55,540.59	–	132,462.66	58,713.95	26,537.41	–	90,446.00
1799	39,048.72	5,468.35	133,553.30	58,715.38	23,791.22	–	113,403.29
1800	36,526.36	–	134,808.55	–	58,595.54	–	142,324.38
1801	40,416.54	5,348.24	–	–	28,531.11	–	154,880.75
1802	53,226.32	8,506.30	134,835.61	58,717.22	25,530.77	–	183,965.01
1803	69,159.67	6,270.53	134,837.82	–	30,697.51	–	–
1804	38,656.49	–	134,838.80	58,708.21	30,707.75	–	184,002.71

Year	Linqin Huguan	Linqin Gongguan	Taiping Guan	Wuchang Guan	Jingzhou Guan	Hubei Xinguan	Kui Guan
1805	38,343.58	8,007.41	133,967.79	58,708.96	30,695.32	–	184,014.41
1806	50,860.99	7,042.26	134,889.89	–	27,036.70	–	184,019.51
1807	53,307.14	11,042.90	134,901.87	58,711.22	24,235.96	–	–
1808	86,905.14	7,692.15	268,967.21	58,712.49	24,240.67	–	184,022.27
1809	72,331.23	8,067.40	134,938.17	58,713.34	23,554.93	–	184,024.39
1810	76,935.52	5,307.64	134,964.21	–	26,669.55	–	184,025.60
1811	35,513.96	4,812.80	135,002.90	–	28,214.18	–	184,029.72
1812	36,466.11	5,673.00	135,033.52	–	23,952.89	–	184,034.83
1813	33,314.79	6,222.37	135,030.40	58,716.92	25,834.41	–	–
1814	117,081.24	7,823.28	135,034.13	58,717.18	22,583.27	–	184,040.05
1815	79,559.13	8,470.04	135,057.37	58,717.60	22,069.86	–	184,045.47
1816	50,805.56	5,884.49	135,075.08	117,438.61	–	–	–
1817	62,221.22	7,148.97	135,079.29	58,720.15	28,820.74	–	184,089.79
1818	63,246.08	6,121.60	135,105.63	58,720.88	24,600.96	–	184,106.59
1819	59,089.01	6,396.16	134,204.14	–	24,663.60	–	184,108.65
1820	27,151.92	4,596.81	135,129.67	–	27,224.33	–	184,114.15
1821	19,415.33	4,402.56	135,103.93	58,721.88	29,749.45	–	–
1822	23,313.22	4,654.63	135,126.27	58,722.19	29,976.12	–	184,117.51
1823	33,900.08	4,435.45	135,184.22	58,722.91	30,103.07	–	184,119.04
1824	63,322.41	6,977.96	134,231.29	58,723.35	30,689.07	–	–
1825	48,422.58	5,509.77	135,176.66	58,723.97	30,690.50	–	–
1826	52,055.17	6,418.03	135,219.34	58,724.25	30,687.23	–	–
1827	50,445.38	6,990.42	135,207.80	–	–	–	–
1828	53,755.57	6,186.98	135,195.70	58,725.44	–	–	184,140.99
1829	41,958.84	5,920.86	134,258.13	–	–	–	184,144.95
1830	47,082.10	9,585.25	–	–	30,687.30	–	184,151.59
1831	58,087.70	6,476.61	135,203.23	58,726.80	–	–	184,164.20
1832	53,376.27	7,371.17	135,157.13	58,726.87	–	–	368,342.17
1833	51,704.33	7,652.43	135,181.04	58,726.93	–	–	–
1834	20,966.17	4,653.75	135,182.84	58,726.92	–	–	184,178.41
1835	47,752.85	7,348.76	135,188.49	58,726.94	–	–	–
1836	60,151.01	6,564.86	135,197.65	58,726.98	–	–	184,182.71
1837	57,068.59	4,441.04	135,198.39	58,727.00	30,687.37	–	184,184.29
1838	43,323.37	5,366.21	135,225.61	58,727.03	–	–	184,185.58
1839	42,556.36	5,619.54	135,227.43	58,727.06	–	–	184,187.10
1840	52,612.67	6,189.17	135,241.84	58,727.09	–	–	184,188.31
1841	55,095.12	4,209.81	265,653.27	58,727.13	–	–	184,190.49

TABLE A.5 *Customs revenues collected at selected* Changguan, *1723–1909* (*taels of silver*) (cont.)

Year	Linqin Huguan	Linqin Gongguan	Taiping Guan	Wuchang Guan	Jingzhou Guan	Hubei Xinguan	Kui Guan
1842	25,436.60	4,103.85	135,268.36	58,727.17	–	–	–
1843	35,731.49	4,741.59	135,243.53	58,727.21	–	–	–
1844	48,036.60	4,607.67	135,252.97	–	–	–	184,201.66
1845	59,739.10	7,998.10	135,253.00	–	–	–	–
1846	98,166.54	3,781.93	119,074.11	58,727.28	30,687.28	–	–
1847	41,865.35	2,884.48	117,696.11	58,727.32	–	–	–
1848	85,441.13	6,611.66	118,643.31	–	–	–	184,220.00
1849	63,144.98	5,477.71	118,970.41	117,454.70	–	–	184,221.01
1850	35,134.24	3,383.83	113,651.88	–	–	–	184,229.02
1851	40,982.12	3,422.98	113,837.74	–	–	–	–
1852	64,694.28	5,501.11	111,735.97	–	–	–	184,242.51
1853	46,310.72	4,583.38	102,646.16	–	–	–	108,099.70
1854	26,611.13	1,452.08	92,671.03	–	–	–	115,801.86
1855	37,494.51	4,490.74	7,467.92	–	–	–	–
1856	37,382.83	2,925.82	49,504.37	–	–	–	119,146.24
1857	38,807.50	4,070.24	53,774.57	–	–	21,800.00	118,619.76
1858	48,211.95	6,338.87	33,411.66	–	–	27,700.00	178,290.14
1859	51,635.47	7,170.26	30,975.99	–	–	27,600.00	184,219.44
1860	83,748.70	7,823.72	41,580.35	23,587.75	–	–	164,833.20
1861	50,075.96	3,753.65	37,286.70	20,691.78	–	–	143,281.38
1862	34,989.95	7,254.44	37,733.71	20,357.16	–	–	180,083.30
1863	36,631.19	3,070.67	39,655.33	–	–	–	184,222.83
1864	26,650.47	5,890.59	38,615.20	23,111.84	23,242.21	–	184,225.18
1865	18,620.35	3,212.88	32,601.02	–	23,242.19	31,252.35	196,705.11
1866	21,712.97	4,997.11	66,996.26	24,786.94	–	35,794.04	184,226.80
1867	32,186.05	5,764.28	189,825.10	–	–	–	184,223.80
1868	32,811.54	3,105.72	189,597.20	25,407.87	–	–	197,613.57
1869	33,813.68	5,148.01	175,260.62	24,513.49	–	39,771.37	172,331.29
1870	42,453.53	3,689.81	175,385.63	20,130.86	–	–	–
1871	29,100.64	6,098.11	175,421.53	18,985.33	–	–	184,226.12
1872	54,352.26	7,827.49	170,071.26	19,554.35	–	39,917.96	174,860.13
1873	65,886.30	4,951.69	168,261.37	19,633.53	–	–	195,906.81
1874	42,173.31	3,450.61	163,074.37	19,097.25	–	39,968.16	–
1875	28,174.17	5,496.52	162,612.83	19,538.29	–	–	–
1876	50,534.80	4,466.58	162,704.72	19,521.59	–	–	196,705.74
1877	46,994.80	2,048.14	155,433.93	19,207.19	–	39,990.00	178,083.20

Year	Linqin Huguan	Linqin Gongguan	Taiping Guan	Wuchang Guan	Jingzhou Guan	Hubei Xinguan	Kui Guan
1878	23,567.52	1,497.95	135,767.54	19,511.13	–	39,991.57	184,165.81
1879	58,121.22	3,972.91	136,701.99	19,505.45	–	–	138,866.48
1880	50,526.83	5,336.05	146,725.44	19,544.59	–	–	139,073.77
1881	23,285.65	2,785.23	147,355.29	19,548.52	–	–	123,471.23
1882	36,538.29	4,664.02	147,794.73	19,570.08	–	–	128,389.58
1883	57,802.15	5,072.81	142,552.21	18,786.55	–	39,998.00	115,188.33
1884	55,568.15	4,946.80	147,728.73	18,833.50	–	27,905.03	138,555.43
1885	63,618.59	6,964.38	144,468.55	19,496.23	–	–	105,752.57
1886	68,976.99	6,535.63	145,622.19	30,998.61	–	–	113,573.34
1887	62,255.68	6,532.36	144,350.97	40,909.43	–	–	106,302.74
1888	63,421.16	6,017.84	146,138.66	41,496.93	–	–	94,656.15
1889	64,635.23	7,368.93	146,081.68	45,728.87	–	–	85,630.10
1890	68,812.28	5,262.85	146,205.93	41,070.02	–	–	62,444.39
1891	66,170.14	6,179.96	145,652.80	–	–	–	50,000.00
1892	62,093.35	6,078.46	291,053.67	41,452.44	–	–	46,308.07
1893	63,074.51	6,024.11	140,155.86	36,380.29	–	–	46,905.61
1894	93,508.25	5,752.82	141,266.22	38,260.36	–	–	37,376.92
1895	92,432.22	7,215.95	140,166.19	34,581.39	–	–	37,595.11
1896	76,093.55	5,761.47	141,221.49	33,645.00	–	–	–
1897	81,917.80	5,545.06	141,424.65	31,258.13	–	–	28,058.28
1898	57,282.23	5,178.03	144,221.82	–	–	–	–
1899	52,358.45	5,709.33	148,355.17	–	–	–	–
1900	58,944.11	2,396.88	154,287.12	–	–	89,516.82	22,680.00
1901	17,507.18	2,972.42	154,281.64	33,810.72	–	89,559.11	15,648.00
1902	93,748.06	5,723.42	152,537.82	–	–	89,871.45	15,756.00
1903	166,582.61	12,876.95	123,441.22	–	–	89,877.53	18,315.00
1904	140,655.07	9,873.74	146,091.15	35,900.06	–	89,896.42	14,357.66
1905	127,215.45	9,418.48	170,493.54	34,706.84	32,380.56	89,903.81	14,512.00
1906	110,409.17	9,431.47	144,862.23	34,882.81	29,319.18	89,908.00	18,243.62
1907	128,769.68	10,508.53	143,328.76	35,880.78	29,928.05	89,910.03	20,141.40
1908	125,291.23	10,790.87	142,812.22	–	–	–	14,760.97
1909	–	–	149,952.41	–	–	–	–

TABLE A.6 *Customs revenues collected at selected* Changguan, *1723–1909* (*taels of silver*)

Year	Yu Guan	Tianjin Guan	Tianjin Haiguan	Donghai Guan	Jianghai Guan	Zhehai Guan
1723	–	–	0.00	–	–	–
1724	–	–	0.00	–	–	–
1725	–	–	0.00	–	–	–
1726	–	–	0.00	–	–	–
1727	–	–	0.00	–	–	–
1728	–	–	0.00	–	–	–
1729	–	–	0.00	–	–	–
1730	–	–	0.00	–	–	–
1731	–	–	0.00	–	–	–
1732	–	–	0.00	–	–	–
1733	–	–	0.00	–	–	–
1734	7,071.21	–	0.00	–	–	–
1735	5,210.62	–	0.00	–	67,673.61	95,222.34
1736	3,473.74	–	0.00	–	62,608.75	67,942.56
1737	–	–	0.00	–	69,078.67	90,073.13
1738	5,687.81	–	0.00	–	65,120.33	90,105.50
1739	5,187.39	–	0.00	–	69,282.42	91,402.77
1740	8,826.00	–	0.00	–	78,914.33	91,392.77
1741	5,132.09	–	0.00	–	79,794.68	93,472.67
1742	6,308.69	–	0.00	–	79,473.92	93,727.87
1743	5,011.71	–	0.00	–	81,809.52	93,798.00
1744	5,166.56	–	0.00	–	81,460.71	93,806.00
1745	5,178.00	–	0.00	–	81,372.92	93,774.00
1746	5,178.31	–	0.00	–	55,632.86	88,159.45
1747	5,265.27	–	0.00	–	52,610.01	93,949.79
1748	5,238.48	–	0.00	–	52,097.52	188,185.49
1749	5,217.28	–	0.00	–	55,422.46	92,754.56
1750	3,522.56	–	0.00	–	77,389.44	99,501.18
1751	3,046.00	–	0.00	–	78,553.49	85,641.40
1752	3,330.00	–	0.00	–	77,186.77	95,412.31
1753	4,441.00	101,214.85	0.00	–	77,509.00	87,654.23
1754	6,317.17	100,695.38	0.00	–	75,759.00	87,667.23
1755	6,960.55	108,008.29	0.00	–	76,775.00	90,553.23
1756	6,543.73	108,169.24	0.00	–	57,925.00	89,692.23
1757	5,215.34	108,072.35	0.00	–	57,926.60	89,737.23

Year	Yu Guan	Tianjin Guan	Tianjin Haiguan	Donghai Guan	Jianghai Guan	Zhehai Guan
1758	6,484.10	109,223.80	0.00	–	72,214.40	89,568.23
1759	6,859.24	109,435.82	0.00	–	73,137.50	89,472.97
1760	6,501.39	109,798.01	0.00	–	73,145.80	89,358.31
1761	6,518.69	110,054.29	0.00	–	73,150.30	89,377.69
1762	6,861.34	219,829.12	0.00	–	76,968.60	89,360.12
1763	5,416.13	121,306.26	0.00	–	69,013.68	89,432.57
1764	6,000.93	128,101.48	0.00	–	69,242.04	89,519.64
1765	5,882.34	126,434.51	0.00	–	71,328.23	89,555.14
1766	5,263.87	121,672.42	0.00	–	71,341.50	89,573.57
1767	5,832.57	122,198.70	0.00	–	71,477.40	89,603.33
1768	6,039.66	126,417.71	0.00	–	71,783.03	89,603.26
1769	5,397.01	127,201.99	0.00	–	71,895.60	89,630.98
1770	5,686.89	111,864.63	0.00	–	143,861.00	89,635.82
1771	5,435.92	108,994.41	0.00	–	71,996.60	89,626.02
1772	5,438.01	115,120.00	0.00	–	72,031.10	89,673.06
1773	5,656.59	112,893.78	0.00	–	72,142.50	89,685.02
1774	5,285.53	115,165.90	0.00	–	72,278.40	89,700.35
1775	5,599.00	113,077.71	0.00	–	72,368.50	89,717.44
1776	5,181.02	115,018.71	0.00	–	72,380.20	89,688.64
1777	5,181.26	112,492.77	0.00	–	72,390.37	89,716.90
1778	5,358.18	109,216.73	0.00	–	72,428.14	89,752.31
1779	5,181.74	109,077.93	0.00	–	72,467.50	90,164.45
1780	5,181.95	110,735.31	0.00	–	72,498.10	90,178.70
1781	5,358.29	110,044.57	0.00	–	72,521.48	180,382.40
1782	5,182.72	109,064.15	0.00	–	72,635.01	90,199.18
1783	5,182.68	106,218.25	0.00	–	72,671.33	90,206.30
1784	5,656.59	108,836.76	0.00	–	72,712.00	90,211.39
1785	5,183.13	98,101.30	0.00	–	72,716.00	90,218.33
1786	5,359.17	101,536.02	0.00	–	72,728.00	90,223.16
1787	5,183.25	99,106.99	0.00	–	72,739.00	90,137.38
1788	5,183.37	99,122.13	0.00	–	72,741.00	90,229.49
1789	5,657.50	107,696.60	0.00	–	72,752.44	90,238.51
1790	5,183.40	107,729.94	0.00	–	72,761.00	90,243.28
1791	5,183.48	107,762.47	0.00	–	72,869.00	90,254.33
1792	5,657.51	107,799.62	0.00	–	72,878.00	90,297.33
1793	5,183.49	107,835.32	0.00	–	72,892.00	90,321.13

TABLE A.6 *Customs revenues collected at selected* Changguan, *1723–1909* (*taels of silver*) (cont.)

Year	Yu Guan	Tianjin Guan	Tianjin Haiguan	Donghai Guan	Jianghai Guan	Zhehai Guan
1794	5,183.51	107,923.69	0.00	–	72,906.00	90,344.33
1795	–	–	0.00	–	72,920.00	90,357.83
1796	5,183.52	103,284.27	0.00	–	72,934.33	59,224.07
1797	5,120.00	107,992.20	0.00	–	72,934.44	56,469.36
1798	5,120.00	–	0.00	–	72,940.83	80,373.29
1799	5,120.00	–	0.00	–	72,954.30	75,123.30
1800	5,120.00	114,874.65	0.00	–	72,957.52	66,697.91
1801	5,120.00	–	0.00	–	73,012.54	75,131.47
1802	5,120.00	–	0.00	–	73,330.33	75,132.63
1803	5,120.00	99,200.44	0.00	–	146,938.25	77,134.70
1804	5,120.00	102,158.99	0.00	–	73,556.58	77,135.28
1805	5,120.00	99,666.21	0.00	–	73,561.58	79,047.62
1806	5,121.09	100,167.05	0.00	–	73,573.82	73,738.73
1807	–	100,140.98	37,941.60	–	73,579.51	73,889.23
1808	–	96,277.06	53,050.60	–	73,582.82	79,918.23
1809	–	90,022.85	69,220.00	–	73,586.73	79,927.98
1810	–	97,125.68	64,137.76	–	73,592.91	79,935.06
1811	–	96,592.04	47,500.00	–	73,606.64	79,943.16
1812	–	–	50,119.00	–	73,612.77	79,952.48
1813	–	94,941.77	53,418.00	–	73,619.63	79,960.51
1814	–	95,783.27	51,517.00	–	73,629.00	159,955.08
1815	–	–	39,102.00	–	73,632.68	79,993.85
1816	–	–	35,643.00	–	73,637.20	80,014.13
1817	–	–	40,154.00	–	73,640.65	79,021.79
1818	–	–	43,664.00	–	73,643.86	80,024.39
1819	–	95,900.95	44,023.00	–	73,647.08	80,039.30
1820	–	95,126.08	41,615.00	–	73,650.97	80,053.78
1821	–	95,874.40	42,034.00	–	73,656.68	79,157.82
1822	–	98,089.90	42,752.00	–	73,661.20	80,063.51
1823	–	96,833.69	43,102.00	–	73,664.59	80,073.19
1824	–	96,865.62	43,016.82	–	73,666.64	79,115.58
1825	–	94,811.15	42,344.53	–	73,669.35	79,187.41
1826	–	94,707.11	41,543.80	–	71,384.79	78,955.40
1827	–	190,717.85	42,416.58	–	73,671.36	79,007.65
1828	–	95,536.04	42,030.39	–	73,672.51	79,183.59

Year	Yu Guan	Tianjin Guan	Tianjin Haiguan	Donghai Guan	Jianghai Guan	Zhehai Guan
1829	–	95,740.87	40,094.49	–	73,673.35	79,301.68
1830	–	–	40,042.89	–	73,674.29	79,352.81
1831	–	95,749.86	40,195.09	–	73,675.19	79,426.38
1832	–	95,622.37	21,056.01	–	73,676.15	79,438.15
1833	–	95,747.44	20,105.33	–	73,677.22	79,504.11
1834	–	105,034.28	40,050.78	–	73,678.23	79,505.52
1835	–	95,854.26	40,123.46	–	147,359.77	79,506.30
1836	–	95,876.56	40,213.56	–	73,681.25	79,506.74
1837	–	95,888.20	41,235.40	–	73,682.26	79,510.12
1838	–	95,898.70	40,213.40	–	73,683.29	79,510.45
1839	5,121.18	96,098.70	24,350.62	–	73,684.39	79,514.36
1840	–	95,999.76	20,766.92	–	57,046.51	79,506.29
1841	–	95,629.74	25,031.30	–	73,685.54	79,512.14
1842	–	74,002.90	0.00	–	32,621.47	0.00
1843	–	94,812.48	9,191.52	–	73,686.06	78,025.76
1844	–	94,908.98	28,045.17	–	79,821.79	77,037.56
1845	–	94,992.50	29,053.85	–	79,788.02	78,018.53
1846	–	95,024.72	30,311.29	–	74,291.14	78,020.03
1847	–	94,841.79	33,863.17	–	81,893.53	76,542.32
1848	–	94,127.58	–	–	77,796.46	78,265.94
1849	–	95,153.27	39,676.45	–	75,731.88	78,376.87
1850	–	95,315.96	39,587.44	–	73,752.31	76,546.70
1851	–	95,356.38	34,982.94	–	72,469.09	76,430.26
1852	–	95,701.77	24,711.67	–	74,011.00	47,053.60
1853	908.85	94,099.30	42,656.28	–	–	62,698.97
1854	948.59	85,259.64	40,391.95	–	14,046.79	62,321.09
1855	42.68	68,345.60	40,025.36	–	45,783.16	62,522.61
1856	281.74	93,936.96	41,795.93	–	53,422.45	64,111.84
1857	1,192.02	93,806.83	41,954.67	–	70,686.03	65,467.18
1858	–	93,561.90	42,563.22	–	71,038.67	66,340.07
1859	5,121.18	93,482.38	41,243.66	–	84,374.33	71,368.58
1860	1,072.00	162,428.48	35,485.00	–	99,892.29	55,267.70
1861	–	74,932.20	14,127.90	–	100,584.58	49,858.30
1862	–	75,393.62	14,668.56	–	140,140.59	32,138.24
1863	–	76,083.40	28,995.20	–	165,138.54	21,593.10
1864	987.00	84,447.27	–	–	121,661.03	40,336.46

TABLE A.6 *Customs revenues collected at selected* Changguan, *1723–1909* (*taels of silver*) (cont.)

Year	Yu Guan	Tianjin Guan	Tianjin Haiguan	Donghai Guan	Jianghai Guan	Zhehai Guan
1865	1,430.00	84,451.81	29,074.90	68,578.11	103,920.61	38,047.52
1866	–	84,591.55	38,858.71	90,299.10	103,809.12	32,800.50
1867	–	84,841.54	38,772.10	94,229.34	42,687.12	29,885.04
1868	–	85,535.02	42,713.89	68,649.29	129,547.56	62,656.75
1869	–	–	43,143.25	80,981.97	60,813.79	31,671.04
1870	–	–	40,545.93	86,662.34	67,392.84	35,335.83
1871	–	–	40,481.87	86,183.68	61,223.64	30,481.50
1872	–	166,633.17	42,055.67	86,183.68	61,652.10	30,061.52
1873	–	92,953.46	40,373.18	81,635.57	61,652.10	35,908.23
1874	–	92,498.89	41,721.82	78,557.35	64,927.22	33,712.20
1875	–	92,979.40	41,460.44	77,957.51	65,083.82	33,139.61
1876	–	93,084.26	41,473.23	118,156.27	62,312.97	33,366.74
1877	5,121.18	93,046.93	41,821.01	61,407.57	64,379.34	28,848.14
1878	–	92,634.04	44,988.77	62,719.94	64,499.20	31,417.60
1879	–	92,966.87	41,740.27	63,113.54	65,037.84	31,472.18
1880	–	94,441.11	40,340.11	62,213.03	70,665.27	31,536.32
1881	–	94,745.39	40,079.96	69,785.30	70,160.10	35,908.23
1882	–	96,487.31	40,104.86	70,122.19	68,542.34	34,628.46
1883	–	92,715.65	40,068.28	68,619.47	67,419.21	34,250.33
1884	–	92,086.31	40,038.45	65,945.75	67,092.67	34,330.80
1885	–	67,711.52	40,071.48	55,202.24	44,111.61	27,812.57
1886	–	101,793.08	40,074.22	59,599.06	66,133.63	31,591.19
1887	–	93,857.91	40,064.87	59,858.41	72,986.96	32,337.83
1888	–	93,713.18	40,080.61	54,582.11	92,823.35	33,816.97
1889	–	106,131.79	40,078.85	61,652.78	87,840.31	33,820.71
1890	–	93,618.53	40,079.25	62,250.30	60,369.14	33,693.53
1891	5,121.18	79,022.05	40,081.21	63,758.57	69,354.86	29,165.70
1892	–	187,778.42	40,071.48	57,446.68	66,288.00	33,761.05
1893	–	93,941.24	40,062.87	57,399.01	65,991.81	33,778.93
1894	–	92,957.04	40,071.48	57,525.58	66,424.97	28,997.43
1895	–	94,122.10	36,603.14	58,374.57	28,437.49	30,669.45
1896	–	94,347.39	37,098.04	67,951.77	35,048.99	33,946.34
1897	–	94,215.55	37,657.73	76,883.41	44,772.89	31,876.81
1898	–	94,398.09	40,067.32	75,814.20	45,077.58	51,292.40
1899	–	94,070.89	40,070.54	68,655.49	42,505.20	32,975.33

Year	Yu Guan	Tianjin Guan	Tianjin Haiguan	Donghai Guan	Jianghai Guan	Zhehai Guan
1900	5,547.00	–	40,068.53	66,699.01	73,763.35	61,205.07
1901	1,214.00	–	–	108,592.93	23,378.03	23,145.72
1902	1,528.00	–	–	123,796.00	89,901.33	133,875.65
1903	5,120.00	510,705.73	4,296.95	148,944.00	132,037.43	106,910.30
1904	1,875.00	444,044.57	1,884.14	132,995.00	140,202.72	122,451.74
1905	–	1,054,023.3	3,965.40	168,946.00	165,236.40	125,777.21
1906	5,547.00	732,648.75	4,053.30	159,159.00	172,856.11	–
1907	5,120.00	676,793.50	3,535.84	143,651.00	174,728.74	–
1908	5,121.00	571,515.65	4,089.13	132,356.00	152,803.73	–
1909	–	–	4,188.12	–	112,012.29	–

TABLE A.7 *Summary table (taels of silver)*

Year	Minghai Guan	Yuehai Changguan	Total Changguan	Contribution *Huguan*	Contribution Gongguan
1723	–	–	175,094.95	163,053.65	12,041.30
1724	106,656.00	–	439,454.08	439,454.08	–
1725	116,419.00		779,876.75	655,984.25	123,892.50
1726	116,111.55	–	802,846.19	668,862.67	133,983.52
1727	123,603.55	–	847,448.46	838,148.46	9,300.00
1728	142,440.55	–	1,157,389.60	1,144,989.60	12,400.00
1729	162,029.00	–	861,575.90	849,075.90	12,500.00
1730	179,013.75		1,429,467.09	1,246,442.60	183,024.49
1731	–		787,349.79	787,349.79	–
1732	–		1,270,733.35	1,242,497.62	28,235.73
1733	166,598.81		1,768,135.29	1,742,067.68	26,067.61
1734	180,825.37		1,776,623.42	1,732,425.35	44,198.07
1735	181,133.37		3,476,387.69	3,130,138.66	346,249.03
1736	203,336.42		3,359,946.35	3,066,973.82	292,972.53
1737	215,506.82		3,153,387.08	2,924,513.33	228,873.75
1738	221,269.78		2,854,240.05	2,644,698.20	209,541.86
1739	251,025.47		3,089,173.26	2,779,954.13	309,219.13
1740	251,099.04		2,797,761.46	2,448,295.53	349,465.92
1741	258,599.04		3,265,201.35	2,915,625.13	349,576.23

TABLE A.7 *Summary table (taels of silver)* (cont.)

Year	Minghai Guan	Yuehai Changguan	Total Changguan	Contribution *Huguan*	Contribution Gongguan
1742	281,199.00		3,450,161.15	3,053,472.05	396,689.10
1743	254,550.00		3,326,543.13	2,945,627.66	380,915.48
1744	241,223.00		3,584,945.54	3,209,707.30	375,238.25
1745	228,618.00		3,826,590.44	3,404,151.91	422,438.54
1746	266,573.00		3,374,869.25	2,970,923.85	403,945.40
1747	277,974.00		3,272,534.10	2,844,351.23	428,182.87
1748	523,058.25		4,610,789.78	4,051,041.69	559,748.09
1749	321,126.12		3,687,158.37	3,278,503.06	408,655.31
1750	326,751.03		3,854,776.35	3,540,930.88	313,845.46
1751	308,883.76		3,412,733.84	3,022,977.00	389,756.84
1752	332,418.12		4,258,399.33	3,855,767.64	402,631.68
1753	314,448.16		4,223,373.62	3,857,165.03	366,208.59
1754	325,481.40		3,841,688.11	3,461,026.71	380,661.40
1755	327,969.10		4,111,806.58	3,744,999.34	366,807.24
1756	326,520.80		4,271,901.75	3,890,292.87	381,608.88
1757	331,910.40		3,422,668.00	3,107,094.69	315,573.31
1758	327,284.00		3,551,366.99	3,235,226.38	316,140.61
1759	318,755.20		4,361,586.06	3,804,050.28	557,535.78
1760	330,663.66		4,284,768.43	3,853,507.43	431,261.00
1761	354,792.02		4,048,835.33	3,635,708.58	413,126.75
1762	352,342.28		4,283,957.54	3,847,651.06	436,306.48
1763	355,497.73		4,408,473.57	3,962,639.50	445,834.06
1764	356,822.89		4,485,854.41	4,101,109.22	384,745.19
1765	356,929.95		4,824,376.77	4,407,818.48	416,558.29
1766	357,173.29		4,443,153.22	4,011,465.01	431,688.21
1767	357,249.67		5,361,169.70	4,784,725.49	576,444.21
1768	343,231.92		4,027,853.69	3,635,221.79	392,631.90
1769	294,581.33		4,322,050.52	3,931,442.49	390,608.03
1770	350,891.71		4,942,461.00	4,552,038.83	390,422.17
1771	364,512.07		4,489,057.77	4,106,275.01	382,782.76
1772	364,519.69		4,459,563.21	4,060,411.81	399,151.40
1773	373,023.97		4,868,521.14	4,463,985.99	404,535.15
1774	368,805.27		4,909,152.45	4,484,077.15	425,075.30
1775	366,415.99		4,573,637.42	4,145,466.35	428,171.08
1776	354,297.64		4,530,296.94	4,115,062.57	415,234.37

Year	Minghai Guan	Yuehai Changguan	Total Changguan	Contribution *Huguan*	Contribution Gongguan
1777	352,861.30		4,854,314.55	4,423,426.96	430,887.59
1778	368,877.55		4,496,970.99	4,064,272.71	432,698.28
1779	374,407.47		4,525,366.01	4,119,254.35	406,111.66
1780	396,938.60		4,494,464.47	4,083,779.54	410,684.93
1781	794,263.24		5,683,362.45	5,271,183.95	412,178.50
1782	365,888.31		4,210,506.54	3,790,082.65	420,423.89
1783	349,706.33		4,402,589.86	3,978,575.54	424,014.32
1784	356,723.54		4,401,897.89	3,960,913.63	440,984.26
1785	365,990.51		4,045,272.83	3,621,575.23	423,697.60
1786	366,045.46		3,781,426.15	3,398,462.35	382,963.80
1787	274,071.82		4,062,671.38	3,734,224.67	328,446.71
1788	312,321.28		4,429,019.85	4,097,062.60	331,957.25
1789	320,967.59		4,883,278.59	4,503,465.54	379,813.06
1790	330,093.04		4,471,225.87	4,039,779.73	431,446.15
1791	330,332.94		4,649,298.23	4,225,400.44	423,897.79
1792	298,018.50		4,922,088.13	4,360,197.92	561,890.21
1793	329,746.59		4,429,746.43	4,016,172.31	413,574.12
1794	327,742.71		4,385,120.29	4,019,107.40	366,012.89
1795	248,723.48		3,889,343.41	3,558,322.86	331,020.55
1796	192,849.87		4,105,193.56	3,802,087.10	303,106.45
1797	198,507.18		4,142,211.93	3,813,762.58	328,449.35
1798	199,163.91		3,808,440.62	3,455,019.47	353,421.15
1799	227,639.64		3,934,493.86	3,570,475.43	364,018.43
1800	195,974.72		4,692,429.86	4,204,851.15	487,578.71
1801	202,152.78		3,331,306.75	3,096,522.82	234,783.93
1802	219,251.00		3,934,812.02	3,558,998.45	375,813.57
1803	201,520.97		4,143,603.81	3,834,140.73	309,463.08
1804	198,851.94		4,224,829.82	3,847,532.14	377,297.68
1805	171,884.80		4,309,959.15	3,949,419.32	360,539.84
1806	175,719.96		3,725,494.85	3,373,276.24	352,218.61
1807	168,923.34		3,824,202.52	3,441,067.69	383,134.83
1808	186,852.86		4,394,358.94	4,010,150.64	384,208.30
1809	193,421.12		4,097,684.49	3,727,916.47	369,768.02
1810	186,617.48		4,198,342.98	3,802,083.81	396,259.17
1811	187,061.00		3,823,611.15	3,434,136.61	389,474.54
1812	189,539.00		3,802,296.09	3,415,174.95	387,121.14

TABLE A.7 *Summary table (taels of silver)* (cont.)

Year	Minghai Guan	Yuehai Changguan	Total Changguan	Contribution *Huguan*	Contribution Gongguan
1813	211,477.86		3,834,349.81	3,446,170.46	388,179.35
1814	430,906.97		4,552,176.62	4,165,858.70	386,317.92
1815	209,672.54		3,872,833.64	3,497,905.00	374,928.65
1816	205,844.72		3,608,316.10	3,271,269.29	337,046.81
1817	235,865.94		3,850,448.89	3,463,319.09	387,129.80
1818	196,855.58		4,061,151.25	3,675,263.38	385,887.86
1819	193,462.45		4,381,215.79	3,982,379.73	398,836.06
1820	195,280.47		3,957,579.19	3,585,762.50	371,816.70
1821	192,688.46		3,707,676.58	3,307,862.52	399,814.07
1822	186,778.08		4,582,059.15	4,183,104.28	398,954.87
1823	186,766.91		3,809,708.29	3,407,721.37	401,986.92
1824	186,770.71		4,012,055.65	3,534,841.57	477,214.09
1825	186,759.12		3,800,705.28	3,465,548.22	335,157.06
1826	188,438.86		3,387,752.81	3,062,308.20	325,444.62
1827	188,913.24		3,395,333.78	3,082,212.04	313,121.74
1828	189,391.58		3,945,040.34	3,602,644.73	342,395.61
1829	187,597.52		4,001,499.58	3,663,017.53	338,482.05
1830	186,873.11		4,002,700.51	3,596,042.86	406,657.65
1831	187,243.56		3,401,557.65	3,083,702.04	317,855.61
1832	186,733.95		4,267,346.74	3,861,443.70	405,903.04
1833	152,939.37		3,383,614.94	3,095,519.95	288,094.99
1834	176,825.19		3,729,902.64	3,469,384.19	260,518.44
1835	186,913.99		4,100,031.48	3,794,235.65	305,795.83
1836	184,095.28		3,533,895.61	3,219,531.94	314,363.67
1837	188,886.64		3,642,312.57	3,304,516.50	337,796.07
1838	191,665.08		4,086,220.82	3,789,788.80	296,432.02
1839	191,391.01		3,826,262.29	3,559,781.47	266,480.83
1840	186,900.94		3,883,113.01	3,603,874.83	279,238.18
1841	181,451.09		3,918,769.19	3,678,229.18	240,540.01
1842	115,953.40		3,187,345.47	2,942,739.15	244,606.31
1843	86,059.68		3,076,396.91	2,786,584.83	289,812.08
1844	127,569.83		3,396,892.60	3,099,378.12	297,514.48
1845	91,462.89		3,333,728.87	3,013,429.81	320,299.06
1846	305,932.19		3,880,028.46	3,546,130.78	333,897.68
1847	146,417.84		2,657,011.78	2,480,381.20	176,630.57

Year	Minghai Guan	Yuehai Changguan	Total Changguan	Contribution *Huguan*	Contribution Gongguan
1848	153,179.60		3,225,211.37	2,892,328.10	332,883.27
1849	150,830.77		3,888,043.03	3,584,283.76	303,759.27
1850	156,091.95		3,001,638.68	2,835,966.26	165,672.42
1851	161,340.16		3,433,436.22	3,172,572.93	260,863.30
1852	132,351.27		2,891,319.90	2,730,898.32	160,421.58
1853	113,028.80		2,382,813.23	2,311,280.82	71,532.41
1854	80,352.87		1,445,568.53	1,403,960.34	41,608.19
1855	102,149.66		1,564,026.92	1,505,321.78	58,705.14
1856	122,220.66		1,783,961.29	1,712,435.57	71,525.72
1857	130,592.64		1,650,651.80	1,573,992.77	76,659.03
1858	145,167.77		1,666,071.73	1,586,033.69	80,038.04
1859	147,400.92		1,680,141.13	1,597,909.29	82,231.84
1860	163,769.47		2,005,044.85	1,950,775.20	54,269.65
1861	129,958.60	60,440.82	1,375,014.22	1,322,477.12	52,537.11
1862	109,494.28	62,253.25	1,369,923.52	1,319,518.87	50,404.65
1863	99,290.71	46,961.86	1,562,564.07	1,515,118.88	47,445.19
1864	104,879.93	47,857.63	1,827,798.69	1,753,299.57	74,499.12
1865	77,261.58	53,941.09	1,867,276.90	1,793,553.59	73,723.31
1866	85,406.22	56,511.94	1,862,089.01	1,812,695.03	49,393.98
1867	94,284.27	66,646.30	1,891,568.22	1,841,394.44	50,173.79
1868	93,897.76	111,770.87	2,173,451.94	2,081,503.25	91,948.69
1869	100,709.26	160,041.34	2,060,004.78	2,010,424.92	49,579.86
1870	115,134.82	156,933.91	1,777,884.24	1,694,905.89	82,978.35
1871	116,649.69	156,884.13	2,007,061.16	1,956,521.63	50,539.53
1872	117,779.21	157,183.12	2,200,618.33	2,148,344.32	52,274.01
1873	126,150.80	157,640.08	2,157,054.47	2,107,651.25	49,403.21
1874	131,068.29	158,611.60	1,978,119.54	1,930,212.91	47,906.63
1875	136,225.34	158,988.79	1,958,528.94	1,908,573.37	49,955.57
1876	159,428.48	168,994.27	2,290,616.87	2,241,687.19	48,929.68
1877	148,719.33	170,553.42	2,343,364.21	2,221,041.74	122,322.47
1878	140,520.31	173,185.60	2,232,407.23	2,128,278.16	104,129.07
1879	351,018.01	347,721.86	2,858,386.22	2,734,774.31	123,611.91
1880	185,842.31	187,761.87	2,329,923.51	2,184,731.73	145,191.78
1881	185,588.07	194,034.10	2,308,990.73	2,183,987.46	125,003.27
1882	186,062.72	192,087.25	2,320,521.22	2,205,545.90	114,975.32
1883	182,888.90	197,048.72	2,295,812.10	2,177,776.54	118,035.56

TABLE A.7 *Summary table (taels of silver)* (cont.)

Year	Minghai Guan	Yuehai Changguan	Total Changguan	Contribution *Huguan*	Contribution Gongguan
1884	158,159.45	199,968.20	2,448,122.73	2,339,751.16	108,371.57
1885	175,792.78	200,735.85	2,193,896.42	2,118,891.84	75,004.58
1886	190,462.82	195,087.10	2,266,249.36	2,154,533.81	111,715.55
1887	189,576.34	201,808.26	2,368,705.31	2,256,321.01	112,384.30
1888	201,135.31	201,860.46	2,437,561.23	2,300,440.12	137,121.12
1889	194,042.70	201,901.84	2,378,189.97	2,263,699.28	114,490.68
1890	178,428.71	202,417.66	2,818,236.54	2,632,507.53	185,729.00
1891	177,030.35	202,690.17	2,271,314.01	2,152,702.96	118,611.06
1892	180,499.02	202,957.81	2,556,720.45	2,443,864.11	112,856.34
1893	175,844.45	192,726.75	1,875,289.27	1,851,942.14	23,347.14
1894	170,680.00	181,996.95	2,237,430.76	2,140,928.30	96,502.46
1895	166,352.93	192,009.62	2,068,087.77	1,959,991.75	108,096.03
1896	172,962.02	192,172.88	2,138,192.49	2,038,258.84	99,933.65
1897	195,813.27	181,352.02	2,207,741.55	2,110,049.09	97,692.46
1898	176,573.96	206,590.97	2,128,385.33	2,028,895.56	99,489.77
1899	178,864.99	206,301.95	2,071,632.63	2,001,774.40	69,858.23
1900	181,244.83	200,676.85	2,293,038.95	2,148,719.92	144,319.03
1901	247,944.47	203,481.48	1,719,952.91	1,645,207.08	74,745.83
1902	283,075.48	302,530.17	2,269,037.63	2,154,854.58	114,183.05
1903	358,400.00	442,592.40	2,618,225.98	2,527,892.53	90,333.44
1904	368,200.00	399,075.72	2,561,706.66	2,421,426.25	140,280.41
1905	396,300.00	560,255.68	3,661,894.54	3,480,977.68	180,916.86
1906	382,770.46	313,005.76	2,912,487.55	2,737,006.32	175,481.23
1907	–	297,437.32	2,473,818.19	2,227,509.61	246,308.59
1908	317,893.57	301,651.45	2,335,880.19	2,189,308.78	146,571.42
1909	438,761.59	462,749.63	1,831,971.47	1,681,805.28	150,166.18
1910	–	–	169,413.02	169,413.02	–

Source: All kinds of archives.

APPENDIX B

Customs Revenue Data for Yuhei Guan, 1723–1911

TABLE B.1 *Customs revenues collected at Yuehai Guan, 1723–1860 (taels of silver)*

Year	Customs revenue	Year	Customs revenue	Year	Customs revenue	Year	Customs revenue
1723	–	1758	370,071.31	1793	885,612.80	1828	1,441,924.60
1724	–	1759	354,694.72	1794	972,948.50	1829	1,499,580.70
1725	97,294.56	1760	356,266.54	1795	1,171,911.00	1830	1,663,635.00
1726	–	1761	382,634.39	1796	981,186.69	1831	1,461,806.20
1727	–	1762	382,652.51	1797	973,172.98	1832	1,532,933.20
1728	–	1763	411,636.51	1798	1,035,757.50	1833	1,477,846.30
1729	–	1764	474,412.79	1799	937,073.00	1834	1,669,712.60
1730	198,062.09	1765	505,138.77	1800	1,201,246.50	1835	1,424,944.20
1731	228,659.70	1766	600,120.81	1801	1,336,171.80	1836	1,674,851.70
1732	309,107.92	1767	546,930.69	1802	1,540,773.10	1837	1,789,424.30
1733	–	1768	547,737.68	1803	1,695,389.00	1838	1,242,044.20
1734	–	1769	549,194.82	1804	1,555,586.40	1839	1,448,559.00
1735	216,000.00	1770	591,067.35	1805	1,641,971.80	1840	1,186,551.90
1736	271,953.53	1771	579,935.97	1806	1,621,376.00	1841	864,232.17
1737	285,154.91	1772	593,869.71	1807	1,663,830.00	1842	1,115,742.40
1738	234,059.50	1773	554,903.08	1808	1,470,460.20	1843	1,182,489.00
1739	270,620.84	1774	541,553.19	1809	1,457,201.80	1844	2,030,543.10
1740	269,454.96	1775	541,863.70	1810	1,408,641.90	1845	2,360,832.20
1741	252,606.05	1776	533,178.41	1811	1,165,263.10	1846	4,158,620.20
1742	296,920.90	1777	588,407.97	1812	1,347,936.90	1847	1,825,223.10
1743	317,168.68	1778	588,453.97	1813	1,246,708.20	1848	1,424,045.90
1744	328,776.00	1779	556,185.10	1814	2,420,719.50	1849	1,471,318.50
1745	415,143.00	1780	556,233.94	1815	1,331,239.90	1850	1,476,868.00
1746	339,618.00	1781	1,130,684.50	1816	1,446,980.00	1851	1,636,574.10
1747	216,023.00	1782	521,110.55	1817	1,421,303.80	1852	1,666,811.90
1748	435,080.00	1783	797,861.57	1818	1,302,911.00	1853	1,274,129.50
1749	447,420.20	1784	748,125.72	1819	1,380,097.10	1854	1,166,492.10
1750	467,562.50	1785	872,150.91	1820	1,479,820.10	1855	404,758.73
1751	461,795.00	1786	953,960.66	1821	1,497,022.50	1856	1,156,805.90
1752	503,303.80	1787	981,686.31	1822	1,485,146.80	1857	101,121.63
1753	514,800.00	1788	1,036,999.30	1823	1,404,913.20	1858	434,272.17
1754	515,300.00	1789	1,101,362.00	1824	1,444,322.60	1859	882,017.68
1755	486,285.80	1790	1,127,562.90	1825	1,298,829.00	1860	991,888.53
1756	405,009.00	1791	995,882.52	1826	1,576,637.20		
1757	320,551.00	1792	1,011,426.30	1827	1,850,046.00		

Source: All kinds of archives.

 | DOI 10.1163/9789004324886_013

Customs Revenues Collected at *Yangguan*, 1844–1910

TABLE C.1 *Customs revenues collected at selected* Yanguan, *1844–1910* (*taels of silver*)

Year	Jianghai Yangguan	Zhehai Yangguan	Xiamen and Fuzhou Yangguan	Suzhou Guan	Jinling Guan	Wuhu Yangguan
1844	42,617.31	6,264.47	15,134.44	–	–	–
1845	187,960.79	6,885.05	48,275.94	–	–	–
1846	1,229,628.42	2,173.38	72,778.25	–	–	–
1847	680,295.19	1,571.93	29,136.25	–	–	–
1848	587,984.93	–	24,599.77	–	–	–
1849	670,603.02	419.89	30,655.62	–	–	–
1850	–	117.63	33,684.40	–	–	–
1851	1,200,000.00	–	–	–	–	–
1852	1,283,377.65	–	–	–	–	–
1853	545,687.48	0.00	49,590.95	–	–	–
1854	646,847.56	–	198,970.68	–	–	–
1855	1,976,953.01	252.00	265,477.20	–	–	–
1856	2,126,956.68	–	387,663.50	–	–	–
1857	2,273,955.58	4,149.38	507,172.04	–	–	–
1858	1,954,739.38	2,153.83	526,122.41	–	–	–
1859	2,365,909.25	4,609.98	578,646.90	–	–	–
1860	2,047,898.70	994.20	711,549.11	–	–	–
1861	2,349,359.56	340,262.34	178,814.73	–	–	–
1862	3,933,304.70	8,644.00	1,947,852.00	–	–	–
1863	2,927,402.51	37,485.00	2,034,424.00	–	–	–
1864	2,150,662.99	19,242.00	2,349,469.00	–	–	–
1865	2,233,486.53	22,266.00	1,979,391.00	–	–	–
1866	2,164,051.57	17,494.00	2,248,242.00	–	–	–
1867	2,439,473.00	21,681.00	2,108,657.00	–	–	–
1868	2,675,717.00	32,733.00	2,512,513.00	–	–	–
1869	2,719,381.00	49,389.00	2,120,906.00	–	–	–
1870	2,821,247.00	67,594.00	2,011,502.00	–	–	–
1871	2,843,674.00	106,387.00	2,358,151.00	–	–	–
1872	3,479,212.00	349,322.00	2,293,308.00	–	–	–
1873	3,294,164.51	169,069.00	2,275,613.00	–	–	–
1874	3,607,757.84	152,504.00	2,403,178.00	–	–	–

 | DOI 10.1163/9789004324886_014

Year	Jianghai Yangguan	Zhehai Yangguan	Xiamen and Fuzhou Yangguan	Suzhou Guan	Jinling Guan	Wuhu Yangguan
1875	3,608,000.27	149,132.51	2,482,195.30	–	–	–
1876	3,691,491.40	165,707.62	2,436,317.00	–	–	–
1877	3,458,087.00	112,454.00	2,482,771.10	–	–	14,108.00
1878	3,606,330.00	204,958.91	2,590,432.80	–	–	28,311.00
1879	4,020,741.33	165,457.49	2,334,599.40	–	–	32,558.00
1880	4,480,998.00	231,196.33	2,579,152.30	–	–	44,826.00
1881	4,653,373.15	338,254.00	2,922,410.00	–	–	68,187.00
1882	4,350,181.14	352,141.29	2,682,131.40	–	–	91,907.00
1883	3,820,888.83	197,873.00	2,506,655.00	–	–	87,399.00
1884	3,819,202.22	148,415.26	2,515,123.80	–	–	57,718.00
1885	4,199,277.28	184,002.11	2,662,224.00	–	–	65,876.00
1886	4,547,976.22	229,511.62	2,639,045.90	–	–	150,600.00
1887	5,142,134.76	609,936.00	2,422,084.50	–	–	542,339.00
1888	6,294,511.00	678,607.00	3,380,988.00	–	–	529,984.00
1889	5,956,248.00	559,334.00	2,877,197.00	–	–	544,153.00
1890	5,835,098.00	601,809.00	2,807,704.00	–	–	474,472.00
1891	6,948,617.00	528,833.00	2,611,746.00	–	–	777,934.00
1892	6,795,068.00	602,346.00	2,564,747.00	–	–	686,615.00
1893	6,017,622.00	673,636.00	2,602,210.00	–	–	637,054.00
1894	6,686,797.00	781,652.00	2,513,803.00	–	–	813,076.00
1895	6,300,891.00	1,408,716.00	2,261,193.00	–	–	395,379.00
1896	7,456,145.00	879,410.00	2,322,308.00	–	–	620,366.00
1897	7,492,930.00	800,939.00	2,342,292.00	27,349.00	–	442,816.00
1898	7,029,330.00	713,757.00	2,099,366.00	27,661.00	–	371,079.00
1899	7,835,122.00	912,598.00	2,200,969.00	77,997.00	31,297.00	832,636.00
1900	7,376,137.00	908,987.00	2,083,028.00	32,217.00	124,864.00	1,008,707.00
1901	7,889,077.00	975,450.00	1,728,601.50	91,602.00	195,947.00	692,209.00
1902	10,094,064.00	1,407,875.00	1,954,580.00	67,408.00	191,541.00	464,384.00
1903	10,317,940.00	1,177,968.00	1,962,730.00	68,617.00	192,034.00	1,140,499.00
1904	10,376,840.00	1,235,260.00	2,025,106.00	71,292.00	235,958.00	895,817.00
1905	11,481,490.00	1,176,155.00	1,974,816.00	98,415.00	204,907.00	1,064,338.00
1906	12,865,262.00	1,266,660.00	1,938,335.00	117,913.00	202,812.00	843,687.00
1907	11,383,108.00	1,271,823.00	1,945,394.00	112,845.00	256,056.00	629,081.00
1908	9,774,908.00	1,239,152.00	1,836,208.00	96,493.00	216,524.00	898,205.00
1909	10,326,203.00	1,196,480.00	1,816,996.00	105,647.00	119,763.00	774,545.00
1910	10,652,382.00	983,272.00	1,719,437.00	107,462.00	131,599.00	576,579.00

TABLE C.2 *Customs revenues collected at selected* Yanguan, *1863–1910* (*taels of silver*)

Year	Jiujiang Yangguan	Jianghan Guan	Yuezhou Guan	Changsha Guan	Shashi Guan	Yichang Guan
1863	478,266.00	932,701.00	–	–	–	–
1864	579,864.00	1,047,055.00	–	–	–	–
1865	490,920.00	855,596.00	–	–	–	–
1866	491,411.00	1,085,195.00	–	–	–	–
1867	470,120.00	985,814.00	–	–	–	–
1868	528,982.00	1,274,303.00	–	–	–	–
1869	513,472.00	1,273,962.00	–	–	–	–
1870	528,458.00	1,306,811.00	–	–	–	–
1871	544,752.00	1,525,102.00	–	–	–	–
1872	448,726.00	1,576,400.00	–	–	–	–
1873	538,783.00	1,510,928.00	–	–	–	–
1874	723,593.00	1,611,006.00	–	–	–	–
1875	675,431.00	1,615,850.00	–	–	–	–
1876	703,221.00	1,884,730.00	–	–	–	–
1877	680,537.00	1,802,665.00	–	–	–	134.00
1878	753,052.00	1,617,333.00	–	–	–	1,794.00
1879	726,595.00	1,775,844.00	–	–	–	17,399.00
1880	727,413.00	2,053,477.00	–	–	–	37,158.00
1881	804,356.00	2,057,111.00	–	–	–	43,717.00
1882	863,755.00	1,940,831.00	–	–	–	94,956.00
1883	785,682.00	1,976,708.00	–	–	–	87,698.00
1884	789,976.00	1,865,485.00	–	–	–	87,893.00
1885	782,526.00	1,899,544.00	–	–	–	94,165.00
1886	849,694.00	2,110,434.00	–	–	–	147,217.00
1887	959,747.00	2,092,691.00	–	–	–	178,879.00
1888	1,107,048.00	2,200,493.00	–	–	–	223,514.00
1889	1,055,225.00	2,100,456.00	–	–	–	221,377.53
1890	1,126,805.00	2,034,327.00	–	–	–	207,418.10
1891	1,180,937.00	1,989,431.00	–	–	–	188,641.00
1892	1,027,899.00	1,924,437.00	–	–	–	107,071.39
1893	1,034,250.00	2,309,698.00	–	–	–	16,574.00
1894	1,000,198.00	2,326,788.00	–	–	–	193,796.97
1895	1,044,465.00	2,332,860.00	–	–	–	341,607.82
1896	1,030,628.00	2,058,591.00	–	–	–	444,272.00
1897	944,247.00	2,139,848.00	–	–	7,468.83	384,845.00
1898	931,568.00	2,306,024.00	–	–	4,882.08	404,107.11

Year	Jiujiang Yangguan	Jianghan Guan	Yuezhou Guan	Changsha Guan	Shashi Guan	Yichang Guan
1899	1,013,657.00	2,511,635.00	–	–	6,073.48	474,037.50
1900	901,184.00	2,315,087.00	602.00	–	5,921.00	603,272.39
1901	822,306.00	1,912,242.00	3,200.00	–	12,314.00	860,573.00
1902	815,148.00	1,971,735.00	22,257.00	–	14,983.95	605,257.39
1903	650,062.00	2,678,152.00	84,137.00	–	5,943.00	277,014.81
1904	710,168.00	2,655,299.00	69,812.00	21,238.00	17,832.06	474,562.16
1905	691,940.00	2,665,815.00	25,166.00	103,197.00	16,859.17	885,962.51
1906	652,382.00	2,640,553.00	14,025.50	79,463.00	14,190.91	722,561.00
1907	774,096.00	2,697,826.00	20,425.00	94,976.00	14,785.38	856,673.00
1908	728,141.00	3,271,499.00	93,561.00	208,635.00	14,999.00	1,359,778.00
1909	634,227.00	2,878,109.00	71,386.00	229,991.00	15,625.00	1,276,567.00
1910	741,999.00	3,148,495.00	29,152.00	226,819.00	12,083.00	1,454,531.00

TABLE C.3 *Customs revenues collected at selected* Yanguan, *1861- 1910* (*taels of silver*)

Year	Chongqing Guan	Hangzhou Guan	Zhehai Yangguan	Ouhai Guan	Taiwan Guan	Wuzhou Yangguan
1861			373256	–	–	–
1862	–	–	220834	–	11814	–
1863	–	–	346060	–	50176	–
1864	–	–	513302	–	69036	–
1865	–	–	407923.88	–	140127	–
1866	–	–	465905.23	–	98207	–
1867	–	–	516255.64	–	111917	–
1868	–	–	608762.56	–	127723	–
1869	–	–	659711	–	121588	–
1870	–	–	700468	–	176736	–
1871	–	–	681745.59	–	213190.79	–
1872	–	–	826740.03	–	227957	–
1873	–	–	754846	–	233076	–
1874	–	–	747564.55	–	249573	–
1875	–	–	770774.03	–	277090.09	–
1876	–	–	709663.05	–	352203	–
1877	–	–	715191.45	2656	387678.59	–

TABLE C.3 *Customs revenues collected at selected* Yanguan, *1861- 1910* (*taels of silver*) (cont.)

Year	Chongqing Guan	Hangzhou Guan	Zhehai Yangguan	Ouhai Guan	Taiwan Guan	Wuzhou Yangguan
1878	–	–	630398.03	2992	384920.99	–
1879	–	–	653876.02	5480	477301.32	–
1880	–	–	679127.13	11344	530189	–
1881	–	–	738059	11941	558638.15	–
1882	–	–	669273.49	17753	490132.41	–
1883	–	–	657136	9319	489062.63	–
1884	–	–	752788.25	9892	578559.88	–
1885	–	–	730251.05	11162	443798.45	–
1886	–	–	704374.3	15661	531696.48	–
1887	–	–	816322	18989	781343	–
1888	–	–	1145320	34977	986332.37	–
1889	–	–	1182191	38046	997525.81	–
1890	–	–	1181252	29428	1028237.9	–
1891	44,886.00	–	1229809	31432	1089846.4	–
1892	202,933.00	–	1198033	35027	1115872.5	–
1893	222,689.00	–	1332161	49427	1078901	–
1894	258,351.00	–	1182609	50856	998859	–
1895	336,716.00	–	1194867	59595	–	–
1896	404,479.00	–	1168672	44234	–	–
1897	409,684.00	229,398.81	1022547	54368	–	46731
1898	383,785.00	342,288.79	702028	55860	–	181615.94
1899	432,567.00	587,576.00	825458	65056	–	311010
1900	452,574.00	521,794.00	710164	48527	–	287874
1901	522,013.00	566,164.00	687767	45872	–	335993.47
1902	399,836.00	587,467.00	639285	64576	–	309728
1903	341,932.00	630,726.00	663021	83863	–	312578.41
1904	444,419.00	712,707.00	702194	59647	–	504728.32
1905	584,521.00	634,072.00	642334	52958	–	553395
1906	577,798.31	580,837.00	599252	62043	–	470602.79
1907	406,204.00	670,173.00	633597	51668	–	513926.8
1908	631,792.00	659,038.00	714440	65765	–	474507
1909	602,774.00	651,044.00	624088	64765	–	519175
1910	772,528.00	648,421.00	602199	65910	–	602747

TABLE C.4 *Customs revenues collected at selected* Yanguan, *1861–1910* (*taels of silver*)

Year	Nanning Guan	Zhennan Guan	Mengzi Guan	Simao Guan	Tengyue Guan	Donghai Yangguan
1861	–	–	–	–	–	14,813.00
1862	–	–	–	–	–	59,255.00
1863	–	–	–	–	–	128,690.00
1864	–	–	–	–	–	214,184.00
1865	–	–	–	–	–	243,801.00
1866	–	–	–	–	–	308,082.00
1867	–	–	–	–	–	264,191.00
1868	–	–	–	–	–	219,042.00
1869	–	–	–	–	–	286,982.00
1870	–	–	–	–	–	301,749.00
1871	–	–	–	–	–	294,851.00
1872	–	–	–	–	–	320,981.00
1873	–	–	–	–	–	286,314.00
1874	–	–	–	–	–	300,545.00
1875	–	–	–	–	–	305,622.00
1876	–	–	–	–	–	233,472.00
1877	–	–	–	–	–	217,016.00
1878	–	–	–	–	–	294,178.00
1879	–	–	–	–	–	339,394.00
1880	–	–	–	–	–	308,881.00
1881	–	–	–	–	–	269,400.00
1882	–	–	–	–	–	292,990.00
1883	–	–	–	–	–	277,059.00
1884	–	–	–	–	–	268,647.00
1885	–	–	–	–	–	264,382.00
1886	–	–	–	–	–	277,489.00
1887	–	–	–	–	–	373,615.00
1888	–	–	–	–	–	328,910.00
1889	–	424	–	–	–	301,584.00
1890	–	1514	39846	–	–	343,024.00
1891	–	1819	54076.784	–	–	312,510.00
1892	–	1782	71876.431	–	–	346,850.00
1893	–	2029	90576	–	–	358,759.00
1894	–	3779.95	73188	–	–	376,200.00
1895	–	5286.582	94605.061	–	–	357,254.00
1896	–	3981	101619	–	–	441,326.00
1897	–	3699.433	107175.18	5,527.00	–	470,993.00

TABLE C.4 *Customs revenues collected at selected* Yanguan, *1861–1910* (*taels of silver*) (cont.)

Year	Nanning Guan	Zhennan Guan	Mengzi Guan	Simao Guan	Tengyue Guan	Donghai Yangguan
1898	–	2841.915	134645.44	8,451.00	–	523,017.00
1899	–	3702.465	167692.15	8,000.50	–	673,172.00
1900	–	5100.824	179119.91	6,914.94	–	560,447.00
1901	–	4404	195365.49	9,259.14	–	734,503.00
1902	–	6463.616	223052	7,322.00	7,371.28	825,508.00
1903	–	3280	155643.07	6,982.05	42,153.57	775,348.00
1904	–	11213.947	215572.6	7,531.51	52,340.19	762,817.00
1905	–	12791.747	240037.09	7,023.39	45,976.60	850,240.00
1906	–	6778.881	288976.48	6,722.81	39,181.30	846,024.00
1907	13588	8007	225466.68	7,045.15	47,063.00	612,297.00
1908	52436	7022	201045	5,859.00	48,460.00	666,935.00
1909	82525	7282	177778	6,407.00	44,045.00	683,710.00
1910	93216	8264	219212	5,991.00	45,737.00	681,958.00

TABLE C.5 *Customs revenues collected at selected* Yanguan, *1861–1910* (*taels of silver*)

Year	Jinhai Guan	Qinhuangaod Guan	Niuzhuang Guan	Andong Guan	Ha'erbin Guan	Yuehai Yangguan	*Yangguan* Total
1861	90,917.00	–	–	–	–	1,553,311.00	6,510,065.60
1862	98,331.00	–	–	–	–	1,279,835.00	7,559,870.00
1863	148,132.00	–	58,822.00	–	–	1,415,318.00	8,557,477.00
1864	175,364.00	–	128,502.00	–	–	1,130,334.00	8,377,015.00
1865	330,013.00	–	167,175.00	–	–	1,067,275.00	7,937,974.00
1866	504,104.00	–	158,942.00	–	–	1,365,057.00	8,906,691.00
1867	456,747.00	–	214,798.00	–	–	1,337,656.00	8,927,310.00
1868	399,728.00	–	221,576.00	–	–	1,286,405.00	9,887,485.00
1869	418,424.00	–	264,454.00	–	–	1,203,262.00	9,631,531.00
1870	407,033.00	–	260,148.00	–	–	1,178,501.00	9,760,247.00
1871	446,149.00	–	185,641.00	–	–	1,517,827.00	10,717,470.00
1872	364,155.00	–	215,508.00	–	–	1,503,610.00	11,605,919.00
1873	350,782.00	–	203,945.00	–	–	1,564,351.00	11,181,872.00
1874	388,909.00	–	204,042.00	–	–	1,521,552.00	11,910,224.00
1875	346,786.00	–	228,653.00	–	–	1,709,578.00	12,169,112.00
1876	318,158.00	–	237,510.00	–	–	1,840,374.00	12,572,847.00

Year	Jinhai Guan	Qinhuangaod Guan	Niuzhuang Guan	Andong Guan	Ha'erbin Guan	Yuehai Yangguan	*Yangguan* Total
1877	350,764.00	–	232,047.00	–	–	1,837,591.00	12,293,700.00
1878	299,679.00	–	267,816.00	–	–	1,773,016.00	12,455,212.00
1879	397,297.00	–	353,435.00	–	–	1,896,219.00	13,196,197.00
1880	424,358.00	–	298,150.00	–	–	1,940,136.00	14,346,406.00
1881	403,000.00	–	298,521.00	–	–	1,885,755.00	15,052,722.00
1882	432,030.00	–	285,236.00	–	–	1,925,454.00	14,488,772.00
1883	432,420.00	–	295,297.00	–	–	1,980,728.00	13,603,925.00
1884	432,480.00	–	322,122.00	–	–	2,090,012.00	13,738,314.00
1885	436,289.00	–	313,229.00	–	–	2,091,503.00	14,178,229.00
1886	518,901.00	–	309,683.00	–	–	2,232,192.00	15,264,476.00
1887	729,587.00	–	356,450.00	–	–	3,423,527.00	18,447,644.00
1888	689,063.00	–	390,085.00	–	–	5,104,435.00	23,094,267.00
1889	650,986.00	–	319,590.00	–	–	5,125,384.00	21,929,721.00
1890	699,589.00	–	459,485.00	–	–	5,114,230.00	21,984,239.00
1891	775,532.00	–	216,373.00	–	–	5,144,113.00	23,126,536.00
1892	769,194.00	–	547,286.00	–	–	4,811,360.00	22,808,397.00
1893	822,732.00	–	493,093.00	–	–	4,324,774.00	22,066,185.00
1894	846,218.00	–	548,208.00	–	–	4,142,648.00	22,797,028.00
1895	877,252.00	–	143,261.00	–	–	3,831,162.00	20,985,110.00
1896	954,168.00	–	398,619.00	–	–	3,711,836.00	22,040,654.00
1897	1,074,696.00	–	527,722.00	–	–	4,137,274.00	22,672,550.00
1898	1,045,922.00	–	594,246.00	–	–	3,965,579.00	21,828,054.00
1899	1,449,710.00	–	844,088.00	–	–	4,751,178.00	26,015,232.00
1900	949,342.00	–	700,418.00	–	–	4,308,308.00	24,090,590.00
1901	500,137.00	–	623,647.00	–	–	4,514,984.00	23,923,631.00
1902	1,839,755.00	36,260.00	910,318.00	–	–	4,911,015.00	28,377,190.00
1903	2,138,684.00	98,371.00	889,002.00	–	–	5,726,524.00	30,423,205.00
1904	1,903,867.00	133,531.00	614,621.00	–	–	5,292,132.00	30,206,506.00
1905	2,858,817.00	262,768.00	916,950.00	–	–	4,624,629.10	32,675,574.00
1906	3,140,318.00	335,605.00	830,826.00	–	–	5,825,176.00	34,967,986.00
1907	3,180,489.00	149,265.00	397,405.00	55,054.00	–	6,169,441.00	33,197,778.00
1908	2,373,963.00	114,051.00	681,720.00	155,291.00	221,906.00	6,117,829.00	32,930,162.00
1909	2,321,750.00	116,441.00	931,070.00	181,398.00	541,232.00	6,204,064.00	33,205,087.00
1910	2,980,297.00	202,283.00	967,576.00	235,212.00	727,720.00	5,875,778.00	34,518,859.00

Source: All kinds of archives.

References

Archival Sources

Chaodang (Copies of the Archives) (抄档), Stored in the library of the Institute of Economics, the Chinese Academy of Social Sciences. Including *Qingdai Guanshui Shouzhi Baogao Biao* (清代关税收支报告表, Revenue and Expenditure Reports of Customs in the Qing Dynasty), *Tiben·Guanshui* (题本关税, Customs Duties Reports to the Emperors), *Geguan Changshui Shizheng Duanzheng Yinliang Shumu* (各关常税实征短征银两数目, The taxed silver number and insufficient silver number in each Changguan).

Chinese Library Material Center (国家图书馆文献中心), *Hu Bu Zou Gao* (户部奏稿, Draft by the Ministry of Revenue of the Qing). Beijing: Xinhua Bookstore, 2004.

The First Historical Archives of China (中国第一历史档案馆, Beijing), *Gong Zhong Dang Zhu Pi Zou Zhe* (宫中档朱批奏折, Palace Midrange Rescript Memorials).

The First Historical Archives of China (中国第一历史档案馆, Beijing), *Guang Xu Chao Zhu Pi Zou Zhe* (光绪朝朱批奏折, Palace Midrange Rescript Memorials of the Guangxu Reign) (Beijing: Zhonghua Bookstore, 1995) .

The First Historical Archives of China (中国第一历史档案馆, Beijing), *Guang Xu Xuan Tong Liang Chao Shang Yu Dang* (光绪宣统两朝上谕档, Edict Records of Guangxu and Xuantong Reigns) (Guilin: Guangxi Normal University Press, 1996).

The First Historical Archives of China (中国第一历史档案馆, Beijing), *Jian Qing Dao Guang Liang Chao Shang Yu Dang* (嘉庆道光两朝上谕档, Edict Records of Jiaqing and Daoguang Reigns) (Guilin: Guangxi Normal University Press, 2000).

The First Historical Archives of China (中国第一历史档案馆, Beijing), *Jun Ji Chu Lu Fu Zou Zhe* (军机处录副奏折, Extra Copies of the Grand Council Memorials).

The First Historical Archives of China (中国第一历史档案馆, Beijing), *Kang Xi Chao Man Wen Zhu Pi Zou Zhe Quan Yi* (康熙朝满文朱批奏折全译, Translation of the Palace Midrange Rescript Memorials in Manchu Language of the Kangxi Reign) (Beijing: Chinese Social Science Press, 1996).

The First Historical Archives of China (中国第一历史档案馆, Beijing), *Kang Xi Chao Han Wen Zhu Pi Zou Zhe Hui Bian* (康熙朝汉文朱批奏折汇编, Collection of the Palace Midrange Rescript Memorials in Han Language of the Kangxi Reign) (Beijing: Archives Press, 1985).

The First Historical Archives of China (中国第一历史档案馆, Beijing), *Qian Long Chao Shang Yu Dang* (乾隆朝上谕档, Edict Records of Qianlong Reign) (Beijing: Archives Press, 1998).

The First Historical Archives of China (中国第一历史档案馆, Beijing), *Shangyu Dang* (上谕档, Edict Records).

The First Historical Archives of China (中国第一历史档案馆, Beijing), *Tiben* (题本, Reports to the Emperors).

The First Historical Archives of China (中国第一历史档案馆, Beijing), *Xian Feng Tong Zhi Liang Chao Shang Yu Dang* (咸丰同治两朝上谕档, Edict Records of Xianfeng and Tongzhi Reigns) (Guilin: Guangxi Normal University Press, 1998).

The First Historical Archives of China (中国第一历史档案馆, Beijing), *Yong Zheng Chao Man Wen Zhu Pi Zou Zhe Quan Yi* (雍正朝满文朱批奏折全译, Translation of the Palace Midrange Rescript Memorials in Manchu Language of the Yongzheng Reign) (Hefei: Huanshan Press, 1998).

The First Historical Archives of China (中国第一历史档案馆, Beijing), *Yong Zheng Chao Han Wen Zhu Pi Zou Zhe Hui Bian* (雍正朝汉文朱批奏折汇编, Collection of the Palace Midrange Rescript Memorials in Han Language of the Yongzheng Reign) (Nanjing: Jiangsu Guji Press, 1991).

National Library Center of Material Copy (全国图书馆文献缩微复制中心), *Hu Bu Zou Gao* (Draft by the Ministry of Revenue of the Qing) (Beijing, 2004).

National Palace Museum in Taiwan (台湾故宫博物院), *Gong Zhong Dang Kang Xi Chao Zou Zhe* (宫中档康熙朝奏折, Palace Midrange Rescript Memorials of the Kangxi Reign) (Taipei: 1976).

National Palace Museum in Taiwan (台湾故宫博物院), *Gong Zhong Dang Guang Xu Chao Zou Zhe* (宫中档光绪朝奏折, Palace Midrange Rescript Memorials of the Guangxu Reign) (Taipei: 1973).

National Palace Museum in Taiwan (台湾故宫博物院), *Gong Zhong Dang Yong Zheng Chao Zou Zhe* (宫中档雍正朝奏折, Palace Midrange Rescript Memorials of the Yongzheng Reign) (Taipei: 1978).

National Palace Museum in Taiwan (台湾故宫博物院), *Gong Zhong Dang Qian Long Chao Zou Zhe* (宫中档乾隆朝奏折, Palace Midrange Rescript Memorials of the Qianlong Reign) (Taipei: Wenhai Press, 1983).

Other Material

Fu Heng (傅恒), *Qian Long Da Qing Hui Dian* (乾隆大清会典, Rules of the Qianlong Reign of the Qing Dynasty) (1764).

He Changling (贺长龄), *Qing Jing ShiWen Bian* (清经世文编, Collections of Economic Essays in the Qing Dynasty) (Beijing: ZhongHua Publising House, 1992).

Ji Zengyun (嵇曾筠), *Zhe Jiang Tong Zhi* (浙江通志, Gazetteer of Zhejiang Province in the Qianlong Reign of the Qing) (1736).

Kun Gang (崑冈), *Guang Xu Da Qing Hui Dian* (光绪大清会典, Rules of the Guangxu Reign of the QingDynasty) (Beijing: Zhonghua Publishing House, 1990).

Li Dongyang (李东阳), *Da Ming Hui Dian* (大明会典, Rules of the Ming Dynasty). (1529).

Li Hongzhang (李鸿章), *Da Qing Hui Dian Shi Li* (大清会典事例, Rules Explanation of the Qing Dynasty) (Shanghai: Shangwu Yinshuguan, 1908).

Jin Fufu (金毓黻), *Feng Tian Tong Zhi* (奉天通志, Gazetteer of Fengtian Province) (Shengyang: Liaohai Publishing House, 2003).

Liang Tingzhan (梁廷枏), *Yue Hai Guan Zhi* (粤海关志, Gazetteer of Yuehai Guan) (1935).

Ling Shouqi (凌寿祺), *Hu Shu Guan Zhi* (浒墅关志, Gazetteer of Hushu Guan) (Shanghai: Shanghai Bookstore, 1992).

Liu Jingzhao (刘锦藻), *Qing Chao Xu Wen Xian Tong Kao* (清朝续文献通考, Another Encyclopaedia of Official Documents of the Qing Dynasty) (Hangzhou: Zhejiang Guji Publishing House, 2000).

Liu Yueyun (刘岳云), *Guang Xu Kuai Ji Biao* (光绪会计表, Accounting Tables of Guangxu Period) (Shanghai: Education World Press,1901).

Min Nin (旻宁), *Qin Ding Hu Bu Zhe Li* (钦定户部则例, Rules of Finance Ministry) (1831).

Mou Quansun (缪荃孙), *Guang Xu Shun Tian Fu Zhi* (光绪顺天府志, Gazetteer of Shuntian Prefecture in the Guangxu timnes of the Qing) (1886).

Qing Shilu (清实录, Veritable records of the Qing Dynasty) (Beijing: Zhonghua shuju, 1986).

Tuo Jin (托津), *Jia Qing Chao Da Qing Hui Dian Shi Li* (嘉庆朝大清会典事例, Rules Explanation of the Jiaqing Reign of the Qing Dynasty) (1818).

Unkonwn, *Ge Guan Chang Shui Shi Zhen Duan Zhen Yin Liang Shu Mu* (各关常税实征短征银两数目, The Taels Number of Real Tax and Shortage Tax in Different Changguan) (Handwriting, sotred in library of the Institute of Economics, the Chinese Academy of Social Sciences).

Wang Qingyun (王庆云), *Shi Qu Yu Ji* (石渠余纪, Financial Records of the Qing) (Beijing: Beijing Guji Publishing House, 1985).

Wang Yanwei (王彦威), *Qing Ji Wai Jiao Shi Liao* (清季外交史料, Diplomacy Materials in the Qing Dynasty) (Beijing: Bibliographic Literature Publishing House, 1987).

Wen Qing (文庆), *Dao Guang Chao Chou Ban Yi Wu Shi Mo* (道光朝筹办夷务始末, The History of Foreign Affairs in Daoguang Reign) (Shanghai: Shanghai Guji Bookstore, 2007).

Wo Ren (倭仁), *Qing Ding Hu Bu Ze Li* (钦定户部则例, Regulations of the Ministry of Revenue) (1865).

Wu Chunli (吴存礼), *Tong Zhou Zhi* (通州志, Gazetteer of Tongzhou Prefecture) (Shanghai: Shanghai Bookstore, 2002).

Xu Song (徐松), *Song Hui Yao Ji Gao* (宋会要辑稿, Collections of Songhiyao) (Beijing: Zhonghua Publising House, 1957).

Yang Shiqi (杨士奇), *Ming Xuan Zhong Shi Lu* (明宣宗实录, Veritable records of the Xuan Zhong of the Ming Dynasty) (1438).

Yi Sang'e (伊桑阿), *Kang Xi Da Qing Hui Dian* (康熙大清会典, Rules of the Kangxi Reign of the Qing Dynasty) (1690).

Zhan Rong (詹荣), *Jia Jing Shan Hai Guan Zhi* (嘉靖山海关志, Gazetteer of Shanhai Guan in the Jiajing Reign of the Ming) (1534).

Zhang Tingyu (张廷玉), *Qing Chao Wen Xian Tong Kao* (清朝文献通考, Encyclopedia of Official Documents of the Qing Dynasty) (Shanghai: Commercial Press, 1936).

Zhang Tingyu (张廷玉), *Yong Zhen Da Qing Hui Dian* (雍正朝大清会典, Rules of the Yongzheng Reign of the Qing Dynasty) (1732).

Zhang Tingyu (张廷玉), *Ming Shi* (明史, Ming History) (Beijing: Zhonghua Publising House, 1974).

Secondary Literature

Cao Shuji (曹树基), *Zhongguo Renkou Shi* (中国人口史, The Population History of Qing China, vol 4 & 5) (Shanghai: Fudan University, 2001).

Deng Shaohui (邓绍辉), *Wan Qing Cai Zhen Yu Zhong Guo Jin Dai Hua* (晚清财政与中国近代化, Fiscal and Social Transformation in the Late Qing) (Chengdu: Sichuan People Publishing House, 1998).

Deng Yibin (邓亦兵), *Qing Dai Qian Qi Shui Ze Zhi Du De Bian Qian* (清代前期税则制度的变迁, The Transformation of Customs Duties System in the Early Qing Dynasty), in *Journal of Chinese Historical Studies*, vol. 3 (Sept., 2003).

Deng Yibin (邓亦兵), "Qing Dai Qian Qi Guan Shui De Fu Jia Shi" (清代前期关税的附加税, Surtax of the Customs Duties of the Early Qing), in *Journal of Tsinghu University*, vol. 6 (Nov., 2007).

Deng Yibin (邓亦兵), *Qing Dai Qian Qi Guan Shui Zhi Du Yan Jiu* (清代前期关税制度研究, Customs Duties System of the Early Qing) (Bejing: Yanshan Presss, 2008).

He Benfang (何本方), "Qing Dai Shang Shui Zhi Du Chu Yi" (清代商税制度刍议, The Tax System of the Qing Dynasty), in *Social Science Research*, vol. 1 (Jan., 1987).

He Benfang (何本方), "Qing Dai Hu Bu Zhu Guan Chu Tan" (清代户部诸关初探, Research of the Hubu Ports in the Qing Dynasty), in *Journal of Nankai University*, vol 3 (Sept., 1984).

Hei Guangju (黑广菊), "Qing Shi Qi De Que Guan Yan Jiu Zong Shu" (清时期的榷关研究综述, Review on the Research of the Changguan of the Qing Dynasty) in *Lishi Jiaoxue*, vol. 4 (Apr., 2004).

Hosea Ballou Morse, *The Chronicles of the East India Company Trading to China (1635~1834)* (Cambridge: Harvard University Press, 1926).

Hosea Ballou Morse, *The Trade and Administration of the Chinese Empire*. Kelly and Walsh, Itd., (Shanghai: 1908).

Huang GuoXin (黄国信), *Ya Pian Zhan Zheng Qian De Dong Nan Si Hai Guan* (鸦片战争前的东南四海关, The Four Custom Ports in East-south of China before Opium War) (Fuzhou: Fujain People's Presss, 2000).

Jiang Zhaochen (蒋兆成), *Ming Qing Hang Jia Hu She Hui Jing Ji Yan Jiu* (明清嘉杭湖社会经济研究, The Social and Economy of Hangjiahu Area in the Ming and Qing Dynasties) (Hangzhou: Zhejiang University Press, 2002).

Kishimoto Mio, *Qing Dai Zhong Guo De Wu Jia Yu Jing Ji Bian Dong* (Price and Economy Changes in the Qing China) (Tokyo: Observations Publishing house, 1997).

Kosaka Masanori, *Qing Dai Zhong Qi De Hang Zhou Guan Shang Pin Liu Tong* (Hangzhou and Commodity Circulatioin in the Mid-Qing Period: Especially Focused on Beixinguan), in *Oriental History Studies*, vol 50 (June, 1991).

Li Jingming (李景铭), *Zhong Guo Cai Zheng Shi* (中国财政史, Chinese Fiscal History) (Beijing: Huabei University, 1936).

Li Xueqing (李学勤), *Zhou Li Zhu Shu* (周礼注疏, Explanation of Zhouli) (Beijing: Peking University Press, 1999).

Liao Shengfen (廖声丰), "Jin Nian Lai Ming Qing Shi Qi De Que Guan Yan Jiu" (近年来明清时期的榷关研究, Review on the Research of the Changguan of the Ming and Qing Dynasties in Recent Years), in *ZhongguoShi Yanjiu Dongtai*, vol. 11 (Nov., 1997).

Liao Shengfen (廖声丰), *Qindai Changguan Yu Quyu Jingji Yanjiu* (清代常关与区域经济研究, The Changguan and the Regional Economy of the Qing Dynasty) (Beijing: People's Press, 2010).

Ma, Y., de Jong, H.J. & Chu, T, *Living standards in China between 1840 and 1912: A new estimate of Gross Domestic Product per capita*, GGDC Research Memorandum No. 147 (2014).

Ni Yuping (倪玉平) (A), Steady Customs Duties in the Daoguang Depression", in *Essays in Economic & Business History*, (Volume XXXI, 2013).

Ni Yuping (倪玉平) (B), *Qing Chao Jia Dao Cai Zhen Yu She Hui* (清朝嘉道财政与社会, Research on the Finance and Society in the Jiaqing and Daoguan Reigns of the Qing Dynasty) (Beijing: The Commercial Press, 2013).

Ni Yuping (倪玉平), *Qing Chao Jia Dao Guan Shui Yan Jiu* (清朝嘉道关税研究, Research On the Customs Duties in the Jiaqing and Daoguang Reigns of the Qing Dynasty) (Beijing: Beijing Normal University Press, 2010).

Ni Yuping (倪玉平) (A), "Wang Qing Yun Shi Qu Yu Ji Suo Zai Dao Guang Guan Shui Bian Xi" (王庆云《石渠余纪》所载道光关税辨析, A Classification of the Daoguang-Era Tariffs Recorded in Wang Qingyun's *Shi Qu Yu Ji*), in (近代史研究, *Modern Chinese History Studies*, 5: 98-105 (Sept., 2008)).

Ni Yuping (倪玉平) (B), "Hu He Jia Qing Shi Qi Nian Ge Zhi Sheng Qian Liang Chu Ru Qing Dan Bian Xi" (汇核嘉庆十七年各直省钱粮出入清单》所载关税额辨析, An Examination of the Amounts of Customs Duties recorded in the List of Money and Grains Sent to and from the Provinces in the Seventeenth Year of Jiaqing in the Qing Dynasty), in (历史研究, *Historical Research*, 5: 184-189 (Oct., 2008).

Ni Yuping (倪玉平), *Qing Dai Cao Liang Hai Yun Yu She Hui Bian Qian* (清代漕粮海运与社会变迁, Sea Transport of Tribute Grain and the Social Transformation in the Qing Dynasty) (Shanghai: Shanghai Bookstore Publishing House, 2005).

Peng Yuxin (彭雨新), *Qing Dai Guan Shui Zhi Du* (清代关税制度, Customs Duties System of the Qing Dynasty) (Wuhan: Hubei People's Press, 1956).

Peng Zeyi彭泽益, "Qing Chu Si Que Guan Di Dian He Mao Yi Liang De Kao Cha"(清初四榷关地点和贸易量的考察, Researches on the Places and Trade Volumes of the Four Costal Ports in the Early Qing), in *Social Science*, vol. 3 (June, 1984).

Qi Meiqin (祁美琴). *Qing Dai Que Guan Zhi Du Yan Jiu* (清代榷关制度研究, The Changguan Sysytem of the Qing Dynasty) (Huhehaote: Namenggu University Press, 2004).

Rosenthal, J. L., and Wong, R. B, *Before and beyond divergence* (Cambridge: Harvard University Press, 2011).

Shi Xiaofeng (时晓峰), *Shan Hai Guan Li Dai Jiu Zhi Jiao Zhu* (山海关历代旧志校注, Annotation on all Kinds of Gazetteers in Shanhai Guan) (Tianjin: Tianjin People Publishing House, 1999).

Shi Zhihong (史志宏), Xu Yi (徐毅) and Ni Yuping (倪玉平), *Shi Jiu Shi Ji Shang Ban Qin De Zhong Guo Jingji Zong Liang Gu Zhi* (Estimates on China's Economy Volume in the First Half of the 19th Century) (Forthcoming).

Sun Xuewen (孙学文), *Zhong Guo Guan Shui Shi* (中国关税史, Chinese Customs Duties History) (Beijing: China Financial and Economic Press, 2003).

Takino Shojiro, *Qing Dai Qian Long Nian Jian Chang Guan Zheng Shui E* (The Quota of Customs Duties in the Qianlong Reign), in *Oriental History Jouranl of Kyushu University*, vol 29 (Apr., 2001).

Tang Xianglong (汤象龙), *Zhong Guo Jin Dai Hai Guan Shui Shou He Fen Pei Tong Ji: 1861–1910* (中国近代海关税收和分配统:1861–1910, Statistics of Customs Revenue and Its Distribution: 1861–1910) (Beijing: Zhonghua Shuju, 2005).

Vries Peer. State, *Economy and the Great Divergence: Great Britain and China, 1680s-1850s* (London: Bloomsbury Publishing, 2015).

Wang Pingzhen (王聘珍), *Da Dai Li Ji Jie Gu* (大戴礼记解诂, Explanation of Liji) (Beijing: Zhonghua Publising House, 1983).

Wu Chengming (吴承明), *Zhong Guo De Xian Dai Hu: Shi Chang Yu She Hui* (中国的现代化: 市场与社会, China's Modernization: Market and Society) (Beijing: Sanlian Bookshop, 2001).

Wu Zhaoshen (吴兆莘), *Zhongguo Guanshui Shi* (中国关税史, Customs Duties of Chinese Hisotry) (Shanghai: Shanghai Bookstore, 1937).

Xu Dixing and Wu Chengming (许涤新、吴承明), *Zhong Guo Zhi Ben Zhu Yi Fa Zhan Shi* (中国资本主义发展史, The Development History of Chinese Capitalism) (Beijing: People's Press, 1985).

Xu Tan and Jing Junjian (许檀、经君健), "Qing Dai Qian Qi Shang Shui Wen Ti Xing Tan" (清代前期商税问题新探, New Research about the Customs Duties in the Early Qing), in *Researches In Chinese Economic History*, vol. 2 (May 1990).

Yang Chaomin (杨朝明), *Kong Zi Jia Yu* (孔子家语, Konzhi's Family Words) (Jinan: Qilu Publishing House, 2009).

Yang Jianting (杨建庭), "Jin Shi Nian Qing Dai Que Guan Yan Jiu Zong Shu" (近十年清代榷关研究综述, Review on the Research of the Changguan of the Qing Dynasty in Recent Ten Years), in *ZhongguoShi Yanjiu Dongtai* (中国史研究动态), vol. 4 (Aug., 2009).

Index

www.ingramcontent.com/pod-product-compliance
Lightning Source LLC
LaVergne TN
LVHW010545300926
849162LV00002B/239
9789004324879